Promoting Entrepreneurship and Innovation Through Business Incubation

Logaiswari Indiran
Universiti Teknologi Malaysia, Malaysia

Ramakrishna Yanamandra
Skyline University College, UAE

Published in the United States of America by
    IGI Global
    701 E. Chocolate Avenue
    Hershey PA, USA 17033
    Tel: 717-533-8845
    Fax: 717-533-8661
    E-mail: cust@igi-global.com
    Web site: https://www.igi-global.com

Copyright © 2025 by IGI Global. All rights reserved. No part of this publication may be reproduced, stored or distributed in any form or by any means, electronic or mechanical, including photocopying, without written permission from the publisher.
Product or company names used in this set are for identification purposes only. Inclusion of the names of the products or companies does not indicate a claim of ownership by IGI Global of the trademark or registered trademark.

                        Library of Congress Cataloging-in-Publication Data

CIP PENDING

ISBN13: 979-8-3693-4302-9
Isbn13Softcover: 979-8-3693-5191-8
EISBN13: 979-8-3693-4303-6

Vice President of Editorial: Melissa Wagner
Managing Editor of Acquisitions: Mikaela Felty
Managing Editor of Book Development: Jocelynn Hessler
Production Manager: Mike Brehm
Cover Design: Phillip Shickler

British Cataloguing in Publication Data
A Cataloguing in Publication record for this book is available from the British Library.

All work contributed to this book is new, previously-unpublished material.
The views expressed in this book are those of the authors, but not necessarily of the publisher.

Table of Contents

Preface xii

Chapter 1
Entrepreneurial Empowerment: Maximizing Potential Through Business Incubators 1
    Lakshmi Prasad Panda, Government College of Engineering, Kalahandi, India
    Kali Charan Rath, Gandhi Institute of Engineering and Technology University, Gunupur, India
    N. V. Jagannadha Rao, Gandhi Institute of Engineering and Technology University, Gunupur, India

Chapter 2
Exploring the Opportunities and Confronting the Challenges Within Business Incubation: Opportunities and Challenges 29
    Saba Inamdar, St. Joseph's Degree and PG College, India
    Sameera Afroze, St. Joseph's Degree and PG College, India

Chapter 3
Promoting Entrepreneurship Through Business Incubation 55
    Neeta Baporikar, Namibia University of Science and Technology, Namibia & SP Pune University, India

Chapter 4
Validating the Push-Pull Theory in the Age of Entrepreneurship: A Conceptual Study 77
    Prachita A. Patil, Dr. Ambedkar Institute of Management Studies and Research, India
    Sushil Gadekar, Dr. Ambedkar Institute of Management Studies and Research, India
    Saket Bansod, Dr. Ambedkar Institute of Management Studies and Research, India

Chapter 5
Business Incubators as Tools for Innovation and Growth of Entrepreneurship:
A Mixed Method Analysis 115
    Dhan Bagiyam, Christ University, India
    Mohammad Irfan, Christ University, India
    Sandhya Singh, GLA University, India
    Rui Dias, ESCAD – Instituto Politécnico da Lusofonia, Lisboa, Portugal

Chapter 6
Economic and Social Impact of Business Incubation in UAE:
Entrepreneurship 145
    Shankar Subramanian Iyer, Westford University College, UAE

Chapter 7
Antecedents and Outcomes of Knowledge Sharing in Business Incubators
From Social Capital Theory's Perspective 177
    Masoumeh Zibarzani, Alzahra University, Iran
    Mohd Zaidi Abd Rozan, Universiti Teknologi Malaysia, Malaysia

Chapter 8
Shaping the Future: Business Incubation and HRM Integration for Optimal
Entrepreneurship and Innovation 207
    Anjali Rai, ICFAI Business School (IBS), IFHE University, Hyderabad, India

Chapter 9
Green Business Incubation: Fostering Green Entrepreneurship and Innovation 231
    Amitab Bhattacharjee, Lincoln University College, Malaysia

Chapter 10
Get-Set-Go- Blockchain Startup: Innovative Business Incubation 269
    Satya Sekhar Venkata Gudimetla, GITAM University (Deemed), India

Chapter 11
Touchdowns to Take-Off: Sporting Ventures on the Incubation Runway.......... 299
   Amitava Pal, ICFAI University, Jharkhand, India
   Kavita Mathad, Presidency University, India

Compilation of References 327

About the Contributors 375

Index 381

Detailed Table of Contents

Preface xii

Chapter 1
Entrepreneurial Empowerment: Maximizing Potential Through Business
Incubators 1
    Lakshmi Prasad Panda, Government College of Engineering,
        Kalahandi, India
    Kali Charan Rath, Gandhi Institute of Engineering and Technology
        University, Gunupur, India
    N. V. Jagannadha Rao, Gandhi Institute of Engineering and Technology
        University, Gunupur, India

Business incubators help the economy of the nation through business growth. It helps to the next generation of entrepreneurs. This chapter explores how incubators help early-stage enterprises with networking, mentorship, resources, and education. It takes a look at how brooding procedures are changing, including the utilization of virtual and cross breed models, new innovation, and an emphasis on friendly impact and supportability. This chapter brings together perspectives from academia, business, and government to improve understanding of the creation of incubation system and its role in promoting development, job creation, and financial development. Practical recommendations are made to improve the manageability and viability of business visionary projects for the upcoming generation of business futurists.

Chapter 2
Exploring the Opportunities and Confronting the Challenges Within Business Incubation: Opportunities and Challenges 29
Saba Inamdar, St. Joseph's Degree and PG College, India
Sameera Afroze, St. Joseph's Degree and PG College, India

Business incubation is a public or private development process that nurtures firms from idea creation to start-ups, providing complete assistance to help them grow and succeed. An incubator offers resources including, physical space, capital guidance, shared services, and networking opportunities. Incubators provide mentoring, business aid, and monitoring services. New enterprises are facilitated by raising awareness of risks and reducing the cost of failure. With over 10,000 incubators globally, the business incubation process has grown more important for start-ups, and extensive research has been conducted on the process, encompassing studies on its interventions and consequences. The current study advances understanding of the processes influencing particular performance and results and the incubation process. It also examines the many kinds of business incubators, benefits, and drawbacks. It clarifies the goals of future research and how policymakers and incubation managers might design interventions according to the particular incubator type and the process setting.

Chapter 3
Promoting Entrepreneurship Through Business Incubation 55
Neeta Baporikar, Namibia University of Science and Technology, Namibia & SP Pune University, India

Many countries and institutions have established business incubators for promoting entrepreneurs and entrepreneurship development. Studies have shown that business incubators aid in enhancing entrepreneurial ecosystems worldwide. Some of the African countries have also established business incubators to promote entrepreneurial development. Adapting an exploratory approach the aim of this chapter is to review and examine to what extent business incubators have promoted entrepreneurship development with a focus on South Africa.

Chapter 4
Validating the Push-Pull Theory in the Age of Entrepreneurship: A
Conceptual Study 77
    Prachita A. Patil, Dr. Ambedkar Institute of Management Studies and
        Research, India
    Sushil Gadekar, Dr. Ambedkar Institute of Management Studies and
        Research, India
    Saket Bansod, Dr. Ambedkar Institute of Management Studies and
        Research, India

Entrepreneurship has emerged as a pivotal force in shaping contemporary economies worldwide. Amidst the dynamic landscape of entrepreneurial endeavors, understanding the underlying motivations and factors influencing entrepreneurial behavior remains a critical area of research. The push-pull theory, originally conceived in the context of migration studies, offers a valuable framework for comprehending the interplay of factors that drive individuals towards entrepreneurship or deter them from it. In this chapter, the authors delve into the validation of the push-pull theory within the realm of entrepreneurship, contextualizing it within the contemporary socio-economic landscape. The push-pull theory posits that individuals are pushed away from their current situation by undesirable factors and pulled towards entrepreneurship by attractive opportunities.

Chapter 5
Business Incubators as Tools for Innovation and Growth of Entrepreneurship:
A Mixed Method Analysis 115
    Dhan Bagiyam, Christ University, India
    Mohammad Irfan, Christ University, India
    Sandhya Singh, GLA University, India
    Rui Dias, ESCAD – Instituto Politécnico da Lusofonia, Lisboa, Portugal

This chapter explores the process of relationships between business incubation and growth and development of entrepreneurship. The researcher has specifically focused on the provision of incubators and their dynamic support along with the financial support provided by the incubation centres for the growth of entrepreneurship. The researcher has focused on investigating the bibliometric investigation among the extracted documents and applications such as SPSS have been used to analyse the significant influence for the growth and development of entrepreneurship. To determine the most recent themes, developments, and trends in the subject, the network collaboration with the incubation centre has been provided.

Chapter 6
Economic and Social Impact of Business Incubation in UAE:
Entrepreneurship 145
    Shankar Subramanian Iyer, Westford University College, UAE

Business incubation programs have emerged as pivotal mechanisms for fostering entrepreneurship and innovation, especially within the rapidly evolving economic landscape of the UAE. This research investigates the multifaceted economic and social impacts of business incubation initiatives and their significance. By fostering a conducive environment, business incubators play a critical role in driving economic diversification. It highlights the role of incubators in fostering community engagement by creating networks of entrepreneurs, mentors, and investors that bolster the entrepreneurial ecosystem. The qualitative research methodology involves expert interviews to gather insights and support for the hypotheses formulated. By analyzing findings from various studies, this research offers valuable insights into the complex and multifaceted impacts of business incubation programs. These insights inform policymakers, practitioners, and stakeholders about effective strategies for supporting entrepreneurship and fostering sustainable development both locally and globally.

Chapter 7
Antecedents and Outcomes of Knowledge Sharing in Business Incubators
From Social Capital Theory's Perspective 177
    Masoumeh Zibarzani, Alzahra University, Iran
    Mohd Zaidi Abd Rozan, Universiti Teknologi Malaysia, Malaysia

Knowledge sharing (KS) is referred to as an important strategy for improving innovation, productivity, efficiency, and competitiveness of organizations. The outcomes of KS are explained from different standpoints. However, previous studies significantly fail to explore the outcomes of KS from a relationship marketing (RM) perspective. This study examined the outcomes of KS on an organization's performance and relationship with customers in business incubators in Malaysia drawing on the social capital theory and RM concepts. The study used a quantitative PLS-SEM approach and using a cross-sectional survey method data was collected from 104 randomly selected respondents. Results reveal that the overall relationship between KS and the customer relationship is significant. The findings indicate that the KS has a positive effect on customer relationships and work performance. This research expands the understanding of the effects of KS on organizations from the RM perspective in business incubators in Malaysia.

Chapter 8
Shaping the Future: Business Incubation and HRM Integration for Optimal
Entrepreneurship and Innovation 207
    Anjali Rai, ICFAI Business School (IBS), IFHE University, Hyderabad, India

Business incubation has become indispensable today as an activator of entrepreneurship and innovation, through which HRM's catalyst role is vital. Incubators offer a much-needed process of services and resources within which startups can be nurtured; HRM, on the other hand, looks into turning individuals into a world-class motivated workforce through effective management. This chapter also explains how bundling financial resources and physical tools with HRM increases the startup's success by incubating a strategic acceptance in the operation continuum to understand operational human capital. It lacks specific metrics, fails to name the market-driven reasons, and offers no insights into future-proofing a career or what technology may soon bring. Furthermore, more research on corporate culture, the role of regulatory frameworks, and the applications of HR policies are needed. This chapter aims to fill the gaps in our understanding with relevant research questions that describe how business incubation and HRM might foster innovation and growth performance.

Chapter 9
Green Business Incubation: Fostering Green Entrepreneurship and Innovation 231
    Amitab Bhattacharjee, Lincoln University College, Malaysia

Business incubators provide a business environment, where incubatee entrepreneurs can nurture their startup ventures successfully. By offering green infrastructural support, networking, green investors, and mentoring, business incubators can assist entrepreneurs in achieving enhanced business performance, successful market penetration, and financial success. Notwithstanding the emerging interest in the business incubation domain, the green incubation process for innovation and entrepreneurial success remains limited. The author therefore proposes the design of a green business incubation ecosystem and incubation process framework (initiative and context, green incubation facilities, and outcomes). Admittedly, establishing green incubation processes would enhance early-stage entrepreneurial success, foster green innovation, minimize startup challenges, and expand employment opportunities. Thus, the contribution of this chapter would broadly support the development of green business incubators, nascent entrepreneurial success, green innovation, and sustainable development worldwide.

Chapter 10
Get-Set-Go- Blockchain Startup: Innovative Business Incubation 269
Satya Sekhar Venkata Gudimetla, GITAM University (Deemed), India

'Blockchain Startup' is an innovative business idea which works with the decentralized financial (Defi) transactions through an encrypted system with the help of initial coin offering (ICO). The ICO is a way for startups and organizations within the crypto market to raise funds through unregulated crowdfunding. Blockchain is technology is used for cryptocurrency as an open-source currency – functioning through a central distribution agency or state lead control. Cryptocurrency helps in reducing intermediation of banking sector. Hence, protecting the Defi-transactions from hacking depends on the incentive-compatible proof-of-work (PoW). However, investors are crazy about digital currency/ crypto currency trading irrespective of risks involved. This chapter addresses the issues 1) to make aware of the status, progress of blockchain startup ventures and 2) to understand the threats and challenges involved in blockchain-startup business.

Chapter 11
Touchdowns to Take-Off: Sporting Ventures on the Incubation Runway 299
Amitava Pal, ICFAI University, Jharkhand, India
Kavita Mathad, Presidency University, India

This study investigates the field of sports entrepreneurship, specifically examining the process of incubation and its impact on innovation. Sports companies have a significant role in fostering economic growth and community development. However, achieving success in this field necessitates strategic support and access to resources. Business incubation offers a well-organized setting for ambitious sports entrepreneurs to enhance their ideas, develop robust strategies, and attain sustainable success. Conducting qualitative research with sports entrepreneurs offered valuable insights for entrepreneurs and incubation practitioners, shedding light on effective strategies and the typical obstacles.

Compilation of References 327

About the Contributors 375

Index 381

Preface

In today's rapidly evolving economic landscape, business incubation has emerged as a pivotal mechanism for fostering entrepreneurship and driving innovation. *Promoting Entrepreneurship and Innovation Through Business Incubation* critically examines this dynamic ecosystem, offering an in-depth exploration of the practices, challenges, and successes that underpin incubation processes worldwide. As editors, we have curated a comprehensive body of knowledge that reflects the growing significance of incubators in shaping not only entrepreneurial ventures but also the broader economic and social fabric.

Business incubators play a crucial role in nurturing early-stage ventures, providing the resources, mentorship, and networks necessary to transform promising ideas into thriving enterprises. In this book, we delve into the incubation ecosystem, tracing its evolution and examining its profound impact on startups. Our aim is to illuminate how incubators have become integral to global economic progression, offering startups the tools they need to navigate the complexities of today's market.

Each chapter presents unique insights into the incubation journey, revealing the multifaceted role of incubators as more than just physical spaces but as catalysts for growth, innovation, and collaboration. We explore various incubation models, their adaptation to diverse sectors such as technology, biotech, and social entrepreneurship, and the tailored support they provide to entrepreneurs in these fields. Furthermore, the book discusses the societal contributions of incubators, highlighting their capacity to empower social ventures and contribute to sustainable development.

Chapter 1 sets the stage by examining how business incubators contribute to national economic growth through nurturing early-stage enterprises. It highlights the evolution of incubation models, including virtual and hybrid approaches, and emphasizes the importance of sustainability and social impact in fostering entrepreneurial development. The chapter offers practical recommendations for enhancing the effectiveness of incubator programs to support the next generation of entrepreneurs.

Chapter 2 delves into the global landscape of business incubation, with over 10,000 incubators worldwide playing a critical role in the success of startups. It provides an in-depth analysis of incubation processes, types of incubators, and their advantages and drawbacks. This chapter also addresses the need for tailored interventions by policymakers and incubator managers based on the specific incubator type and setting.

Chapter 3 shifts the focus to Africa, particularly South Africa, where business incubators are instrumental in promoting entrepreneurial ecosystems. Through an exploratory approach, this chapter reviews the extent to which incubators have supported entrepreneurship development, offering a regional perspective on the global phenomenon of business incubation.

Chapter 4 explores entrepreneurial motivations through the lens of the push-pull theory, which originally stems from migration studies. This chapter adapts the theory to understand the factors that drive or deter individuals from pursuing entrepreneurship, providing a socio-economic context for the analysis of entrepreneurial behavior.

Chapter 5 offers a bibliometric investigation into the relationship between business incubation and entrepreneurial growth. It highlights the dynamic support incubators provide, including financial aid, and utilizes analytical tools such as SPSS to identify trends and themes in incubation research. The findings emphasize the significance of network collaboration in enhancing the entrepreneurial ecosystem.

Chapter 6 focuses on the UAE, where business incubators play a crucial role in economic diversification and social impact. Through qualitative research, the chapter investigates the economic and social contributions of incubation programs, providing valuable insights for policymakers and stakeholders on strategies to foster sustainable development and entrepreneurship.

Chapter 7 addresses the role of knowledge sharing (KS) within business incubators in Malaysia, examining its effects on organizational performance and customer relationships through the lens of relationship marketing (RM). Using a quantitative approach, this chapter provides evidence of the positive impact of KS on business incubators and expands the understanding of its influence from an RM perspective.

Chapter 8 examines the intersection of business incubation and human resource management (HRM), highlighting how bundling financial resources and physical tools with HR strategies enhances startup success. The chapter identifies gaps in research related to corporate culture, regulatory frameworks, and HR policies, offering research questions that address these issues and contribute to a better understanding of the HRM-incubation relationship.

Chapter 9 introduces the concept of green business incubation, proposing a framework for green innovation and sustainability. The chapter emphasizes the importance of green infrastructure, networks, and investors in supporting entrepreneurial success, advocating for a greener incubation ecosystem to enhance startup growth, job creation, and sustainable development.

Chapter 10 explores blockchain startups, focusing on decentralized financial transactions and the role of Initial Coin Offerings (ICO) in raising funds. It addresses the challenges and risks involved in blockchain startups, particularly in the context of cryptocurrency trading, and provides an overview of the progress and potential of blockchain ventures.

Chapter 11 investigates sports entrepreneurship and the role of incubation in driving innovation within the sports industry. Through qualitative research, the chapter examines the support systems provided by incubators to sports entrepreneurs, offering insights into strategies for success and common obstacles faced in the industry.

This collection of chapters brings together a diverse range of perspectives, research methodologies, and regional case studies, offering a comprehensive understanding of the evolving role of business incubation in promoting entrepreneurship, innovation, and sustainable development across various sectors and geographies.

The objectives of *Promoting Entrepreneurship and Innovation Through Business Incubation* are fourfold:

1. Comprehensive Evaluation: To offer an in-depth evaluation of business incubation's role in stimulating entrepreneurial spirit and innovation across various sectors.
2. Exploration of Success Factors: To examine the specific practices, processes, and strategies that contribute to the success of business incubators, enriched with case studies from different industries.
3. Societal and Economic Impact: To explore the far-reaching societal and economic effects of business incubation, particularly its role in fostering social entrepreneurship, promoting community development, and advancing sustainability.
4. Actionable Insights: To provide stakeholders with practical knowledge and insights that can influence incubation practices, academic research, policy formulation, and entrepreneurial strategies.

This book is crafted to serve a wide spectrum of stakeholders. Entrepreneurs will find valuable guidance on leveraging incubation for business growth. Incubator managers can draw from real-world examples and strategic insights to enhance their programs. Policymakers and economic development professionals will gain a deeper understanding of how incubators contribute to economic prosperity, while researchers and students in business and economics will find this work a rich resource for academic exploration. Investors and venture capitalists will discover how incubation primes startups for market success, and corporate innovation teams can explore models for collaboration with startups. Additionally, community development organizations, social entrepreneurs, and educational institutions will benefit from the book's emphasis on the broader social and educational impact of incubation.

Ultimately, *Promoting Entrepreneurship and Innovation Through Business Incubation* offers a holistic view of the incubation process, shedding light on its transformative potential for entrepreneurship and innovation. We hope this book serves as a valuable resource for anyone invested in the entrepreneurial journey, providing the knowledge and inspiration needed to foster a vibrant, innovation-driven economy.

Logaiswari Indiran
Universiti Teknologi Malaysia, Malaysia

Ramakrishna Yanamandra
Skyline University College, UAE

Chapter 1
Entrepreneurial Empowerment:
Maximizing Potential Through Business Incubators

Lakshmi Prasad Panda
https://orcid.org/0000-0002-9185-2967
Government College of Engineering, Kalahandi, India

Kali Charan Rath
Gandhi Institute of Engineering and Technology University, Gunupur, India

N. V. Jagannadha Rao
Gandhi Institute of Engineering and Technology University, Gunupur, India

ABSTRACT

Business incubators help the economy of the nation through business growth. It helps to the next generation of entrepreneurs. This chapter explores how incubators help early-stage enterprises with networking, mentorship, resources, and education. It takes a look at how brooding procedures are changing, including the utilization of virtual and cross breed models, new innovation, and an emphasis on friendly impact and supportability. This chapter brings together perspectives from academia, business, and government to improve understanding of the creation of incubation system and its role in promoting development, job creation, and financial development. Practical recommendations are made to improve the manageability and viability of business visionary projects for the upcoming generation of business futurists.

DOI: 10.4018/979-8-3693-4302-9.ch001

INTRODUCTION

A person who starts and takes the risk of business with little funding is called an entrepreneur. The person bears accountability for the advantages and disadvantages of their business venture (Daraojimbaet al. (2023); Korang (2024)). An innovative product or service is the emphasis of a company idea as opposed to an established business model. The Batavia Industrial Centre is located in New York. It was the first business incubator. The various models and tactics that have been discussed for the improvement of business and entrepreneurship have helped new entrepreneurs. Because of this, a large number of entrepreneurs (Mian (2021), Kilcrease (2012), Galbraith et al, (2019)) are encouraged to do their business in an improved manner and are in the ladder of growth. Business planning gives an explicit road map for success. It has a clear business system purpose, mission, and vision in order to reach the target market. Business owners who have a well-defined goal are better able to deploy resources, make wise decisions, and reduce risks.

Academic institutions and well-versed incubator centers possess the expertise to offer entrepreneurs more insightful recommendations on how to proceed with their firm. A range of resources (Peters, et al. (2004)), including lab space, startup money, technology resources, architectural design, and advising services are provided by these successive entrepreneurs through their incubator centers (Himanen et al. (2011); Toganel & Zhu (2017); Keenan et al. (2018)). Network links, mentorship, and other services are offered by well-established incubators. There are a lot of technology companies in Silicon Valley. The Indian Silicon Valley is referred to as Bangalore. The hub of India's high-tech sector is here. These centers help with the creation of new businesses.

According to the International Business Incubation Association, there are more than 7000 incubators in the world. The main goal of the incubators is to encourage new business entrepreneurs. These incubators are company created and supports not only for the expansion but also to success of new ventures by offering mentorship, access to investors, expertise, free or inexpensive workspace, and in some situations, loans for operating capital (Assenova (2020) ; Odeyemi et al. (2024), Hervieux et al. (2018)).

Research shows that incubators are playing a crucial role for fostering an entrepreneurial culture. They help entrepreneurs grow their companies, particularly in the early phases. According to International Business Innovation Association (IBIA), the business Incubator is defined as the process of lifting up early-stage companies through various key development processes until they become self-driven system. In general business incubators provides tool for the successive entrepreneur. In order to aid in the incubation of new technological firms, numerous nations across the world are promoting "innovation orchards" through partnerships between University, government and industry (Robinson, et. al. (2014); William et al (2023)).

India's Department of Science and Technology's Innovation & Entrepreneurship division created the National Initiative for Developing and Harnessing Innovations (NIDHI). Through innovation scouting, assistance, and scaling, NIDHI seeks to foster start-ups. Principal funders of the NIDHI program include a number of federal departments and agencies, state and local governments, financial institutions, research and educational institutions, mentors, the private sector, angel investors, and venture capitalists. One of the most important tools for creating jobs and advancing the economy is business incubators. Innovation and Entrepreneurship of the Department of Science and Technology supports technology-related company incubators in the academic sector. Utilizing the infrastructure and expertise that the host institution already held to create businesses, it also required access to concepts and technologies through a variety of technical and management schools.

Business Incubators to Empowering Entrepreneurs

Every day, the population grows, which raises the need for a range of products and services. Building several manufacturing and service facilities as a core economic hub is essential to meeting these objectives. Such enterprises require a knowledgeable and skilled team to be established. Through skill-leveraging, people are motivated to start new businesses and support the growth of their country. The field of startup incubators and accelerators include various prominent entities that provide essential support to early-stage companies. These organizations provide critical support in the form of advice, funding, and connections to a large network of professionals and investors, greatly impacting the development of innovative enterprises (Browne (2021); Roundy (2021)).

Most people agree that Y Combinator is the greatest location to launch a business. Through their fiercely competitive accelerator program, they have assisted in the launches of numerous successful firms, including Dropbox and Airbnb. Y Combinator provides start-ups with capital, mentorship, and access to a vast network in order to help them develop into large enterprises. Similarly, Businesses that operate at the intersection of advertising and marketing are the focus of Collider. Collider has access to a network of industry professionals, financing, and coaching through its program. Liveposter and Unruly are in their portfolio. Another example can be provided as a British early-stage accelerator, Ignite Accelerator supports start-ups in a variety of industries, education, technology developer and healthcare. It consists of a three-month active stage program that provides links to seasoned entrepreneurs from various sectors, as well as initial funding and mentorship. Chicago-based TechNexus is a company that links entrepreneurs and startups with other businesses.

See more about us. Thousands of companies from all around the world have already partnered with us by becoming members of our community. Few more examples are, Rock Health, Blue Startups, Le Camping, Dreamit Ventures, NUMA, etc. are supporting for the growth of startups by providing seed money, mentorship, and customized programs. They put a lot of emphasis on encouraging creativity and making it possible for firms to prosper.

Thus the new entrepreneurs and existing business ventures serve as the society's front tire leaders. They make it easier to start new businesses. Through them, new companies are emerging and aiming to open other locations, which will support their continued growth and provide additional employment possibilities for the general public. They are becoming the backbone of the country's economy by fostering growth in it.

The Challenges Faced by Entrepreneurs During the Startup Stage

Entrepreneurs can overcome the common obstacle of limited funding by focusing on a solid business plan and financial foundation. This includes creating detailed financial forecasts, outlining a clear path to profitability, and building relationships with investors or creditors willing to take on more risk. By showcasing their unique value proposition and innovative ideas, business visionaries can attract investors interested in financing new ventures or disruptive technologies. A well-prepared business plan and financial strategy can help entrepreneurs secure the necessary funds to achieve their objectives.

Entrepreneurs can overcome the common obstacle of limited funding by focusing on a solid business plan and financial foundation. This includes creating detailed financial forecasts, outlining a clear path to profitability, and building relationships with investors or creditors willing to take on more risk. By showcasing their unique value proposition and innovative ideas, business visionaries can attract investors interested in financing new ventures or disruptive technologies. A well-prepared business plan and financial strategy can help entrepreneurs secure the necessary funds to achieve their objectives.

Scope, Objective, and Novelty of the Work

Entrepreneurial empowerment provides individuals with the necessary resources and support to successfully start and grow their businesses, fostering economic growth and job creation. By cultivating self-confidence, independence, and adaptability, it enables entrepreneurs to turn innovative ideas into profitable ventures, promoting economic expansion and community development. Programs promoting entrepreneurial empowerment, such as those supporting women and minority entrepreneurs in the US, have led to increased business initiatives and job opportunities (Akpuokwe et al. (2024)).

Scope of the work: This painting's breadth delves into the vital role that business incubators play in empowering and assisting entrepreneurs, with a particular emphasis on their influence throughout the initial stages of startup creation. This article discusses the several obstacles that entrepreneurs have when launching and managing their own businesses. It offers in-depth information about conferences, seminars, mentorship programs, and other growth initiatives offered by reputable incubators. The emphasis also includes the provision of different forms of seed finance, technological development, strategy planning, and other policies that one must follow in order to become a successful entrepreneur. The main focus of the research is still commercial enterprise incubators, but in order to give a complete picture of startup ecosystems, it may also reveal linked issues with accelerator packages and entrepreneurship education. Understanding the evolving role that business incubators play in fostering innovation and economic success is the goal of the study.

Objective of the work: Business incubators assist and facilitate marketing throughout the first phases of their projects. The resources, connections, and mentoring of these incubators promise to support businesses in becoming successful in the cutthroat world of business, no matter what challenges they face. The incubator's role was highlighted in the study as it examined the initial challenges that marketers encounter.

Novelty of the work: This work looked at how company incubators increase the power of marketers. The supply of specialist guiding offers and the construction of collaborative places help the development of entrepreneurs. It shows the significance of incubators. Through reading about various worldwide entrepreneurial ecosystems and success stories, the study emphasizes the revolutionary impact and immense relevance of empowering entrepreneurs through business incubators.

ADVANCEMENT AND OTHER FORMS OF ASSISTANCE TO BUSINESS INITIATORS

These days, entrepreneurs can choose from a multitude of support options. Originally designed to provide all the physical infrastructure needed, business incubators now offer a wide range of specialized services to cater to the different needs of enterprises (Lesakova (2012); Dhochak, et al. (2019)). For instance:

a) Infrastructure: Traditional business incubators originated from sharing office space and facilities, offering affordable resources, and fostering a collaborative environment where entrepreneurs could connect, exchange ideas, and learn from each other to grow their businesses.
b) Mentorship: A startup mentor provides guidance, support, and direction to early-stage entrepreneurs, helping them develop their skills and knowledge, and navigate business challenges. Mentorship programs, often offered by business incubators, provide valuable networking opportunities, guidance, and support, empowering entrepreneurs to grow their businesses. E-mentoring platforms also enable convenient connections across distances and time zones, fostering meaningful relationships and networking opportunities. Example: Mentors are highly demanded in market due to their expertise in business. They are providing assistance through their contact and communication, vast networks and skills. By using AI technologies in business they are accelerating their mentorship in a strong manner and offer even more individualized advice. As a result of this mentees get assurance to success in their business and they expand their plan to workout.
c) Funding: Entrepreneurs with promising ideas seek mentors for guidance and funding. A solid proposal can secure startup capital, and investors may provide financial support by investing in the venture, helping entrepreneurs overcome the financing hurdle.

Example: With the goal of fostering a more inclusive and sustainable society, Techstars cultivates startup cultures locally by expanding entrepreneurial communities via live events, mentorship, and education.

d) Networking: Venture capital incubators help arrange connections with profitable merchants, industry experts, and other business owners. These networks present opportunities for collaboration, collaborative ventures, and future funding rounds. Building relationships with investors and business experts helps speed up the number of businesses by facilitating alliances, teamwork, and future funding rounds.

Example: Networking events are not just for an opportunity to make small talk and trade business cards. They also offer enterprises advantageous discussion and various nodes to build connections for joint ventures to foster partnerships. This leads to high their business not in national level but in an international manner.

e) *T*raining and Workshops: Incubators support entrepreneurs by refining their ideas and business plans, providing services like funding, training, office space, and mentorship, to help them commercialize their innovations and scale their businesses.
f) Administrative Support: Incubators provide legal support to entrepreneurs, offering access to specialized legal knowledge, intellectual property protection, and regulatory guidance, enabling them to navigate complex laws and build successful businesses.

Example: Berkeley Law's startup criminal storage gives early-stage startup with loose criminal services to help them with legal issues and compliance concerns.

g) Industry Support: The focus of certain business incubators is certain industries or sectors.

Example: CleanTech Open provides clean age marketers with access to industry contacts, investment opportunities and mentorship.

h) International Support: A growing number of business incubators offer services and projects to help businesses expand into foreign markets as globalization continues.

Example: Entrepreneurs can get early access to a global network of investors with the help of the startup bootcamp.

Analysis of Y Combinator Case

Corporate incubators have changed over time and the range of services they now offer to companies is shown in the illustration. The Y Combinator program gave entrepreneurs with funding, guidance, and a network of potential customers to help them launch their businesses successfully. Y Combinator has improved with time and now offers a full range of support services that are specifically designed to meet the requirements of early-stage businesses.

- *Seed Funding: Well-known startup accelerator Y Combinator is providing seed money to early-stage firms in exchange for equity. By helping with the initial investment, marketers are able to pay for their essentials and concentrate on expansion and improvement.*
- *Networking: Startups can join the large community of business partners, traders, and graduates. Meetings with possible partners and customers can*

be arranged through regular pitch sessions, demo days and networking events. Online communities can be expanded by businesses through the use of forums and online frameworks.
- *Mentorship:* The mentorship program is one of the benefits of Y Combinator. The experienced business owners and executives who provide guidance and support throughout the program are matched with the selected startup.
- *Resources:* A range of resources for entrepreneurs, including office space, help with administration and prisons,cloud services, and software tools, are provided by Y Combinator.
- *Workshops and Training:* Product development, marketing tactics, funding, and legal compliance are some of the topics addressed in the workshops and training sessions.
- *Follow-up Support:* When this scheme ends, Y Combinator will continue to support and mentor its alumni. The challenges of expanding their company could be overcome. The association helps alumni grow and sustain their businesses.

From being basic infrastructure suppliers, enterprise incubators have developed into all-encompassing steerage environments that satisfy the many needs of marketers as they go. The way Y Combinator promotes entrepreneurship has propelled the startup scene worldwide.

Various Types of Business Incubators (e.g., Government-Sponsored, University-Affiliated, and Private)

Business incubators help new and early-stage companies in their expansion and development by
offering a variety of tools, services, and coaching. There are different types of incubators, each with its own characteristics and principles. An example of a special kind of business incubator, along with actual instances from India and other nations, can be found here.

a) Government-sponsored incubators: To sell financial improvement, innovation, and entrepreneurship in a selected region or enterprise, authorities departments or agencies set up and preserve government-sponsored incubators.

Startups can have access to mentorship, funding and office space at United Kingdom's Innovation Warehouse and London, an innovation incubator supported by the central government.

Example in India: The NITI Aayog lunched ATAL Incubation Centers, which are running by the Government of India's ATAL Innovation Mission. Infrastructure, finance, mentoring, and other resources are provided to companies by these organizations.

All types of incubators greatly enhance the national and international entrepreneurial landscape.

b) University-affiliated incubators: Incubators connected to universities are typically installed within or in conjunction with educational institutions. They use the university's resources, research facilities, faculty knowledge, and networks-to direct business endeavors.

Stanford University is one of the popular University and facilitate such platform for better improvement of entrepreneurs and incubators. The Incubation Cell of the Indian Institute of Technology Madras gives entrepreneurs access to research facilities, money, mentorship and networking opportunities.

c) Private sector incubators: Private companies, assignment capital firms, and associations of traders are the ones who set up personal zone incubators. Financial support, mentoring, and networking opportunities are offered in return for equity or other forms of return on investment.

One of the most famous personal sector incubators in the world is located in Silicon Valley, California. Entrepreneurs get seed money, mentorship, and access to traders in exchange for ownership. The startup support provided by the Bangalore-based Axilor Ventures is in the form of capital, mentorship, marketplace access, and other resources.

Business Incubators Initiatives

There are a lot of resources offered by incubators in the development of new businesses. Access to financing sources, networking opportunities, and mentorship from knowledgeable experts are included in these resources (Pompa (2013) ; Uhm et al. (2018)). In India and abroad, business incubators offer support services to help companies grow and prosper.

a) Mentorship: In locations like Silicon Valley, America, and London, enterprise incubators have excellent networks of seasoned marketers, enterprise professionals, and professional experts who act as mentors. Several aspects of business development, approach, product improvement, and market penetration are offered by the mentors.

Indian entrepreneurship incubators offer mentorship packages that pair up aspiring business owners with experienced mentors. The Indian College of company in Hyderabad provides assistance to startup companies through its mentorship software.

b) Funding assistance: Funding availability is important for startup growth. Get right of entry to different types of funding can be provided by enterprise incubators in different international locations. They help startup with pitch deck instruction, investor relations, and investment acquisition (Phani & Khandekar (2017)).

New businesses are helped by India's business incubators. In-house finance is provided by some incubators, while others help entrepreneurs apply for grants or arrange introductions to investors. The KSUM in India has a number of funding initiatives.

INCUBATORS EMPOWERMENT

The creation of jobs and economic growth in India are dependent on incubators. Office space, financial chances, and networking opportunities are some of the tools provided by the incubators. The support network supports entrepreneurship, creates jobs, and propels economic growth. cubated companies can play a role in the growth of India's business landscape, promoting innovation and strengthening the country's standing in the international economy India's entrepreneurial talent is able to reach its full potential through incubators working together (Sharma et al. (2019); Surana et al. (2020)).

Table 1. List of Indian Incubators With Jobs Creation

Year	Incubator Name	Number of Incubators	Startups Supported	Jobs Created
2015	Venture Catalysts	500	5,000	20,000
2016	Axilor Ventures	600	6,500	25,000
2017	9Unicorns Accelerator Fund	700	8,000	30,000

continued on following page

Table 1. Continued

Year	Incubator Name	Number of Incubators	Startups Supported	Jobs Created
2018	10,000 Start-Ups (initiative launched by the Government of India under the Ministry of Electronics and Information Technology (MeitY)	800	10,000	40,000
2019	JITO Angel Network	900	12,000	50,000
2020	IIM Calcutta Innovation Park	1,000	15,000	60,000
2021	T-Hub	1,200	18,000	70,000
2022	NSRCEL, IIM Bangalore	1,400	22,000	80,000
2023	NASSCOM 10,000 Startups	1,600	25,000	90,000

Let Us Discuss the Case Study of Incubators Empowerment in India

India has seen a rise in the number of incubators. The government, businesses, and educational institutions might fund these incubators. They want to build innovative standards and turn them into successful businesses. The ATAL Incubation centers were hooked up all over the kingdom in the ATAL innovation project. New agencies get entry to capital, networking possibilities, mentorship, and infrastructure aid from the accelerators. Bangalore, also known as India's Silicon Valley, is domestic to this type of AICs.

AIC Bangalore as a case study example. The explanation of the results follows.

Modern workspaces, labs, and prototype facilities are all provided by AIC Bangalore. These are essential for resource-poor early-stage firms.

Through collaborations with government initiatives, angel investors, and venture capital firms, AIC Bangalore makes investment more accessible. Startups get assistance in creating pitch decks, company plans, and networking with possible investors.

Business experts and advisors work with startup companies to provide guidance on business strategy, product creation, market entry, and capital raising. This mentorship increases the likelihood that this startup will succeed.

Networking events, workshops, and industry links are arranged by the incubators to facilitate the formation of partnerships, collaborations, and access to new consumers and markets for entrepreneurs.

Impact: AIC Bangalore has an influence that goes beyond economic growth and job creation. They help to advance society by creating a culture of creativity. Some of significant effects are:

a) By promoting collaboration between startups, companies, investors, and institutions, AIC Bangalore plays a vital role in supporting the entrepreneurial ecosystem. The results of this interaction include knowledge sharing, skill development, and generational transition.
b) Growth in wealth creation, creativity, and productivity can be attained by startups supported by AIC Bangalore. These startups create cutting-edge goods and services, upend established markets, and boost GDP.
c) A great job opportunities are provided by AIC Bangalore in the recent year 2024 also. The organization not only supports startup but also create vacancies on various positions for new fellows in different departments like: ales, marketing, technology developer etc..

The mentioned significances reflect the potential support of AIC Bangalore for the emplobility and a ladder of economic growth of nation. These incubators also acts as catalyst of the nation who promotes various entrepreneurs to play a major role for national growth through business incubation.

Overcoming Obstacles to Implementing Effective Incubator Programs

To accelerate various entrepreneur towards incubators, need experience. So, various skills have been trained and critically evaluated to foster various entrepreneur by overcoming challenges.

Various challenges that Indian incubators are facing are: funding constrains, lack of advanced technological tools, policy and regulatory barriers, high turnover rate, lack of awareness between entrepreneurs, startup ecosystem, proper collaboration, limited to market access, ineffective outreach, scaling difficulties, less MOU with academic institutions, less supportive communities etc. Few of these are explained below.

a) Geographical Inequalities:

Challenge: Industry professionals can get assistance with market validation from the

DLabs at Indian School of Business. HealthifyMe has been helped by DLabs to improve

their business strategy.

Solution: Making use of virtual resources and putting up incubators in tier 2 and tier 3

cities.

Example: By situating their centers in smaller cities, Atal Incubation Centers aim to reduce
   geographical disparities. The Greater Noida branch of AIC-BIMTECH provides incubation
   support to local businesses in an effort to promote entrepreneurship outside of metropolitan
   centers.

b) Talent and skills:

   Challenge: It's difficult to find skilled talent in specialized fields.
   Solution: Preparing seminars for skill development and providing assistance with recruitment are some of the things that are done with academic institutions.
   Example: Technical institutes and the Nasscom Startup Warehouse work together to close
   the talent gap. Flipkart has been able to get highly trained personnel through Nasscom's
   talent programs.

c) Technological Infrastructure:

   Challenge: An inadequate technical infrastructure is one of the biggest obstacles to a startup's growth.
   Solution: There is access to cutting-edge technology.
   Example: The KTIZ offers access to state-of-the-art research facilities. Sastra Robotics
   uses KTIZ's infrastructure to develop new products.

d) Regulatory and compliance:

   Challenge: Finance and healthcare are some of the industries where regulatory problems
   and compliance problems are common.
   Solution: Legal advice, compliance courses, and interactions with regulatory bodies are
   offered.
   Example: Entrepreneurs can get help navigating legal frameworks from T-Hub. T-Hub
   helps with regulatory matters. Stan Plus is a healthcare company.

e) Scalability and Sustainability:

Challenge: The long-term efficacy of many incubators is affected by the issues of sustainable and scalability.
Solution: Making money via business alliances and equity investments is one of the self-
sustaining strategies.
Example: Revenue is generated by equity investments in entrepreneurs through the self-
sustaining business model employed by IIM Bangalore's NSRCEL. The long-term viability
of NSRCEL is ensured by its cooperation with commercial groups.
The application of strategic solutions to overcome these challenges and the use of an Indian success incubator case study could be used to promote financial growth and innovation in the nation.

Trends for Business Incubation Sector

Business incubators support entrepreneurs from concept to commercialization, offering expertise and resources through mentoring programs. This public or private process fosters entrepreneurial, social, and economic development. Incubators help startups conserve cash and secure external assistance to accelerate growth. Notable Indian incubators include Amity Innovation Incubator, IIM Calcutta Innovation Park, Forge Accelerator, TIDES Business Incubator, IIIT-B Innovation Centre, and Centre for Incubation and Business Acceleration at Goa, providing guidance and support to new ventures.

a) **Zone based incubators:** Physical or virtual spaces that provide resources, support, and networking opportunities to entrepreneurs and startups, typically focused on a specific industry or geographic region.

Trend: There is growing attention to industry-specific incubators.
Example: Villgro is a well-known incubator that focuses on social entrepreneurs in the agricultural sectors, healthcare and renewable energy. It is a quarter-unique.

b) **Programs for corporate Incubation:** Internal initiatives by established companies to foster innovation and entrepreneurship, providing resources and support to develop new ideas, products, and businesses within the company.

Trend: Expansion of business-backed incubator initiatives.

Example: Google's resources (Launchpad Accelerator) and knowledge are used to mentor and develop companies in India.

c) **Remote assistance and virtual incubation:** Online platforms and programs that provide entrepreneurs and startups with access to resources, mentorship, and support services remotely, without the need for physical presence in a traditional incubator setting.

Trend: Companies can access resources from any location with the implementation of remote support systems.
Example: Entrepreneurs can get remote networking and coaching through NUMA Bengaluru.

d) **Entrepreneurship for women:** Initiatives and programs aimed at empowering and supporting women to start and grow their own businesses, addressing gender-specific challenges and providing resources, mentorship, and networking opportunities.

Trend: Women who wish to launch their own businesses can get assistance. It has been difficult for women to start their own businesses. We can help achieve parity by offering focused assistance. Funding possibilities, networking events, and mentorship are some of the tools we can provide for women's business success. There are obstacles that prevent women from starting businesses, such as lack of funding or gender bias. Specific emphasis is put on encouraging and assisting female entrepreneurs through targeted programs and activities.
Example: Through the KSUM Women Startup Program, women-led firms can access networking opportunities, funding, and mentorship.

e) **Deep tech startups:** Early-stage companies that leverage cutting-edge technologies like AI, blockchain, quantum computing, and biotechnology to develop innovative solutions and products, often requiring significant research and development.

Trend: The growth of deep tech incubators. Artificial intelligence, quantum computing, etc.
Example: The Incubation Cell of the Indian Institute of Technology Madras offers cutting-edge research facilities and mentorship to deep tech businesses.

f) **Government-funded programs for incubation:** Initiatives sponsored by government agencies to support entrepreneurship and innovation, providing resources, funding, and infrastructure to incubators and startups, aiming to stimulate economic growth and job creation.

Trend: There is an increase in government-sponsored programs to support innovation and entrepreneurship.
Example: Businesses in a variety of industries can receive incubation help from NITI Aayog's Tal Innovation Mission.

g) **Assessment of incubator:** A systematic evaluation of an incubator's performance, impact, and effectiveness in supporting startups, typically assessing metrics such as job creation, funding raised, survival rates, and economic impact.

Trend: The effectiveness of incubation programs is evaluated through impact evaluation and measurement.
Example: The social effect measurement of the businesses in its portfolio is tracked by the Villgro effect Report.

h) **Rural and social impact:** Programs that support entrepreneurs and startups developing solutions addressing social and environmental challenges in rural or underserved areas, aiming to drive positive change and sustainable development.

Trend: Rural entrepreneurship and social impact ventures have been targeted by incubators.
Example: Through grassroots innovation, the Deshpande Foundation supports social entrepreneurs and rural innovators.

i) **Entrepreneurship Ecosystem:** A network of interconnected resources, institutions, and stakeholders that support and foster entrepreneurship, innovation, and economic growth, including incubators, accelerators, investors, mentors, and government agencies.

Trend: There should be more cooperation between government agencies, corporations, universities, and incubators.
Example: Business executives, academic institutions, and government agencies collaborate with Nasscom's Bengaluru Center of Excellence for IoT and AI.

j) **International linkages and access to markets:** Connections and partnerships that enable startups to expand globally, access new customers, and tap into international networks, resources, and expertise, facilitating cross-border collaborations and trade.

Trend: Companies can connect with the world through alliances and programs.
Example: Techstars India is a program that gives entrepreneurs the chance for global expansion and market penetration by collaborating with foreign corporations and investors.
In India, a range of creative models and new techniques are propelling entrepreneurship and promoting innovation in multiple industries.

Importance of Empowering Entrepreneurs

Encouraging entrepreneurship is crucial for innovation, job creation, and economic growth. Successful entrepreneurs possess skills like effective communication, adaptability, and strategic planning, leading teams to achieve their full potential. By aligning company objectives with vision and values, entrepreneurs create a roadmap for success, drive employee engagement, and contribute to national prosperity.

Some of important entrepreneur steps have been taken care by India and also in foreign countries are:

a) The empowerment of female entrepreneurs: Encouraging and assisting women to engage in business endeavors advances gender equality.

Example: According to a report by Bain & Company, the number of women-led businesses in India grew by 50%.

b) Transition to digital enterprise: The emergence of digital entrepreneurship has been made possible by the digital revolution.

Example: The surge in internet access and smartphone usage resulted in a 30% increase in revenue for ecommerce enterprises.

c) Inclusive growth for rural development: entrepreneurship fosters growth and development across the nation by empowering people in remote locations.

Example: The creation of businesses in Tier II and Tier III towns has been accelerated by initiatives like "Startup India, Standup India".

d) GDP growth: The GDP of a nation is influenced by entrepreneurial activity.

Example: The Ministry of Exchange and Enterprise has released data showing that between 2018 and 2024, the GDP contribution of startups in India increased from 1.8% to 4.5%.

e) Technological Innovation and Advancements: Entrepreneurs drive innovation and technical improvements.

Example: Indian companies submitted over 15,000 patents by the year 2022, demonstrating a boom in innovation.

f) Infrastructure and ecosystem development: The framework and resources are provided by the government.

Example: Various corporates and new venture established so many Startup Hubs and Incubation Centers in various areas. As a result of this, various prospective business owners can now access mentorship, funding, and networking opportunities.

g) sustainable development and social effect: A growing number of entrepreneurs are focusing on social impact projects that support the SDGs.

Example: More than 40% of Indian companies will have social impact projects integrated into their business strategies by the year 2023.

h) adaptability and resilience: Entrepreneurial endeavors adapt when faced with economic downturns.

Example: Indian entrepreneurs were able to recover quickly in the years that followed by changing their business strategies in the face of the COVID-19 pandemic.

i) Investments and Global recognition: Local and foreign investors give funding to successful startups.

Example: Indian entrepreneurs received $10 billion in funding in 2020.

Table 2. Startup with Their GDP Contribution, No of IPRS Filed and Women – Led Startup

Year	Startup Contribution to GDP (%)	Number of Patents Filed	Funding Received (in billions USD)	Growth in Women-led Startups (%)
2018	1.8	5,000	5.2	-
2019	2.5	7,500	7.8	20
2020	3.2	10,000	10.6	30
2021	3.9	12,500	9.5	40
2022	4.2	15,000	12.3	45
2023	4	16,500	11.8	48
2024 (April)	4.5	17,500	8.9	50

Figure 1. Startup contribution to GDP (%)

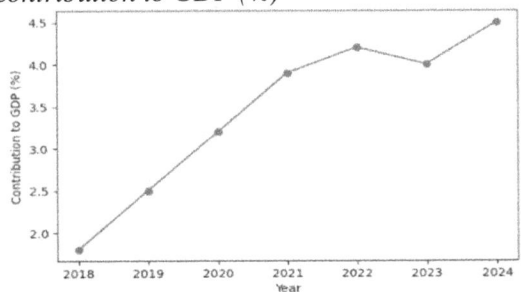

Figure 2. Number of patents filed

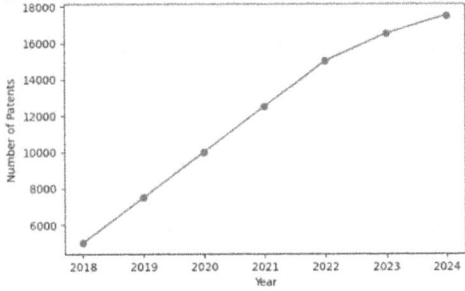

Figure 3. Funding received (in billions USD)

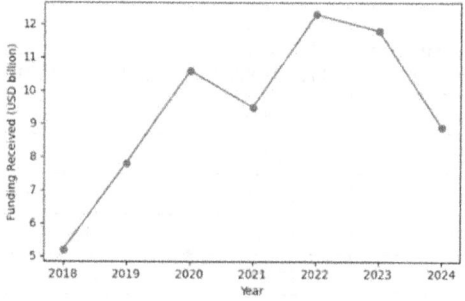

Figure 4. Growth in women startup (%)

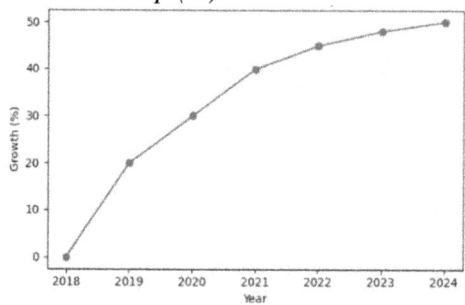

Result Analysis

The graph-1 shows that the startup contribution to GDP is rising between the year 2018 and April 2024.

The culture of invention and technological growth can be seen in the rising number of patents filed by startups as shown in figure-2.

Although the amount of funds received (figure-3) peaked in 2020, there is a minor fall in the years that follow, which could indicate changes in investor attitude or market circumstances.

The rise in female-led businesses shows that the entrepreneurial environment is moving in the direction of gender inclusion (Figure-4).

Strategies to Run Business Incubators

Effective business incubators foster creativity, accelerate startup growth, and drive economic development by providing comprehensive support, including physical space, training, networking, mentorship, and access to funding. The incubation process consists of three stages: pre-incubation (concept development), incubation (prototype refinement), and post-incubation (launch preparation), helping startups succeed and contributing to economic growth. Best practices of Indian incubators are:

a) Government Collaboration: Government programs such as Startup India can be used to take advantage of incentives.

Example: The Atal Incubation Centers (AICs) are one of the programs that the Atal Innovation Mission (AIM) works with.

b) Market Access and Validation: Promote market validation by means of pilot programs, corporate collaborations, and access to prospective clientele.

Example: Market access and pilot opportunities for its portfolio firms are made easier by collaborating with corporate entities.

c) Infrastructure Support: To meet the needs of entrepreneurs, coworking spaces, labs, and prototype facilities are provided.

Example: The NSRCEL at IIM Bangalore is a great place for startups to use cutting edge facilities.

d) Networking and Community Building: Peer-to-peer learning, networking, and cooperation can be provided.

Example: The Kerala Startup Mission organizes gatherings to encourage networking and cooperation amongst businesses.

e) International Exposure: Exposure to foreign markets, investors, and ecosystems can be provided by means of alliances, exchange programs, and international gatherings.

Example: The DLabs at the Indian School of Business works with international companies such as Techstars and 500 firms to offer their firms visibility abroad.

f) Feedback and Impact Measurement: Provide systems to gauge how the incubator affects the expansion, employment, and income of entrepreneurs.

Example: The social and economic effects of the foundation's programs are regularly monitored.

ENTREPRENEURS, PARTNERSHIPS, AND INNOVATION

Collaboration, innovation, and business incubators are crucial elements in fostering entrepreneurship and economic development in India. Startup ecosystems, enterprises, government agencies, academia, and other stakeholders have come together to support startups and promote innovation through national and international programs. These initiatives aim to enhance the start-up environment by leveraging the strengths of all stakeholders. Ultimately, these programs aim to contribute to India's long-term economic growth by promoting innovation and success (Phani, et al., (2017)).

Business incubators are establishments that offer resources, assistance, and direction to fledgling and early stage businesses to facilitate their growth and success. These incubators are essential to encourage innovation and entrepreneurship in India. They provide a variety of services including market exposure, infrastructural support, capital access, networking opportunities, and coaching. They provide a variety of services including market exposure, infrastructural support, capital access, networking opportunities, and coaching, such as mentorship programs and business development workshops (Kulal (2022), Dasgupta (2022)).

For Example: Indian Angel Network (IAN) is a notable and leading angel investor network business incubator that offers funding, mentorship, and strategic guidance to startups. For instance, they have recently invested in GreenTech, an innovative startup focused on developing eco-friendly solutions for the agricultural industry. IAN has been providing a valuable mentorship with unique products and services, such as Health Tech, which is developing cutting-edge medical devices to enhance patient outcomes. IAN incubation program supports startups in various sectors with the necessary resources and support to thrive in today's competitive business environment. enabling them to scale up their businesses and access new markets.

Findings, Discussions, and Implications

Collaboration between diverse entities sparks innovation, boosts productivity, and expands market reach by sharing resources, expertise, and networks. By working together, stakeholders can develop cutting-edge solutions, reduce costs, and accelerate time-to-market, achieving better results than they would alone. Collaboration can be national, as seen in India's CoInnovate program, or international, as seen in the US-India Business Council's efforts. These partnerships drive innovation, trade, and investment, fostering growth and progress (Patil (2020)).

Innovation is the successful commercialization of an invention through a novel business model, product, process, or service that meets customer needs. It encompasses various types, including organizational, marketing, and social innovation, and is crucial for long-term sustainability and competitiveness in today's industry.

Findings: Business incubators have a positive impact on entrepreneurial empowerment, leading to improved business performance and job creation. Incubators provide essential resources, mentorship, and networking opportunities that enhance entrepreneurs' skills and confidence. Entrepreneurs in incubators show higher levels of innovation, risk-taking, and adaptability.

Discussions: The study highlights the importance of business incubators in fostering entrepreneurial empowerment, particularly in emerging economies. The incubator model can be replicated and scaled up to support more entrepreneurs, promoting economic growth and development.

Implications: Governments and policymakers should invest in creating and supporting business incubators, especially in underserved regions. Incubators should focus on providing tailored support to entrepreneurs, addressing their specific needs and challenges. Entrepreneurs should be encouraged to seek out incubator programs to maximize their potential and contribute to economic growth.

By creating a nurturing environment that encourages collaboration, rewards innovation, and supports startups, India can maintain its status as a global hub for entrepreneurship and innovation, driving sustainable growth and prosperity.

CONCLUSION

The essential component for fostering entrepreneurs and companies are business incubators. These are acting as a catalyst agent in promoting their efficiency at the early stages of the venture for their expansion and growth. This chapter assesses the different forms of assistance that incubators offer and looks at new developments such as virtual models and sustainability integration. It provides a perspective for the incubation ecosystem by combining insights from scholars, business executives, and legislators. The novelty of this chapter is to promote a vibrant entrepreneurial environment that stimulates innovation, job creation, and economic growth by deepening our understanding of the incubation process and providing actionable recommendations for enhancing its efficacy and sustainability.

Future Scope of the Work

Incubators play a vital role in fostering entrepreneurship, providing resources, support, and guidance to help businesses grow. They connect entrepreneurs with partners, customers, and investors, contributing to economic development. To promote entrepreneurship, institutions should establish their own incubators, leveraging expertise and research. Rural entrepreneurship is also crucial for sustainable businesses, and this chapter will focus on strategies to support rural entrepreneurs and attract government and incubator support.

REFERENCES

Akpuokwe, C. U., Chikwe, C. F., & Eneh, N. E. (2024). Innovating business practices: The impact of social media on fostering gender equality and empowering women entrepreneurs. Magna Scientia Advanced Research and Reviews, 10(2), 032-043.

Assenova, V. A. (2020). Early-stage venture incubation and mentoring promote learning, scaling, and profitability among disadvantaged entrepreneurs. Organization Science, 31(6), 1560-1578.

Browne, E. (2021). Social and commercial enterprise interactions: Insights from UK business incubators (Doctoral dissertation, University of Plymouth).

Daraojimba, C., Abioye, K. M., Bakare, A. D., Mhlongo, N. Z., Onunka, O., & Daraojimba, D. O. (2023). Technology and innovation to growth of entrepreneurship and financial boost: A decade in review (2013-2023). *International Journal of Management & Entrepreneurship Research*, 5(10), 769–792. DOI: 10.51594/ijmer.v5i10.593

Dasgupta, T. (2022). Analysis of Strategies followed by New-Age Indian Entrepreneurs for seeking Business Opportunities and Competitive Advantage (Doctoral dissertation, ICFAI University Jharkhand).

Dhochak, M., Acharya, S. R., & Sareen, S. B. (2019). Assessing the effectiveness of business incubators. *International Journal of Innovation and Learning*, 26(2), 177–194. DOI: 10.1504/IJIL.2019.10022108

Galbraith, B., McAdam, R., & Cross, S. E. (2019). The evolution of the incubator: Past, present, and future. *IEEE Transactions on Engineering Management*, 68(1), 265–271. DOI: 10.1109/TEM.2019.2905297

Hervieux, C., & Voltan, A. (2018). Framing social problems in social entrepreneurship. *Journal of Business Ethics*, 151(2), 279–293. DOI: 10.1007/s10551-016-3252-1

Himanen, P., Au, A., & Margulies, P. (2011). The new incubators. *World Policy Journal*, 28(3), 22–34. DOI: 10.1177/0740277511425351

Keenan, J., Wein, J., & Willis, T. (2018). Economic Assessment of Startup Accelerators.

Kilcrease, K. (2012). The Batavia industrial center: The hatching of the world's first business incubator. *New York History*, 93(1), 71–93.

Korang, V. (2024). Establishing a Network for Promoting and Developing Entrepreneurship Education. *Convergence Chronicles*, 5(1), 343–353.

Kulal, A. (2022). Business Incubator: Seeding Start-ups Awareness among Post Graduation students with reference to CEOL, Mangalore.

Lesakova, L. (2012). The role of business incubators in supporting the SME start-up. *Acta Polytechnica Hungarica*, 9(3), 85–95.

Mian, S. A. (2021). Whither modern business incubation? Definitions, evolution, theory, and evaluation. In *Handbook of research on business and technology incubation and acceleration* (pp. 17–38). Edward Elgar Publishing. DOI: 10.4337/9781788974783.00008

Odeyemi, O., Oyewole, A. T., Adeoye, O. B., Ofodile, O. C., Addy, W. A., Okoye, C. C., & Ololade, Y. J. (2024). Entrepreneurship in Africa: A review of growth and challenges. *International Journal of Management & Entrepreneurship Research*, 6(3), 608–622. DOI: 10.51594/ijmer.v6i3.874

Patil, K. (2020). Indo-US S&T cooperation and the role of innovation diplomacy. *Science & Diplomacy*, 15.

Peters, L., Rice, M., & Sundararajan, M. (2004). The role of incubators in the entrepreneurial process. *The Journal of Technology Transfer*, 29(1), 83–91. DOI: 10.1023/B:JOTT.0000011182.82350.df

Phani, B. V., & Khandekar, S. (2017). *Innovation, Incubation and Entrepreneurship*. Springer. DOI: 10.1007/978-981-10-3334-6

Pompa, C. (2013). Literature review on the impact of business incubation, mentoring, investment and training on start-up companies. EPS PEAKS--Economic and Private Sector Professional Evidence and Applied Knowledge Services.

Robinson, S., & Stubberud, H. A. (2014). Business incubators: What services do business owners really use? *International Journal of Entrepreneurship*, 18, 29.

Roundy, P. T. (2021). Leadership in startup communities: How incubator leaders develop a regional entrepreneurial ecosystem. *Journal of Management Development*, 40(3), 190–208. DOI: 10.1108/JMD-10-2020-0320

Sharma, A. R., Shukla, B., & Joshi, M. (2019). *The Role of Business Incubators in the Economic Growth of India*. Walter de Gruyter GmbH & Co KG. DOI: 10.1515/9783110640489

Surana, K., Singh, A., & Sagar, A. D. (2020). Strengthening science, technology, and innovation-based incubators to help achieve Sustainable Development Goals: Lessons from India. *Technological Forecasting and Social Change*, 157, 120057. DOI: 10.1016/j.techfore.2020.120057

Thomas, J., & Reddy, R. (2013). Evaluation of social entrepreneurship educational programs in india. Social Innovation in Social Entrepreneurship: Strengthening the Ecosystem for Scaling Social Innovation, Villgro & IDRC. http://www. villgro. org/~ villgrouser/images/social%20innovation%20paper

Toganel, A. R. M., & Zhu, M. (2017). Success factors of accelerator backed ventures: Insights from the case of TechStars Accelerator Program.

Uhm, C. H., Sung, C. S., & Park, J. Y. (2018). Understanding the accelerator from resources-based perspective. *Asia Pacific Journal of Innovation and Entrepreneurship*, 12(3), 258–278. DOI: 10.1108/APJIE-01-2018-0001

William, P., Shrivastava, A., Aswal, U. S., Kumar, I., Gupta, M., & Rao, A. K. (2023, May). Framework for implementation of android automation tool in agro business sector. In *2023 4th International Conference on Intelligent Engineering and Management (ICIEM)* (pp. 1-6). IEEE. DOI: 10.1109/ICIEM59379.2023.10167328

Chapter 2
Exploring the Opportunities and Confronting the Challenges Within Business Incubation:
Opportunities and Challenges

Saba Inamdar
https://orcid.org/0000-0001-5917-4070
St. Joseph's Degree and PG College, India

Sameera Afroze
https://orcid.org/0000-0002-9162-1712
St. Joseph's Degree and PG College, India

ABSTRACT

Business incubation is a public or private development process that nurtures firms from idea creation to start-ups, providing complete assistance to help them grow and succeed. An incubator offers resources including, physical space, capital guidance, shared services, and networking opportunities. Incubators provide mentoring, business aid, and monitoring services. New enterprises are facilitated by raising awareness of risks and reducing the cost of failure. With over 10,000 incubators globally, the business incubation process has grown more important for start-ups, and extensive research has been conducted on the process, encompassing studies on its interventions and consequences. The current study advances understanding of the processes influencing particular performance and results and the incubation

DOI: 10.4018/979-8-3693-4302-9.ch002

process. It also examines the many kinds of business incubators, benefits, and drawbacks. It clarifies the goals of future research and how policymakers and incubation managers might design interventions according to the particular incubator type and the process setting.

INTRODUCTION

Business incubation, a multibillion-dollar sector involving accelerators and incubators, has evolved from a 1950s concept to become an essential part of the modern corporate landscape, providing entrepreneurs with resources and mentorship to transform their ideas into profitable businesses. This chapter discusses the importance of business incubation in corporate innovation, highlighting its stages (pre-incubation, incubation, acceleration) and the need for support structures. It also discusses the challenges and opportunities of business incubation. Further, it also discusses government support's strengths and role in fostering successful programs. The business incubation process consists of three stages: pre-incubation, incubation, and acceleration. Pre-incubation involves developing a technology-focused business idea or project for companies working alone or with a team. Forming a capable team and creating a viable business strategy to save money is crucial. Incubation involves entrepreneurs who have completed their business plan and are ready for incorporation. Business incubation is a public or private development process that nurtures firms from idea creation to start-ups, providing complete assistance to help them grow and succeed. An incubator offers resources including physical space, capital guidance, shared services, and networking opportunities. Incubators offer mentoring, business aid, and monitoring services. New enterprises are facilitated by raising awareness of risks and reducing the cost of failure. Business incubation was first introduced in the US in 1942 to address the issue of high transaction costs and limited social networking among inventors, which prevented many innovations from becoming practical goods. This resulted in the founding of the first business incubator, Student Agencies Inc., in Ithaca. In 1946, an MIT alumnus founded American Research Development (ARD), a business incubator. Business incubators have gained popularity worldwide since their inception. The top business incubators are located in Silicon Valley, New York, Berlin, and Singapore.

National Business Incubation Association (NBIA) of the United States of America (US) defined business incubation as "Business incubators nurture the development of entrepreneurial companies, helping them survive and grow during the start-up period, when they are most vulnerable. Their programs provide client companies with business support services and resources tailored to young firms. The most common goals of incubation programs are creating jobs in a community, enhancing a community's entrepreneurial climate, retaining businesses in a community, building or accelerating growth in a local industry and diversifying local economies."

Business incubators are essential in connecting fledgling entrepreneurial companies to the rest of the business world. Incubators operate as a buffer mechanism, internally supplying critical resources while protecting initiatives from external dangers and problems. The protective role allows enterprises to focus on growing their core skills, goods, services, or business strategies free of external influences. Incubators also act as bridges, connecting emerging companies to their surroundings when appropriate. They promote interactions and align norms, allowing entrepreneurs to access and collect critical resources that would be difficult or expensive to acquire (Isher, 2024). This bridging position strengthens the enterprises' capacity to thrive and expand in their competitive environment (Mrkajic, 2017). The technique creates a supportive atmosphere for entrepreneurs during the early stages of their business growth. This environment may save start-up costs, boost entrepreneur confidence and capacity, and provide access to necessary resources for successful growth.

Entrepreneurs at business incubators typically stay until they accomplish a certain milestone, such as sales income or profitability. Business incubation is a mechanism for promoting innovation and company growth. Complementary intermediaries include company development service providers and technology parks. Incubation is a continuing interaction between an incubator and an early-stage entrepreneur. Graduation occurs when the firm reaches maturity. The incubator's assistance evolves with the business's development needs, including prototypes, pilot goods, and sales. Legally, entrepreneurs must understand intellectual property and other regulations, including patent, trademark, copyright, and international business restrictions and the tax implications of running a business. Various factors influence entrepreneurship success, including community support, networking opportunities, educational resources, and university collaborations. Incubators play a crucial role in fostering success through financial support, guidance, managerial assistance, and transparent entry/exit policies. They also shape entrepreneurs' market expertise, foster social connections, and provide insights into emerging trends.

LITERATURE REVIEW

Incubators vary from business centers in that the latter simply provide renting space, access to office equipment and conference rooms. Incubators, on the other hand, often provide comprehensive business assistance to their customers, guiding them through the difficult formative years while allowing them to grow their enterprises and focus on bringing products and services to market (Rice, 2002). Several studies in the entrepreneurial literature have highlighted the role of incubators in entrepreneurial activity (Theodoraki et al., 2020; Audretsch et al., 2021) and the influence of the incubation process (Albort-Morant & Ribeiro-Soriano, 2016; Mas-Verdú et al., 2015). One of the primary goals of the incubator process is to help businesses in their early phases boost their chances of survival and Growth (Aernoudt, 2004). Growth in the business incubation process led to various business incubators, such as corporate incubators, technology incubators, university incubators, accelerators, innovation centres, and working and co-working spaces. The incubation process occurs inside the "black box" of an incubator, where the incubator engages in value-added activities. (Startupblink, 2023). Campbell et al. (1985) pioneered the business incubation process paradigm. Their methodology consists of four basic value-adding activities or services that incubators provide to help incubate function better. The incubator's new business concept requires diagnosing needs as the first step. After performing the tests, they closely monitor the incubated companies. Throughout the incubation process, incubatees gain access to cash investment and expert networks. The incubatees eventually graduate as successful ventures. The most common forms of support include:

1. **Infrastructure:** Most incubators have "easy in, easy out" arrangements, which are monthly leasing terms that provide clients flexibility when entering or leaving. Some incubators, particularly sector-specific incubators, include technical facilities such as laboratories and equipment, which may be extremely beneficial, especially for a technology-based start-up firm. This topic is covered in full in Module 3 of the training program, "Planning an Incubator".
2. **Business Services**: Incubators offer administrative and communication services, sometimes at "pay as you go" prices, such as Internet, telecommunications, copier, fax, binding, reception, mail, document receiving and dispatch, and secretarial support. These support services enable clients to focus on their primary business rather than the supporting infrastructure. Furthermore, start-up companies are not required to make initial investments in costly office equipment or front-of-house personnel, which can be provided by the incubation.
3. **Financing:** Incubators help entrepreneurs have access to a variety of financing options. Depending on the business's growth stage, the incubator may connect its customer with government grant programs, banks, or venture capitalists. As a result, financing options range from seed grants to loans and equity. Some incubators may also provide their customers with access to their own sources of capital, such as managing their own seed fund to invest in their clients' enterprises. Module 9 of the training curriculum delves deeply into the subject of funding incubator customers.

4. **People Connectivity:** Incubators promote advising connections between the start-up company's management team and an experienced member of the incubator management team or an external expert in the appropriate field or industry (the mentor). In this approach, incubators assist clients develop their own entrepreneurial and business talents (Bøllingtoft & Ulhøi, 2005). Personal talents, such as financial, marketing, and managerial abilities, as well as general sound business judgment, are vital to any company's success. As a result, incubators strive to help their clients enhance these talents. The experienced incubator manager or mentor advises and guides the start-up throughout its development. The mentor may also assist the entrepreneur with links to his or her own networks.

Incubators can help their customers arrange meetings, talks, connections, and partnerships with professionals like as accountants, communications and marketing consultants, and attorneys. Furthermore, incubators enable relationships between their clients and industry leaders in their respective marketplaces. These networks and relationships may assist client organizations in acquiring new consumers or entering new markets, as well as identifying possible partners and investors.

Process of Business Incubation

Business incubation is a systematic procedure that aims to foster and accelerate the growth of early-stage companies or startups (Azih & Inanga, 2014). It starts with a rigorous screening and evaluation of talented entrepreneurs, including their business concepts and preparedness. Accepted businesses receive extensive support, including mentorship, access to resources such as office space and investment options, and specialized training in critical areas for company development (Ayatse et al., 2017). Throughout the incubation stage, continued assistance and networking opportunities allow businesses to fine-tune strategy, overcome obstacles, and pivot strategically as necessary. The ultimate objective is to assist entrepreneurs in becoming self-sustaining and market-ready by graduating from the program or adapting to market demand (Universidade Comunitária da Região de Chapecó, Santa Catarina, Brazil et al., 2017). Business incubators boost economic growth and competitiveness in various industries by encouraging innovation and entrepreneurship. The process of business incubation is discussed as under.

Pre-incubation: Pre-incubation is the process of developing a technology-focused company idea or project for companies that have begun working alone or with a team but have not yet been incorporated to make this notion a reality. Entrepreneurs in the pre-incubation process require specialized training, coaching, and consulting services to determine whether their ideas are feasible, commercializable, scalable, and so on. Pre-incubation centers offer these chances to early-stage entrepreneurs for a period of six months to a year. Pre-incubation centers can give entrepreneurs with the physical amenities they require, such as open offices and shared workspaces. The duration of these possibilities for entrepreneurs varies depending on the sector in which they will operate. While software-focused firms are anticipated to finish this phase in six months on average, health-related start-ups may take longer. Entrepreneurs develop an appropriate and practical company strategy by clarifying their ideas with the assistance of pre-incubation centers. At this point, a large proportion of entrepreneurs shift their company plan in favor of a more practical one by using the knowledge and experience of mentors and advisors. In the pre-incubation phase, the key thing is to form a team that can accomplish the task and create the correct business plan that will save money. At the conclusion of the pre-incubation period, entrepreneurs are prepared to enter the firm with a correct and complete business plan and implement their ideas. After then, they resume their work on the incubation phase. Because the pre-incubation process is at an early stage, entrepreneurs frequently obtain financial backing from government bodies.

Incubation: At the conclusion of the pre-incubation period, entrepreneurs who have completed the business plan and are ready for incorporation enter the incubation phase. During the incubation era, entrepreneurs require physical facilities as well as training, consulting, and mentoring services, just as they did before. These entrepreneurs' requirements are covered while in the incubation facility. The incubation time ranges from one to three years, depending on the industry of the firm. Start-ups in industries such as health, food, and others that require more time to get certifications and patents are incubated longer than software start-ups.

Entrepreneurs form their firms at the incubation stage and create a minimal viable product. Incubation facilities give the technical help that entrepreneurs require, particularly while creating goods. Following product development, one of the most difficult stages of company process and management begins: commercialization. The primary reason for this stage's difficulty is because commercialization efforts are pricey. Companies' financial demands grow as a result of the expenditures spent, and they must seek new sources of funding. This method might vary based on the sector or product that the entrepreneurs produce. For example, licenses and certifications impose significant expenses for health-care enterprises. Entrepreneurs who stand out with their business plans and the capabilities of their teams and who have high awareness of the functioning of the entrepreneurship ecosystem can skip the pre-incubation stage and settle directly in the incubation center.

Acceleration: Acceleration is the method by which firms that has developed their goods and begun commercialization studies but are having difficulty acquiring market share and internationalization may resolve these issues with the assistance of acceleration programs during this phase. The notion of acceleration may be viewed as a new model for the entrepreneurship community. It is incorrect to define it as a continuation of the incubation phases since it is a new model that continually evolves to meet the demands of entrepreneurs. Acceleration programs differ significantly from pre-incubation and incubation methods. Institutions that organize the program usually restrict the duration of the program to 6-12 months and want all companies to start the program at the same time. As a result, all firms attend the same trainings and events and present to investors at the same time. This environment assures that competition and engagement among businesses are high.

Companies participating in accelerator programs often begin to earn money after their goods are ready for commercialization. Furthermore, because the company's sales, turnover, profit, and other expectations may be compared to its actual values at this point, venture capital funds and angel investors are interested in these enterprises. Private corporations and funds not only invest in accelerator start-ups, but they also frequently conduct acceleration programs. To summarize, entrepreneurs vary from hierarchically structured private organizations that make sluggish judgments by utilizing new business concepts and rapid, flexible frameworks. Because of these characteristics, they have a significant role both economically and socially. As a result, it is critical that entrepreneurs get governmental and private sector support based on their stage of development, including business strategies, product status, commercialization status, and so on. When companies have the required backing, they may be extremely successful for their investors. As a result, the budgets and numbers of the entrepreneurial ecosystem and pre-incubation, incubation, and acceleration programs will continue to grow, increasing their relevance in the economy even more.

History of Business Incubation

Business incubation concepts began in the U.S. in 1959 when Joseph L. Mancuso came up with the Batavia Industrial Center in Batavia, New York. Then, the idea of incubation expanded in the U.S. in the 1980s, leading it to spread in the U.K. and Europe with different forms, such as innovation centres, technopolis/science parks, and pepinieres enterprises. The U.S.-based International Business Innovation Association states that more than 7,000 incubators are functional worldwide. According to the European Commission's 2002 estimation, approximately 900 incubation environments exist in Western Europe. Nowadays, incubation environments are also popular in developing countries, as interest in financial support from organizations such as UNIDO and the World Bank is gaining prevalence worldwide. Campbell et al (1985) were the first to develop business incubation model. Their methodology consists of four basic value-added activities or services that incubators provide to incubatees to improve their success. The incubator's new business concept outlines operations that begin with diagnostics. After the tests are performed, these incubatee companies are watched. Throughout the incubation process, incubatees get access to cash investment and expert networks. Successful enterprises emerge from incubation programs. Campbell model was later extended by Smilor (1987) who visualised incubator as "a system that confers 'structure' and 'credibility' on incubatees while controlling a set of assistive resources". Business incubators provide services and are associated with private sector, colleges, government, and non-profit organizations, as per the author. Incubators offer secretarial, business knowledge, and administrative services to promote innovative product development, profitability, job creation, technological diversity, and economic growth. Hackett & Dilts (2004) stated that the procedure begins with choosing incubatees from a pool of prospective individuals. Selected applicants participate in "black box" operations such as resource allocation, monitoring, and business help. Start-ups exit the incubator with either success or failure. Other parameters to consider are incubator size, development level, population size, and economic status. As per Cooper & Park (2008) incubators generate social capital, provides direction to entrepreneur's market experience and provides availability of technological solution.

TYPES OF BUSINESS INCUBATORS

Venture Capital Incubators

Venture Capital Incubators invest in new firms and offer funding in exchange for equity (Chen, 2009). They provide mentorship, connect management teams with investors, and offer financial management support as part of their incubation package.

For instance, Y Combinator is a renowned Silicon Valley-based startup accelerator that has supported over 2,000 firms, providing seed funding, mentorship, and access to a vast network of investors.

Startup Studio

Startup Studios, or startup foundries, focus on constructing multiple businesses sequentially (Sansone et al., 2023). They work with start-ups in the early stages, providing mentorship and planning support to bring ideas to reality.

For instance, ShiftPixy Labs operates Fast Pitchen, a ghost kitchen incubator program that supports restaurant operators in developing innovative concepts and succeeding in the competitive restaurant industry.

Seed Accelerators

Seed Accelerators are programs similar to incubators but with a fixed timeline and a focus on fast-tracking start-ups (Yagüe-Perales et al., 2024). They land on a pitch day, where start-ups present their progress.

For instance, Techstars, a global network of business incubators, has offices in over 20 countries and has supported over 2,000 start-ups since its inception, providing mentorship and investor access.

Corporate Incubators

Corporate Incubators, or corporate accelerators, are initiatives by large companies to foster innovation by supporting start-ups (Gonthier & Chirita, 2019). They provide office space, funding, mentorship, and collaboration opportunities to emerging businesses.

For instance, Google for Start-ups is an initiative by Google that provides support, mentorship, and resources to start-ups globally, enhancing innovation and collaboration within the tech ecosystem.

Kitchen Incubators

Kitchen *Incubators* offer entrepreneurs, chefs, and restaurateurs a space to develop culinary ideas and concepts (Dent, 2008). They provide commercial kitchen facilities, mentorship, funding access, and educational opportunities to nurture food-related start-ups.

For instance, ShiftPixy Labs operates Fast Pitch, a ghost kitchen incubator program that supports restaurant operators in developing innovative concepts and succeeding in the competitive restaurant industry

Virtual Business Incubators

Virtual Business Incubators provide mentorship, networking, and support to start-ups in a digital environment (Freiling et al., 2022). They offer guidance and resources remotely, fostering entrepreneurship and business growth virtually.

For instance, Startup Chile is a virtual business incubator program by the Chilean government that supports start-ups globally through mentorship, funding, and access to the Latin American market.

Academic Incubators

Academic Incubators are programs set up by colleges and universities to encourage entrepreneurship among students, faculty, and alums. They provide resources, mentorship, and support to help develop business ideas and launch start-ups (Blank, 2021).

For instance, Stanford-StartX is a non-profit start-up accelerator affiliated with Stanford University, offering funding, mentorship, and resources to student-led start-ups across various industries.

Social Incubators

Social Incubators support start-ups and entrepreneurs addressing social or environmental challenges. They provide resources, mentorship, and funding to develop sustainable and impactful businesses (Mair et al., 2006).

For instance, Ashoka is a global network of social entrepreneurs and change makers that provides funding, mentorship, and support to start-ups addressing social and environmental challenges.

Medical Incubators

Medical Incubators focus on supporting start-ups developing medical technologies, devices, or services (Braun & Hentschel, 2011). They provide specialized resources, mentorship, and funding to navigate the complex healthcare industry (Rotenstein et al., 2019).

For instance, MedTech Innovator is a medical technology incubator and accelerator program that offers funding, mentorship, and support to start-ups developing innovative medical devices and technologies.

Advantages of Business Incubators

1. **Cost Savings:** Incubators offer start-ups affordable office space and access to shared resources like internet and administrative support (Pattanasak et al., 2022). By providing these essentials at lower costs, start-ups can significantly reduce their operating expenses, allowing them to allocate more resources to business development.
2. **Educational Resources:** Start-ups benefit from educational programs, workshops, and mentorship incubators provide. These resources offer invaluable learning opportunities, enabling entrepreneurs to gain insights from experienced

professionals, acquire new skills, and navigate the challenges of starting and growing a business effectively.
3. **Funding Access:** Incubators often maintain strong connections with investors and facilitate start-up funding opportunities (Markley & McNamara, 1995). By offering a structured environment, mentorship, and networking events, incubators increase start-ups' chances of securing investment, accelerating their growth and development.
4. **Networking Opportunities:** Joining an incubator provides start-ups with access to a diverse network of entrepreneurs, investors, and industry experts. These connections offer collaboration, partnerships, and mentorship opportunities, boosting growth and expansion within the start-up ecosystem (Schwartz & Hornych, 2012).
5. **Structured Environment:** An incubator's structured environment and curriculum help start-ups maintain focus, develop productive work habits, and achieve their business objectives systematically. This disciplined approach enhances start-ups' efficiency and productivity, driving progress toward their goals.
6. **Product Testing and Development**: Incubators offer start-ups a supportive environment to test their products or services, gather feedback, and refine their offerings before launching them. This iterative process permits start-ups to detect and address potential challenges early on, increasing their chances of success (Gandhi et al., 2022).
7. **Enhanced Credibility:** Associating with a reputable incubator can enhance a start-up's credibility, visibility, and brand recognition within the entrepreneurial community. This association signals to investors, customers, and partners that the start-up has undergone rigorous vetting and is poised for success in the market.

MAIN FOCUS OF THE CHAPTER

Challenges

While offering a robust platform for startups and emerging companies, business incubation faces many challenges that can hinder incubation effectiveness and sustainability. Key among these challenges is the issue of sustainability itself, as many incubators need continuous support to maintain long-term viability. The need for essential skills among incubates further complicates the incubation process, often requiring additional resources and training. Securing adequate funding remains a significant hurdle, impeding growth and innovation. The digital divide presents another barrier, limiting access to critical technological resources and knowledge.

Legal complications can create complex hurdles, diverting focus and resources from core business activities. Talent acquisition challenges exacerbate the situation, as incubators must compete with established firms for top-tier talent. Additionally, the absence of comprehensive success metrics makes it difficult to gauge the true impact of incubation programs. Lastly, the lack of post-incubation support leaves many startups vulnerable once they exit the incubator, undermining their ventures' long-term success and sustainability. The aforementioned are discussed as under:

Sustainability: One major difficulty for business incubators is the lack of growth and sustainability, which can prevent them from meeting their objectives. Lack of sustainability occurs when the incubator is unable to maintain and sustain itself. The research adds that the effectiveness of the business incubator management is judged by his or her ability to obtain funding, hire suitable personnel, and maintain the resources required to run the incubator efficiently and successfully. It is crucial for the administration of a business incubator to seek out partnerships and investors who can offer financial support and make the incubator sustainable in order for it to be economically sustainable (Denktas-Sakar & Karatas-Cetin, 2012). It is crucial for the administration of a business incubator to seek out partnerships and investors who can offer financial support and make the incubator sustainable in order for it to be economically sustainable.

Lack of Skills: Some business incubators have a mind-set of offering training programs based on what they offer rather than what entrepreneurs demand, they lack the ability to adapt to entrepreneurs' needs (Jordan, 1998 in InfoDev, 2010, p. 29). In the same vein, Wilber and Dixon (2003) stated that business incubators have the difficulty of providing small business owners and managers with the skills required to succeed in a competitive market.

Funding: In developing countries where the business incubators are still evolving, funding is available only through government agencies, it's very difficult for start-ups to raise funds on their own. Running a start-up requires a large quantity of finance. The majority of companies are supported with their own money or by borrowing from friends and relatives. Not every start-up needs external investment, the issue arises when they intend to expand their firm. Even if the response to the product is positive, collecting financing from the proper investors is challenging. However, many incubators have difficulty collecting adequate funding for their programs, restricting the financial resources available to the firms they sponsor. This typically occurs when an incubator has not established a market reputation or has not worked with a large number of clients. This can stifle the growth and viability of developing businesses, undermining the whole aim of incubators.

Digital Divide: The digital gap is caused by unequal access to technology and digital infrastructure and can hinder the development of businesses. In addition to all of this, start-ups frequently struggle to enter and compete in established marketplaces that are controlled by bigger, more established businesses. While it is undeniable that businesses have transformed the way we live, work, and interact, their unbridled influence and monopolistic practises pose a severe threat to the entrepreneurs. The problem of data is one area that warrants special attention. Big IT companies have an unfair advantage as compared to start ups when it comes to creating new products and services since they have access to a vast amount of customer data.

Legal complications: Legally, entrepreneurs must understand the complexity of intellectual property and other regulations that may influence their operations. This entails comprehending the complexities of patent law, trademark law, copyright law, and international business restrictions. Furthermore, entrepreneurs must understand the tax ramifications of conducting a firm.

Talent Acquisition: Skilled job seekers avoid start-ups due to inherent risk, instead prefer to work for large corporations. Even if they manage to join the start-up eventually they switch to established companies. Another challenge in acquiring talent is that many job applicants lack the necessary qualifications. Start-ups notice a knowledge gap between what is taught in schools and what is required for work, particularly in fields where technology advances quickly. New graduates are typically not immediately employable since they are not familiar with market demands. As a result, when employing new personnel, companies must commit a sizable amount of time and money to training them.

Limited Success Metrics: Measuring business incubator success is difficult, as many programs lack established indicators. Without well-defined benchmarks, assessing the impact of these incubators on the firms they help becomes difficult. This lack of accountability can result in inefficiencies and impede the on-going progress of incubation programs.

Lack of Post-Incubation Support: This absence of on-going support after incubation frequently leaves firms struggling to scale and navigate market complexity. Creating a structure for on-going advice and resources beyond the initial program is critical to ensure the long-term viability of these new initiatives.

Opportunities

The present economy considers every job a valuable contribution, warranting compensation with few exceptions. The mindset of integrating everyone into the economic cycle has fuelled a rise in business ventures, thereby generating employment opportunities. Interestingly, the scarcity of traditional job openings has given rise to a paradox in keeping the economic engine running and encouraging start-ups. Instead of waiting for existing positions to become available, those unemployed are empowered to create jobs. This shift addresses the immediate need for employment and fosters innovation and entrepreneurial spirit, driving further economic growth and diversification.

Many factors, spanning various dimensions, influence success in entrepreneurship. These elements encompass the support of the community within the entrepreneurial ecosystem, opportunities for networking, access to educational resources, and collaborations with universities (Vardhan & Mahato, 2022). Additionally, the success of incubators is highlighted by critical factors such as financial backing, continuous support for start-ups, managerial guidance, and straightforward entry and exit strategies (Allahar & Brathwaite, 2016). For start-ups undergoing incubation, factors like business expertise and success metrics are crucial for progress (Pettersen et al., 2015). Incubators act as catalysts for innovation, shaping entrepreneurs' market knowledge, building social networks, providing insights into emerging trends, and facilitating access to technological resources (Dhiman & Arora, 2024). The strengths of incubators vary between developed and developing countries (Allahar & Brathwaite, 2016).

Developed nations prioritize developing business incubation due to its pivotal role in facilitating innovation, entrepreneurship, and economic growth. These nations typically possess robust government support systems that provide funding, infrastructure, and regulatory frameworks conducive to nurturing start-ups. Developed nations aim to maintain and enhance their global competitiveness across technology, biotech, and advanced manufacturing sectors by supporting business incubators. Moreover, incubators contribute significantly to job creation, economic stability, and the diversification of economies away from traditional industries. With access to extensive resources, including high-speed internet, research institutions, and skilled labour pools, these nations create environments where start-ups can thrive, benefiting from mentorship, networking opportunities, and access to capital (Hassan, 2020). This strategic focus on business incubation reflects a commitment to fostering a dynamic entrepreneurial ecosystem that drives cutting-edge innovations and sustainable economic development (Yuan et al., 2022). In developed nations, incubators often receive substantial government support to achieve self-sustainability. They excel in assisting entrepreneurs with comprehensive tangible and intangible services. Cultural factors such as innovation, creativity, digital entrepreneurship, skill development, and education quality play a significant role. Considering the aforementioned factors, incubators play a crucial role in supporting such underserved businesses like small and handmade products by offering mentoring, training, networking, investment, and market access. However, they face challenges such as diverse demands, limited resources, and a volatile market environment. They must be adaptable and versatile to meet diverse business needs (Egbetokun, 2023).

In contrast, developing countries often show modest to low levels of these cultural indicators. Incubators in these regions frequently face policy challenges, with considerable involvement from the government and universities in their management and funding. Despite these hurdles, there is moderate policy engagement in developing countries, suggesting potential for future growth and improvement (Chandra & Medrano Silva, 2012, Mubaraki & Busler, 2015). Business incubators in emerging nations like China and Brazil have encouraged entrepreneurship and innovation. The government has aggressively promoted incubators in China through regulations and subsidies, emphasizing the technology and industrial sectors. China's incubators frequently give entrepreneurs access to excellent research facilities and industry networks. In contrast, Brazil's incubator strategy emphasizes the importance of public-private cooperation. Brazilian incubators commonly work with universities and firms to offer entrepreneurs mentorship, resources, and market access. Both nations use their incubators to boost economic growth, generate employment, and increase global competitiveness (Lalkaka, 2003). When well-planned, supported, and performed, business incubators can significantly improve the supportive conditions for entrepreneurship (Sanyal & Hisam, 2018). Identifying inadequacies, determining which sectors are underperforming, and developing plans to close these gaps are critical to success. The rigorous identification procedure establishes the foundation for a thriving economy (Wasdani et al., 2022).

DISCUSSION

Business incubation is a complex process filled with opportunities and obstacles, including financial constraints, regulatory hurdles, and market entry obstacles. Despite these challenges, incubators offer significant benefits such as a structured environment, access to mentors, and a supportive community that encourages creativity and problem-solving skills. They also act as intermediaries for potential investors, enhancing the chances of obtaining crucial funding. Despite these challenges, incubators provide a supportive environment for startups to grow and thrive. The government should consider creating a single system capable of tracking business incubators around the country and coordinating the efforts of all organizations and companies involved in new venture creation. Furthermore, there is an urgent need to build sector-specific incubators to promote manufacturing, as most start-ups today operate on a service model (Li et al., 2020). Accelerators and incubators programs help start-ups and small companies by offering tools, coaching, and finance. They boost members' employability and make it simpler for firms to obtain financing, allowing quick development (Madaleno et al., 2022). These initiatives' effectiveness depends on variables like university engagement, which provides research expertise and resources, and the economic situation of their respective communities (Etzkowitz, 2002). Academics and program organizers are currently endeavouring to design and implement interventions that optimize their influence on job creation and company growth, though sometimes the most effective design for each component of these programs still needs to be determined (Mian, 1996, Kolympiris & Klein, 2017, Leal et al., 2023). Further, understanding the interaction of social, geographical, and material aspects within organizations is crucial for comprehending incubation activity dynamics (Van Erkelens et al., 2024). Social factors, such as connections between entrepreneurs, mentors, and support personnel, influence collaborative norms and information exchange. Spatial aspects, like the context, affect resource accessibility and community. Material components, like financing, technology, and infrastructure, provide entrepreneurs with the necessary support to prototype and expand their enterprises which helps refine support systems and improve incubation outcomes. Financial stability is critical for incubators' long-term viability since it assures essential services such as mentorship and infrastructure availability. Incubators play an important role in emerging economies, handling a variety of difficulties and possibilities (Narayanan & Shin, 2019). They deal with legal and regulatory issues, cultural dynamics, economic variables, and the entrepreneurial ecosystem. Understanding these environments is critical for managing difficulties and opportunities, assuring business registration, intellectual property protection, investment practices, and the overall health of the entrepreneurial ecosystem, including talent availability and investor participation (Bitzer et al., 2008). Developing countries can learn from developed countries' environmental mistakes, particularly regarding natural resource depletion and degradation. By incorporating academia in business incubators, developing countries may thoroughly examine these examples and incorporate sustainable methods into their company incubation procedures. This method encourages innovation and assures that economic expansion does not harm the environment. Emphasizing sustainability from the start can result in long-term advantages such as protected natural resources, better ecosystems, and a higher standard of living for future generations. Furthermore, this proactive approach may position emerging nations as pioneers in sustainable development, establishing a worldwide benchmark for balancing economic advancement with environmental care (Hernández & Carrà, 2016). Creating a supportive environment within the incubator strengthens its value offer, recruiting fresh talent and investment (Bergek & Norrman, 2008). By concentrating on these pillars, incubators may thrive and continue to foster long-term innovation and economic growth (Jha & A, 2024).

FUTURE RESEARCH DIRECTIONS

Over the past three decades, research on the incubation process has solidified and considerably enhanced our understanding of the type of services and value supplied by the incubation process and the processes of start-up support and growth. Consequently, there are no studies concerning comparative study across regions. There is scope for future researchers to focus on the processes that facilitate incubator performance and inputs, as well as which mechanisms and interventions work best for distinct incubator kinds and circumstances. Researchers can also focus on various performance indicators of incubators and incubates. Future researching can also be for a socially conscious and sustainable business practices in incubators for long-term success and positive societal impact with focus on using advanced technology and addressing structural issues. Integrating artificial intelligence and machine learning can optimize incubation resource allocation and performance tracking. Blockchain technology can improve financial and operational security and transparency.

CONCLUSION

The current study on business incubation provides details of the incubation process and the mechanisms that influence specific outcomes and performance. It also explores the types of business incubators and their advantages and challenges. However, there is no one-size-fits-all process. Different mechanisms exist for incubators across industries. Various factors influence startups, such as the context in which they operate and the availability of resources, competencies, and skills that influence the final output of the incubation process. Different dynamics concern incubators; however, the methods used at each stage determine the dynamics of incubator growth and the functioning of the incubation process. The policymakers must offer a more dynamic and customised approach across diverse sectors rather than a one-size-fits-all approach. Other stakeholders, such as universities, financiers, and philanthropists, must also support and cater to the diverse demands of different incubators. Incubators and innovation programs have gained popularity throughout the world and have helped to boost economic growth. The successful adaptation of incubators and innovation programs results in high outcomes when reaching a higher stage of economic development, as measured by the number of graduate companies, client companies with high survival rates, and high added value for innovative products and services, as well as fostering an entrepreneurship environment and commercializing technology transfer. Incubators have enabled start-ups for thousands of young people to work for several enterprises through new employment channels, thereby producing resources for growth. This information is based on successful global deployments in developed and developing nations. Apart from the aim to achieve self-sufficiency, business incubators encountered many obstacles, such as inadequate funding, limited production space, sophisticated technology amenities, and diversification into new domains, which are identified as the primary issues business incubators face. Building strong links with academics, businesses, and local governments strengthens the incubator's ecosystem, providing entrepreneurs with more access to knowledge and financing possibilities. This study concludes the need for governments and businesses to identify barriers to economic development, it also highlights the collaborative efforts among businesses, universities, and government entities in utilizing effective business incubation for achieving optimal economic outcomes.

REFERENCES

Aernoudt, R. (2004). Incubators: Tool for Entrepreneurship? *Small Business Economics*, 23(2), 127–135. DOI: 10.1023/B:SBEJ.0000027665.54173.23

Al-Mubaraki, H. M., & Busler, M. (2017). Challenges and opportunities of innovation and incubators as a tool for knowledge-based economy. *Journal of Innovation and Entrepreneurship*, 6(1), 15. DOI: 10.1186/s13731-017-0075-y

Allahar, H., & Brathwaite, C. (2016). Business Incubation as an Instrument of Innovation: The Experience of South America and the Caribbean. *International Journal of Innovation*, 4(2), 71–85. DOI: 10.5585/iji.v4i2.107

Ayatse, F. A., Kwahar, N., & Iyortsuun, A. S. (2017). Business Incubation Process and Firm Performance: An Empirical Review. *Journal of Global Entrepreneurship Research*, 7(1), 2. DOI: 10.1186/s40497-016-0059-6

Azih, E., & Inanga, E. L. (2014). Performance Effectiveness of Technology Incubation in Nigeria. Business and Economics Journal. https://www.semanticscholar.org/paper/Performance-Effectiveness-of-Technology-Incubation-Azih-Inanga/46f293fc34a532194097484f2ec1cb718992cb6a

Bergek, A., & Norrman, C. (2008). Incubator Best Practice: A Framework. *Technovation*, 28(1–2), 20–28. DOI: 10.1016/j.technovation.2007.07.008

Bitzer, V., Francken, M., & Glasbergen, P. (2008). Intersectoral Partnerships for A Sustainable Coffee Chain: Really Addressing Sustainability or Just Picking (Coffee) Cherries? *Global Environmental Change*, 18(2), 271–284. DOI: 10.1016/j.gloenvcha.2008.01.002

Blank, T. H. (2021). When Incubator Resources are Crucial: Survival Chances of Student Startups Operating in an Academic Incubator. *The Journal of Technology Transfer*, 46(6), 1845–1868. DOI: 10.1007/s10961-020-09831-4

Bøllingtoft, A., & Ulhøi, J. P. (2005). The Networked Business Incubator—Leveraging Entrepreneurial Agency? *Journal of Business Venturing*, 20(2), 265–290. DOI: 10.1016/j.jbusvent.2003.12.005

Braun, G., & Hentschel, R. (2011). Incubators. In Kramme, R., Hoffmann, K.-P., & Pozos, R. S. (Eds.), *Springer Handbook of Medical Technology* (pp. 1285–1290). Springer. DOI: 10.1007/978-3-540-74658-4_71

Campbell, C., Kendrick, R. C., & Samuelson, D. S. (1985). Stalking the Latent Entrepreneur: Business Incubators and Economic Development. *Economic Development Review (Schiller Park, Ill.)*, 3(2), 43–49.

Chandra, A., & Medrano Silva, M. A. (2012). Business Incubation in Chile: Development, Financing and Financial Services. *Journal of Technology Management & Innovation*, 7(2), 1–13. DOI: 10.4067/S0718-27242012000200001

Chen, C.-J. (2009). Technology Commercialization, Incubator and Venture Capital, and New Venture Performance. *Journal of Business Research*, 62(1), 93–103. DOI: 10.1016/j.jbusres.2008.01.003

Cooper, S. Y., & Park, J. S. (2008). The Impact of 'Incubator' Organizations on Opportunity Recognition and Technology Innovation in New, Entrepreneurial High-Technology Ventures. *International Small Business Journal*, 26(1), 27–56. DOI: 10.1177/0266242607084658

Denktas-Sakar, G., & Karatas-Cetin, C. (2012). Port Sustainability and Stakeholder Management in Supply Chains: A Framework on Resource Dependence Theory. *The Asian Journal of Shipping and Logistics*, 28(3), 301–319. DOI: 10.1016/j.ajsl.2013.01.002

Dent, B. (2008). The Potential for Kitchen Incubators to Assist Food-Processing Enterprises. *International Journal of Entrepreneurship and Small Business*, 6(3), 496. DOI: 10.1504/IJESB.2008.019141

Dhiman, V., & Arora, M. (2024). Exploring the Linkage between Business Incubation and Entrepreneurship: Understanding Trends, Themes and Future Research Agenda. LBS Journal of Management & Research. DOI: 10.1108/LBSJMR-06-2023-0021

Egbetokun, A. (2023). Business Incubators in Africa: A Review of the Literature. *Innovation and Development*, 1–28. DOI: 10.1080/2157930X.2023.2295090

Freiling, J., Marquardt, L., & Reit, T. (2022). Virtual Business Incubators: A Support for Entrepreneurship in Rural Areas? In Hornuf, L. (Ed.), *Diginomics Research Perspectives: The Role of Digitalization in Business and Society* (pp. 65–88). Springer International Publishing. DOI: 10.1007/978-3-031-04063-4_4

Gandhi, V., Syed, A. A., & Kumar, S. (2022). A study of performance indicators of technology business incubators (Tbis) in india. *Management Dynamics*, 21(1), 14–23. DOI: 10.57198/2583-4932.1006

Global Startup Accelerator Map and List of Startup Accelerators. (n.d.). StartupBlink; StartupBlink. Retrieved 20 July 2024, from https://www.startupblink.com/accelerators

Gonthier, J., & Chirita, G. M. (2019). The Role of Corporate Incubators as Invigorators of Innovation Capabilities in Parent Companies. *Journal of Innovation and Entrepreneurship*, 8(1), 8. DOI: 10.1186/s13731-019-0104-0

Hackett, S. M. (2004). Real Options and the Option to Incubate: An Exploratory Study of the Process of Business Incubation. *SSRN*. DOI: 10.2139/ssrn.1260438

Hackett, S. M., & Dilts, D. M. (2004). A Systematic Review of Business Incubation Research. *The Journal of Technology Transfer*, 29(1), 55–82. DOI: 10.1023/B:-JOTT.0000011181.11952.0f

Hannon, P. D., & Chaplin, P. (2003). Are Incubators Good for Business? Understanding Incubation Practice—The Challenges for Policy. *Environment and Planning. C, Government & Policy*, 21(6), 861–881. DOI: 10.1068/c0215

Hassan, N. A. (2020). University Business Incubators as a tool for Accelerating Entrepreneurship: Theoretical Perspective. Review of Economics and Political Science. DOI: 10.1108/REPS-10-2019-0142

Hernández, R., & Carrà, G. (2016). A Conceptual Approach for Business Incubator Interdependencies and Sustainable Development. *Agriculture and Agricultural Science Procedia*, 8, 718–724. DOI: 10.1016/j.aaspro.2016.02.054

Isher, A. K. (2024). Driving Innovation and Economic Development: The Role of Business Incubators in Agri-Tech Start-Up Ecosystems. *Economic Affairs*, 69(2). Advance online publication. DOI: 10.46852/0424-2513.3.2024.7

Jha, S. K., & A, T. R. (2024). The Future of Incubation. *IIMB Management Review*, 36(1), 48–55. DOI: 10.1016/j.iimb.2024.03.003

Kolympiris, C., & Klein, P. G. (2017). The Effects of Academic Incubators on University Innovation. *Strategic Entrepreneurship Journal*, 11(2), 145–170. DOI: 10.1002/sej.1242

Kurode, T., Kurode, A. V., & Moitra, K. (2016). A Study of Critical Challenges in Startup Management. *SSRN*. DOI: 10.2139/ssrn.3348534

Lalkaka, R. (2003). Business Incubators in Developing Countries: Characteristics and Performance. *International Journal of Entrepreneurship and Innovation Management*, 3(1/2), 31. DOI: 10.1504/IJEIM.2003.002217

Leal, M., Leal, C., & Silva, R. (2023). The Involvement of Universities, Incubators, Municipalities, and Business Associations in Fostering Entrepreneurial Ecosystems and Promoting Local Growth. *Administrative Sciences*, 13(12), 245. DOI: 10.3390/admsci13120245

Li, C., Ahmed, N., Qalati, S. A., Khan, A., & Naz, S. (2020). Role of Business Incubators as a Tool for Entrepreneurship Development: The Mediating and Moderating Role of Business Start-Up and Government Regulations. *Sustainability (Basel)*, 12(5), 1822. DOI: 10.3390/su12051822

Madaleno, M., Nathan, M., Overman, H., & Waights, S. (2022). Incubators, Accelerators and Urban Economic Development. *Urban Studies (Edinburgh, Scotland)*, 59(2), 281–300. DOI: 10.1177/00420980211004209

Mair, J., Robinson, J., & Hockerts, K. (Eds.). (2006). *Social Entrepreneurship.*, DOI: 10.1057/9780230625655

Markley, D. M., & McNamara, K. T. (1995). Economic and Fiscal Impacts of a Business Incubator. *Economic Development Quarterly*, 9(3), 273–278. DOI: 10.1177/089124249500900307

Mian, S. A. (1996). The University Business Incubator: A Strategy for Developing New Research/Technology-Based Firms. *The Journal of High Technology Management Research*, 7(2), 191–208. DOI: 10.1016/S1047-8310(96)90004-8

Mrkajic, B. (2017). Business Incubation Models and Institutionally Void Environments. *Technovation*, 68, 44–55. DOI: 10.1016/j.technovation.2017.09.001

Mubaraki, H. M. A., & Busler, M. (2015). The Importance of Business Incubation in Developing Countries: Case Study Approach. *International Journal of Foresight and Innovation Policy*, 10(1), 17. DOI: 10.1504/IJFIP.2015.070054

Narayanan, V. K., & Shin, J. (2019). The Institutional Context of Incubation: The Case of Academic Incubators in India. *Management and Organization Review*, 15(3), 563–593. DOI: 10.1017/mor.2018.52

Pattanasak, P., Anantana, T., Paphawasit, B., & Wudhikarn, R. (2022). Critical Factors and Performance Measurement of Business Incubators: A Systematic Literature Review. *Sustainability (Basel)*, 14(8), 4610. DOI: 10.3390/su14084610

Pettersen, I. B., Aarstad, J., Høvig, Ø. S., & Tobiassen, A. E. (2015). Business Incubation and the Network Resources of Start-Ups. *Journal of Innovation and Entrepreneurship*, 5(1), 7. DOI: 10.1186/s13731-016-0038-8

Ramchandani, P. H. (2017). A Descriptive Study of Opportunities and Challenges of Startup India Mission. *International Journal of Advanced Research and Innovative Ideas in Education*, 3, 61–65.

Rice, M. P. (2002). Co-production of Business Assistance In Business Incubators: An Exploratory Study. *Journal of Business Venturing*, 17(2), 163–187. https://doi.org/ (00)00055-0DOI: 10.1016/S0883-9026

Rizzi, D. I., Wescinski, J. V., Poli, O., & Jacoski, C. A.Universidade Comunitária da Região de Chapecó. (2017). The Importance of Incubation Processes from the Perspective of Incubated and Graduated Companies. *Journal of Information Systems and Technology Management*, 14(2), 263–279. DOI: 10.4301/S1807-17752017000200007

Rotenstein, L. S., Wickner, P., Hauser, L., Littlefield, M., Abbett, S., Desrosiers, J., Bates, D. W., Dudley, J., & Laskowski, K. R. (2019). An Academic Medical Center-Based Incubator to Promote Clinical Innovation and Financial Value. *Joint Commission Journal on Quality and Patient Safety*, 45(4), 259–267. DOI: 10.1016/j.jcjq.2018.12.004 PMID: 30665836

Sansone, G., Viglialoro, D., Ughetto, E., & Landoni, P. (2023). What is a Startup Studio? Evidence from Europe. *Proceedings - Academy of Management*, 2023(1), 13027. DOI: 10.5465/AMPROC.2023.13027abstract

Sanyal, S., & Hisam, M. W. (2018). The Role of Business Incubators in Creating an Entrepreneurial Ecosystem: A Study of the Sultanate of Oman. *Indian Journal of Commerce and Management Studies*, 9(3), 10–17. DOI: 10.18843/ijcms/v9i3/02

Schwartz, M., & Hornych, C. (2012). Specialisation versus Diversification: Perceived Benefits of Different Business Incubation Models. *International Journal of Entrepreneurship and Innovation Management*, 15(3), 177. DOI: 10.1504/IJEIM.2012.046599

Sohail, K., Belitski, M., & Castro Christiansen, L. (2023). Developing Business Incubation Process Frameworks: A Systematic Literature Review. *Journal of Business Research*, 162, 113902. DOI: 10.1016/j.jbusres.2023.113902

Tengeh, R. K., & Choto, P. (2015). The Relevance and Challenges of Business Incubators that Support Survivalist Entrepreneurs. Investment Management and Financial Innovations, 12(2), 150–161. https://philarchive.org/rec/TENTRA-3

Theodoraki, C., Messeghem, K., & Audretsch, D. B. (2022). The Effectiveness of Incubators' Co-Opetition Strategy in the Entrepreneurial Ecosystem: Empirical Evidence from France. *IEEE Transactions on Engineering Management*, 69(4), 1781–1794. DOI: 10.1109/TEM.2020.3034476

Van Erkelens, A. M., Thompson, N. A., & Chalmers, D. (2024). The Dynamic Construction of an Incubation Context: A Practice Theory Perspective. *Small Business Economics*, 62(2), 583–605. DOI: 10.1007/s11187-023-00771-5

Vardhan, J., & Mahato, M. (2022). Business Incubation Centres in Universities and their Role in Developing Entrepreneurial Ecosystem. *Journal of Entrepreneurship and Innovation in Emerging Economies*, 8(1), 143–157. DOI: 10.1177/23939575211034056

Wasdani, K. P., Vijaygopal, A., & Manimala, M. J. (2022). Business Incubators: A Need-Heed Gap Analysis of Technology-Based Enterprises. *Global Business Review*, 097215092210740, 09721509221074099. Advance online publication. DOI: 10.1177/09721509221074099

Wilber, P. L., & Dixon, L. (2003). The Impact of Business Incubators on Small Business Survivability. *Journal of Business Venturing*, 10(5), 349–370.

Yagüe-Perales, R. M., March-Chorda, I., & López-Paredes, H. (2024). Assessing the Impact of Seed Accelerators in Start-Ups from Emerging Entrepreneurial Ecosystems. *The International Entrepreneurship and Management Journal*, 20(2), 1323–1345. Advance online publication. DOI: 10.1007/s11365-024-00956-8

Yuan, X., Hao, H., Guan, C., & Pentland, A. (2022). Which Factors Affect The Performance of Technology Business Incubators in China? An Entrepreneurial Ecosystem Perspective. *PLoS One*, 17(1), e0261922. DOI: 10.1371/journal.pone.0261922 PMID: 35015766

KEY TERMS AND DEFINITIONS

Acceleration: Acceleration is the method by which firms that has developed their goods and begun commercialization studies but are having difficulty acquiring market share and internationalization may resolve these issues with the assistance of acceleration programs during this phase. The notion of acceleration may be viewed as a new model for the entrepreneurship community

Business Incubation: Business incubation is a public or private development process that nurtures firms from idea creation to start-ups, providing complete assistance to help them grow and succeed. An incubator offers resources including physical space, capital guidance, shared services, and networking opportunities.

Incubation: At the conclusion of the pre-incubation period, entrepreneurs who have completed the business plan and are ready for incorporation enter the incubation phase. During the incubation era, entrepreneurs require physical facilities as well as training, consulting, and mentoring services, just as they did before. These entrepreneurs' requirements are covered while in the incubation facility.

Preincubation: Pre-incubation is the process of developing a technology-focused company idea or project for companies that have begun working alone or with a team but have not yet been incorporated to make this notion a reality. Entrepreneurs in the pre-incubation process require specialized training, coaching, and consulting services to determine whether their ideas are feasible, commercializable, scalable, and so on.

Chapter 3
Promoting Entrepreneurship Through Business Incubation

Neeta Baporikar
https://orcid.org/0000-0003-0676-9913
Namibia University of Science and Technology, Namibia & SP Pune University, India

ABSTRACT

Many countries and institutions have established business incubators for promoting entrepreneurs and entrepreneurship development. Studies have shown that business incubators aid in enhancing entrepreneurial ecosystems worldwide. Some of the African countries have also established business incubators to promote entrepreneurial development. Adapting an exploratory approach the aim of this chapter is to review and examine to what extent business incubators have promoted entrepreneurship development with a focus on South Africa.

INTRODUCTION

Business incubators are perceived to be a mainstay of economic development programs. They create value by combining the entrepreneurial drive of a startup with resources generally available to new ventures. Among the primary objectives of business incubators are creating employment opportunities in the local economy and commercializing technologies. More and more nations, especially emerging economies have put high-growth, innovative businesses at the heart of its econom-

DOI: 10.4018/979-8-3693-4302-9.ch003

Copyright © 2025, IGI Global. Copying or distributing in print or electronic forms without written permission of IGI Global is prohibited.

ic agenda. Business incubators began in the 1960s and really took off in the late 1990s as support for start-up companies who need advice and venture capital to get their ideas off the ground. Business incubators are programs measured to step up the successful development of entrepreneurial companies through a selection of business maintain wealth and services. The major purpose of a business incubator is to promote the development of innovative business within the local society. By assisting a local entrepreneur to start a company in the area, the community is likely to benefit from an increase in the number of available jobs in the region and the further profits that is bring to the metropolitan or town because of the new business actions. Both elements can help to revitalize a local economy and thus enhance the quality of life for everyone who lives and works in the area.

The role of business incubation in fostering entrepreneurship and SMEs development has generated a strong interest among policymakers in recent years. Even among scholars, there is a consensus that entrepreneurship is pivotal to economic growth in both developing and developed countries. Business incubation from a layman point of view is to help train startup enterprises in order for them to survive the modern business competitive environment. Incubator can be seen from the angle of premature birth, when a premature baby would be put in an incubator for a period in order for the baby to develop. Such process applies to a startup business that needs to develop and survive the challenges in the modern business environment towards its success. Business incubation have proven to be an effective tool for promoting economic growth throughout the world, as they serve as catalysts in the process of starting and growing companies by providing entrepreneurs with the expertise, networks, and tools needed to make their ventures successful (Alavi, and Leidner, 2001). Oshewolo (2010) posit that Business Incubation generally in particular contribute to the economic development of a country by the creation of new enterprises, employment increased or creation of job, improvement of industry structure, acquisition, commercialization and/or transfer of technology owned by universities and research institutions, wealth creation, and the promotion of techno-entrepreneurship culture (Naude, 2011; UN Bakar et al, 2015; Okafor et al., 2015).

Business Incubation is a unique and highly flexible combination of business development processes, infrastructure and people, designed to support entrepreneurs, nurture, and grow new and small businesses, products and innovations through the early stages of development (Omoh, 2015). Small and medium scale enterprises (SMEs) are businesses whose personnel numbers fall below certain limits. Small enterprises outnumber large companies by a wide margin and employ many more people. The SMEs are responsible for driving innovation and competition in many economic sectors. For instance in Nigeria, SMEs have been able to contribute to Gross Domestic Product (GDP) of the country, helps to reduce unemployment, thereby increasing the standard of living of the people (Omoh, 2015; NBS, 2014;

Agboola, 2010). SMEs is considered as an impediment to further economic development and growth, SMEs often fail within their first three years of operations as a result of low technical capabilities, low entrepreneurial skills, limitation of their sizes among others (Baporikar, 2018a; 2018b). SMEs adduced to their low survival rate, therefore for SMEs to survive in this modern age of global market, business incubation programs was introduced to help give advice, assistance and to nurture SMEs for survival (Baporikar, 2020; 2024). Thus, adopting an exploratory approach the aim of this chapter to review and examine to what extent business incubators have promoted entrepreneurship development with focus on South Africa.

LITERATURE REVIEW

The pre-incubation phase is critical in the forming of entrepreneur's intention and however it is almost missing in literature (Martínez, Fernández-Laviada, & Crespo, 2018). Several changes in the global economy resulting from globalization, advancement in technology, accelerated innovations, and trends in demographics calls for the need to improve levels of entrepreneurship which also plays a crucial role in their improvement of growth and development. Entrepreneurship is an important factor in facilitating poverty reduction, creation of employment opportunities, and structural changes within its context. In essence, entrepreneurship is an important tool for improving living standards and the general well-being of the society. Additionally, the creation of new ventures is an important strategy applied by governments in the quest for attaining sustainable national economic growth and development. It is also important for the development and achievement of competitive economies in the national and international levels.

Real driven-options theory of business incubation (Hackett, & Dilts, 2004), seeks to predict and explain how business incubators and the process of business incubation increase the likelihood that new ventures will survive the early stages of development. It conceptualizes the incubator as an entrepreneurial firm that sources and macro-manages the innovation process within emerging organizations, infusing these organizations with resources at various developmental stage-gates while containing the cost of their potential failure. The incubator is the unit of analysis while incubation outcomes-measured in terms of incubatees growth and financial performance at the time of incubator exit-provide indicators of success. Our model of the incubation process and specification of the range of possible incubation outcomes offer implications for managerial practice and policy-making vis-à-vis incubator management and good entrepreneurial failure. It further asserts that decision-makers create low-cost options to initiate (but not fully commit to) risky investments; subsequent investments are based on reductions in uncertainty and the perceived likelihood of return on option investment.

Structural contingency theory (Ketchen, Thomas, & Snow, 1993), suggests that the configuration of the incubator must obtain "fit" with environmental needs in order to achieve incubation success. This contingency theory also relate to decision making. According to these models, the effectiveness of a decision procedure depends upon a number of aspects of the situation:

- the importance of the decision quality and acceptance;
- the amount of relevant information possessed by the leader and subordinates;
- the likelihood that subordinates will accept an autocratic decision or cooperate in trying to make a good decision if allowed to participate;
- the amount of disagreement among subordinates with respect to their preferred alternatives

Although the incubator configuration studies were theoretical, inductive compilations of variables of the incubator-incubation phenomenon, implicitly this approach rests on structural contingency theory. The primary assumption of structural contingency theory is that the configuration of an organization and the external environment must achieve "fit" in order to obtain "success" (Ketchen et al., 1993). Although most configuration studies do not test for success, structural contingency theory provides a theoretical underpinning for the often-asserted need for the incubator to be tailored to meet local needs and norms. This theory of contingency is an organizational theory that claims that there is no best way to organize a corporation to lead a company, or to make decisions, instead, the optimal course of action is contingent (dependent) upon the internal and external situation.

Study on the impact of governmental Business Incubation program on entrepreneurship performance in the EU, approximately 900; help create 40,000 new (net) jobs. The UK has a well-established network of approximately 300 business incubators that support over 12,000 high-growth technology businesses in sectors such as biomedical, IT and the creative industries. The range reported is between 25-40 supported businesses per incubator, and between 44-91 jobs created per year per incubator. However, these figures typically include a mix of technology and other types of incubators (Al-Mubaraki and Busler, 2010).

Statistics compiled by Australia Industry show that Australian incubators have graduated 3,500 businesses, facilitating more than $785 million in SME sales and created a minimum of more than 10,500 jobs. The New Zealand Trade and Enterprise Incubator Support Programme, regarded as one of the best incubation programmes, reported that over the past 10 years, more than 250 ventures graduated from an incubator; 69 percent of these have raised external investment, 71 percent are still trading, and 57 percent are exporting. Along the way over 1100 high value jobs were created.

The World Bank Information for Development Program (infoDev's) Business Incubation Network consists of nearly 300 incubators in over 80 developing countries assisting 20,000 enterprises, which have created more than 220,000 jobs. In 2010, 150 business incubators in infoDev's Business Incubation Network reported that they were assisting 12,500 early-staged enterprises, and 92 business incubators reported they had graduated 4,200 enterprises. According to the Monitoring and Impact Assessment Report (MEIA), which assessed over 49 incubators, one third of the incubators helped to start more than 50 new businesses. Three incubators in Costa Rica, Panama and Uruguay, have together graduated 63 companies with an annual turnover of $90,000. These enterprises had no, or less than $15,000 annual turnover at the start of the incubation process and on average were incubated for three years.

According to a study conducted in 2011 by Anprotec, in partnership with the Ministry of Science, Technology and Innovation (MCTI), Brazil has 384 incubators in operation, home to 2,640 companies, generating 16,394 jobs. These incubators have graduated 2,509 enterprises, with revenues of $2.1 billion and employing 29,205 people. The same study revealed another important fact: 98% of incubated companies innovate, 28 of them at the local level, 55% at the national level and 15% at the global level. The Tianjin Women's Business Incubator (TWBI) specializes in assisting women entrepreneurs and fostering growth in the employment of women made redundant through economic reform and restructuring. It currently has 48 on-site tenants and 7 off-site tenants and, to date, has graduated eight enterprises.

Seoane, Rodriguez, & Rojo, (2014) in a study in Spain on the influence of training and gender in entrepreneurship through business incubators in Galicia, established a positive relationship on incubators assisting incubates to begin business, note that mainstream of the citizen prefer civil service jobs to free enterprise. The transportation is simultaneous to access to finance, export direction and employment establishment. There have been studies on incubation in South Africa. Incubation started in South Africa in the 1990's with hives of Industry model. Familiarity in South Africa shows that incubation wants administration, Market and currency to be successful. Where management mean having business incubator managers with strong business management skills in book keeping, business plan development, marketing skills, networking linkages able to link tenant firms with markets, venture capital as well as business development trainings (Masutha & Rogers, 2014). Al-Mubaraki and Hamad (2010) concluded that the incubator organizations or innovation programs are model accelerator tools for the 21st century. This study has obviously positive that business incubation programs are considered to step up the successful improvement of entrepreneurial companies through an arrangement of business support property and services, industrial by incubator management. According to Meckel (2014), the study has a number of implications for incubator managers. Firstly attention and scarce resources should be focused on providing relevant information and encouraging an atmosphere of learning and mutual support. Secondly, managers should adopt a less managerial; approach and be prepared to act as mentors to support and encourage incubates. Thirdly recruitment practices should be revised to include a more holistic appreciation of potential incubates contribution to the learning community as well as an assessment of their business plans.

The National Business Incubators Association (NBIA) (2014) state that BI is a dynamic process of business enterprise growth and business assistance that accelerates the successful development of start-up enterprises by giving particular resources to entrepreneurs. These resources are often created by BI management and distributed through its network of connections. In developed countries, entrepreneurs benefit greatly from affiliation or management of a BI program within a university because these institutions can provide links to industry, society, and government entities. In these countries, universities have been urged to become more accountable to the public and to contribute directly to local, regional, and national economic development by engaging in a variety of "third mission" activities. Incubation of start-up firms, knowledge commercialization, the development of knowledge transfer partnerships, and the provision of entrepreneurship courses are examples of such activities.

Business Incubation Concept

Significant economic and technological developments, innovations and inventions influence and shape the business incubation concept (Baporikar, 2015). Since its inception, and its governance, value proposition and configuration have evolved. In their early development, business incubators were primarily seen as an instrument of urban renewal and community development. First business incubators were conceived because of the difficulty some property owners faced finding tenants for their vacant buildings. These buildings were factories that had curtailed or ceased operation because of industrial restructuring and re-location of production facilities, schools experiencing declining enrolment or other types of buildings left vacant by emigrating companies. Faced with the difficulty of finding a single tenant for the entire building, their owners started partitioning them and renting them out as units to different tenants. Thus the use of the term 'tenant' to describe residents of a business incubator, which emphasizes the rental relationship, is not entirely coincidental (Bollingtoft, 2012). It is a reflection of the focus of the early incubators' activities, although it continues to be used even today when provision of rental space is one of their many activities. Given government concern with revitalizing decaying urban areas and creating employment opportunities in close proximity to where communities lived, combined with the fact that some of these buildings were public property, the early business incubators tended to be joint private-public partnerships or were subsidized by government. In the mid-1980s, in the U.S. the Small Business Administration undertook a number of initiatives to strengthen the incubation movement, including regional conferences, handbooks and newsletters on business incubation, and supporting the formation of a national association. The World in which research, development and innovation take place has changed fundamentally. Today, open science and open innovation coexist, creating new opportunities and interdependences (Baporikar, 2016). Figure 1 gives the conceptual framework.

Figure 1. Conceptual Framework

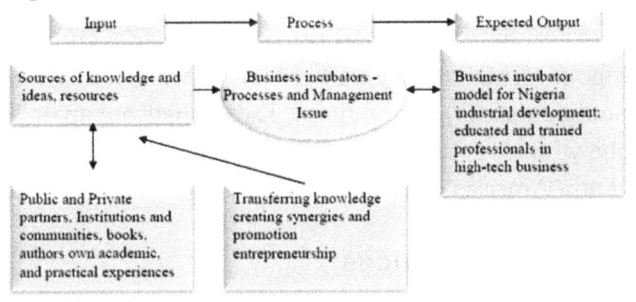

Source: Verheugen, 2007

Evolution of Business Incubation

The term 'incubator' was derived from the fundamental meaning of the term: The artificial nurturing of the chicken egg in order to hatch them faster in a sheltered environment. The same hatching concept is applied to the incubating of companies; it speeds up new ventures' establishments and increases their chances of success. An incubator thus hatches new ideas by providing new ventures with physical and intangible resources. Despite the efforts to develop a general definition for business incubation, there are still varieties of models of business incubators. In business incubation, there is some degree of Government, Academia and industry involvement (Baporikar, 2024).

The most common classification of business incubators is based on funding. There are those that are:

- public funded such as those set up by government agencies in science/technology/business parks, research institutions and universities

- privately funded such as those in privately run organizations and enterprises

Recent studies introduced the mixed-models of business incubators such as public private partnerships incubators. The first incubator was established in 1959 in the United States. This concept had since spread to other part of the world for development with significant improvement in the process of conducting it. As at 2000, there were 900 incubators of different categories in the United States, while in 2006, the number has increased to about 1,200. As per the NBIA estimates, since 1980 the North American incubators have generated 500,000 jobs and every 50 jobs created by an incubator has generated another 25 jobs in the community. Incubator graduates create jobs, revitalize neighborhoods and commercialize new technologies, which strengthen local, regional and even national economies. The survival rates of the U.S. incubators graduates are in the average of 87% and it have also brought down the start-up cost by nearly 40-50 per cent. Similarly, OECD countries have also reported high survival rate ranging from 80-85 per cent as against 30-35% survival rates of non-incubators start-up firms. Today, there are up to 7000 incubators around the globe with close to half in North America and other half spread across Europe, Asia, Latin America and a few in Africa (Omoh, 2015; Matuluko, 2015).

Business Incubation Services

Business incubators have proliferated since their emergence over 50 years ago. Over this time business incubation has evolved to include a range of incubation practices. In the developed world, business incubators play a key supportive role for businesses and have continued to grow. The growth in the number of business incubators worldwide demonstrates their perceived value. The United Kingdom has a well-established network of approximately 300 business incubators supporting around 12,000 businesses. Globally, business incubators have been shown to play a key role in business growth. In the United Kingdom, across a portfolio of incubator tenants around 23 per cent identify the incubator as important to business performance. Majority did identify the incubator as critical; while just few regard the incubator as unimportant to performance. Since the 1980s business incubators have become a popular policy instrument to foster entrepreneurship, innovation, and regional development. Incubation can be viewed as a way of addressing market failures, which limit the ability of small start-ups to overcome uncertainty and obstacles associated with the early stages of firm development. Market failures stem from the relatively high costs and risks associated with providing support to start-up companies. Incubators can also be viewed as a catalyst to accelerate the entrepreneurial process systematically, thereby institutionalizing the support of ventures with potential for high growth. Thus, the primary incubator function has been described as increasing the chances of an incubatee firm surviving its formative years.

Reasons for Business Incubation

There are a number of studies in the literature that evaluate the usefulness of the incubators by assessing their value-added contributions. One fact that makes the assessment challenging is the selection of appropriate criteria. On what grounds can an incubator be labeled as successful? Answering this question requires a brief summary of the aims of establishing incubators. Incubators are established and supported for different reasons:

- To reduce start-up and early stage operational costs, and the risk of doing business by providing a protective environment for start-ups. (Al-Mubaraki and Busler, 2010). Most incubators offer managerial and administrative assistance as well as physical infrastructure to their tenants. Previous studies showed that incubator services are important for tenant firms (Barney, 1991). For instance, one of the main reasons behind the low performance of incubators is poor and insufficient incubator services. Especially managerial assistance could be an asset to entrepreneurs who lack managerial skills.
- As a means of regional (technology) development policy. Incubators were used as an effective policy tool in various countries for reducing unemployment, new job and venture creation.
- Enhancing university-industry collaboration via university incubators. Especially in the mid-1990s, incubators were established with the aim of increasing commercialization of research and transfer of technology. University incubators also serve as a role model for university students and act as an in-house (part-time) employment opportunity for students (Nwekeaku and Ozioko, 2011).
- Stimulating networking among firms (Naude, 2011). Tenant firms and entrepreneurs can benefit from peer groups effects. The idea is based on synergies among entrepreneurs who share similar problems, businesses and work environment. For instance, Bakar et al. (2015) argue that among the existing incubator models, the networked incubator (incubators in which networking is organized and deliberately fostered) is likely to be more successful. In a similar manner,
- Reversing or preventing brain drain. For instance, in Israel high tech incubators were effectively used as a tool for absorbing immigration. Between 1989 and 1995, more than 11.000 high skilled scientists and engineers emigrated from the former Soviet Union some of which were employed in incubator

firms. Incubators can also help scientists to commercialize their work and to increase the financial means of scientific research. For instance, one particular goal of the Zelenograd Scientific and Technology Park in Russia is to make scientific work financially worthwhile to gain scientists back. Russian science has faced a within country 'brain drain' in the sense that most Russian scholars gave up scientific research for more profitable non-scientific work such as managing western retail stores in Moscow (Barney,1991). Similarly, China established 'Innovation Parks for Returned Scholars' to attract talented researchers and students who live abroad. Various subsidies are provided for returned scholars to set up high technology-oriented businesses in China (Chen, 2009).

Benefits of Business Incubation

The benefits of a well-managed incubator can be many-fold for different stakeholders (NBIA, 2014; Agboola, 2010; Omoh, 2015, Okafor et al, 2015; Akpoviroro, Oba-Adenuga, and Akanmu, 2021):

- For tenants: it enhances the chances of success, raises credibility, helps improve skills, creates synergy among client-firms, and facilitates access to mentors, information and seed capital;
- For governments: the incubator helps overcome market failures, promotes regional development, generates jobs, incomes and taxes, and becomes a demonstration of the political commitment to small businesses;
- For research institutes and universities: the BIC helps strengthen interactions between university-research-industry, promotes research commercialization, and gives opportunities for faculty/graduate students to better utilize their capabilities;
- For business: the BIC can develop opportunities for acquiring innovations, supply chain management and spin-offs, and helps them meet their social responsibilities;
- For the local community: creates self-esteem and an entrepreneurial culture, together with local incomes as a majority of graduating businesses stay within the area;
- For the international community: it generates opportunities of trade and technology transfer between client companies and their host incubators, a better understanding of business culture, and facilitated exchanges of experience through associations and alliances.

ROLE OF BUSINESS INCUBATORS IN PROMOTING ENTREPRENERUSHIP

An incubator is an organization designed to help startup businesses grow and succeed by providing free or low-cost workspace, mentorship, expertise, access to investors, and in some cases, working capital in the form of a loan. The incubation process allows entrepreneurs to preserve capital and gain external support to accelerate their businesses growth. Through business incubation, the enterprises captures each entrepreneur's uniqueness and offers support and customized services to maximize businesses potential. Moreover, business incubation in entrepreneurship fosters innovation by providing entrepreneurs with the tools and knowledge necessary to bring their ideas to life. Furthermore, these programs facilitate connections with industry leaders and potential customers, which is crucial for any growing business. At their most basic level, incubators help entrepreneurs by providing practical, concrete resources that may be difficult for a new business to obtain or afford, including: office space. Incubators usually maintain office facilities that young businesses can use at a fraction of the cost of a traditional office. Thus, business incubation acts as a catalyst for startups, offering a supportive ecosystem for their development. This process is crucial for fostering entrepreneurship and ensuring that innovative ideas have the support they need to thrive.

Business incubation in entrepreneurship programs vary widely, yet they all share a common goal: accelerating the growth and success of entrepreneurial ventures. Figure 2 gives basic components of business incubation.

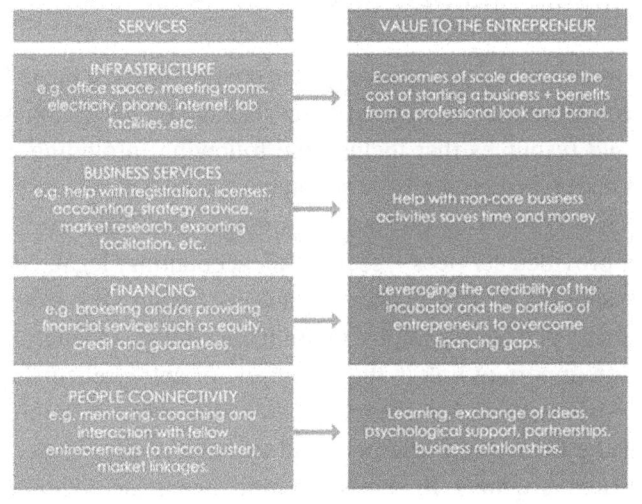

Figure 2. Basic Components of Business Incubation

SERVICES	VALUE TO THE ENTREPRENEUR
INFRASTRUCTURE e.g. office space, meeting rooms; electricity, phone, internet, lab facilities, etc.	Economies of scale decrease the cost of starting a business + benefits from a professional look and brand.
BUSINESS SERVICES e.g. help with registration, licenses; accounting, strategy advice, market research, exporting facilitation, etc.	Help with non-core business activities saves time and money.
FINANCING e.g. brokering and/or providing financial services such as equity, credit and guarantees.	Leveraging the credibility of the incubator and the portfolio of entrepreneurs to overcome financing gaps.
PEOPLE CONNECTIVITY e.g. mentoring, coaching and interaction with fellow entrepreneurs (a micro cluster), market linkages.	Learning, exchange of ideas, psychological support, partnerships, business relationships.

Source: Adopted from Barrow, 2001.

Given below is the general framework on how incubators work:

- **Selection Criteria:** Incubators often have a rigorous selection process to identify startups with the most potential. This critical step ensures that resources are allocated to businesses with the highest likelihood of success and impact.
- **Tailored Support:** Once selected, these startups receive customized support, including mentorship and network access. This support is tailored to the specific needs of each startup, addressing their unique challenges and opportunities.
- **Continuous Guidance:** Lastly, ongoing guidance ensures startups navigate the early challenges of entrepreneurship effectively. This continuous support helps entrepreneurs make informed decisions, pivot when necessary, and maintain momentum toward achieving their business goals.
- **Funding Opportunities:** Incubation programs frequently facilitate connections to early-stage investors. For example, startup incubators assist companies in securing funding and providing essential services for effective operations. This is provided they fulfill specific requirements and appeal to investors, making incubators a growing choice for entrepreneurs.
- **Resource Provision:** Business incubation in entrepreneurship programs provides critical resources like office space and technical support. These resources allow startups to reduce overhead costs and focus on their core business activities.

Benefits of Business Incubation for Entrepreneurship and Startups

A business incubator is an organization that creates the most favorable conditions for starting development of small enterprises through the provision of comprehensive services and resources that include the following: providing companies the area on preferential terms, as well as communication means, office equipment, and necessary facilities; providing personnel training, consulting, etc. Availability of broad range of provided services – secretarial, accounting, legal, educational, and consulting is one of the most important conditions, because it is exactly the service comprehensiveness that is very important for launching small enterprises. Business incubators are an important link in the ecosystem of entrepreneurship support and development. The business hatching process is designed to inspire and provoke people for starting their own businesses and to support start-up companies in developing innovative products. Business hatching means the creation of conditions that enable and foster the development of entrepreneurship and start-up companies. Salient benefits of business incubation include:

- **Access to Expertise:** Primarily, business incubation in entrepreneurship gives startups direct access to industry experts. These mentors offer invaluable insights, guiding young companies through complex challenges. Moreover, this mentorship helps entrepreneurs refine their business strategies, ensuring they are on the path to success. Additionally, the guidance received is often personalized, catering to the specific needs of each startup.
- **Networking Opportunities:** Incubation programs create environments where startups can connect with a vast network of peers, advisors, and investors. This networking is crucial because it opens doors to potential partnerships, funding opportunities, and valuable collaborations. Furthermore, being part of a community of like-minded individuals fosters a sense of support and camaraderie among entrepreneurs.
- **Resource Availability:** Startup support within incubators includes access to physical and technical resources. These resources can range from office space to high-speed Internet and even to specialized equipment. Moreover, readily available resources allow startups to focus more on their core activities rather than worrying about logistical issues.
- **Increased Credibility:** Finally, being associated with a reputable incubator enhances a startup's legitimacy in the eyes of customers, investors, and partners. This increased credibility can be a game-changer for young companies looking to establish themselves in competitive markets.

SOLUTIONS AND RECOMMENDATIONS

1. Business incubation programs assists entrepreneurs in the cost of running a startup venture towards its survival in the first three years of operation. Therefore, it is very important for entrepreneurs to enroll for the incubation programs to get the necessary knowledge as regards business setting.
2. Incubation centers should emphasize more on their coaching and technical knowledge, as coaching and technical knowledge acquisition contributes substantial towards entrepreneurship performance in terms of human capital management and their productivity performance level.
3. Another recommendation is that the business incubators should find ways of understanding and sustaining customers' relationship to encourage more incubatees into the incubation programs in terms of service quality and knowledge-

delivering system to the incubatees because findings showed that knowledge acquisition has a significant impact to incubatees' performance.
4. In addition, the incubators should ensure that they have adequate records of their incubatees in order to facilitate incubatees' operation checkup, i.e. the incubator trying to examine the performance of the incubatees after graduation from the incubation program so that they can become more competitive.

FUTURE RESEARCH DIRECTIONS

Future research needs to take into account the concept of (relative) absorptive capacity when studying knowledge acquisition of incubatees. This can improve the understanding of the extent to which incubatees acquire knowledge from business incubation. Another suggestion for future research is to address the long-term impact of business incubation by means of longitudinal research methods. Business incubators have always created the necessary infrastructure for the development of new business ideas, set the entrepreneurial tone and atmosphere. University incubation programs are seen as an important resource for finding and growing talents, and can also be regarded as the center of power that positively influences the economy of the region. But there is need to do detailed studies on how university incubation programs have fared so far and identify successful models and frameworks for replication. Business incubator is treated by the most contemporary scholars as an economic entity (organization) created to support emergent entrepreneurs. However, there are definitions in which the term 'business incubator' is considered more widely. There is also need to identify, develop a more acceptable and holistic definition based on appropriate underlying theories.

CONCLUSION

As the SMEs are seen as engines and bedrock of the industrial and economic development and growth in many dynamic economies, government of various evolving nations have been performing a vital function in outlining strategies and agenda which sustain the enhancement of entrepreneurs from grassroots to medium enterprises. In this agenda, business incubation programs are recognized by various national governments as the particular mechanism used to achieve such SMEs outcomes as incubators have been observed to fostering the enhancement of the entrepreneur way of life as well as performing as a mechanism intended for the growth of incorporated firm support arrangement which comprise along with others, institutions of higher education, entrepreneurial business, professionals and government bodies.

The success and survival of every startup venture in the global world cannot be over-emphasized. Businesses all over the world go as far as possible to survive the challenges and the global market competition. This study is an important study that helps to evaluate the role of governmental incubation programs on entrepreneurship performance and SMEs development. The study found that startup businesses often fail within their first few years of operations because of low technical capabilities, low entrepreneurial skills and limitation of their sizes among others and so on. Because of all these challenges being faced by startup ventures, this study provides information for entrepreneurs to know the essence of incubation programs towards achieving result with less stress. This study will also assist entrepreneurs in the incubation programs to know that they cannot handle all services alone, as they need to undertake some coaching under the incubation programs. Since the study, will equipped entrepreneurs in order to survive the early challenges of startup to be able to cope and adapt to changes in the global market competition. Finally, this study has clearly stated that business incubators is aimed at promoting economic development of its community by supporting start-up companies and their business development and offers services to support the establishment and development of new as well as existing small and medium companies.

REFERENCES

Akpoviroro, K. S., Oba-Adenuga, O. A., & Akanmu, P. M. (2021). The role of business incubation in promoting entrepreneurship and SMEs development. *Management and Entrepreneurship: Trends of Development*, 2(16), 82–100. DOI: 10.26661/2522-1566/2021-1/16-07

Al-Mubaraki, H., & Busler, M. (2010). Business incubators models of the USA and UK: A SWOT analysis. *World Journal of Entrepreneurship, Management and Sustainable Development*, 6(4), 335–354. DOI: 10.1108/20425961201000025

Alavi, M., & Leidner, D. E. (2001). Review: Knowledge Management and Knowledge Management Systems: Conceptual Foundations and Research Issues. *Management Information Systems Quarterly*, 25(1), 107. DOI: 10.2307/3250961

Albort-Morant, G., & Ribeiro-Soriano, D. (2016). A bibliometric analysis of international impact of business incubators. *Journal of Business Research*, 69(5), 1775–1779. DOI: 10.1016/j.jbusres.2015.10.054

Allen, D. N., & Rahman, S. (1985). Small business incubators: A positive environment for Entrepreneurship. *Journal of Small Business Management*, 23(3), 12–22.

Arogundade, B. B. (2011). Entrepreneurship education: An imperative for sustainable development in Nigeria. *Journal of Emerging Trends in Educational Research and Policy Studies*, 2(1), 26–29.

Arokiasamy, A. R. (2012). The Influence of Globalization in Promoting Entrepreneurship in Malaysia. *South East European Journal of Economics and Business*, 7(2), 149–157. DOI: 10.2478/v10033-012-0021-7

Autio, E., Sapienza, H. J., & Almeida, J. G. (2000). Effects of age at entry, knowledge intensity, and imitability on international growth. *Academy of Management Journal*, 43(5), 909–924. DOI: 10.2307/1556419

Bakar, R., Islam, M. A., & Lee, J. (2014). Entrepreneurship Education: Experiences in Selected Countries. *International Education Studies*, 8(1), 80–88. DOI: 10.5539/ies.v8n1p88

Baporikar, N. (2015). Drivers of Innovation. In Ordoñez de Pablos, P., Turró, L., Tennyson, R., & Zhao, J. (Eds.), *Knowledge Management for Competitive Advantage During Economic Crisis* (pp. 250–270). IGI Global. DOI: 10.4018/978-1-4666-6457-9.ch014

Baporikar, N. (2016). *Handbook of Research on Entrepreneurship in the Contemporary Knowledge-Based Global Economy*. IGI Global. DOI: 10.4018/978-1-4666-8798-1

Baporikar, N. (2018a). Entrepreneurship Development and Project Management (Text & Cases). Himalaya Publishing House.

Baporikar, N. (Ed.). (2018b). *Knowledge Integration Strategies for Entrepreneurship and Sustainability*. IGI Global. DOI: 10.4018/978-1-5225-5115-7

Baporikar, N. (2020). *Handbook of Research on Entrepreneurship Development and Opportunities in Circular Economy*. IGI Global. DOI: 10.4018/978-1-7998-5116-5

Baporikar, N. (Ed.). (2024). *Ecosystem Dynamics and Strategies for Startups Scalability*. IGI Global. DOI: 10.4018/979-8-3693-0527-0

Barney, J. (1991). Firm Resources and Sustained Competitive Advantage. *Journal of Management*, 17(1), 99–120. DOI: 10.1177/014920639101700108

Barrow, C. (2001). *Incubators, A Realist's Guide to the World's New Business Accelerators*. Wiley.

Bøllingtoft, A. (2012). The bottom-up business incubator: Leverage to networking and cooperation practices in a self-generated, entrepreneurial-enabled environment. *Technovation*, 32(5), 304–315. DOI: 10.1016/j.technovation.2011.11.005

Booth-Jones, L. (2012). *Assessing small business training programme effectiveness in an incubator setting and beyond*. Masters dissertation, Nelson Mandela Metropolitan University.

Chen, X. (2009). *Students Who Study Science, Technology, Engineering, and Mathematics (STEM) in Postsecondary Education. Stats in Brief. NCES 2009-161*. National Center for Education Statistics.

Giordano Martínez, K., Fernández-Laviada, A., & Herrero Crespo, Á. (2018). Influence of Business Incubators Performance on Entrepreneurial Intentions and Its Antecedents during the Pre-incubation Stage. *Entrepreneurship Research Journal*, 8(2), 20160095. DOI: 10.1515/erj-2016-0095

Hackett, S. M., & Dilts, D. M. (2004). A real options-driven theory of business incubation. *The Journal of Technology Transfer*, 29(1), 41–54. DOI: 10.1023/B:-JOTT.0000011180.19370.36

Hitt, M. A., Ireland, R. D., & Lee, H. (2000). Technological learning, knowledge management, firm growth and performance: An introductory essay. *Journal of Engineering and Technology Management*, 17(3-4), 231–246. DOI: 10.1016/S0923-4748(00)00024-2

Ketchen, D. J. Jr, Thomas, J. B., & Snow, C. C. (1993). Organizational configurations and performance: A comparison of theoretical approaches. *Academy of Management Journal*, 36(6), 1278–1313. DOI: 10.2307/256812

Masutha, M., & Rogers, C. M. (2014). *Small enterprise development in South Africa: role of Business Incubators. Bulletin of Geography, Social –Economic Series No. 26*. Nicholas Copernicus University.

Matuluko, M. (2015). Nigeria's Communications Minister to release new ICT Blueprint in January. Available at: https://techpoint.ng

Mecke, P. (2014). *The role of business incubators in developing entrepreneurship*. Centre for Enterprise Manchester Metropolitan University Business School.

Moses, Ch., Ola-David, O., Steven, O., Olumuyiwa, O., Mosunmola, A., Mayowa, A., & Achugamonu, U. (2015). Entrepreneurship Education and Poverty Alleviation: Impact Analysis of Covenant University Graduate between 2006- 2013, *2nd Covenant University Conference on African Development Issues (CU-ICADI)*, 11th - 13th May, 2015, Africa Leadership Development Center, Covenant University, Ota, Nigeria.

National Bureau of Statistics. (2014). *Measuring Better: Presentation of Preliminary Results of the Rebased Nominal Gross Domestic Product (GDP) Estimates for Nigeria 2010 to 2013*. National Bureau of Statistics.

National Business Incubation Association. (2014). *The History of Business Incubation: What is Business Incubation?* National Business Incubation Association.

Naudé, W. (2011). Entrepreneurship and Economic Development: An Introduction. *Entrepreneurship and Economic Development*, 3-17.

Nwabueze, A. U., & Ozioko, R. E. (2011). Information and communication technology for sustainable development in Nigeria. *Library Philosophy and Practice*, (1), 92.

Nwekeaku, C. (2013). Entrepreneurship education and challenges to Nigerian universities. *Journal of Education and Practice*, 4(3), 51–56.

Okpara, J. O., Halkias, D., Nwajiuba, C., Harkiolakis, N., & Caracatsanis, S. M. (2011). Challenges facing women entrepreneurs in Nigeria. *Management Research Review*, 34(2), 221–235. DOI: 10.1108/01409171111102821

Omoh, G. (2015). *Youth unemployment in Nigeria up to 50% - Mckinsey & Co.* Vanguard.

Oshewolo, S. (2010). Galloping poverty in Nigeria: An appraisal of government interventionist Policies. *Journal of Sustainable Development in Africa*, 12(6), 264–274.

Seoane, F. J. F., Rodriguez, G. R., & Rojo, D. A. (2014). The Influence of Training and gender in entrepreneurship through Business Incubators in Galicia (Spain). *International Journal of Social Science and Entrepreneurship*, 1(9), 611–623.

Verheugen, G. (2007). CSR and competitiveness: A view from the European Commission. *The State Of Responsible Competitiveness*, 2007, 111.

ADDITIONAL READINGS

Baporikar, N. (2018). *Global Practices in Knowledge Management for Societal and Organizational Development*. IGI Global. DOI: 10.4018/978-1-5225-3009-1

Eshun, J. P.Jr. (2009). Business incubation as strategy. *Business Strategy Series*, 10(3), 156–166. DOI: 10.1108/17515630910956570

Hackett, S. M., & Dilts, D. M. (2004). A systematic review of business incubation research. *The Journal of Technology Transfer*, 29(1), 55–82. DOI: 10.1023/B:-JOTT.0000011181.11952.0f

Hausberg, J. P., & Korreck, S. (2021). *Business incubators and accelerators: a co-citation analysis-based, systematic literature review*. Edward Elgar Publishing.

Hewitt, L. M., & Van Rensburg, L. J. J. (2020). The role of business incubators in creating sustainable small and medium enterprises. *The Southern African Journal of Entrepreneurship and Small Business Management*, 12(1), 9. DOI: 10.4102/sajesbm.v12i1.295

Lala, K. (2024). *The Role of Incubation in India's Innovation and Development Ecosystem*. Cambridge Scholars Publishing.

Nicholls-Nixon, C. L., Singh, R. M., Hassannezhad Chavoushi, Z., & Valliere, D. (2024). How university business incubation supports entrepreneurs in technology-based and creative industries: A comparative study. *Journal of Small Business Management*, 62(2), 591–627. DOI: 10.1080/00472778.2022.2073360

Obaji, N. O., Onyemerela, C., & Olugu, M. U. (2015). Entrepreneurship and business incubation programme: The sure couple. *Int. J. Sci.Tech. and Mgt*, 4, 1627–1633.

Ramar, M. N., Muthukumaran, C. K., Manida, M. M., Nandhini, M. B., & Parkavi, M. C. (2020). Role Of Business Incubation Centres In Promoting Entrepreneurship With Special Reference To Tamilnadu. *Technology*, 68(34), 34.

KEY TERMS AND DEFINITIONS

Barriers: Anything serving to obstruct, or preventing, access, or progress. Anything or something, which limits a quality or achievement or the act of limiting or the condition of being limited or cause delay. Barriers come in many forms and from many sources. They can be temporary or permanent. When evaluating a barrier, it is necessary that one looks at all the activities that precede the delay as well as the activities that follow the delay.

Business: Pertains broadly to commercial, financial, and industrial activities.

Challenges: Something that by its nature or character serves as a call to make special effort, a demand to explain, justify, or difficulty in a undertaking that is stimulating to one engaged in it.

Entrepreneur: An individual engaged in the process of starting and growing one's own business or idea. One undertakes risk to start an enterprise not only for profits.

Entrepreneurial Process: Creativity and its links to enterprise, the three-stage process of entrepreneurship; opportunity screening; innovation and competitive advantage; acquiring resources.

Entrepreneurship: The capacity and willingness to develop organize and manage a business venture along with any of its risks in order to make a profit. The most obvious example of entrepreneurship is the starting of new businesses.

Environment: Important or essential in relation to a plan of action; highly important to an intended objective.

Government: The organization, machinery, or agency through which a political unit exercises authority and performs functions and which is usually classified according to the distribution of power within it.

Innovation: Something new or different introduced, it is the act of innovating which includes introduction of new things or methods. Innovation is also introduction of a new idea into the marketplace in the form of a new product or service, or an improvement in organization or process. The process of translating an idea or invention into a good or service that creates value or for which customers will pay.

Process: A systematic series of actions directed to some end, it is a continuous action, operation, or series of changes taking place in a definite manner. A natural phenomenon marked by gradual changes that lead toward a particular result, a natural progressively continuing operation or development marked by a series of gradual changes that succeed one another in a relatively fixed way and lead toward a particular result or end. A process is thus a series of progressive and interdependent steps by which an end is attainable.

Small and Medium Enterprises (SMEs): is a term for segmenting businesses and other organizations that are somewhere between the "small office-home office" size and the larger enterprise. Country to country this term may vary, but the basis or criteria for the term is usually the investment, number of employees and turnover, etc.

Strategies: Method chosen and plans made to bring about a desired future, achievement of a goals or solutions to a problem. Strategies are a result of choices made. It is set of managerial decisions and actions that determine the long-term performance of a business enterprise.

Technology: The branch of knowledge that deals with the creation and use of technical means and their interrelation with life, society, and the environment, drawing upon such subjects as industrial arts, engineering, applied science, and pure science; method for convening resources into goods and services.

Chapter 4
Validating the Push-Pull Theory in the Age of Entrepreneurship:
A Conceptual Study

Prachita A. Patil
Dr. Ambedkar Institute of Management Studies and Research, India

Sushil Gadekar
Dr. Ambedkar Institute of Management Studies and Research, India

Saket Bansod
Dr. Ambedkar Institute of Management Studies and Research, India

ABSTRACT

Entrepreneurship has emerged as a pivotal force in shaping contemporary economies worldwide. Amidst the dynamic landscape of entrepreneurial endeavors, understanding the underlying motivations and factors influencing entrepreneurial behavior remains a critical area of research. The push-pull theory, originally conceived in the context of migration studies, offers a valuable framework for comprehending the interplay of factors that drive individuals towards entrepreneurship or deter them from it. In this chapter, the authors delve into the validation of the push-pull theory within the realm of entrepreneurship, contextualizing it within the contemporary socio-economic landscape. The push-pull theory posits that individuals are pushed away from their current situation by undesirable factors and pulled towards entrepreneurship by attractive opportunities.

DOI: 10.4018/979-8-3693-4302-9.ch004

INTRODUCTION

"Chase the vision, not the money, the money will end up following you." – Tony Hsieh, Zappos CEO"

Entrepreneurship has become fundamental to driving economic growth and fostering innovation in today's global context. The rise in entrepreneurial activity is propelled by a convergence of socio-economic factors, such as rapid technological advancements, dynamic shifts in market conditions, and evolving perspectives on career trajectories. Within this dynamic environment, there is a growing scholarly interest in understanding the fundamental motivations and cognitive processes that lead individuals to embark on entrepreneurial ventures.

Entrepreneurship has become a pivotal driver of economic growth and innovation in today's global landscape. The rise in entrepreneurial endeavours is spurred by a confluence of socio-economic factors, such as technological advancements, evolving market dynamics, and shifting perceptions of career trajectories. In this dynamic environment, there is a growing scholarly focus on understanding the intrinsic motivations and decision-making mechanisms that propel individuals towards entrepreneurship. The role of individual characteristics, such as personality traits, prior experiences, and personal circumstances, will be examined to understand how these factors shape the push-pull dynamics in entrepreneurial decision-making.

Firstly, we will investigate the push factors that propel individuals towards entrepreneurship. Key push factors include economic instability, job dissatisfaction, and limited opportunities for career advancement. Additionally, we will consider socio-cultural influences, such as evolving attitudes towards risk-taking and the desire for greater autonomy, to gain a comprehensive understanding of these push dynamics.

Secondly, we will examine the pull factors that attract individuals to entrepreneurship. These factors include perceived opportunities for wealth creation, autonomy, flexibility, and the allure of pursuing one's passion. Additionally, advancements in technology and the growth of start-up ecosystems enhance the appeal of entrepreneurial ventures.

Furthermore, we will investigate how individual characteristics, including personality traits, prior experiences, and personal circumstances, influence the manifestation of push-pull dynamics in entrepreneurial decision-making.

Through empirical research spanning diverse geographical and cultural contexts, our objective is to validate the relevance and applicability of the push-pull theory in elucidating entrepreneurial motivations and behaviours. By undertaking this endeavour, our analysis aims to provide valuable insights for policymakers, educators, and aspiring entrepreneurs striving to navigate the intricate terrain of entrepreneurship in the 21st century.

Moreover, this analysis will explore the intricate interplay between push and pull factors, recognizing that they are often intertwined and context-dependent. By examining the role of individual characteristics, such as personality traits, prior experiences, and personal circumstances, we aim to elucidate how these factors shape the manifestation of push-pull dynamics in entrepreneurial endeavours.

Through secondary research drawn from diverse geographical and cultural contexts, we seek to validate the relevance and applicability of the push-pull theory in explaining entrepreneurial motivations and behaviours. By doing so, this analysis endeavours to offer valuable insights for policymakers, educators, and aspiring entrepreneurs seeking to navigate the complex landscape of entrepreneurship in the 21st century.

On the other hand, "Pull" entrepreneurs are attracted to the challenges and potential rewards associated with launching a successful venture. Their entrepreneurial skills and attributes make them more suited for professional fulfilment outside traditional corporate settings.

The Chapter is structured as follows: It begins with a theoretical review and general Introduction followed by a detailed description of the research methodology, including Conclusion, discussion and Practical Implications. The implications for both research and practice are addressed in the summary section.

Lastly, this Chapter analyses how push factors influence the relationship between entrepreneurial identity and intentionality. While much theory exists on the impact of push factors on entrepreneurship, empirical research on how specific push factors affect the intentions of different personality types is limited. This Chapter aims to fill this gap by examining how push factors influence various groups of individuals.

PUSH -PULL THEORY

The push-pull theory, originally developed in migration studies, offers a valuable framework for comprehending the intricate dynamics that shape entrepreneurial behaviour. This theory posits that individuals are motivated to pursue entrepreneurship by a blend of push factors, which push them away from their current situations, and pull factors, which draw them towards new entrepreneurial opportunities.

Although the push-pull theory has found broad application across different fields, its specific validation within the realm of entrepreneurship presents a promising area for further investigation. In today's entrepreneurial landscape, marked by rapid technological advancement, globalization, and evolving socio-cultural norms, it becomes imperative to scrutinize the theory's relevance and applicability in elucidating the motivations and behaviours driving entrepreneurs.

This comprehensive analysis aims to explore and corroborate the push-pull theory within the current entrepreneurial environment. By integrating theoretical frameworks with empirical research, our goal is to illuminate the complex dynamics that influence entrepreneurial decision-making. We will investigate various push factors, such as economic instability, dissatisfaction with current employment, and societal influences. Additionally, we will examine pull factors, such as perceived opportunities for financial gain, autonomy, and pursuing personal passions. Through this exploration, we seek to offer a nuanced understanding of the diverse motivations that propel individuals towards entrepreneurship.

Furthermore, this analysis will delve into the complex interaction between push and pull factors, acknowledging their intertwined nature and sensitivity to context. By investigating individual characteristics such as personality traits, past experiences, and personal circumstances, we aim to clarify how these elements influence the dynamics of push-pull in entrepreneurial pursuits.

The push-pull theory posits that individuals are driven away from their current situations by undesirable factors and attracted towards entrepreneurship by enticing opportunities. In the current age of entrepreneurship, marked by rapid technological advancements, evolving market dynamics, and shifting work paradigms, this theory's applicability necessitates thorough investigation. This Chapter outlines a comprehensive approach authenticating the push-pull theory within the contemporary entrepreneurial landscape.

This Chapter aims to validate the push-pull theory in modern entrepreneurial endeavours by examining the push factors, such as economic instability, job dissatisfaction, and lack of career advancement, alongside the pull factors, such as perceived opportunities for wealth creation, autonomy, flexibility, and passion pursuit. Additionally, it will explore how socio-cultural influences and technological advancements contribute to these dynamics.

While the push-pull theory has been widely applied in various domains, its validation within the context of entrepreneurship remains an area ripe for exploration. In the age of entrepreneurship, characterized by unprecedented technological innovation, globalization, and evolving socio-cultural norms, it is essential to examine the relevance and applicability of this theory in explaining the motivations and behaviours of entrepreneurs.

This comprehensive analysis seeks to delve into the validation of the push-pull theory in the contemporary entrepreneurial landscape. By synthesizing theoretical insights with empirical evidence, we aim to shed light on the multifaceted dynamics that underpin entrepreneurial decision-making processes. Through an exploration of push factors, such as economic instability, job dissatisfaction, and societal pressures, as well as pull factors, including perceived opportunities for wealth creation, autonomy, and passion pursuit, we aim to provide a nuanced understanding of the forces that drive individuals towards entrepreneurship.

The push-pull theory, initially conceptualized within the field of migration studies, provides a valuable framework for understanding the complex interplay of factors that influence entrepreneurial behaviour. According to this theory, individuals are propelled towards entrepreneurship by a combination of push factors, which drive them away from existing circumstances, and pull factors, which attract them towards entrepreneurial opportunities.

Finally, through empirical research our aim is to validate the relevance and applicability of the push-pull theory in explaining entrepreneurial motivations and behaviours across diverse contexts. By integrating theoretical insights with empirical evidence, this abstract strives to enhance understanding of the nuanced dynamics of push-pull factors in contemporary entrepreneurship. These insights are intended to provide valuable guidance for policymakers, educators, and aspiring entrepreneurs navigating the complex background of entrepreneurship in today's environment.

LITERATURE REVIEW

In differentiating between pull and push factors, Uhlaner and Thurik (2007) characterize pull factors as leading to either material or non-material benefits. These factors entice individuals towards entrepreneurship by offering rewards that can be tangible (such as financial gains) or intangible (such as autonomy or personal fulfilment).

Conversely, push factors, as explained by Huisman and De Ridder (1984), stem from dissatisfaction with one's current situation and a desire for change. These factors often arise from frustrations with wage-employment, experiences of unemployment, or personal crises that prompt individuals to seek alternative paths, such as starting their own ventures.

According to Verheul et al. (2010), the distinction is nuanced: necessity entrepreneurs are primarily motivated by push factors, while opportunity entrepreneurs are predominantly driven by pull factors. However, self-employment often involves a blend of both types of motivations rather than fitting strictly into one category or the other.

In study on push and pull factors influencing entrepreneurship orientation, Giacomin et al. (2007) observed that younger individuals are motivated by a combination of push factors, such as the desire for independence, and pull factors, including profit objectives and social status. On the other hand, older unemployed individuals are primarily driven by the necessity of finding employment. Additionally, the research indicates that older individuals who are not unemployed often pursue entrepreneurship as a hobby.

The push-pull theory has been a significant framework in entrepreneurship research since the seminal work of Gilad and Levine (1986). Motivations related to employment are typically categorized as push factors and play a crucial role in shaping preparation for an entrepreneurial career (Dobrev and Barnett, 2005; Winn, 2004). These factors encompass issues such as unemployment, layoffs, and limited job or career opportunities. While some studies indicate gender differences in work-related motivations (Borooah et al., 1997; Cromie, 1987a; DeMartino and Barbato, 2003; Hakim, 1989), prior research generally suggests minimal gender disparities in these motivators.

The literature presents various concepts exploring the motivations behind entrepreneurial pursuits. One prominent concept is the push-pull dichotomy, as discussed by Shapero (1975) and Solymossy (1997), among others. This framework categorizes aspiring entrepreneurs into two groups: those who are "pulled" into entrepreneurship by voluntary motives, such as a desire to pursue a business idea, and those who are "pushed" into entrepreneurship due to external, typically unfavorable circumstances (Storey, 1991; Clark & Drinkwater, 2000; Caliendo & Kritikos, 2010; Kautonen et al., 2014).

A related categorization, aligned with the push-pull approach, is employed by the Global Entrepreneurship Monitor (GEM), which distinguishes between opportunity entrepreneurs and necessity entrepreneurs (Reynolds et al., 2022).

Pull factors are commonly used to categorize motivations in entrepreneurship research (DeMartino and Barbato, 2003; Fischer et al., 1993; Rosa and Dawson, 2006). This approach acknowledges that not all aspiring entrepreneurs are primarily driven by financial gain or economic necessity; rather, self-dedication plays a significant role in their decision-making process.

Family-related motives are considered significant push factors for both men and women entering entrepreneurship, reflecting a growing global trend (Verheul et al., 2006). According to Still and Timms (2000, p. 3), women entrepreneurs often start businesses with the aim of making a societal impact, demonstrating a stronger focus on customer needs and social goals alongside financial objectives.

Taylor (1996) and Clark and Drinkwater (2000) highlight that individuals are often drawn to self-employment by the potential for higher earnings. However, this view is contested by others, such as Gill (1988) and Earle and Sakova (2000), who question the primacy of financial incentives. Amit et al. (2001) suggest that financial motives may hold secondary importance in entrepreneurial decisions.

Financial motivations in entrepreneurship are typically categorized as "pull" factors, indicating attraction towards opportunities rather than necessity. Yet, the conceptual distinction between opportunity and necessity based on financial motivation remains ambiguous. In occupational choice analysis, self-employment may become more appealing either due to perceived higher returns from entrepreneurship (pull factors), reduced perceived earnings from traditional employment (push factors), or a combination of both.

According to the "push" hypothesis, rising unemployment diminishes prospects for finding traditional employment, thereby increasing the attractiveness of entrepreneurship as an alternative (Storey, 1982; Storey and Johnson, 1987). However, analyzing motivation should extend beyond the sole impact of unemployment (Mason, 1989).

Based on a GEM report from 2001, Vivarelli (2004) notes that while opportunity entrepreneurs (who start firms due to perceived opportunities and personal interests) are more prevalent, necessity entrepreneurs (who start firms due to lack of better employment alternatives, involuntarily) still constitute a significant portion of potential and actual entrepreneurs (Reynolds et al., 2001).

Castles, S., & Miller, M. J. (2009) provide a comprehensive overview of global migration patterns, highlighting the complexity and multifaceted nature of migration, thus emphasizing the need for a more nuanced approach to the push-pull theory, De Haas (2010) critiques traditional push-pull models for their oversimplification and advocates for a more dynamic approach that incorporates the changing nature of migration drivers over time.

Carling, J., & Collins, F. (2018), explored how aspirations and desires shape migration decisions, suggesting that traditional push-pull factors need to be expanded to include subjective and psychological dimensions. Hagen-Zanker, J. (2020) initiated reviews various migration theories, including push-pull models, and calls for more comprehensive frameworks that integrate economic, social, and environmental factors. Czaika, M., & Reinprecht, C. (2020), synthesizes recent research on migration drivers, highlighting the importance of integrating multiple factors, such as policy changes and transnational networks, into the push-pull framework. Van Hear, N., Bakewell, O., & Long, K. (2018), propose an extended push-pull model that includes additional drivers like social networks and individual agency, advocating for a more nuanced and comprehensive understanding of migration. 5. De Haas, H., Castles, S., & Miller, M. J. (2020) incorporates recent migration trends and theoretical developments, emphasizing the need for dynamic and multidimensional approaches to understanding migration.

MAIN FOCUS OF THE CHAPTER

The classification of motivations such as "to be autonomous" and "get out of unemployment" as push factors is supported by earlier studies (Ritsilä & Tervo, 2002; Evans & Leighton, 1989; Mason, 1989; Harrison & Hart, 1983). These motivations reflect circumstances where individuals are compelled to pursue entrepreneurship due to external pressures or constraints, such as the need for autonomy or the necessity to find alternative employment.

Moreover, previous literature has consistently delineated a clear distinction between push and pull motives in the context of self-employment and entrepreneurship. Researchers have also categorized motives as either external or internal, depending on whether they are driven by external opportunities or constraints versus personal goals and aspirations. This categorization helps structure and analyse available data effectively.

Furthermore, motivations like "meet family expectations" and "carry on the family tradition" are categorized under push factors because they represent situations where individuals are influenced or pressured by family and social expectations to start a business.

However, it's important to recognize that these dimensions can often overlap, especially between push and pull motivations. Individuals may cite multiple reasons for choosing self-employment that span both categories and can be influenced by external and internal factors alike. Additionally, occupational choice plays a significant role, as self-employment may be a deliberate career choice or may arise incidentally within specific occupations, such as trades or professions, which can also be influenced by gender-related occupational segregation.

In summary, while distinct categorizations help in organizing and understanding motivations for entrepreneurship, the reality often involves a complex interplay of push and pull factors, external and internal motivations, and considerations related to occupational choices and gender dynamics.

ISSUES, CONTROVERSIES, AND PROBLEMS

The push-pull theory, initially developed in the field of migration studies, offers a framework for understanding how individuals are propelled towards entrepreneurship. It suggests that push factors, which urge individuals away from their current situations, and pull factors, which attract them towards entrepreneurial opportunities, jointly influence entrepreneurial decision-making. Despite its widespread application, the validation of this theory within the dynamic context of contemporary entrepreneurship remains a critical area of investigation.

In today's socio-economic landscape characterized by rapid technological advancements, globalization, and evolving attitudes towards career paths, there is a growing need to rigorously examine and validate the relevance of the push-pull theory. This theory's applicability in explaining the motivations and behaviours of entrepreneurs requires thorough empirical scrutiny and theoretical refinement. By doing so, scholars aim to enhance our understanding of how various factors interact to shape entrepreneurial intentions and actions in modern times. Therefore, a comprehensive analysis is warranted to explore how push and pull dynamics manifest in entrepreneurial contexts today, considering the nuanced influences of socio-economic trends and individual aspirations. Such research not only contributes to theoretical advancements but also informs practical strategies for fostering entrepreneurship amidst contemporary challenges and opportunities.

The research problem lies in elucidating the nuanced dynamics of push and pull factors that influence entrepreneurial decision-making processes in the age of entrepreneurship. Specifically, the following research questions guide this investigation:

1. What are the main motivators for prospective entrepreneurs in the current socioeconomic environment?
2. In what ways do social pressures, job discontent, and unstable economies influence the desire to start their own business?
3. What are the main draw elements that entice people to become entrepreneurs?
4. How do entrepreneurial intentions and practices are influenced by perceived chances for wealth creation, autonomy, pursuing passions, and technology advancements?
5. How do push and pull variables combine to shape the motivations and actions of entrepreneurs? What part do personal factors, such as personality traits, life experiences, and circumstances, play in mediating how push-pull dynamics manifest?
6. How well does the push-pull theory offer an all-encompassing framework for comprehending the motivations and actions of entrepreneurs in various geographic and cultural contexts? How is it possible?

AIM OF THE PROPOSAL

The aim of the proposal is to validate the push pull theory in the era of Entrepreneurship.

OBJECTIVES OF THE PROPOSAL

This chapter targets to delve into the core of push pull motivational factor, exploring its principles, methodologies, and implications within the framework of an entrepreneurial era. The purpose of the chapter will underpin the need, necessity and passion of aspiring entrepreneurs endorsing the entrepreneurial concern.

Here are the key objectives of validating the push-pull theory:

1. Theory Development and Refinement
2. Predictive Accuracy
3. Policy Formulation and Implementation
4. Entrepreneurial Ecosystem Development.
5. Educational Curriculum Design
6. Cross-cultural Understanding

Figure 1. Objectives of the Proposal-Authors elaboration

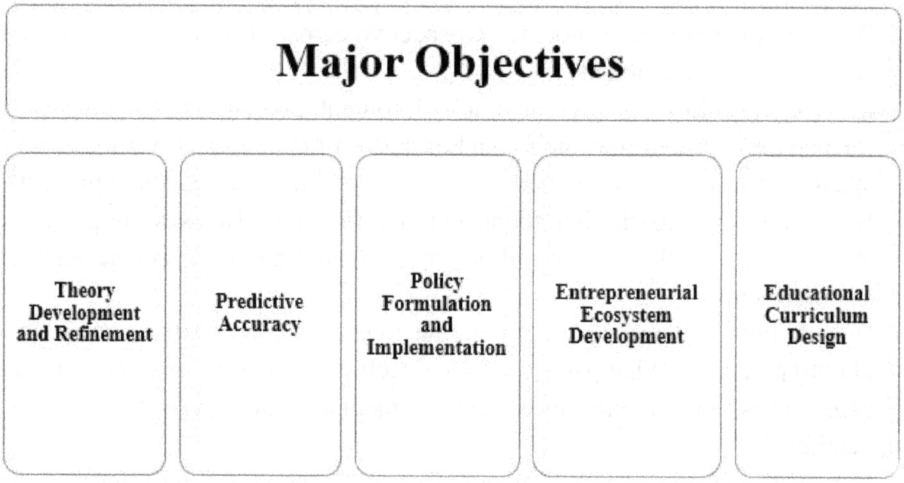

Major Objectives

| Theory Development and Refinement | Predictive Accuracy | Policy Formulation and Implementation | Entrepreneurial Ecosystem Development | Educational Curriculum Design |

OBJECTIVES

1. **Understanding Entrepreneurial Processes**: To gain deeper insights into how entrepreneurial activities and decisions are made, understanding the nuances of opportunity recognition, resource mobilization, and innovation.

2. **Guiding Entrepreneurial Practice**: To provide frameworks and models that can be applied by entrepreneurs to improve their chances of success.
3. **Academic Contribution**: To contribute to the body of knowledge within the field of entrepreneurship, aiding in the education of future scholars and practitioners.
4. **Policy Development**: To inform policy makers with evidence-based insights that can help shape supportive environments for entrepreneurial ventures.

OUTCOMES

1. **Enhanced Theoretical Frameworks**: Refined theories that better explain the dynamics of entrepreneurship, incorporating factors such as market conditions, individual traits, and socio-economic influences.
2. **Practical Tools and Models**: Development of practical tools, such as business model canvases and strategic planning frameworks, that entrepreneurs can use to plan and execute their ventures more effectively.
3. **Improved Educational Content**: Enhanced curricula for entrepreneurship education, incorporating the latest theories and practical insights, preparing students better for entrepreneurial challenges.
4. **Evidence-Based Policies**: Formulation of policies that are based on rigorous academic research, aimed at fostering entrepreneurial ecosystems and reducing barriers to entry for new ventures.

PUSH AND PULL THEORY IN ENTREPRENEURSHIP: THEORY AND PRACTICE PUSH FACTORS

- **Necessity-Driven Entrepreneurship**: Individuals are 'pushed' into entrepreneurship due to lack of employment, job dissatisfaction, or economic necessity.
- **Theoretical Perspective**: Research focuses on how economic downturns, unemployment rates, and personal crises trigger entrepreneurial activities.
- **Practical Implications**: Policies and support systems aimed at unemployed individuals can help them transition into entrepreneurship, such as unemployment benefits converted into start-up capital or retraining programs.

PULL FACTORS

- **Opportunity-Driven Entrepreneurship**: Individuals are 'pulled' into entrepreneurship by recognizing market opportunities, personal aspirations, or the desire for independence.
- **Theoretical Perspective**: Examines how market opportunities, innovation, and individual aspirations influence the decision to start a venture.
- **Practical Implications**: Encouraging innovation through incubators, providing access to funding, and fostering a culture that celebrates entrepreneurial success can attract individuals to start businesses.

INTEGRATION OF PUSH AND PULL THEORY IN PRACTICE

1. **Hybrid Models**: Many entrepreneurs experience a mix of push and pull factors. Understanding this interplay can lead to more effective support systems.
2. **Customized Support Programs**: Tailoring entrepreneurship programs to address both push and pull motivations, such as combining financial support with opportunity recognition training.
3. **Policy Design**: Developing policies that recognize the dual nature of push and pull factors can create a more inclusive entrepreneurial ecosystem, supporting both necessity-driven and opportunity-driven entrepreneurs.

PREDICTIVE ACCURACY

Objectives

1. **Improving Decision-Making**: To enhance the decision-making processes of entrepreneurs by providing accurate predictions about market trends, customer behaviour, and business outcomes.
2. **Resource Allocation**: To optimize the allocation of resources such as time, capital, and human resources by predicting the most promising opportunities and potential risks.
3. **Risk Management**: To identify and mitigate risks early on by predicting potential challenges and failures.
4. **Strategic Planning**: To aid in the development of more effective strategic plans based on reliable forecasts of future conditions.
5. **Enhancing Success Rates**: To increase the overall success rate of entrepreneurial ventures by using predictive tools to guide crucial business decisions.

Outcomes

1. **Data-Driven Strategies**: Entrepreneurs are able to develop strategies based on concrete data and predictive models, leading to more informed and potentially successful ventures.
2. **Reduced Uncertainty**: Lower levels of uncertainty in business decisions due to more accurate forecasts about market and industry trends.
3. **Increased Efficiency**: More efficient use of resources by avoiding investments in less promising opportunities and focusing on high-potential areas.
4. **Higher Success Rates**: Improved success rates of start-ups and new ventures by aligning efforts with predictive insights.
5. **Scalable Models**: Development of scalable predictive models that can be adapted and used across various sectors and industries within entrepreneurship.

PREDICTIVE ACCURACY

Market Analysis

o **Objective**: Predict market trends and consumer demand to identify viable business opportunities.
o **Outcome**: Entrepreneurs can enter markets with higher potential for growth and profitability.

2. **Customer Behaviour**:

o **Objective**: Anticipate customer needs, preferences, and behaviours to tailor products and services effectively.
o **Outcome**: Enhanced customer satisfaction and loyalty, leading to sustained business growth.

3. **Financial Projections**:

o **Objective**: Forecast financial performance, including revenue, expenses, and profitability.
o **Outcome**: Better financial planning and management, reducing the risk of financial shortfalls.

4. **Competitive Analysis**:

- **Objective**: Predict competitor actions and market positioning.
- **Outcome**: Development of competitive strategies that effectively counteract competitor moves.

  5. **Operational Efficiency**:

- **Objective**: Forecast operational challenges and resource requirements.
- **Outcome**: Streamlined operations and optimized use of resources, improving overall business efficiency.

Practical Implications

1. **Tools and Technologies**:
   - **Big Data Analytics**: Leveraging large datasets to identify patterns and trends that can inform predictive models.
   - **Machine Learning and AI**: Using advanced algorithms to enhance the accuracy of predictions related to various aspects of entrepreneurship.
2. **Application in Business Planning**:
   - **Scenario Analysis**: Developing multiple potential scenarios based on predictive models to prepare for different future conditions.
   - **Real-Time Adjustments**: Continuously updating predictions with real-time data to adapt strategies quickly.
3. **Education and Training**:
   - **Curriculum Development**: Integrating predictive analytics into entrepreneurship education to prepare future entrepreneurs for data-driven decision-making.
   - **Workshops and Seminars**: Offering practical training on the use of predictive tools and technologies.
4. **Policy and Support Systems**:
   - **Government Initiatives**: Encouraging the use of predictive analytics in entrepreneurship through grants and support programs.
   - **Incubator and Accelerator Programs**: Providing access to predictive tools and expertise to help start-ups thrive.

POLICY FORMULATION AND IMPLEMENTATION

Objectives

1. **Promote Entrepreneurial Activity**: To create a favourable environment that encourages the initiation and growth of new businesses.
2. **Support Innovation and Competitiveness**: To foster innovation and enhance the competitiveness of start-ups and SMEs (small and medium-sized enterprises).
3. **Economic Growth and Job Creation**: To stimulate economic growth and generate employment through the development of a robust entrepreneurial ecosystem.
4. **Reduce Barriers to Entry**: To identify and eliminate obstacles that hinder entrepreneurial ventures, making it easier for individuals to start and sustain businesses.
5. **Ensure Inclusive Growth**: To promote inclusivity by supporting underrepresented groups in entrepreneurship, such as women, minorities, and disadvantaged communities.
6. **Facilitate Access to Resources**: To ensure entrepreneurs have access to essential resources like funding, training, mentorship, and infrastructure.

   Outcomes:

   1. **Increased Start-up Rates**: Higher rates of new business formation as a result of a more supportive and conducive policy environment.
   2. **Enhanced Innovation**: Greater levels of innovation within the economy due to policies that encourage research and development (R&D) and the adoption of new technologies.
   3. **Economic Development**: Positive economic impact through increased GDP, job creation, and higher productivity driven by entrepreneurial activities.
   4. **Reduced Failure Rates**: Lower business failure rates due to improved access to support services and resources, as well as policies that mitigate risks for new ventures.
   5. **Social Equity**: More equitable distribution of entrepreneurial opportunities across different social groups, leading to balanced economic growth.
   6. **Sustainable Ecosystems**: The development of sustainable entrepreneurial ecosystems that can support long-term economic resilience and adaptability.

KEY AREAS OF POLICY FORMULATION AND IMPLEMENTATION

1. **Access to Finance**:
   - **Objective**: Ensure that entrepreneurs have access to various funding sources, including venture capital, loans, grants, and crowdfunding.
   - **Outcome**: Increased availability of financial resources for startups, leading to higher business creation and expansion rates.
2. **Regulatory Environment**:
   - **Objective**: Simplify and streamline regulations and compliance requirements for new and existing businesses.
   - **Outcome**: Reduced administrative burden and costs, making it easier to start and operate businesses.
3. **Tax Policies**:
   - **Objective**: Implement tax incentives and reliefs to encourage investment in new ventures and support business growth.
   - **Outcome**: Enhanced profitability and sustainability of start-ups due to favourable tax conditions.
4. **Education and Training**:
   - **Objective**: Provide entrepreneurship education and training programs to equip individuals with the necessary skills and knowledge.
   - **Outcome**: A more skilled and capable entrepreneurial workforce, leading to higher success rates and innovation.
5. **Infrastructure Development**:
   - **Objective**: Develop and maintain physical and digital infrastructure that supports entrepreneurial activities.
   - **Outcome**: Improved access to essential infrastructure, such as co-working spaces, broadband internet, and transportation, facilitating business operations and growth.
6. **Support Networks and Mentorship**:
   - **Objective:** Foster networks of support, including mentorship programs, incubators, and accelerators.
   - **Outcome**: Enhanced guidance and support for entrepreneurs, contributing to better business strategies and increased chances of success.
7. **Market Access and Internationalization**:
   - **Objective**: Facilitate access to domestic and international markets for startups and SMEs.
   - **Outcome**: Expanded market reach and growth opportunities for entrepreneurial ventures.

POLICY IMPLEMENTATION

1. **Government Initiatives**:
   o Programs such as grants, subsidies, and incentives aimed at reducing the financial burden on new businesses.
   o Establishing one-stop shops for business registration and compliance to simplify administrative processes.
2. **Public-Private Partnerships**:
   o Collaborations between government and private sector to create entrepreneurship hubs and innovation districts.
   o Leveraging private sector expertise and resources to support government-led entrepreneurship initiatives.
3. **Monitoring and Evaluation**:
   o Continuous assessment of policy impact through metrics and feedback from the entrepreneurial community.
   o Adjusting policies based on real-time data and feedback to ensure they remain effective and relevant.

ENTREPRENEURIAL ECOSYSTEM DEVELOPMENT

Objectives:

1. **Enhance Collaboration and Networking**: To build a cohesive network of stakeholders, including entrepreneurs, investors, educators, policymakers, and support organizations, facilitating mutual support and collaboration.
2. **Improve Resource Accessibility**: To ensure entrepreneurs have easy access to critical resources such as capital, mentorship, education, and infrastructure.
3. **Promote Innovation and Creativity**: To create an environment that encourages innovative thinking and supports the development and commercialization of new ideas.
4. **Facilitate Market Entry and Expansion**: To help startups and small businesses access local and global markets, enhancing their growth opportunities.
5. **Supportive Regulatory Environment**: To advocate for policies and regulations that reduce barriers to entry and provide ongoing support for entrepreneurial ventures.
6. **Cultural Shift towards Entrepreneurship**: To foster a culture that values and supports entrepreneurship, risk-taking, and innovation within the community.

Outcomes:

1. **Increased Start-up Creation**: Higher rates of new business formation as a result of a more supportive and connected ecosystem.
2. **Sustainable Business Growth**: Enhanced growth and sustainability of start-ups and small businesses due to continuous access to necessary resources and support.
3. **Boosted Innovation**: Increased levels of innovation, leading to the development of competitive products and services.
4. **Economic Growth and Job Creation**: Significant contributions to economic growth, job creation, and overall economic development in the region.
5. **Resilient and Adaptive Ecosystem**: Development of a resilient entrepreneurial ecosystem capable of adapting to changes and challenges in the business environment.
6. **Inclusive and Diverse Entrepreneurship**: Greater inclusivity in entrepreneurship, ensuring diverse participation across different demographics and socioeconomic groups.

Key Components of Entrepreneurial Ecosystem Development

1. **Access to Capital**:
   - **Objective**: Ensure a variety of funding options are available, including venture capital, angel investors, grants, and loans.
   - **Outcome**: Increased funding availability for startups, leading to higher business creation and growth rates.
2. **Education and Training**:
   - **Objective**: Provide comprehensive entrepreneurship education and training programs at all levels.
   - **Outcome**: A more knowledgeable and skilled entrepreneurial workforce capable of driving innovation and business success.
3. **Mentorship and Support Networks**:
   - **Objective**: Establish robust mentorship and support networks to guide entrepreneurs through their journey.
   - **Outcome**: Enhanced guidance, reduced failure rates, and accelerated business growth due to experienced mentorship.
4. **Infrastructure Development**:
   - **Objective**: Develop essential infrastructure, including co-working spaces, incubators, accelerators, and digital infrastructure.
   - **Outcome**: Improved operational efficiency and support for start-ups, facilitating business development and innovation.

5. **Regulatory Framework**:
   o **Objective**: Create a regulatory environment that supports entrepreneurship through streamlined processes and favourable policies.
   o **Outcome**: Reduced administrative burden and legal obstacles, making it easier to start and grow businesses.
6. **Market Access**:
   o **Objective**: Help businesses access local and international markets through trade facilitation, export support, and market linkage programs.
   o **Outcome**: Expanded market opportunities and increased business revenues from diverse markets.
7. **Cultural Support**:
   o **Objective**: Foster a culture that celebrates entrepreneurship, innovation, and risk-taking.
   o **Outcome**: Greater societal support for entrepreneurs, leading to increased entrepreneurial activity and a dynamic ecosystem.

ENTREPRENEURIAL ECOSYSTEM DEVELOPMENT

1. **Public-Private Partnerships**:
   o **Collaboration**: Encouraging collaborations between government, private sector, and academic institutions to support entrepreneurial activities.
   o **Initiatives**: Launching joint initiatives such as innovation hubs, startup competitions, and accelerator programs.
2. **Policy and Advocacy**:
   o **Supportive Policies**: Developing policies that provide tax incentives, reduce regulatory burdens, and offer financial support to start-ups.
   o **Advocacy Groups**: Forming advocacy groups to represent the interests of entrepreneurs and influence policy-making.
3. **Community Engagement**:
   o **Events and Workshops**: Organizing events, workshops, and seminars to promote entrepreneurship and provide learning opportunities.
   o **Networks**: Building community networks that connect entrepreneurs with mentors, investors, and other stakeholders.
4. **Monitoring and Evaluation**:
   o **Impact Assessment**: Continuously assessing the impact of ecosystem initiatives and making data-driven adjustments.
   o **Feedback Mechanisms**: Implementing feedback mechanisms to gather insights from entrepreneurs and stakeholders for ongoing improvement.

EDUCATIONAL CURRICULUM DESIGN

Objectives

1. **Develop Entrepreneurial Skills and Mind-set**: To equip students with the skills, knowledge, and mind-set needed to succeed as entrepreneurs.
2. **Foster Innovation and Creativity**: To encourage innovative thinking and creativity, enabling students to identify and exploit business opportunities.
3. **Enhance Practical Knowledge and Experience**: To provide hands-on learning experiences that simulate real-world entrepreneurial challenges.
4. **Encourage Risk-Taking and Resilience**: To build students' confidence in taking calculated risks and developing resilience in the face of failure.
5. **Promote Ethical and Socially Responsible Entrepreneurship**: To instill a sense of ethical responsibility and social consciousness in entrepreneurial activities.
6. **Facilitate Networking and Collaboration**: To create opportunities for students to network with peers, mentors, investors, and industry professionals.
7. **Integrate Interdisciplinary Learning**: To combine knowledge from various disciplines to provide a comprehensive understanding of entrepreneurship.

Outcomes:

1. **Skilled and Knowledgeable Entrepreneurs**: Graduates who are well-equipped with the necessary skills and knowledge to start and run successful businesses.
2. **Increased Start-up Creation**: A higher number of students starting their own ventures, contributing to the entrepreneurial ecosystem.
3. **Innovative Solutions and Products**: Development of innovative solutions and products that address market needs and societal challenges.
4. **Resilient and Adaptive Entrepreneurs**: Entrepreneurs who are capable of adapting to changes and bouncing back from setbacks.
5. **Ethical and Socially Responsible Ventures**: Businesses that prioritize ethical practices and contribute positively to society.
6. **Strong Professional Networks**: A robust network of contacts that students can leverage for support, advice, and business opportunities.
7. **Holistic Understanding of Entrepreneurship**: Graduates with a well-rounded perspective on the various aspects of entrepreneurship, including finance, marketing, operations, and strategy.

Educational Curriculum Design in Entrepreneurship

1. **Core Entrepreneurial Skills**:
   - **Objective**: Teach essential skills such as business planning, financial management, marketing, and operations.
   - **Outcome**: Students who can effectively plan, launch, and manage business ventures.
2. **Innovation and Creativity**:
   - **Objective**: Encourage creative problem-solving and innovative thinking.
   - **Outcome**: Students capable of developing unique business ideas and solutions.
3. **Experiential Learning**:
   - **Objective**: Provide hands-on experiences through internships, projects, and simulations.
   - **Outcome**: Practical knowledge and skills that are directly applicable to real-world entrepreneurship.
4. **Risk Management and Resilience**:
   - **Objective**: Teach students how to assess risks, handle failures, and build resilience.
   - **Outcome**: Entrepreneurs who are prepared to navigate challenges and persist in the face of adversity.
5. **Ethics and Social Responsibility**:
   - **Objective**: Instill values of ethical behaviour and social responsibility in business practices.
   - **Outcome**: Graduates who prioritize ethical considerations and societal impact in their ventures.
6. **Networking and Collaboration**:
   - **Objective**: Facilitate connections with mentors, industry experts, and fellow entrepreneurs.
   - **Outcome**: Strong professional networks that support entrepreneurial endeavours.
7. **Interdisciplinary Approach**:
   - **Objective**: Integrate knowledge from various fields such as technology, economics, and social sciences.
   - **Outcome**: A comprehensive understanding of the multifaceted nature of entrepreneurship.

Practical Implications of Curriculum Design

1. **Project-Based Learning**:

- **Implementation**: Incorporate projects that require students to develop business plans, conduct market research, and launch pilot ventures.
- **Outcome**: Enhanced problem-solving skills and practical experience.

2. **Mentorship Programs**:
   - **Implementation**: Pair students with experienced entrepreneurs and industry professionals.
   - **Outcome**: Guidance, inspiration, and valuable insights from seasoned experts.
3. **Start-up Incubators and Accelerators**:
   - **Implementation**: Provide access to incubator and accelerator programs that offer resources, funding, and support.
   - **Outcome**: Increased chances of start-up success and growth.
4. **Guest Lectures and Workshops**:
   - **Implementation**: Regularly invite successful entrepreneurs and experts to share their experiences and conduct workshops.
   - **Outcome**: Exposure to real-world challenges and learning from the experiences of others.
5. **Competitions and Pitch Events**:
   - **Implementation**: Organize business plan competitions and pitch events to encourage students to present their ideas.
   - **Outcome**: Improved pitching skills and opportunities to secure funding and support.
6. **Global Perspectives**:
   - **Implementation**: Include courses and modules on global entrepreneurship, cross-cultural management, and international markets.
   - **Outcome**: Entrepreneurs prepared to operate in a globalized business environment.

CROSS-CULTURAL UNDERSTANDING

Objectives

1. **Enhance Global Competence**: To equip entrepreneurs with the knowledge and skills to operate effectively in diverse cultural environments.
2. **Improve Communication and Negotiation Skills**: To develop the ability to communicate and negotiate across cultural boundaries, fostering better relationships and business deals.
3. **Foster Inclusive Leadership**: To cultivate leadership qualities that respect and leverage cultural diversity within teams and organizations.

4. **Promote Ethical Business Practices**: To ensure that entrepreneurs conduct business ethically and responsibly, respecting cultural norms and values.
5. **Increase Market Access and Penetration**: To enable entrepreneurs to enter and thrive in international markets by understanding and adapting to local cultural contexts.
6. **Facilitate Innovation through Diversity**: To leverage diverse cultural perspectives to drive creativity and innovation in business practices and product development.
7. **Mitigate Cultural Risks and Conflicts**: To anticipate and manage potential cultural misunderstandings and conflicts that could impact business operations.

Outcomes

1. **Culturally Competent Entrepreneurs**: Entrepreneurs who are adept at understanding and navigating different cultural environments.
2. **Improved Cross-Cultural Communication**: Enhanced ability to communicate effectively with partners, clients, and teams from diverse cultural backgrounds.
3. **Inclusive and Diverse Workplaces**: Organizations that foster inclusive cultures, benefiting from diverse perspectives and talents.
4. **Ethical and Respectful Business Operations**: Business practices that are culturally sensitive and ethically sound, enhancing reputation and trust.
5. **Successful International Expansion**: Increased success in entering and operating in international markets due to better cultural adaptation.
6. **Innovative Business Solutions**: Development of innovative products and services that cater to diverse cultural needs and preferences.
7. **Reduced Cultural Conflicts**: Fewer misunderstandings and conflicts arising from cultural differences, leading to smoother business operations.

Cross-Cultural Understanding in Entrepreneurship

1. **Cultural Awareness Training**:
    - **Objective**: Educate entrepreneurs about the cultural norms, values, and business practices of different regions.
    - **Outcome**: Entrepreneurs who can navigate cultural differences with ease and respect.
2. **Language Skills**:
    - **Objective**: Encourage learning key languages to facilitate better communication in international markets.
    - **Outcome**: Improved ability to communicate and build relationships in non-native languages.

3. **Global Market Research**:
   o **Objective**: Conduct thorough market research to understand cultural preferences and consumer behaviour.
   o **Outcome**: Products and services that are tailored to meet the needs of diverse markets.
4. **Diverse Teams**:
   o **Objective**: Build and manage teams with diverse cultural backgrounds.
   o **Outcome**: Enhanced creativity, problem-solving, and decision-making through diverse perspectives.
5. **Cross-Cultural Leadership Development**:
   o **Objective**: Develop leadership skills that are inclusive and respectful of cultural differences.
   o **Outcome**: Leaders who can effectively manage and inspire diverse teams.
6. **Ethical Business Practices**:
   o **Objective**: Ensure business practices are ethical and culturally sensitive.
   o **Outcome**: Enhanced reputation and trust with international stakeholders.
7. **International Networking**:
   o **Objective**: Build networks and relationships with international partners and clients.
   o **Outcome**: Expanded business opportunities and collaborations across borders.

Practical Implications of Cross-Cultural Understanding

1. **Cultural Awareness Workshops**:
   o **Implementation**: Regularly organize workshops and training sessions focused on cultural awareness and sensitivity.
   o **Outcome**: Entrepreneurs who are well-versed in cultural nuances and capable of operating in diverse environments.
2. **Language Learning Programs**:
   o **Implementation**: Provide access to language learning resources and courses.
   o **Outcome**: Entrepreneurs who can communicate more effectively in key international markets.
3. **Market-Specific Business Strategies**:
   o **Implementation**: Develop business strategies that consider cultural preferences and consumer behaviour.
   o **Outcome**: Higher success rates in international markets through culturally tailored approaches.

4. **Diversity and Inclusion Policies**:
   o **Implementation**: Establish policies that promote diversity and inclusion within the organization.
   o **Outcome**: A more inclusive workplace that harnesses the benefits of diverse perspectives.
5. **Ethical Guidelines and Training**:
   o **Implementation**: Create guidelines and training programs focused on ethical business practices in different cultural contexts.
   o **Outcome**: Businesses that are trusted and respected globally for their ethical standards.
6. **International Partnerships and Alliances**:
   o **Implementation**: Form strategic partnerships with international businesses and organizations.
   o **Outcome**: Broader market access and collaborative opportunities.

MAJOR PARAMETERS

Push and Pull entrepreneurship apart from determining the major objectives include major parameters such as:

Figure 2. Push and Pull factor of Entrepreneurship-Authors elaboration

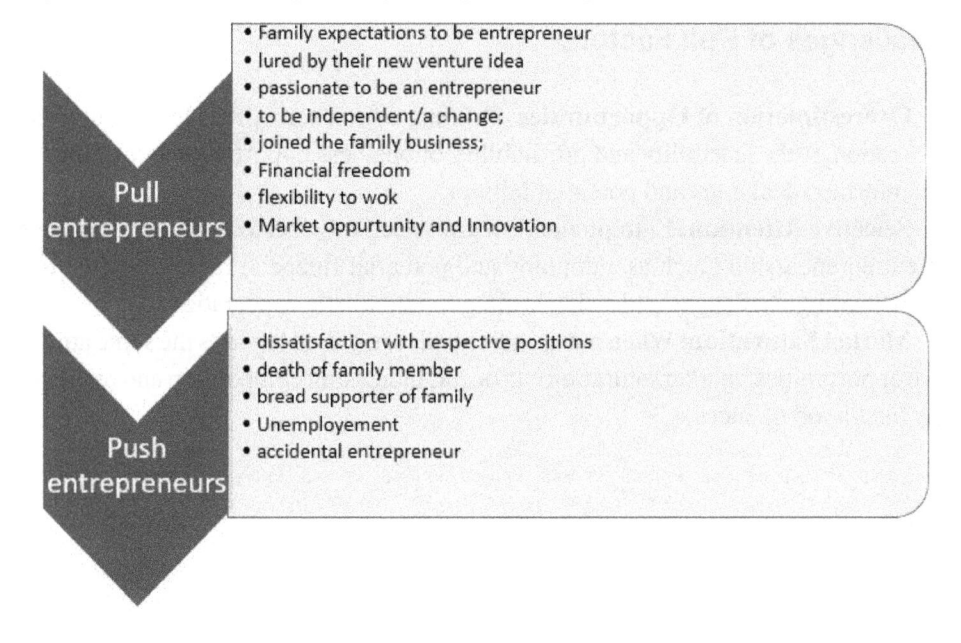

Pull entrepreneurs
- Family expectations to be entrepreneur
- lured by their new venture idea
- passionate to be an entrepreneur
- to be independent/a change;
- joined the family business;
- Financial freedom
- flexibility to wok
- Market oppurtunity and Innovation

Push entrepreneurs
- dissatisfaction with respective positions
- death of family member
- bread supporter of family
- Unemployement
- accidental entrepreneur

CHALLENGES OF PUSH PULL FACTOR

The push-pull theory in entrepreneurship refers to the two different approaches entrepreneurs take to create and market their products or services. The push-pull theory in entrepreneurship posits that individuals are motivated to start their own businesses due to push factors (negative conditions or circumstances that push them out of their current situation) and pull factors (positive attractions or opportunities that pull them towards entrepreneurship). Despite its usefulness, this theory faces several challenges:

Challenges of Push Factors

Economic Pressure Variability: The intensity of economic pressures can vary greatly among individuals. Not everyone facing unemployment or job dissatisfaction will turn to entrepreneurship, making it difficult to predict entrepreneurial behaviour solely based on push factors.

Psychological Factors: Not all individuals respond to negative situations in the same way. Some might lack the psychological resilience or risk tolerance required to pursue entrepreneurship, even when faced with strong push factors.

Lack of Resources: Individuals pushed into entrepreneurship due to negative circumstances might lack the necessary financial resources, skills, or networks to succeed, leading to high failure rates.

Challenges of Pull Factors

Overestimation of Opportunities: Pull factors can sometimes lead to an overestimation of the feasibility and profitability of business opportunities, resulting in misinformed decisions and potential failures.

Selective Attention: Entrepreneurs might selectively focus on attractive aspects of entrepreneurship (such as autonomy and potential financial rewards) while underestimating challenges and risks, leading to unrealistic expectations.

Market Saturation: When many individuals are pulled towards the same attractive opportunities, market saturation can occur, increasing competition and reducing the likelihood of success.

Figure 3. Challenges of Push pull theory (Source: Author)

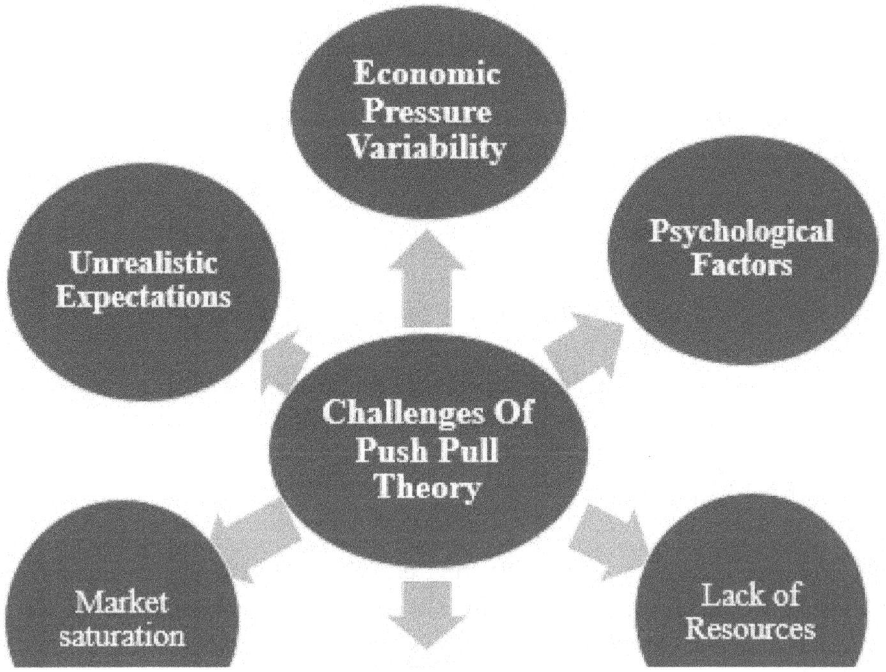

POTENTIAL CHALLENGES AND SUCCESS FACTORS

The Push-Pull Theory, driven by "push" factors that drive people away from their current location and "pull" factors that attract them to a new location. While this theory offers a useful framework for understanding migration, it has several potential challenges and associated success factors.

Oversimplification

Challenge: The push-pull theory can oversimplify the complex and multifaceted nature of migration by reducing it to binary factors.

Success Factor: Incorporating additional layers of analysis, such as socio-cultural and political contexts, can provide a more nuanced understanding.

Economic Focus

Challenge: The theory often emphasizes economic factors, potentially neglecting other important aspects like social networks, safety, and personal aspirations.

Success Factor: Broadening the scope to include non-economic factors can offer a more comprehensive view of migration dynamics.

Static Perspective

Challenge: The theory can imply a static perspective, ignoring how push and pull factors evolve over time.

Success Factor: Adopting a dynamic approach that considers temporal changes in push and pull factors can improve the theory's applicability.

Contextual Variability

Challenge: The factors influencing migration can vary greatly between different regions and populations, making it difficult to apply a one-size-fits-all model.

Success Factor: Customizing the analysis to specific contexts and conducting localized studies can make the theory more relevant and accurate.

Policy Implications

Challenge: Policymakers may misinterpret or oversimplify the theory, leading to ineffective or harmful migration policies.

Success Factor: Engaging with policymakers to ensure they understand the complexities and nuances of the theory can lead to better-informed decisions.

SOLUTIONS AND RECOMMENDATIONS

Our study reveals that individuals embarking on entrepreneurial activities often encounter or perceive disruptive situations and opportunities. These experiences position them along a spectrum of push and pull dynamics, varying in intensity and nature. Notably, the disruptive factors and opportunities that drive entrepreneurial ventures can manifest in diverse forms, illustrating the multifaceted nature of push and pull dynamics in entrepreneurship.

Furthermore, our findings underscore the significant influence of social position and biographical background on how individuals align with push and pull motivations. These factors shape both the intensity and the specific manifestations of push-pull dynamics among entrepreneurs. By considering social status and personal history, our study enhances understanding of how external circumstances and internal motivations interact to propel individuals towards entrepreneurial endeavours. In essence, our research contributes insights into the complex interplay of factors driving entrepreneurial engagement, emphasizing the variability and contextual sensitivity of push and pull dynamics in entrepreneurial decision-making.

IMPLICATIONS

Our study contributes significantly to the literature on entrepreneurial intention by addressing several key gaps and advancing theoretical understanding. Firstly, we respond to the scholarly call articulated by Carsrud and Brännback (2011) to delve into the influence of motivation on entrepreneurial intention. While previous research has explored push-pull motivations among established entrepreneurs (Caliendo & Kritikos, 2010; Giacomin et al., 2011; Ismail et al., 2012), our study uniquely focuses on undergraduate students, allowing us to examine how these motivations shape entrepreneurial intention as a precursor to actual venture initiation.

Our findings underscore the distinct impacts of push and pull motivational factors on entrepreneurial intention. Pull motivations, such as autonomy, challenge, and self-realization, are found to positively influence entrepreneurial intention. These motivations resonate deeply with individuals who prioritize aspects inherent in venture creation, thereby fostering a genuine desire to embark on entrepreneurial ventures (Fayolle et al., 2014). In contrast, push factors, which view venture creation as a means of earning a livelihood or as an alternative due to external pressures, exhibit a negative indirect effect on entrepreneurial intention. This suggests that individuals driven primarily by necessity or external circumstances may not perceive entrepreneurship as aligned with their personal values and priorities.

Furthermore, our study contributes to expanding Krueger's Model of Entrepreneurial Intention (Krueger, 2009) by incorporating new perceptual variables that go beyond the traditional constructs of perceived feasibility and desirability of venture creation (Krueger et al., 2000). By examining these nuanced motivational dynamics, our research enriches the understanding of how environmental and personal factors intersect to shape entrepreneurial intentions.

In conclusion, our findings underscore the pivotal role of intrinsic motivations, particularly pull factors, in fostering entrepreneurial intention among young individuals. This advances existing literature by highlighting the importance of aligning personal values and aspirations with entrepreneurial pursuits, thereby informing educational programs, policy initiatives, and practitioner strategies aimed at fostering a thriving entrepreneurial ecosystem.

PRACTICAL IMPLICATIONS

Our findings offer practical implications for entrepreneurship education, public policy, and practitioners across various domains. Firstly, in the realm of entrepreneurship education, our study supports the need for curriculum designers to focus on fostering internal motivations for venture creation. Pull-related motivations, which are inherently personal (such as self-realization, personal satisfaction, autonomy, independence, and sense of achievement), should be emphasized. Research underscores that these internal drivers can cultivate a genuine desire to pursue entrepreneurial ventures (Staniewski & Awruk, 2015). By highlighting these intrinsic motivations, entrepreneurship courses can inspire students to engage with entrepreneurship as a fulfilling and personally meaningful endeavour, rather than merely a reactive response to external pressures like unemployment or dissatisfaction.

Moreover, effective entrepreneurship education should transcend traditional classroom instruction by integrating experiential and discovery-based learning approaches. Programs that encourage "learning-by-doing" and hands-on experiences, such as creating small ventures on campus or participating in simulations, can significantly enhance students' practical skills and entrepreneurial mind-set (Shirokova et al., 2018). These experiential learning opportunities not only impart practical knowledge but also imbue students with a deeper emotional and intellectual connection to entrepreneurship, fostering a sense of ownership and identity in their entrepreneurial pursuits (Costa et al., 2018).

Furthermore, our results suggest implications for public policy aimed at supporting entrepreneurship. Policymakers can use insights from our study to design initiatives that promote the intrinsic rewards of entrepreneurship and reduce barriers associated with external push factors. Policies should be crafted to incentivize and facilitate entrepreneurial activities that align with individuals' personal aspirations and motivations, thereby nurturing a conducive environment for sustainable venture creation.

In conclusion, by aligning entrepreneurship education, public policies, and practitioner strategies with the internal motivations of aspiring entrepreneurs, stakeholders can foster a more vibrant and resilient entrepreneurial ecosystem. This approach not only enhances the likelihood of entrepreneurial success but also contributes to broader economic growth and societal innovation.

TARGET AUDIENCE

This chapter aims to provide valuable insights into the push-pull theory and its implications for entrepreneurial endeavours, catering to entrepreneurs, business leaders, policymakers, researchers, and students alike. It serves as a comprehensive resource for understanding motivational dynamics and offers innovative strategies for navigating them in today's dynamic business environment.

LIMITATIONS AND FUTURE RESEARCH DIRECTIONS

While our study contributes valuable insights to entrepreneurship literature, it is essential to acknowledge several limitations that temper our conclusions. Firstly, our use of cross-sectional data restricts our ability to establish causal relationships definitively. While established theories like the Theory of Planned Behavior (Ajzen, 1991) suggest causality from attitudes to intentions, longitudinal studies would provide more robust evidence on the causal pathways leading individuals to start ventures.

Secondly, the reliance on self-reported data introduces potential biases due to subjective reporting. Individuals may not accurately perceive or disclose their true motivations for entrepreneurship, particularly under external pressures or challenging circumstances (Staniewski & Awruk, 2015; van der Zwan et al., 2016). This limitation underscores the need for diverse sampling across age segments and alternative measurement methods to ensure objectivity in future research.

Moreover, the cultural context of our study influences the desirability of entrepreneurial traits such as independence and risk-taking (Shirokova et al., 2018). Given that entrepreneurial endeavours entail inherent risk and uncertainty (Sanchez, 2013), our findings may be more applicable to countries with similar cultural traits characterized by high uncertainty avoidance (Hofstede Center, 1967–2010). Replicating our study in different cultural contexts would enhance external validity and broaden the generalizability of our findings.

Lastly, our study suggests avenues for further exploration into specific factors that could mitigate or amplify the impact of push and pull motivations through perceptions of risk and opportunity recognition. For instance, individuals with higher risk tolerance may perceive risk differently, potentially influencing their entrepreneurial intentions positively (Sanchez, 2013). Additionally, social networks play a pivotal role in both pushing individuals towards entrepreneurship by recognizing innovative opportunities (Hsieh & Kelley, 2016).

In conclusion, while our study contributes to understanding the push-pull dynamics in entrepreneurship, addressing these limitations through longitudinal studies, diversified sampling, and cross-cultural comparisons will provide deeper insights into entrepreneurial motivations and behaviours. This approach will enable more robust conclusions and inform targeted policies and strategies to support entrepreneurs across varied contexts.

CONCLUSION

In conclusion, validating the push-pull theory within the context of entrepreneurship provides crucial insights into the diverse motivations and behaviours driving individuals to establish businesses. Through empirical research and theoretical development, the push-pull framework offers a comprehensive lens for understanding how disruptive situations and opportunities propel entrepreneurial activities. Our study has illuminated several key findings:

Our findings challenged conventional categorizations by demonstrating that certain factors initially perceived as pull or push motivations can exhibit opposite effects depending on individual circumstances. For instance, motivations traditionally classified as pull factors, such as social status enhancement, may actually function as push factors for certain groups, like public sector employees transitioning into entrepreneurship.

Furthermore, our study highlighted that unemployment does not universally drive necessity entrepreneurship. Instead, unemployed individuals from entrepreneurial backgrounds may choose entrepreneurship not out of necessity but as a strategic career move.

Moving forward, our research suggests avenues for deeper exploration. Addressing potential selection biases and enhancing theoretical frameworks will refine our understanding of entrepreneurial motivations. Qualitative methods could provide richer insights into the identity and strategic decision-making processes of entrepreneurs, elucidating how personal narratives shape entrepreneurial ventures.

Additionally, future studies could investigate whether push-pull dynamics influence sectoral choices, strategic approaches, employment evolution within firms, and resource allocation among new entrepreneurs. This holistic approach promises to advance our comprehension of entrepreneurial behaviour and inform tailored policies and strategies to support diverse entrepreneurial journeys. In conclusion, our ongoing research aims to delve further into these areas, contributing to a more nuanced understanding of entrepreneurial motivations and behaviours in diverse contexts.

REFERENCES

Ahmad, N., & Seymour, R. G. (2008). Defining Entrepreneurial Activity: Definitions Supporting Frameworks for Data Collection, *OECD Statistics Working Papers, 2008/1, OECD Publishing*. DOI: 10.1787/18152031

Amit, R., MacCrimmon, K., Zietsma, C., & Oesch, J. M. (2001). Does money matter? Wealth attainment as the motive for initiating growth-orientated technology businesses. *Journal of Business Venturing*, 16(2), 119–143. DOI: 10.1016/S0883-9026(99)00044-0

Amit, R., & Muller, E. (1994). *Push and pull entrepreneurship, Frontiers in Entrepreneurship Research*. Babson College.

Amit, R., & Muller, E. (1995). Push and Pull Entrepreneurship. *Journal of Small Business and Entrepreneurship*, 12(4), 64–80. DOI: 10.1080/08276331.1995.10600505

Autio, E., Keeley, R. H., Klofsten, M., & Ulfstedt, T. (1997). Entrepreneurial intent among students: Testing an intent model in Asia, Scandinavia, and USA. *Frontiers of Entrepreneurship Research*, 17(5), 95–109.

Borooah, V. K., Collins, G., Hart, M., & MacNabb, A. (1997). Women in business. In Deakins, D., Jennings, P., & Mason, C. (Eds.), *Small Firms: Entrepreneurship in the Nineties*. Paul Chapman Publishing.

Boyd, N. G., & Vozikis, G. S. (1994). The influence of self-efficacy on the development of entrepreneurial intentions and actions. *Entrepreneurship Theory and Practice,* 18(4), 63-77. *Business Review (Federal Reserve Bank of Philadelphia)*, 6, 273–295. DOI: 10.1007/s40821-016-0065-1

Caliendo, M., & Kritikos, A. (2010). Start-Ups by the Unemployed: Characteristics, Survival and Direct Employment Effects. *Small Business Economics*, 35(1), 71–92. DOI: 10.1007/s11187-009-9208-4

Carling, J., & Collins, F. (2018). Aspiration, Desire and Drivers of Migration. *Journal of Ethnic and Migration Studies*, 44(6), 909–926. DOI: 10.1080/1369183X.2017.1384134

Castles, S., & Miller, M. J. (2009). *The Age of Migration: International Population Movements in the Modern World*. Guilford Press.

Clark, K., & Drinkwater, S. (2000). Pushed out or pulled in? Self-employment amongst Britain's ethnic minorities. *Labour Economics*, 7(5), 603–628. DOI: 10.1016/S0927-5371(00)00015-4

Collins, C., Hanges, P., & Locke, E. A. (2004). The Relationship of Achievement Motivation to Entrepreneurial Behaviour: A Meta-Analysis. *Human Performance*, 17(1), 95–117. DOI: 10.1207/S15327043HUP1701_5

Cromie, S. (1987a). Motivations of aspiring male and female entrepreneurs. *Journal of Organizational Behavior*, 8(3), 251–261. DOI: 10.1002/job.4030080306

Czaika, M., & Reinprecht, C. (2020). Drivers of Migration: A Synthesis of Knowledge. *Regional Studies*, 54(1), 10–18.

Davidsson, P. (2006). *Nascent Entrepreneurship: Empirical Studies and Developments*. Springer.

Dawson, C., & Henley, A. (2012). Push versus pull entrepreneurship: An ambiguous distinction? *International Journal of Entrepreneurial Behaviour & Research*, 18(6), 697–719. DOI: 10.1108/13552551211268139

De Haas, H., Castles, S., & Miller, M. J. (2020). *The Age of Migration: International Population Movements in the Modern World* (6th ed.). Guilford Press.

DeMartino, R., & Barbato, R. (2003). Differences between women and men MBA entrepreneurs: Exploring family flexibility and wealth creation as career motivators. *Journal of Business Venturing*, 18(6), 815–832. DOI: 10.1016/S0883-9026(03)00003-X

Dobrev, S., & Barnett, W. (2005). Organizational roles and transition to entrepreneurship. *Academy of Management Journal*, 48(3), 433–449. DOI: 10.5465/amj.2005.17407910

Earle, J. S., & Sakova, Z. (2000). Business start-ups or disguised unemployment? Evidence on the character of self-employment from transition economies, *Labour Economics*.

Giacomin, O., Guyot, J. L., Janssen, F., & Lohest, O. (2007, June). Novice creators: personal identity and push pull dynamics. In 52th *International Council for Small Business (ICSB) World conference* (pp. 1-30).

Giacomin, O., Janssen, F., Pruett, M., Shinnar, R. S., Llopis, F., & Toney, B. (2011). Entrepreneurial intentions, motivations and barriers: Differences among American, Asian and European Students. *The International Entrepreneurship and Management Journal*, 7(2), 219–238. DOI: 10.1007/s11365-010-0155-y

Gilad, B., & Levine, P. (1986). A behavioural model of entrepreneurial supply. *Journal of Small Business Management*, 24(4), 45–53.

Gill, A. M. (1988). Choice of employment status and the wages of employees and the self-employed: Some further evidence. *Journal of Applied Econometrics*, 3(3), 229–234. DOI: 10.1002/jae.3950030306

Hagen-Zanker, J. (2020). Why Do People Migrate? A Review of the Theoretical Literature. *Migration Studies*, 8(3), 314–330.

Hakim, C. (1989). New recruits to self-employment in the 1980s. *Employment Gazette*, (June), 286–297.

Harrison, R., & Hart, M. (1983). Factors influencing new business formation: A case study of Northern Ireland. *Environment & Planning A*, 15(10), 1395–1412. DOI: 10.1068/a151395

Hessels, J., van Gelderen, M., & Thurik, A. R. (2008). Entrepreneurial aspirations, motivations and their drivers. *Small Business Economics*, 31(3), 323–339. DOI: 10.1007/s11187-008-9134-x

Hisrich, R. D., Peters, M. P., & Shepherd, D. (2005). Entrepreneurship 6ed. *Tata McGraw-Hill Publishing Company Limited.*

Hofstede Center. (2010). Geert hofstede cultural dimensions. Available *at*https://geerthofstede.com/

Hsieh, R. M., & Kelley, D. J. (2016). The Role of cognition and information access in the recognition of innovative opportunities. *Journal of Small Business Management*, 54(S1), 297–311. DOI: 10.1111/jsbm.12300

Huisman, D., & De Ridder, W. J. (1984). *Vernieuwend Ondernemen* [Innovative Business]. SMO.

Kolvereid, L., & Isaksen, E. (2006). New business start-up and subsequent entry into self-employment. *Journal of Business Venturing*, 21(6), 866–885. DOI: 10.1016/j.jbusvent.2005.06.008

Krueger, N. F. Jr. (1993). The impact of prior entrepreneurial exposure on perceptions of new venture feasibility and desirability. *Entrepreneurship Theory and Practice*, 18(1), 5–21. DOI: 10.1177/104225879301800101

Krueger, N. F. Jr, & Carsrud, A. L. (1993). Entrepreneurial intentions: Applying the theory of planned behavior. *Entrepreneurship and Regional Development*, 5(4), 315–330. DOI: 10.1080/08985629300000020

Liñán, F., & Chen, Y. W. (2009). Development and cross-cultural application of a specific instrument to measure entrepreneurial intentions. *Entrepreneurship Theory and Practice*, 33(3), 593–617. DOI: 10.1111/j.1540-6520.2009.00318.x

Lüthje, C., & Franke, N. (2003). The 'making 'of an entrepreneur: Testing a model of entrepreneurial intent among engineering students at MIT. *R & D Management*, 33(2), 135–147. DOI: 10.1111/1467-9310.00288

Patil, P., & Deshpande, Y. (2018). Women entrepreneurship: A road ahead. *International Journal of Economics, Business, and Entrepreneurship*, 1(1). Advance online publication. DOI: 10.31023/ijebe.101.0004

Patil, P., & Deshpande, Y. (2019). Why women enter into entrepreneurship? An exploratory study. *Journal of Organizational studies and Innovation*, 6(2), 30-40.

Patil, P., & Deshpande, Y. (2021). Understanding perception of women entrepreneurs toward employees with reference to quality of work life balance (QWLB). *Journal of Small Business and Entrepreneurship*, 33(4), 475–488. DOI: 10.1080/08276331.2021.1949831

Patil, P. A., & Deshpande, Y. M. (2021). Women entrepreneurship: a journey begins. In *Research Anthology on Challenges for Women in Leadership Roles* (pp. 36–56). IGI Global. DOI: 10.4018/978-1-7998-8592-4.ch003

Reynolds, P. D., Camp, S. M., Bygrave, W. D., Autio, E., & Hay, M. (2001). *Global Entrepreneurship Monitor 2001* Executive Report, Babson College.

Reynolds, P. D., Camp, S. M., Bygrave, W. D., Autio, E., & Hay, M. (2001). *Global Entrepreneurship Monitor 2001 Executive Report*. Kauffman Centre for Entrepreneurial Leadership.

Ritsilä. (2002). Effects of Unemployment on New Firm Formation: Micro-level Panel Data Evidence from Finland. *Small Business Economics*, (19), 31–40.

Sanchez, J. C. (2013). The Impact of an entrepreneurship education program on entrepreneurial competencies and intention. *Journal of Small Business Management*, 51(3), 447–465. DOI: 10.1111/jsbm.12025

Segal, G., Bogia, D., & Schoenfeld, J. (2005). The Motivation to Become an Entrepreneur. *International Journal of Entrepreneurial Behaviour & Research*, 11(1), 42–57. DOI: 10.1108/13552550510580834

Shane, S. A. (2003). *A General Theory of Entrepreneurship: The Individual-Opportunity Nexus*. Edward Elgar Publishing. DOI: 10.4337/9781781007990

Shirokova, G., Osiyevskyy, O., & Bogatyreva, K. (2016). Exploring the Intention-Behavior Link in Student Entrepreneurship: Moderating Effects of Individual and Environmental Characteristics. *European Management Journal*, 34(4), 386–399. DOI: 10.1016/j.emj.2015.12.007

Staniewski, M., & Awruk, K. (2015). Motivating factors and barriers in the commencement of one's own business for potential entrepreneurs. *Ekonomska Istrazivanja*, 28(1), 583–592. DOI: 10.1080/1331677X.2015.1083876

Storey, D., & Johnson, S. (1987). Regional variations in entrepreneurship in the UK. *Scottish Journal of Political Economy*, 34(2), 161–173. DOI: 10.1111/j.1467-9485.1987.tb00276.x

Storey, D. J. (1982). *Entrepreneurship and the New Firm*. Praeger Publishers.

Taged, P., & Ajzen, I. (1991). The Theory of Planned Behaviour. *Organizational Behavior and Human Decision Processes*, 50(2), 179–211. DOI: 10.1016/0749-5978(91)90020-T

Taylor, M. P. (1996). Earnings, independence or unemployment: Why become self-employed? *Oxford Bulletin of Economics and Statistics*, 58(2), 253–265. DOI: 10.1111/j.1468-0084.1996.mp58002003.x

Thurik, A. R., Carree, M. A., van Stel, A., & Audretsch, D. B. (2008). Does self-employment reduce unemployment? *Journal of Business Venturing*, 23(6), 673–686. DOI: 10.1016/j.jbusvent.2008.01.007

Uhlaner, L., & Thurik, R. (2007). Post materialism Influencing Total Entrepreneurial Activity across Nations. *Journal of Evolutionary Economics*, 17(2), 161–185. DOI: 10.1007/s00191-006-0046-0

Van der Zwan, P., Thurik, R., Verheul, I., & Hessels, J. (2016). Factors influencing the entrepreneurial engagement of opportunity and necessity entrepreneurs. *Eurasian Business Review*, 6(3), 273–295. DOI: 10.1007/s40821-016-0065-1

Van Hear, N., Bakewell, O., & Long, K. (2018). Push-Pull Plus: Reconsidering the Drivers of Migration. *Journal of Ethnic and Migration Studies*, 44(6), 927–944. DOI: 10.1080/1369183X.2017.1384135

Verheul, I., Thurik, R., Hessels, J., & van der Zwan, P. (2010). Factors Influencing the Entrepreneurial Engagement of Opportunity and Necessity Entrepreneurs. *In EIM. Research Reports (Montgomery)*.

Winn, J. (2004). Entrepreneurship: Not an easy path to top management for women. *Women in Management Review*, 19(3), 143–153. DOI: 10.1108/09649420410529852

KEY TERMS AND DEFINITIONS

Entrepreneurial Activity: Entrepreneurship is characterised activity in new markets, processes and/or products, which in turn is characterised by the creation of new businesses. Entrepreneurial activity is the enterprising human action in pursuit of the generation of value, through the creation or expansion of economic activity, by identifying and exploiting new products, processes or markets.

Entrepreneurship: Entrepreneurship refers to any attempt at creating new business or venture such as self-employment, a new business organization or the expansion of existing business by an individual, group of individuals or established businesses (Reynolds et al., 2001). Entrepreneurship involves a complex and dynamic activity that requires cognitive processes such that individuals are able to think about future outcomes and determine the desirability and feasibility of such outcomes (Hisrich et al. 2005; Segal et al. 2005).

Motivation: Motivations to become an entrepreneur that relate to work are usually considered to be push factors and are often a key factor that can influence the preparation for an entrepreneurial career (Dobrev and Barnett, 2005; Winn, 2004). This category includes issues such as unemployment, redundancy, and a lack of job or career prospects. Some gender differences are found with respect to work (Borooah et al., 1997; Cromie, 1987a; DeMartino and Barbato, 2003; Hakim, 1989) but generally prior studies have shown few gender differences in work-related motivators.

Pull Factor: Pull factors are the motivators that "attract" individuals to create a new venture through their own personal desire, while push factors are motivators that, drawing on external factors unrelated to the individuals' entrepreneurial characteristics, "force" these individuals to engage in entrepreneurship. While pull factors have positive roots (e.g., need for achievement, opportunities for social development),

Push Factor: Push factors have negative connotations (e.g., unemployment, dissatisfaction with the current situation) such that push-driven individuals opt for self-employment not because it is their preferred option but because it is a better option than those available, or their only option (van der Zwan et al., 2016).

Chapter 5
Business Incubators as Tools for Innovation and Growth of Entrepreneurship:
A Mixed Method Analysis

Dhan Bagiyam
 https://orcid.org/0000-0002-5268-178X
Christ University, India

Mohammad Irfan
 https://orcid.org/0000-0002-4956-1170
Christ University, India

Sandhya Singh
 https://orcid.org/0000-0001-7337-5557
GLA University, India

Rui Dias
 https://orcid.org/0000-0002-6138-3098
ESCAD – Instituto Politécnico da Lusofonia, Lisboa, Portugal

ABSTRACT

This chapter explores the process of relationships between business incubation and growth and development of entrepreneurship. The researcher has specifically focused on the provision of incubators and their dynamic support along with the financial support provided by the incubation centres for the growth of entrepreneurship. The researcher has focused on investigating the bibliometric investigation among the

DOI: 10.4018/979-8-3693-4302-9.ch005

extracted documents and applications such as SPSS have been used to analyse the significant influence for the growth and development of entrepreneurship. To determine the most recent themes, developments, and trends in the subject, the network collaboration with the incubation centre has been provided.

INTRODUCTION

In current scenario, the stable economic development happens by increase of start-ups, government needs to promote entrepreneurship to develop the economy of the country. Many research studies support to maintain a stable economy, the government needs to promote start up and their contribution can increase the economy of the developing and the developed countries. Many research literatures suggest that the substantial economic growth happens only due to innovative ideas of knowledge entrepreneurs. Entrepreneurship is a key source of economic revolution, business development and Job creation. It is a pivotal to attract the young and educated to become entrepreneurs. As Schumpeter said, entrepreneurs are willing and able to turn new ideas or inventions into successful innovations. The idea of entrepreneurship led to economic growth, is one of the explanations in remaining parts of the theory of endogenic growth. So, it continues to be debated in academic economics. Current research is carried in India ranked 130 out of 189 countries on the 2023 HDI index with a 0.650 score, stays in the "medium" category of development, Next to the drop of HDI Value in 2021. India has maintained a consistent trend over the past few years, resulting in the country being ranked 134th out of 193 countries and territories in the recently published 2023/24 Human Development Report (HDR). The process of nurturing and developing new businesses is known as startup incubation. Start-up incubation has been shown to be beneficial for fostering innovation and economic growth by both researchers and policymakers. In an unpredictable business climate, a start-up is defined as (Wang, 2022). According to Schumpeter (1934), start-up companies are essential to the advancement of the economy and society through creative destruction. According to Fini et al. (2018), startups provide novel goods and services that improve clients' lives, create jobs, increase revenue, and tackle global issues. According to Gnawable and Fogel (1994) and Spigel & Harrison (2018), startups collaborate with their surroundings and use both abundant and limited resources, as well as trade with other businesses, to maintain a tight relationship with their surroundings.

According to Gnawable and Fogel (1994) and Spigel & Harrison (2018), start-ups don't exist in a vacuum; rather, they interact closely with their surroundings by continuously using both limited and abundant resources and swapping with other businesses. A Start-up Incubation Ecosystem (SUPIE) is made up of the individuals and elements that work together to support the creation and development of start-ups (Novotny, 2020). At the national and university levels, more money is being allocated to support the formation, expansion, and influence of start-ups (Audretsch et al., 2020; Eesley & Lee, 2021).

These programmes include company development services, technology transfer, and access to office and laboratory space through government programs, incubators, and accelerators (Breznitz & Feldman, 2012; Soetanto & Jack, 2016). They also include entrepreneurial education (Belitski & Heron, 2017). Despite the numerous reviews of the literature on licencing, patenting (Astebro et al., 2012), and university spin-offs (Corsi & Prencipe, 2016; Miller & Acs, 2017), there is comparatively little information on how to successfully incubate a variety of start-ups and the importance of the incubation context or ecosystem (Novotny, 2020; Wright et al., 2017).

According to McIver-Harris & Tatum (2020), the number of jobs created, the number of ecosystem connections made, and the rate at which business support is utilised are all indicators of incubator success. Conversely, a range of metrics related to advancement and progress are typically employed to assess the success of incubated startups, alongside their graduation. (Hackett & Dilts, 2004). According to certain research (Schmutzler & Presse, 2021; Stokan et al., 2015), incubation improves start-up performance. But while incubators provide several forms of assistance to startups (Bruneel et al., 2012; Teodorakopoulos et al., 2014; van Rijnsoever, 2020), it is unclear whether type of support is most beneficial to the development of the business (Van Rijnsoever & Eveleens, 2021).

The absence of theories in the area to base future research on is a significant problem (Kraus et al., 2022). As a result, our understanding of "what" the crucial support services are at various stages of the startup process is limited and inconsistent, and we also don't know "how," "why," or "in what context" these aspects are connected (Hackett & Dilts, 2004). Research reveals nothing about the relationship between the kind and calibre of services and the various performance interpretations. For example, depending on the kind of benefit and the performance metric employed, intermediary benefits (such as resources, expertise, learning, and social capital) can either help or impair start-up performance (Eveleens et al., 2017). Numerous scholars have categorised incubators and their offerings (Barbero et al., 2014; Leitão et al., 2022). But it's still unclear which services in each category are best for startups, and there are no differences between services and incubators located in different countries, socioeconomic environments, or ecological zones. (Zedtwitz & Grimaldi, 2006). Further study on how different types of incubators affect different stages of the entrepreneurial process in different situations might also be beneficial for identifying effective practices (Pauwels et al., 2016).

A deeper knowledge of the advantages of incubators to entrepreneurial learning and the most effective tactics (e.g., assertive vs laissez-faire) for incubating different enterprises may be gained by comparing samples of incubated and non-incubated entrepreneurs. According to Vincent and Zakkariya (2021), longitudinal investigations are necessary to uncover patterns and predictabilities and advance incubator theory since incubation is rarely a brief process. Accelerators are becoming more and more popular within the start-up incubation ecosystem; nevertheless, there is currently no taxonomy for innovation and entrepreneurship intermediaries, which makes it difficult to evaluate various assistance programmes (Cohen et al., 2019).

Furthermore, it must be made clear how sustainability-focused innovations help startups prosper and move markets in the direction of sustainable development (Horne & Fichter, 2022). Though our knowledge of start-ups as facilitators of a wider social influence is limited, they frequently generate technologies that have an impact on the economy, society, culture, health, and quality of life (Fini et al., 2018; Guckenbiehl et al., 2021). A few incubators are concentrating on helping new businesses make a good social effect (Sonne, 2012).

A few incubators are concentrating on helping new businesses make a good social effect (Sonne, 2012). However, there is still a need to define social incubators and specify the services that set them apart from other kinds of incubators (Sansone et al., 2020). Another explanation would be that some successful businesspeople start and fund initiatives that improve the business climate, such lobbying the government or founding organizations that encourage entrepreneurship (Mason and Brown, 2013; Mason and Brown, 2013).

known as the triple helix, where university, industry and government create networks for new companies (Etzkowitz, 2002) or the role of innovation and knowledge for entrepreneurship and regional development (Kraus et al., 2021). Universities are crucial components of entrepreneurship ecosystems as well, although not a prominent role often attributed to them as educators but as business incubators (Astebro and Bazzazian, 2010; Freire-Rubio and Rosado-Cubero, 2015) as well as the collaboration between universities and industry (Atta-Owusu et al., 2021).

Academic scholars and many researcher been found there is a wide gap in entrepreneurial intention by theory of planed behavior and social cognitive theory. the correlation factor between the entrepreneurial intention and career is missing. Extensive literature survey been done to develop the comprehensive model for behavioural research (M Murad, SB Othman, MAIB Kamarudin 2024).

Scuotto, A. C. (2023) Social entrepreneurship (SE) efforts, which combine conventional business models with a specified social goal to grow the welfare of communities, are expanding beyond the structure and its members. Social firms have two goals: financial success and achieving social objectives. To achieve these objectives, social entrepreneurs (SEs) frequently use IT resources in novel ways and develop their digital literacy to accomplish both social and financial objectives. However, there is a lot of interest in illuminating the mechanisms or processes that result in long-lasting societal transformation. Therefore, its necessary to explain how sustainability issues relate to digitalizing SE. In addition, the value of spending money on digital technology is being questioned (Dhanabagiyam et al., 2024).

Because of its substantial impact on global socioeconomic growth during the last 20 years, interest in SE research has grown. Previous research highlights a number of important challenges, though. The literature on sustainable development, for example, gives little emphasis to SE and instead concentrates on sustainable companies. Other notable organisational types, Such social businesses, however, have gotten less focus from previous research since it has focused mostly on for-profit companies that compete in commercial marketplaces. It has been discuss that SE is not always sustainable development because its primary objective is to produce benefits for society and the economy that are "double bottom line" and do not negatively impact the environment. Deciding how social entrepreneurship affects the environment is therefore among the study's key objectives.

It is challenging to match market pricing for labor, materials, and other assets while working in unpredictable environments with fluctuating revenue models, as SEs experience. consequently, SEs are required to consider both goals very often compared to their usual behavior. On the other side, a heavy dependence on volunteers and convoluted government regulations also contribute to the uncertain environment in the social sector. According to experts, IT can strike a balance between social and commercial sustainability in the context of digital social businesses. However, this promise remains mostly unrealized in the case of generic or non-digital SEs. Even though SE research has mostly focused on non-profit-making components, many academics have asked for further study on nonmarket tactics that may empower consumers and favorably impact society and markets. Conversely, SE's core principle is to create social value and uses market-driven strategies and tactics to turn that value creation into reality. In order to provide a comprehensive understanding of the subject, future researchers must resolve these controversial discoveries.

Additionally, SE has been connected to problem-solving skills related to society, while DE has been connected with a flexible approach to utilizing new ventures and creative business models to capitalize on possibilities given by the twenty-first century. This implies that in order to solve socioeconomic issues, integration of the DE and SE is required. DSE may help reduce poverty and promote economic progress, hence it is important to research how social entrepreneurship is becoming more digital in developing nations. This is because entrepreneurship is encouraged to enter new markets by digitalization, which also establishes a positive feedback loop between digitalization and entrepreneurship. Furthermore, digitization can boost the economy and lower poverty, but it may not assist the very poor.

As such, providing a comprehensive understanding of the digitalization of social entrepreneurship is crucial. Furthermore, the digitalization of social entrepreneurship in developing nations is critical to improving access to well-being for the country as a whole because it leverages digital technologies, supports regional social enterprises, and improves access to critical services for communities with limited resources. That is, by utilizing sufficient educational systems, sound governance, and being financially oriented towards charity, digitalization can enhance access to healthcare and education through social enterprise. Therefore, measures should be taken to guarantee that the very poor benefit from digitalization.

There are major theoretical and practical contributions made by this work. This paper is among the first in theory to offer a thorough framework of digital social entrepreneurship and the many constitutes associated with this concept. It explains the need of digitizing SE and lists several considerations that need to be made in line with DSE, such as industry 4.0, social innovations, sustainable development, and socioeconomic effect. This study also demonstrates the benefits of DSE, including sustainability, economic growth, and environmental preservation. However, as one of the SEs' objectives is economic growth, the connection between DSE and business performance is equally crucial.

All things considered, this study contributes to our growing awareness of the digitalization of social entrepreneurship and helps us paint a whole picture of it. Understanding the scholarly literature on "digitalization of social entrepreneurship" is made easier with the assistance of a bibliometric review. The study focuses on identifying significant trends, patterns, and gaps in the current literature on digitalizing social entrepreneurship. Innovation and entrepreneurship are crucial to promoting economic success and social progress. They have an important part in the creation of the creation of innovative products and services, technological innovations, and jobs.

However, starting a business and navigating the entrepreneurial path might be difficult, particularly for individuals without the required resources, guidance, or support. This is the situation when business incubation is beneficial. Company incubation programs offer entrepreneurs a secure and supportive environment in which to refine their business ideas, polish their business strategies, and accelerate their growth. These programs offer a range of resources and support, including co-working spaces, networking opportunities, funding access, and mentorship. Through the course of several decades, business incubation has played a significant role in supporting innovation and entrepreneurship. The systematic process of business incubation has undergone substantial change in response to the shifting demands of entrepreneurs and the business landscape. Here is a thorough examination of business incubation's past:

BACKGROUND / LITERATURE REVIEW

The literature review is framed with the deep insights of objectives related with role of incubators, networking service, funding option, training programme and entrepreneurship development. The study's objective (Alayoubi et al., 2020) aimed to ascertain how the use of strategic entrepreneurship criteria affected the achievement of technical innovation in The employees' perspective of Palestine Technical College-Deir al-Balah. The logical descriptive method was employed by the investigator. Every member of the college's academic and administrative personnel makes up the study community. The complete inventory approach was employed by the researchers.

(Lupiyoadi & Kurniawan, 2019) explains the growth of technopreneurs in Indonesia has had a largely favourable effect, dramatically lowering the proportion of educated jobless people Technopreneurs, however, had to overcome several challenges, including management issues brought on by goods or services that didn't meet the market, an absence of capital, and inadequate business plans (CB Insights, 2019). In this instance, the technopreneur's limitations are addressed by the business incubator. This is due to the fact that it meets a variety of demands for business owners, including workspaces and shared services like internet, office supplies, and professional assistance. (MIKTI, 2018)

The investigation of objective (Owda et al., 2019) was to identify entrepreneurs in the Gaza Strip. The investigators employed the analytical descriptive method to fulfil the study's aims. The three incubators in the Gaza Strip—the Palestinian Information Technology Incubator, the Technology Incubator, the Business Incubator, and Technology—benefit 92 pilot projects that make up the study community. The approach of thorough inventory was employed by the researchers.

After a quiz, the research questions were answered and their hypotheses were investigated using arithmetical averages, standard deviation, T-test, and analysis of variance is the study's primary concern. The most significant finding from the study was that men are more inclined toward entrepreneurship than women. And the impact of that scientific certification on entrepreneurship is zero.

Additionally, a lot of them are trying to find business owners who lack real-world work experience but are yet susceptible to educational programs offered by the business incubator. The researchers advise encouraging male entrepreneurship and supporting female entrepreneurship in light of the findings. and to create educational initiatives that hone entrepreneurial abilities. With the requirement that the majority of university courses include an entrepreneurship course Research by V. O. Ogutu (2016) on a strategy for fostering entrepreneurship is called "business incubation," which gives startups access to networks for forming connections. Training, infrastructure, technical support, business assistance, and mentorship are all provided by incubators. These components are vital for start-ups with little funding to survive and grow into fully-fledged businesses. Incubators take care of the workspace, furnishings, legal matters, and back-office services so that incubates don't have to.

Meru et al. (2011) found a substantial association between entrepreneurs' perceptions of the value of business incubators in Kenya, notwithstanding a discrepancy between the actual services provided and the tenants' expectations. The renter's expectations were not fulfilled by the services rendered. Global interest in business incubators and the alleged role they play in helping start-ups survive to synthesize. According to studies, BIs are essential to the development and growth of some technology-intensive firms. These types of firms frequently lack the skills needed to stay in business, therefore the second generation of incubators began offering knowledge-based services in addition to physical infrastructure (Jamil, Ismail, as well as Mahmood (2015b); Wonglimpiyarat (2014) have discovered by the experts that BIs offer significant services including coaching and training.

As per Somsuk and Laosirihongthong (2014), coaching is deemed essential for the continuous process of learning and skill development, which in turn leads to exceptional performance. According to research done to assess BIs' effectiveness, its clients can obtain financing, receive coaching, or receive other business support services from them. Among their best qualities is that They offer specialized services based on each entrepreneur's needs. It has been discovered that incubators aid in the development of an entrepreneurial culture. They encourage the growth of interconnected business and support networks that include government agencies, big businesses, financial corporations, universities, and business schools. Nonetheless, the expertise and credentials of incubator employees are more crucial to delivering efficient services to enterprises. This is because a vicious cycle of low skill levels will result if the incubator personnel lacks sophisticated knowledge and abilities. (Jamil, Ismail, and Mahmood, 2015a; European Commission, 2013)

Entrepreneurship incubators are considered to be the "magic bullet" that would, in three years, put an end to the high failure rate of small and medium-sized firms (SME), which is estimated to be over 75% in the developing world (Longnecker et al., 2006; Bowen et al., 2009; Klapper et al., 2009). Based on experience with incubated enterprises, it is estimated that up to 70% of them survive after the incubation period. Raising the survival rate of SMEs and start-ups can significantly decrease poverty and promote economic development, and create jobs (Aerts et al., 2007). According to Aerts et al.'s (2007) research, there is consistency in the incubator filtering process when activities with greater tenant survival rates are selected. Although this is a crucial signal for incubator management to comprehend the filtering process, it doesn't show how incubator assistance is applied since the filtering process adds significant selection variables in contrast to incubators that aren't filtered.

Research on (Kareem and Adman, 2006), which sought to investigate the idea of incubators and their significance for Algerian small business growth, as well as the research on Several global experiences, have led to the conclusion that It takes new technology to replace these establishments, such as incubators, which are designed to support small businesses and require comprehensive care and attention in order to be qualified for the future and have the means of success.

Research by Bouziane and Ziani (2006) suggest identifying the success criteria that industrialized nations used to set up different types of incubators, and

The study's conclusion emphasized the value of IT incubators in assisting small businesses, noting that Arab nations still have plenty of opportunities to use this technology to launch and grow small businesses. It also discussed the opportunities for incubator use and the difficulties faced by business incubators.

The research of (Khalil and Hanaa, 2006) aims to investigate the idea, the significance of small businesses and their function in accomplishing economic growth, as well as the what part they play in attaining the intended level of economic growth, how business incubators may assist start and expand small businesses, how to use them, and what global and Arab experiences that According to the study's findings, Arab nations still have a lot of chances to gain from global business incubator experiences that encourage entrepreneurship.

Peters et al. (2004) is highlighted by The impact of incubation services, such as networks, infrastructure, and mentorship, on the proportion of incubates who graduate, they discovered that merely comparing the different kinds of services provided was insufficient to emphasize the variations in the graduation rates between incubators. As an alternative, they draw inferences from your study that the relationships between co-tenants are crucial in determining incubator performances in terms of graduation rates, and that screening actions and literacy resources are required through networks.

Mian (1997) suggests that in addition to supporting program creation and sustainability, Performance evaluations must to consider consideration the environmental repercussions, the implications for the University's mission sponsor, the survival and growth of the tenant's company, and evaluate the performance of the incubator. Studying the incubation process, which includes knowledge-sharing, innovation diffusion, and individual creativity—all of which are essential for the new ventures' developmental process—allows one to examine the findings on technology business incubator performance (Binsawad et al., 2019).

(Mahmood et al., 2016) suggest Several theories of entrepreneurship have been put forth by experts. Schumpeter, in 1949, defined an entrepreneur as a person who both starts and contributes to the process of growth through the cyclical flow of the economy. However, the entrepreneurial economic theory states that

While some studies have offered an exposure theory of entrepreneurship, which holds that exposure to new chances and ideas leads to the creation of entrepreneurial activity in the economy, entrepreneurship can only succeed in a favorable economic environment.

The origins of business incubators (BI) may be found in the middle of the 20th century, during a period of heavy unemployment brought on by the Great Recession in the United States and the United Kingdom, which resulted in the significant collapse of industrial sectors. At that time, there was a growing perception that fresh approaches were required to assist boost revenue. levels of industries and boost the economies' entrepreneurial activity.

MAIN FOCUS OF THE CHAPTER / METHODOLOGY

Because of the rising unemployment rate, industrialized and developing nations alike are giving significant consideration to providing new work prospects for the jobless.

The most significant of these strategies are business incubators, which, in our opinion, may help small businesses overcome several obstacles, particularly when they are just starting out, developing, operating, or starting up.

Issues

Although the concept of incubators is not new, it was first proposed in the United States of America around the close of 1959. as well as the American Business Incubators Association, which claims that the incubators offer small businesses support throughout their start-up phase so they may thrive. In this sense, the concept extended to other developing nations, and incubators were seen as one of the key tools supporting economic development and expansion (Majid and Arif, 2006), (Shalaby,2004) explain It may also be described as: An integrated system that treats each tiny project like a newborn in need of thorough attention and careful care. It is then progressively led by a powerful, capable of growing, and equipped for the future via the experiences and methods. Business incubators are developmental and economic institutions that aim to support and nurture entrepreneurs, innovators, and innovators of the ideas of ambitious projects. It is evident from the previous two definitions that the name of an incubator is borrowed from the incubator in which the children are placed and who need immediate support and help to overcome the difficulties of the circumstances surrounding them.

Due to the employment of several criteria, the notion of small firms was not defined clearly and the notion of small firms: Due to the employment of several criteria, the notion of small firms was not defined in a The notion of Small firms: Due to the employment of several criteria, the notion of small firms was not defined in a clear and explicit way.

One group of people refers to standards of quality, and they include the management standard and the technical standard. Another group uses quantitative criteria, like the number of workers, capital, or sales volume, to differentiate between small projects. We use the International Training Centre of the ILO's standard number of workers for these projects' categorization and definition in our research, which was adopted as follows: clear and explicit way. One group of people refers to standards of quality, and they include the management standard and the technical standard. Another group uses quantitative criteria, like the number of workers, capital, or sales volume, to differentiate between small projects. We use the International Training Centre of the ILO's standard number of workers for these projects' categorization and definition in our research, which was adopted as follows:

Minor projects: These are organizations or initiatives that are often run by their proprietors with assistance from their families. The total number of workers between one and four employees. Local clients are the primary target market for small firms.

Small projects: These are operations run by the proprietors, with anywhere from 5 to 19 employees. Small businesses are characterized by the active involvement of the owners in both technical operations and staff supervision, along with a direct relationship between the owners, their assistants, and employees.

Medium-sized projects: They cover those that are supervised by their proprietors, with staffing levels ranging from 20 to 100, and an organizational framework that calls for a degree of Regarding implementation management in the owner-manager relationship workers to oversee financial management, human resources, marketing, and manufacturing (Cap, 2013).

Controversies

Ahmad and Tatar (2010) explain the role of business incubators is crucial in assisting small businesses in their leadership of innovation by providing them with technological and scientific resources, as well as a range of services and facilities that are required to help the first batch of start-up projects overcome the challenges of the start-up and start-up stage, as many small projects early failure as a result of not having custody, which offers some opportunity. Modern technology and creative approaches and tools are provided by business incubators to small businesses.

One of the instruments that helps a project deal with quick changes, open up new markets, and adapt to new technology and its applications is innovation. Not only do incubators provide money for these tiny businesses, but they also serve as hubs for innovation.By offering the following services, business incubators seek to assist recent college and university graduates in starting new ventures or expanding already-existing ones (Bouziane and Ziani, 2006):

1. Generate fresh concepts for starting new initiatives or growing current ones.
2. Make resources, facilities, and extension services available to its staff.
3. Transform the culture of knowledge sharing and risk sharing through networks.
4. Assisting business owners in the first phases of establishing small businesses.
5. Establishing connections between the relevant institutions and the domestic and global business and industrial sectors.

Problems

Due to the many purposes, they were discovered for, incubators fall into a number of categories follows: According to (Rahim 2003) Initial Categorization: First-generation incubators (basic technology incubators):

1. These are incubators that provide funding to ventures whose primary capital is knowledge, such as It surpasses all internal technical components used in labor and raw material expenses; these incubators are typically associated with research centres, universities, and technical schools.
2. Second-generation incubators, often known as incubators with conventional bases: It is connected to regional organizations and business associations and encompass manual, mechanical, agricultural, industrial, food, and research centre assistance.
3. Third-generation incubators, also known as rehab centres, offer specialized services such as technical education in addition to unique offerings.

According to (Mazi, 2003): It consists of the following items (Mazi, 2003):

1.INCUBATORS FOR GENERAL BUSINESSES: It is focused on the

By expanding the firm, it will contribute to the economic growth of the surrounding area.

2. SPECIALIZED BUSINESS INCUBATORS: These centres aim to improve certain economic characteristics of the region in which they operate by promoting particular sectors, generating employment opportunities for particular job seekers, or drawing particular types of investments.

3. TECHNICAL INCUBATORS: These organizations support researchers at universities and research institutions and work with technology, creating specialized facilities.

According to Shalaby (2002) He lists the following as part of it:

1. The Global Incubator. It wants to draw in people. To attain quality and export capability, technological transfer and foreign money are needed.

2. Regional incubator: This type of incubator focuses on using local raw materials and resources to develop a specific geographic area. It also invests in the potential of jobless youth in the area or supports certain minorities or segments of society, such as women.

3. Industrial incubator: Located in an industrial zone, this facility was established after assessing the needs of feeder industries. It emphasizes expertise and technical assistance from major companies in exchange for advantages for each of the large and small connected firms.

4. Specific sector incubator: Run by professionals with experience in the targeted industry, it serves a particular sector or activity, such as the software or engineering sectors.

5. Technical Incubator: Its goals include advancing the incubated institution's technical capabilities and purchasing new goods and supplying cutting-edge machinery aids in the transition of research findings from the level of laboratory innovation to the stage of commercial promotion.

6. Research Incubator: Typically found at universities or research facilities, these spaces let researchers advance their concepts and studies while also utilizing the facilities' workshops and labs.

7. Virtual Incubator: These are incubators without physical walls that offer all the standard services except for location; small business development centres within Chambers of Commerce are one example.

8. Internet Incubator: A company that assists other online businesses in becoming established, full-fledged businesses. David Wetherhol, who established the CMJI Incubator in 1995, serves as the director of the Internet Incubator.

STEPS FOR ORGANIZATION

The following procedures are used to guarantee the incubators' proper functioning.

1. **THE INITIAL ACTION:** It can be broken down into several stages: the first involves analysing the project and having discussions with applicants about their projects to ensure that the test criteria apply; the second looks at the services that the project needs to be accepted and whether it can provide them; and the third looks at the product's marketing potential and its ability to create marketing strategies for the project's future growth.
2. **THE SECOND STEP**: The project begins in this step once the initial encouraging results from the previous step are demonstrated. The beneficiary prepares his project plan with the incubator's assistance and guidance in order to join the incubator after it accepts his plan and the sponsor gives its approval. The beneficiary also determines where in the incubator to best utilize its services.
3. **THE THIRD STEP**: The incubated project's last stage lasts for one to three years. It is anticipated that the project will have grown and succeeded to the point where it can now function outside of the incubator (Majid and Arif, 2006).

Technopreneur ship has a lengthy history of growth, beginning in Silicon Valley, California, where it first gained traction. Silicon Valley is the birthplace of several globally recognized technology-based businesses. In the 1990s, the impact extended to Indonesia and other parts of Asia. In Indonesia, technology-driven businesses began to emerge in the early 2000s.

Any nation's development of its economic, social, and human capital is greatly aided by entrepreneurship (Brandstätter, 2011; Bruton, Ahlstrom, & Obloj, 2008). Through launching and growing new businesses, innovating current ones, and seizing opportunities, entrepreneurship generates a large number of jobs in a variety of economic sectors. In addition to its practical significance, Numerous studies have been carried out in the academic community on the formation of new businesses and introducing innovation into already-existing companies—that is, on the development of new technologies, products, procedures, and techniques. Pursuing business prospects through entrepreneurship leads to increased business volume, technical improvement, and wealth creation for both new and established companies (Lumpkin & Dess, 1996). According to Rodríguez-Gutiérrez, Moreno, and Tejada (2015), studies in the Small and medium-size industry.

The pursuit of entrepreneurship as a means of seizing economic opportunities promotes technical improvement, the growth of businesses, and the production of profit for both parties. both new and established businesses (Lumpkin & Dess, 1996). According to Rodriguez-Gutiérrez, Moreno, and Tejada (2015), research studies on small and medium-sized enterprises (SMEs) have exploded in the last few Era because this industry has made a significant contribution to the global economy. Between 90 and 99 percent of businesses worldwide are SMEs, with the majority being small, single-owner businesses. Economic success is seen to be significantly influenced by SMEs (Henderson & Weiler, 2009; Richter, Kraus, Eggers, & Jensen, 2014). In emerging markets, growth-oriented businesses in particular represent a major source of income and jobs economy (Vallée, 2006; Parker, 2004).

Researchers, business professionals, and governments everywhere have taken steps to promote industry-academic linkage and collaboration in order to meet the needs of start-ups as enablers for generating employment opportunities, realizing the growing significance of creativity, innovation, and entrepreneurship.

Entrepreneurship education plays a crucial role in motivating students and providing them with essential entrepreneurial skills, making it important not only for business graduates but also for those in other academic disciplines (Shah, Anwar, & Khan, 2018).However, over the past three decades, the literature on entrepreneurship development has undergone a change that emphasizes the function of business incubation as a tool for policymakers to establish new businesses, support them during their initial stages of growth, and provide them with the facilities and favorable environment they need for long-term success (Lewis, Harper-Anderson, & Molnar, 2011; Theodorakopoulos, K. Kakabadse, & McGowan, 2014). Business incubators are designed to assist in the development of new companies and to give them the business assistance that startups require in order to survive and grow.

Business incubators are designed to assist in the development of new companies and to provide them the business assistance they require in order to survive and expand. Furthermore, it is important to note that during the past 20 years, business incubators worldwide have shifted their emphasis from traditional services like office space and administrative support to more innovative and efficient business support services that are less tangible but offer start-ups higher value-added services (Bruneel, Ratinho, Clarysse, & Groen, 2012; Luke\, Longo, & Zouhar, 2018).

Business incubation is a very organized and methodical attempt to support newly established businesses in a regulated setting throughout their formative years. It is a dynamic process that provides a combination of professional skills, development-support procedures, and infrastructure to incubate enterprises and direct them toward a path of growth and sustainability while preventing failure (Khorsheed, Alhargan, & Qasim, 2012). Accordingly, business incubators are organizations that assist entrepreneurs in starting new businesses and incorporating creativity and innovation into already-existing endeavors to enhance the value of their offerings (Wann, Lu, Lozada, & Cangahuala, 2017).

Furthermore, the networks, kinds, and services of business incubation differ between nations and areas based on the native environment, customs, and possibilities accessible to business owners. A variety of business incubators are operating under the direction of governments, universities, non-profit organizations, and private sector consultants to assist entrepreneurs with their start-up needs, including office space, seed money, provision of various services, and consultancy for obtaining trademarks, registration, and patents.

SOLUTIONS AND RECOMMENDATIONS/DISCUSSION

Early Beginnings (1950s - 1970s) The concept of business incubation can be traced back to 1959 with the establishment of the Batavia Industrial center in Batavia, New York. Founded by Joseph Mancuso, BIC is considered the world's first business incubator. Mancuso transformed an old Massey-Ferguson tractor factory into a space where fledgling businesses could access affordable space and shared services. Experimentation and Growth (1960-1970) During the 1960s and 1970s, the idea of business incubation started to gain traction. Various models of incubators emerged, including technology incubators, which focused on high-tech startups and innovation.

University Involvement (1990) Universities began to recognize the potential of incubators to commercialize research and foster innovation. This led to the establishment of university-affiliated incubators, which provided resources and support to student and faculty entrepreneurs.

Expansion and Formalization (1980s - 1990s) National Business Incubation Association (NBIA): Established in 1985 in the United States, NBIA (now the International Business Innovation Association, INDIA) played a crucial role in promoting best practices and supporting the growth of business incubators globally.

Public and Private Sector Involvement Governments and private sector organizations began to see the value of incubators in economic development. This led to increased funding and support for incubator programs.

Global Expansion (1990) The concept of business incubation spread internationally, with countries in Europe, Asia, and Latin America establishing their own incubators. These programs adapted the incubation model to fit their unique economic and cultural contexts. Diverse Models: Incubators started to diversify, focusing on different types of businesses such as technology startups, creative industries, and social enterprises. This diversification allowed incubators to cater to specific needs and foster innovation in various sectors. The rise of accelerate programme (2000) saw the emergence of accelerator programs, a variation of the traditional incubator model. Accelerators like Y Combinator (founded in 2005) and Techstars (founded in 2006) offered short, intensive programs that included seed funding, mentorship, and access to networks in exchange for equity. Increased Investment The success of accelerators in producing high-growth startups attracted significant investment from venture capitalists and other investors.

Technological Advancements and Global Networks (2010), Technological Integration: Advances in technology allowed incubators to offer more sophisticated services, including virtual incubation, online mentorship, and global networking opportunities International Collaboration Incubators and accelerators began to collaborate more across borders, sharing resources, expertise, and market access. Focus on Sustainability and Social Impact (2020) Sustainable Development Goals (SDGs) Many modern incubators align their missions with the United Nations' Sustainable Development Goals, emphasizing the importance of social and environmental impact alongside economic growth. Inclusivity and Diversity: There is a growing focus on inclusivity, with incubators developing programs specifically for underrepresented groups such as women entrepreneurs, minority-owned businesses, and entrepreneurs from developing regions.

NETWORKING SERVICES

Getting Exposure to entrepreneurial development opportunities is an great advantage for the successful business man. Being a great player in the market they also can experience formal and informal communication and connection with the institutions and communities Hernandez-Gantes (2020). More of strategic planning most of the successful business is a form of integrating the work of preparing entrepreneurs to build successful businesses Pearce.J (2020). Business incubators can provide lot of support in the focus specialization for theentrepreneurs Inc (2024). Regional economy transformation undergo adaption of new technologies in ecosystem, global transformation causes renewal with UBI ecosystem and it is essential (Taiwo,2023).

HYPOTHESIS 1 (H1): Incubators provide support for the growth and development of the entrepreneur.

FUNDING SUPPORT

The majority of fin-tech and tech start-up enterprises in the United States receive funding from venture capitalists; in recent years, financial assistance has started to become increasingly important in European and Asian nations. A. Pfeil (2001). Given that capital assistance is viewed as a vital source of innovation, jobs, and economic growth, policymakers must give entrepreneurship and capital support careful consideration. A Mittelstadt (1998). A 2016 Entrepreneur's Annual Survey indicates that just 5–10% of salaried workers do not require capital raising when launching a firm. Thus, in order to launch a firm, 90–95 percent of entrepreneurs require a specific amount of funding.

.The development of distinction about the venture capitalist and maintaining cooperation among the partnering companies gives lot of confidence for the development of the entrepreneur, Swati panda and Sridhar das (2016).

HYPOTHESIS 2 (H2): Incubators and Venture capitalist provide the funding support for entrepreneurial development.

TRAINING PROGRAMME

Jamil.F (2015) Incubators play a crucial role in creation and promotion of some technology-intensive enterprise to execute the business survival and to upskill the knowledge of the entrepreneur for business survival and also, they can use the physical infrastructure provided by the incubators

Today many of the business incubator play a very crucial role in creating and promoting some technology based intensive enterprise. Many if the organizations lack required skill and talent, So, many of the second-generation incubators begin offer various capacity building programme to enhance the knowledge-based services and long tenure usage of physical facilities. Alpenidze and Sanyal (2019) found that mentoring services is an essential service for business incubators, services are measured as essential for consistent skill development of entrepreneurship. There are proven research about the incubators and their excellence of support for the entrepreneurs to excel in their business performance and highly incubators hand hold the entrepreneurs to success in their career being a start-up entrepreneur.

According to Hernandez-Gantes, Sorensen and Nieri (2020) there are consultant for suggesting and creating a very good business model which comes in the third rank, through this consultant also guide the entrepreneurs thought provoking insights and excellent support for the business.

ENTREPRENEURSHIP DEVELOPMENT

To measure the entrepreneurship development, the four attributes been involved in the study like networking services, capital support and training programmes. Ecosystem creators always supports entrepreneurs and start-up company to measure the network services blended from the incubators to incubate Li, C, Ur Rehman, H

& Asim, S (2019). In order to measure the capital, support the study has also rented about the self-generated funds and borrowed funds.

OBJECTIVES OF THE STUDY

RQ1: To identify the key components and services provided by business incubators.

RQ2: To evaluate the impact of business incubators on startup success and innovation.

RQ3: To analyse the challenges faced by the stat-ups and entrepreneurs for entrepreneurial development.

RESEARCH METHODOLOGY

Research design been executed by mixed method by analysing the incubators along with data collection among the respondents of about 765 Sample size. The bibliometric study has involved retrieving a total of 143 articles from the Scopus database. To determine the most recent themes, developments, and trends in the subject, the network collaboration and intellectual structures such as bibliographic coupling, co-occurrence analysis, word clouds, and trending topics have been provided. Along, with this SPSS Analysis is also been applied to understand the significant difference among the data collection executed by using convenience sampling method for a sample size about 765.

ANALYSIS AND DISCUSSION

RQ1: To identify the key components and services provided by business incubators

Table 1. Creation of innovation and incubation entrepreneurship

INCUBATOR	HOST OF PARTNER	HOST TYPE	LOCATION	FOCUS
Amity Innovation and Incubation centre	DST, GOI	Business Type	Noida	Rural innovation and social entrepreneurship, Mobile computing technologies, Analytical and cloud computing.
Angel prime	DST, GOI	Business Type	Bengaluru	Mobile Apps, Mobile internet and E-commerce.
Centre for Innovation and Entrepreneurship (CIIE)	Indian Institute of Management (IIM-A)	Business Type	Ahmedabad	Energy, water, agriculture, IoT, Fintech, Entrepreneurship and Biotechnology, Informative technology,
Centre - Cellular and Molecular Platforms (C-Camp)	Bangaluru biotech cluster	Central Government Research Lab Foundation	Hyderabad	Hardware products, healthcare, medical devices and Biotechnology,
Incubator- IKP Knowledge Park (IKP)	IKP-Foundation	Foundation	Hyderabad	Biotechnology, hardware products, healthcare, medical sciences
Society- Innovation & Entrepreneurship	Indian Institute of Technology-Mumbai (IITB)	Engineering College	Mumbai	Information technology, intellectual property-based ventures, students' entrepreneurship, Information technology, acceleration, electronics.

Figure 1. Innovation, incubation centre

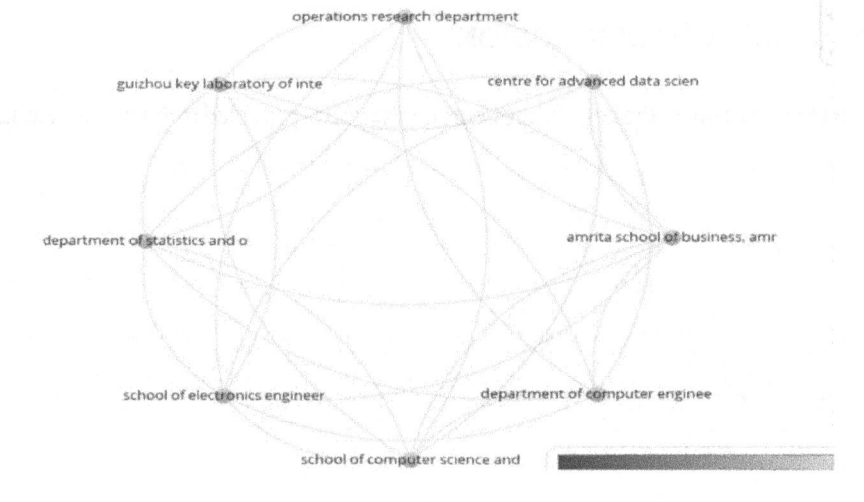

RQ2: To Evaluate the Impact of Business Incubators on Startup Success and Innovation.

To find the impact of incubators on startup success the attributes of the attributes like capital support, entrepreneurship development, Government regulation of the entrepreneurship, training model, network service, business model, the attributes are been calculated with model summary and regression model. The results are shown as

Table 2. Model summary

MODEL	R	R SQUARE	ADJUSTED R SQUARE	STD. ERROR OF THE ESTIMATE
1	0.633[a]	0.369	0.260	0.058

Note: a: Predictors: (Constant) capital support, entrepreneurship development, Government Regulation of the entrepreneurship, training model, network service, business model.

From Table 2, the Regression Coefficient 'R'=0.633 or 63.3% relationship exists in between the independent variables and the dependent variable. The coefficient of the determination R^2=0.369 which shows that 36.9% of variation in the capital support and government regulation of the entrepreneurship, training model, network service and business model for the success of the entrepreneurship development.

Table 3. **Anova**[a]

	SUM OF SQUARES	DF	MEAN	F	SIG.
Regression	0.0313	4	0.01134	3.0244	0.042[b]
Residual	0.066	19	0.0034		
Total	0.1064	23			

The results have been analysed with the most prolific authors, nations, and highly prominent journals that make the most contributions to the subject matter, as well as the pieces that are most frequently referenced. Note: a: Predictors: (Constant) capital support, entrepreneurship development, Government regulation of th entrepreneurship, training model, network service, business model.

Dependent Variable is success and innovation of the incubator.

From Table 3, it can be seen that the F value is 0.0313 and is significant because the significance level is=0.042 which is less than $P \leq 0.05$. this proves that overall, the independent and the dependent variable are highly significant.

The below Table-3, gives the coefficient of regression between the capital support, entrepreneurship development, Government regulation of the entrepreneurship, training model, network service and business model for the dependent variable as success and innovation of the incubator is with the Sig value of 4.23 (p value of 0.025) is greater than the critical value.

RQ3: To analyse the challenges faced by the stat-ups and entrepreneurs for entrepreneurial development.

Table 4. Regression coefficients

	UNSTANDARDIZED COEFFICIENTS		STANDARDIZED BETA COEFFICIENT	T	SIG.
	B	STD. ERROR			
CONSTANT	10.716	1.13		8.92	
BUSINESS MODEL (SUCCESS AND INNOVATION OF THE ENTREPRENEUR)	0.23	0.046	0.294	4.22	0.025

In the table 4, coefficient of regression between constant the factors capital support, entrepreneurship development, Government regulation of the entrepreneurship, training model, network service, business model like at a confidence interval level of 95%. The value of 4.22 (p value of 0.025) is greater than the critical value. From the beginning through continuous analysis it is evident that there is a significant relationship between the constant and the business model (Success and innovation of the entrepreneur)

FUTURE RESEARCH DIRECTIONS/IMPLICATIONS

The results from the beginning of the analysis through bibliometric analysis it shows the ample number of research work with yearly publication, with the highly potential authors, nations, and highly prominent journals with the highest contributions to the subject matter are most frequently referenced. Bibliometric approach in this research work shows the intellectual framework has been designed and highlights of importance of technology transfer and the support of the incubator centre and their mentorship for the growth and development of the entrepreneur. Policymakers and administrative officials may strengthen the foundations of education and entrepreneurship for the overall growth of the economy by following the important advice these studies offer, Also, there is a significant difference existing among the level of education groups of the respondents for the factors motive, issues and challenges, financial and entrepreneurial growth and development (Dhanabagiyam et al., 2024).

CONCLUSION

The results have been analysed with the most prolific authors, nations, and highly prominent journals that make the most contributions to the subject matter, as well as the pieces that are most frequently referenced. By using bibliographic coupling and co-occurrence analysis, the intellectual frameworks have been designed to pinpoint research topics and trends. The research findings highlight the importance of technology transfer, mentorship initiatives, entrepreneurship education, and a focus on innovation and creativity via academic institutions that foster entrepreneurship. Policymakers and administrative officials may strengthen the foundations of education and entrepreneurship for the overall growth of the economy by following the important advice these studies offer. This research also looks for the most recent developments in the field of business incubation, as well as the most significant and pertinent articles. A well developed and possible academic institution can develop the business incubation, as today in India more start-up companies are being promoted by the Ecosystem creators, venture capitalist and Angel investors are emerging to support and give knowledge service for the start-up companies. This mixed method of research provides more in-depth information on the most important advancements in the field of incubation through a comprehensive bibliometric analysis for the past three decades. Furthermore, the researcher has also used various significant analysis to prove the independent and their impact for the growth and development of the entrepreneur.

REFERENCES

Aerts, K., Matthyssens, P., & Vandenbempt, K. (2007). Critical role and screening practices of European business incubators. *Technovation*, 27(5), 254–267. DOI: 10.1016/j.technovation.2006.12.002

Alayoubi, M. M., Shobaki, M. J. A., & Abu-Naser, S. S. (2020). *Requirements for Applying the Strategic Entrepreneurship as an Entry Point to Enhance Technical Innovation: Case Study - Palestine Technical College- Deir al-Balah*. http://dstore.alazhar.edu.ps/xmlui/handle/123456789/580

Alayoubi, M. M., Shobaki, M. J. A., & Abu-Naser, S. S. (2020b). *Requirements for Applying the Strategic Entrepreneurship as an Entry Point to Enhance Technical Innovation: Case Study - Palestine Technical College- Deir al-Balah*. http://dstore.alazhar.edu.ps/xmlui/handle/123456789/580

Alpenidze, O., Pauceanu, R. M., & Sanyal, S. (2019). Key success factors for business incubators in Europe: an empirical study. *Academy of Entrepreneurship Journal*, 25(1), 1. https://www.abacademies.org/articles/Key-success-factors-for-business-incubators-in-europe-an-empirical-1528-2686-25-1-211.pdf

Arafat, M. Y., Saleem, I., Dwivedi, A. K., & Khan, A. (2018). Determinants of agricultural entrepreneurship: A GEM data based study. *The International Entrepreneurship and Management Journal*, 16(1), 345–370. DOI: 10.1007/s11365-018-0536-1

Astebro, T. B., Bazzazian, N., & Braguinsky, S. (2012). Startups by recent university graduates and their faculty: Implications for university entrepreneurship policy. *Research Policy*, 41(4), 663–677. DOI: 10.1016/j.respol.2012.01.004

Audretsch, D., Colombelli, A., Grilli, L., Minola, T., & Rasmussen, E. (2020). Innovative start-ups and policy initiatives. *Research Policy*, 49(10), 104027. DOI: 10.1016/j.respol.2020.104027

Banerji, D., & Reimer, T. (2019). Startup founders and their LinkedIn connections: Are well-connected entrepreneurs more successful? *Computers in Human Behavior*, 90, 46–52. DOI: 10.1016/j.chb.2018.08.033

Barbero, J. L., Casillas, J. C., Wright, M., & Garcia, A. R. (2013). Do different types of incubators produce different types of innovations? *The Journal of Technology Transfer*, 39(2), 151–168. DOI: 10.1007/s10961-013-9308-9

Belitski, M., & Heron, K. (2017). Expanding entrepreneurship education ecosystems. *Journal of Management Development*, 36(2), 163–177. DOI: 10.1108/JMD-06-2016-0121

Breznitz, S. M., & Feldman, M. P. (2010). The engaged university. *The Journal of Technology Transfer*, 37(2), 139–157. DOI: 10.1007/s10961-010-9183-6

Bruneel, J., Ratinho, T., Clarysse, B., & Groen, A. (2012). The Evolution of Business Incubators: Comparing demand and supply of business incubation services across different incubator generations. *Technovation*, 32(2), 110–121. DOI: 10.1016/j.technovation.2011.11.003

Chen, N., Chiang, N., & Storey, N. (2012). Business Intelligence and Analytics: From Big Data to Big Impact. *Management Information Systems Quarterly*, 36(4), 1165. DOI: 10.2307/41703503

Corsi, C., & Prencipe, A. (2016). Improving Innovation in University Spin-Offs: The Fostering Role of University and Region. *Journal of Technology Management & Innovation*, 11(2), 13–21. DOI: 10.4067/S0718-27242016000200002

Dhanabagiyam, S., Doe, M. B., Thamizhselvi, M., Irfan, M., Thalari, S. K., & Libeesh, P. (2024). Factors influencing growth of micro-entrepreneurship in the hospitality industry: An empirical study in India. *Cogent Business & Management*, 11(1), 2285260. Advance online publication. DOI: 10.1080/23311975.2023.2285260

Eesley, C. E., & Lee, Y. S. (2020). Do university entrepreneurship programs promote entrepreneurship? *Strategic Management Journal*, 42(4), 833–861. DOI: 10.1002/smj.3246

Eveleens, C. P., Van Rijnsoever, F. J., & Niesten, E. M. M. I. (2016). How network-based incubation helps start-up performance: A systematic review against the background of management theories. *The Journal of Technology Transfer*, 42(3), 676–713. DOI: 10.1007/s10961-016-9510-7

Fernández-Alles, M., Camelo-Ordaz, C., & Franco-Leal, N. (2014). Key resources and actors for the evolution of academic spin-offs. *The Journal of Technology Transfer*, 40(6), 976–1002. DOI: 10.1007/s10961-014-9387-2

Fini, R., Grimaldi, R., Santoni, S., & Sobrero, M. (2011). Complements or substitutes? The role of universities and local context in supporting the creation of academic spin-offs. *Research Policy*, 40(8), 1113–1127. DOI: 10.1016/j.respol.2011.05.013

Fini, R., Rasmussen, E., Siegel, D., & Wiklund, J. (2018). Rethinking the Commercialization of Public Science: From Entrepreneurial Outcomes to Societal Impacts. *The Academy of Management Perspectives*, 32(1), 4–20. DOI: 10.5465/amp.2017.0206

Gao, Y., Tsai, S. B., Du, X., & Xin, C. (2020). *Sustainability in the Entrepreneurial Ecosystem: Operating Mechanisms and Enterprise Growth*. IGI Global. http://books.google.ie/books?id=6kjmDwAAQBAJ&pg=PA316&dq=A+gateway+to+an+entrepreneurial+society.+J.+Econ.+Sustain.+Dev.+2015,+6,+153%E2%80%93160.&hl=&cd=1&source=gbs_api

Gnyawali, D. R., & Fogel, D. S. (1994). Environments for Entrepreneurship Development: Key Dimensions and Research Implications. *Entrepreneurship Theory and Practice*, 18(4), 43–62. DOI: 10.1177/104225879401800403

Grimaldi, R., & Grandi, A. (2005). Business incubators and new venture creation: An assessment of incubating models. *Technovation*, 25(2), 111–121. DOI: 10.1016/S0166-4972(03)00076-2

Guckenbiehl, P., De Zubielqui, G. C., & Lindsay, N. (2021). Knowledge and innovation in start-up ventures: A systematic literature review and research agenda. *Technological Forecasting and Social Change*, 172, 121026. DOI: 10.1016/j.techfore.2021.121026

Hackett, S. M., & Dilts, D. M. (2004). A Systematic Review of Business Incubation Research. *The Journal of Technology Transfer*, 29(1), 55–82. DOI: 10.1023/B:JOTT.0000011181.11952.0f

Hernandez-Gantes, V. M., & Others, A. (n.d.). *Fostering Entrepreneurship through Business Incubation: The Role and Prospects of Postsecondary Vocational-Technical Education. Report 2: Case Studies*. https://eric.ed.gov/?id=ED399396

Horne, J., & Fichter, K. (2022). Growing for sustainability: Enablers for the growth of impact startups – A conceptual framework, taxonomy, and systematic literature review. *Journal of Cleaner Production*, 349, 131163. DOI: 10.1016/j.jclepro.2022.131163

Hwang, V. (2019). *Access to Capital for Entrepreneurs*. http://books.google.ie/books?id=b9gBzwEACAAJ&dq=Access+to+Capital+for+Entrepreneurs:+Removing+Barriers%3B+Elsevier:+Amsterdam,+The+Netherlands,+2019&hl=&cd=1&source=gbs_api

Kareem, Q., & Adman, M. (2006). The Role of Incubators for Small and Medium Enterprises, International Forum: Requirements for the Qualification of Small and Medium Enterprises in the Arab Countries, 17-18 / 4/2006, Hassiba Ben Ali University, Chlef, Algeria.

Khan, A. M., Arafat, M. Y., Raushan, M. A., Saleem, I., Khan, N. A., & Khan, M. M. (2019). Does intellectual capital affect the venture creation decision in India? *Journal of Innovation and Entrepreneurship*, 8(1), 10. Advance online publication. DOI: 10.1186/s13731-019-0106-y

Khan, M. R. (2013). Mapping entrepreneurship ecosystem of Saudi Arabia. *World Journal of Entrepreneurship, Management and Sustainable Development*, 9(1), 28–54. DOI: 10.1108/20425961311315700

Khorsheed, M. S., Alhargan, A., & Qasim, S. M. (2012). A Three-Tier service model for national ICT incubator in Saudi Arabia. Paper presented at the Proceedings of IEEE International Conference on Management and Service Science.

Lewis, D., Harper-Anderson, E., & Molnar, L. A. (2011). *Incubating Success: Incubation Best Practices That Lead to Successful New Ventures*. https://doi.org/ DOI: 10.13140/RG.2.1.2732.6881

Madichie, N. O. (2010). Business incubation in the UAE: Prospects for enterprise development. *International Journal of Entrepreneurship and Innovation Management*, 12(3/4), 291. DOI: 10.1504/IJEIM.2010.035085

. Mahmood, N., Jianfeng, C., Jamil, F., Karmat, J., Khan, M., & Cai, Y. (2015). Business Incubators: Boon or Boondoggle for SMEs and Economic Development of Pakistan. *International Journal of U- and E- Service Science and Technology*, 8(4), 147–158. https://doi.org/DOI: 10.14257/ijunesst.2015.8.4.15

. Mahmood, N., Jianfeng, C., Munir, H., & Yasir, N. (2016). Impact of Factors that Inhibit the Drive of Entrepreneurship in Pakistan: Empirical Evidence from Young Entrepreneurs and Students. *International Journal of U- and E- Service Science and Technology*, 9(12), 163–174. https://doi.org/DOI: 10.14257/ijunesst.2016.9.12.15

Majid, H. I., & Arif, M. T. (2006) The Role of Productive Incubators in the Development of Small Enterprises, International Forum: Requirements for the Qualification of Small and Medium Enterprises in the Arab Countries.. *Hassiba Ben Ali University, Chlef, Algeria*, 1.

McDonald, R. M., & Eisenhardt, K. M. (2019). Parallel Play: Startups, Nascent Markets, and Effective Business-model Design. *Administrative Science Quarterly*, 65(2), 483–523. DOI: 10.1177/0001839219852349

McIver-Harris, K., & Tatum, A. (2020). Measuring Incubator Success During a Global Pandemic: A Rapid Evidence Assessment. SSRN *Electronic Journal*. https://doi.org/DOI: 10.2139/ssrn.3687712

Mian, S. A. (1997). Assessing and managing the university technology business incubator: An integrative framework. *Journal of Business Venturing*, 12(4), 251–285. DOI: 10.1016/S0883-9026(96)00063-8

Murad, M., Othman, S. B., & Kamarudin, M. a. I. B. (2024). Entrepreneurial university support and entrepreneurial career: the directions for university policy to influence students' entrepreneurial intention and behavior. *Journal of Entrepreneurship and Public Policy*. DOI: 10.1108/JEPP-08-2023-0082

Pearce, J., Grafman, L., Colledge, T., & Legg, R. (2019b, May 6). *Leveraging Information Technology, Social Entrepreneurship, and Global Collaboration for Just Sustainable Development*. https://hal.archives-ouvertes.fr/hal-02120513/

Sánchez, J. C. (2013). The impact of an Entrepreneurship Education program on entrepreneurial competencies and intention. *Journal of Small Business Management*, 51(3), 447–465. DOI: 10.1111/jsbm.12025

Singh, S., & Saxena, A. (2023). The impact that employee performance is influenced by organisational citizenship behaviour and workplace happiness variable intervention in organizations. *Institute of Business Management, GLA University Mathura*.

Singh, S., & Saxena, A. (2024). Professional allegiance and beyond a comprehensive study of organization commitment and citizenship behaviour in ncr region. *Institute of Business Management, GLA University Mathura*. https://seyboldreport.net/

SMEs. (2010). In *OECD studies on SMEs and entrepreneurship*. DOI: 10.1787/9789264080355-en

Spigel, B. (2017). The Relational Organization of Entrepreneurial Ecosystems. *Entrepreneurship Theory and Practice*, 41(1), 49–72. DOI: 10.1111/etap.12167

The Role of Incubators for Small and Medium Enterprises, International Forum: Requirements for the Qualification of Small and Medium Enterprises in the Arab Countries. (2006). *Hassiba Ben Ali University, 1*.

KEY TERMS AND DEFINITION

Business Incubation: Creating a supportive environment where startups can thrive. Incubators provide a range of services like mentorship, office space, funding advice, and networking opportunities, which can be crucial for early-stage companies trying to navigate the challenging path from concept to a fully operational business. They help reduce the risks and increase the chances of success by offering resources and guidance tailored to the needs of nascent enterprises.

Entrepreneurial Support: Entrepreneurial support organizations (ESOs) support, mentor, train, and sometimes fund entrepreneurs and early-stage businesses. ESOs help spur innovation and economic growth by providing business development services and resources to help founders develop, scale, and sustain viable businesses.

Entrepreneurship: Entrepreneurship is the process of starting and running a new business, often with the aim of solving a problem, fulfilling a need, or capitalizing on an opportunity. Entrepreneurs are individuals who identify these opportunities, take risks, and innovate to create and manage new ventures.

Innovation: Absolutely, innovation is a broad and multifaceted concept that goes beyond the latest gadgets. It often involves novel ideas, processes, or approaches that can transform various aspects of our lives and industries. Here are some dimensions of innovation beyond just new products.

Chapter 6
Economic and Social Impact of Business Incubation in UAE:
Entrepreneurship

Shankar Subramanian Iyer
https://orcid.org/0000-0003-0598-9543
Westford University College, UAE

ABSTRACT

Business incubation programs have emerged as pivotal mechanisms for fostering entrepreneurship and innovation, especially within the rapidly evolving economic landscape of the UAE. This research investigates the multifaceted economic and social impacts of business incubation initiatives and their significance. By fostering a conducive environment, business incubators play a critical role in driving economic diversification. It highlights the role of incubators in fostering community engagement by creating networks of entrepreneurs, mentors, and investors that bolster the entrepreneurial ecosystem. The qualitative research methodology involves expert interviews to gather insights and support for the hypotheses formulated. By analyzing findings from various studies, this research offers valuable insights into the complex and multifaceted impacts of business incubation programs. These insights inform policymakers, practitioners, and stakeholders about effective strategies for supporting entrepreneurship and fostering sustainable development both locally and globally.

DOI: 10.4018/979-8-3693-4302-9.ch006

INTRODUCTION

Business incubation programs have emerged as pivotal instruments for nurturing entrepreneurship and innovation, particularly within the dynamic and rapidly evolving economic landscape of the United Arab Emirates (UAE). As global competition intensifies and economies become more interconnected, fostering a robust entrepreneurial ecosystem is essential for sustainable economic growth and diversification. Business incubators provide a supportive environment for startups and small enterprises, offering resources such as mentorship, funding, networking opportunities, and physical space. These programs are designed to reduce the barriers to entry for new businesses and enhance their chances of success. In the UAE, where the government actively promotes entrepreneurship as a means to diversify the economy away from oil dependence, understanding the impacts of business incubation is of paramount importance (Hamdan et al., 2020). This research delves into the economic and social ramifications of business incubation in the UAE, aiming to shed light on how these programs contribute to job creation, economic development, and social well-being. The UAE has made significant strides in fostering a conducive environment for entrepreneurship and innovation (Alhajeri, 2022). Government initiatives such as Vision 2021 and the UAE National Innovation Strategy underscore the nation's commitment to becoming a global hub for business and innovation. Business incubators are integral to this vision, serving as catalysts for the growth of new enterprises. These incubators provide startups with critical support during their formative stages, which is crucial for their survival and growth. The concept of business incubation involves providing nascent businesses with resources and services that can significantly increase their chances of success, including office space, funding opportunities, mentorship, and access to a network of business contacts (Alawad, 2023). In the UAE, the proliferation of business incubators has been supported by both public and private sector initiatives. Notable examples include the Dubai Technology Entrepreneur Centre (DTEC), IN5, and the Sharjah Entrepreneurship Center (Sheraa). These incubators have facilitated the growth of numerous startups, contributing to the diversification of the economy and fostering innovation across various sectors (Hojeij, 2024). Despite the increasing prevalence of business incubation programs, there remains a need for comprehensive research to quantify their economic and social impacts systematically. This study seeks to fill this gap by examining how business incubators in the UAE influence economic growth, job creation, and social dynamics (Mishrif et al., 2023), (Hasanov, 2024).

Research Scope

This research focuses on business incubation programs within the UAE, analyzing their economic and social impacts over the past decade. The study includes a review of the literature on business incubation, case studies of specific incubators in the UAE, and empirical analysis of data related to job creation, economic growth, and social outcomes. The scope encompasses various sectors, including technology, healthcare, education, and renewable energy, reflecting the diverse nature of the UAE's entrepreneurial landscape. The study aims to provide actionable insights for policymakers, business leaders, and stakeholders involved in entrepreneurship and economic development.

Research Questions

a. What is the economic impact of business incubation programs on job creation and economic growth in the UAE?
b. How do business incubation programs in the UAE influence social factors such as community engagement, diversity, and inclusion?
c. What strategies and practices can business incubators in the UAE adopt to maximize their economic and social impact?

Research Objectives

a. To evaluate the economic impact of business incubation programs in the UAE, focusing on job creation and economic growth.
b. To assess the social impact of business incubation, particularly in terms of community engagement, diversity, and inclusion within the entrepreneurial ecosystem.
c. To identify effective strategies and best practices for business incubators in the UAE to enhance their contributions to sustainable economic and social development.

LITERATURE REVIEW

Business incubators are structured systems designed to support the creation of new entrepreneurial enterprises by providing a range of value-added services beyond mere office space. These services, aimed at improving the success rate of their clients, include shared administrative facilities, marketing support, legal assistance, access to funding, laboratories and equipment, and networking resources. Some Researchers highlighted that such services are essential due to new ventures often lacking critical success factors like sufficient capital, networking, and technical assistance. Over the last 15 years, incubators have evolved to meet new market competition challenges. Klofsten et al., (2021) noted that while earlier generations of incubators focused more on satisfying policymakers than tenants, the third generation balances the needs of both, offering extensive services to enable the creation of start-ups. For instance, in Malaysia, identified services like affordable and flexible space, shared administrative services, business counseling, networking, and post-graduation outreach to sustain growth. Scholars like Kakabadse et al., (2020) emphasized funding and experienced management as critical for incubator success. Flanschger et al., 2023, further listed 15 typical services, including partner advisories, management consultation, venture capital exposure, funding access, educational guidance, ICT services, financial management, market guidance, mentoring, networking, business support, soft skills training, regulatory compliance support, technology transfer, and start-up training. Clayton, P. (2024) categorized these services into pre-incubation (idea development), incubation (technical consultancy, networking, logistics), and post-incubation (funding access, customer acquisition) phases. The National Business Incubation Association (NBIA) also identified essential services such as networking exposure, technical expertise, funding access, and shared services, emphasizing that incubators should provide unique, customized services to differentiate themselves from traditional property management and support clients in becoming self-sufficient in the market (Nicholls-Nixon et al., 2024).

Business incubation programs have become integral to fostering economic growth and job creation worldwide, and the UAE is no exception. These programs support startups by providing essential resources, mentoring, and networking opportunities, thereby enhancing their chances of success. The economic impact of business incubation programs can be measured through various indicators, including job creation, the survival rate of startups, and overall economic growth. Several studies highlight the significant economic contributions of business incubators. A report by the International Business Innovation Association (InBIA) emphasizes that incubated businesses tend to have higher survival rates and generate more jobs compared to non-incubated businesses. In the UAE, the Khalifa Fund for Enterprise Development and Dubai SME have been pivotal in driving entrepreneurship and economic diversification. According to the UAE Ministry of Economy, SMEs contribute to 53% of the GDP and employ 86% of the private sector workforce, showcasing the crucial role of business incubators in economic development (Marsal et al., 2024). Beyond economic metrics, business incubation programs also have profound social impacts. These impacts include enhancing community engagement, promoting diversity and inclusion, and fostering a vibrant entrepreneurial ecosystem. Incubators serve as catalysts for social change by supporting diverse entrepreneurs, including women, minorities, and underrepresented groups, thus contributing to a more inclusive economy. To maximize their contributions to sustainable economic and social development, business incubators in the UAE must adopt effective strategies and best practices. Successful incubation strategies include providing comprehensive support services, fostering strong networks, and ensuring access to funding and market opportunities (Trethewey-Mould et al., 2024).

Best practices identified in the literature emphasize the importance of mentorship, tailored support, and collaboration with stakeholders. For instance, a report by the European Commission highlights that incubators with strong mentorship programs tend to have higher success rates. Additionally, access to funding is critical, as evidenced by the success of the DIFC FinTech Hive, which connects startups with investors and financial institutions.

Integrating Resource-Based View (RBV) and Social Capital Theory has been used to explore the Economic and Social Impact of Business Incubation in the UAE. When integrating the Resource-Based View (RBV) and Social Capital Theory to analyze the economic and social impacts of business incubation programs in the UAE, we identify several independent and dependent factors. The independent factors under the Resource-Based View (RBV) include financial resources such as funding, grants, and investment opportunities provided by incubators; human capital, including access to mentorship, training programs, and industry expertise; physical resources like office space and technological infrastructure; and technical support. The Social Capital Theory highlights networking opportunities with entrepreneurs, investors, and industry experts; the quality and availability of mentorship programs; community engagement initiatives fostering collaboration; and the strength of relationships and trust within the incubator ecosystem (Nafari et al., 2024). The dependent factors reflecting the economic impact encompass job creation, economic growth through revenue generation, market expansion, and GDP contribution, as well as the business survival and growth rates of startups post-incubation. Social impact factors include the level of community involvement and contribution to local social initiatives by incubated businesses, the promotion and support of diversity and inclusion within the entrepreneurial ecosystem, and the enhancement of the broader entrepreneurial ecosystem through supportive policies, programs, and networks. By understanding how these independent factors—resources and social capital provided by incubators—influence the dependent factors of economic and social outcomes, the research aims to provide insights into the effectiveness of business incubation programs in the UAE. This will help identify which resources and practices are most beneficial for fostering sustainable economic and social development (Neto et al., 2024). To enhance the scope and novelty of this research study on the economic and social impacts of business incubation programs in the UAE, several key elements will be integrated. A comparative analysis with global best practices from leading entrepreneurial ecosystems such as Silicon Valley, Israel, and Singapore will be conducted. This will provide insights into how the UAE can adopt and adapt successful strategies to its unique socio-economic context. The research will evaluate how technology and innovation are fostered within incubated startups by assessing metrics such as patent filings, product launches, and technological advancements. The study will investigate the influence of cultural factors on the effectiveness of business incubation programs, considering the diverse expatriate and local entrepreneur demographics in the UAE. This will reveal unique challenges and opportunities in fostering entrepreneurship in a multicultural environment (Nafari et al., 2024).

Comparative Analysis: UAE Business Incubators vs. Global Leaders

Here's an analysis comparing UAE business incubators with leading entrepreneurial ecosystems (Silicon Valley, Israel, Singapore) to identify best practices for enhancing their economic and social impact.

Table 1. Comparative analysis of UAE Business incubators vs. Global Leaders

Area	UAE	Silicon Valley	Israel	Singapore	UAE Improvement
Focus	Often general or industry-specific	Highly specialized (Tech, Biotech, etc.)	Diverse, with a strong focus on R&D	Innovation-driven attracts global talent	Specialize in high-growth sectors aligned with UAE's vision (e.g., Cleantech, AI)
Selection	Competitive, but may lack rigorous screening	Rigorous due diligence, focus on high-potential ventures	Selective, strong emphasis on innovation and scalability	Meritocratic selection prioritizes innovative ideas	Implement stricter selection criteria for high-impact ventures
Services	Business plan development, mentoring, networking	Comprehensive support: legal, marketing, fundraising	Strong mentorship network, access to angel investors	Business development, commercialization support, government grants	Offer tailored support throughout the entrepreneurial journey
Networking	Access to events, some connections	An extensive network of investors, VCs, and industry leaders	Robust network of entrepreneurs, mentors, and investors	Strong connections to global markets and corporations	Facilitate deeper connections for fundraising and scaling
Funding	Limited access to seed funding	Venture capital (VC) heavy ecosystem	Government grants and angel investments strong	A mix of government funding, VC, and corporate partnerships	Develop a robust funding ecosystem with angel investors and VC firms

continued on following page

Table 1. Continued

Area	UAE	Silicon Valley	Israel	Singapore	UAE Improvement
Exit Strategy	Focus on local market growth	Focus on IPOs and acquisitions by larger companies	Strong M&A activity and exits through IPOs	Emphasis on global expansion and scaling	Develop strategies to help startups go global and achieve high-value exits.
Social Impact	Growing focus on social enterprises	Limited social impact focus	Strong social entrepreneurship ecosystem	Dedicated incubators for social impact ventures	Increase support for social enterprises and track their social impact

Additional Considerations:

- Metrics and Evaluation: Implement stronger evaluation methods to measure impact on job creation, economic diversification, and social progress.
- Collaboration: Foster collaboration between startups, universities, research institutions, and corporations to accelerate innovation.
- Government Support: Establish policies and regulations that incentivize entrepreneurship, attract talent, and facilitate access to capital.
- Infrastructure: Develop co-working spaces, innovation hubs, and research facilities to support startups at all stages.

Research Gaps

While the UAE has made significant strides in fostering entrepreneurship through various business incubation programs, there remains a lack of comprehensive studies that evaluate both the economic and social impacts of these programs in a holistic manner. Existing research tends to focus predominantly on economic outcomes such as job creation and startup success rates, often overlooking the broader social implications, including community engagement, diversity, and inclusion. Additionally, there is limited empirical evidence on the effectiveness of specific strategies and best practices tailored to the unique socio-economic context of the UAE. This research aims to fill these gaps by providing an integrated assessment of the economic and social impacts of business incubation programs and identifying effective strategies to enhance their contributions to sustainable development.

Environmental Factors

Environmental factors encompass the broader ecosystem within which business incubators operate, including regulatory frameworks, market dynamics, and technological advancements. In the UAE, the government has implemented several initiatives to create a conducive environment for startups. For instance, the UAE

Vision 2021 emphasizes innovation, research, and technology-driven growth, providing fertile ground for business incubation. The presence of free zones, such as Dubai Silicon Oasis and Abu Dhabi's Masdar City, offers startups tax exemptions, full foreign ownership, and streamlined business setup processes, thereby reducing entry barriers and fostering entrepreneurship. Moreover, the UAE's strategic geographical location, connecting East and West, facilitates access to a diverse market and attracts international investors. The well-developed infrastructure, including state-of-the-art logistics and communication networks, further enhances the operational efficiency of startups. These environmental factors collectively contribute to the economic impact by attracting foreign direct investment, creating jobs, and boosting GDP growth (Razavi Hajiagha et al., 2022).

Resource-Based Factors

Resource-based factors refer to the tangible and intangible assets available to startups through incubators. In the UAE, incubators provide critical resources such as funding, mentorship, office space, and access to advanced technologies. Financial support is a significant resource, with government-backed programs like the Khalifa Fund and Dubai SME offering grants, loans, and equity investments. These financial resources help mitigate the risks associated with new ventures and enable startups to scale their operations. Additionally, incubators in the UAE often provide access to cutting-edge technologies and R&D facilities. For example, the Dubai Future Accelerators program connects startups with government entities to pilot innovative solutions, thereby driving technological advancements. The availability of such resources not only enhances the competitiveness of startups but also promotes innovation, leading to the development of new industries and economic diversification (Lose, 2021).

Social Capital Factors

Social capital factors highlight the importance of networks, relationships, and community support in the incubation process. In the UAE, business incubators serve as hubs for networking and collaboration, bringing together entrepreneurs, investors, industry experts, and academia. These networks facilitate knowledge exchange, mentorship, and partnership opportunities, which are crucial for the growth and sustainability of startups. Furthermore, the multicultural environment of the UAE, with its large expatriate population, fosters a diverse and inclusive entrepreneurial ecosystem. This diversity enhances creativity and innovation, as entrepreneurs from different backgrounds bring unique perspectives and ideas. The social capital generated through these networks not only aids in business development but also contributes to social cohesion and cultural integration, enhancing the overall social fabric of the country (Daskalopoulou et al., 2023).

Governance Factors

Governance factors pertain to the policies, regulations, and institutional frameworks that support business incubation. The UAE government plays a proactive role in fostering a supportive governance structure for startups. Regulatory reforms, such as the introduction of long-term visas for entrepreneurs and investors, create a stable and attractive environment for business ventures. The establishment of entities like the UAE Ministry of Economy and various innovation councils ensures continuous support and monitoring of the entrepreneurial ecosystem. Moreover, public-private partnerships (PPPs) are prevalent in the UAE's incubation landscape, with collaborative efforts between government agencies and private sector players driving the growth of incubators. These partnerships leverage the strengths of both sectors, providing startups with comprehensive support ranging from funding and mentorship to market access and policy advocacy. The robust governance framework thus ensures the sustainability and scalability of business incubation efforts, driving significant economic and social impacts (Bergmann et al., 2021).

Business incubation's economic and social impacts in the UAE are profound and multifaceted, driven by environmental, resource-based, social capital, and governance factors. The UAE's strategic initiatives and supportive ecosystem have created fertile ground for startups, leading to increased foreign investment, job creation, and economic diversification. The provision of critical resources, strong networks, and inclusive policies further enhance the viability and success of new ventures (Shepherd et al., 2021). All the variables influencing the Social Economic Impact Factors of Business Incubation in UAE have been used to conceive the conceptual model as shown in Figure 1.

Figure 1. Conceptual Model Conceptual model based on Integrating the Resource-Based View (RBV) and Social Capital Theory

Conceptual model based on Integrating the Resource-Based View (RBV) and Social Capital Theory

Environmental Factors
- Infrastructure
- Technology
- Security and Political Stability
- Collaboration
- Sustainability
- Cultural

Resource-Based Factors
- Financial Resources
- Human Capital
- Physical Resources
- Technical Support

Social Capital Factors
- Networking Opportunities
- Mentorship and Guidance
- Community Engagement
- Relational Capital

Social Economic Impact Factors of Business Incubation in UAE
- Job Creation,
- Economic Growth,
- Business Survival
- Community Engagement,
- Diversity and Inclusion,
- Entrepreneurial Ecosystem Development

Governance Factors
- Regulatory Framework
- Government Support Programs
- Transparency and Accountability
- Urban Planning and Development
- Environmental and Social Governance

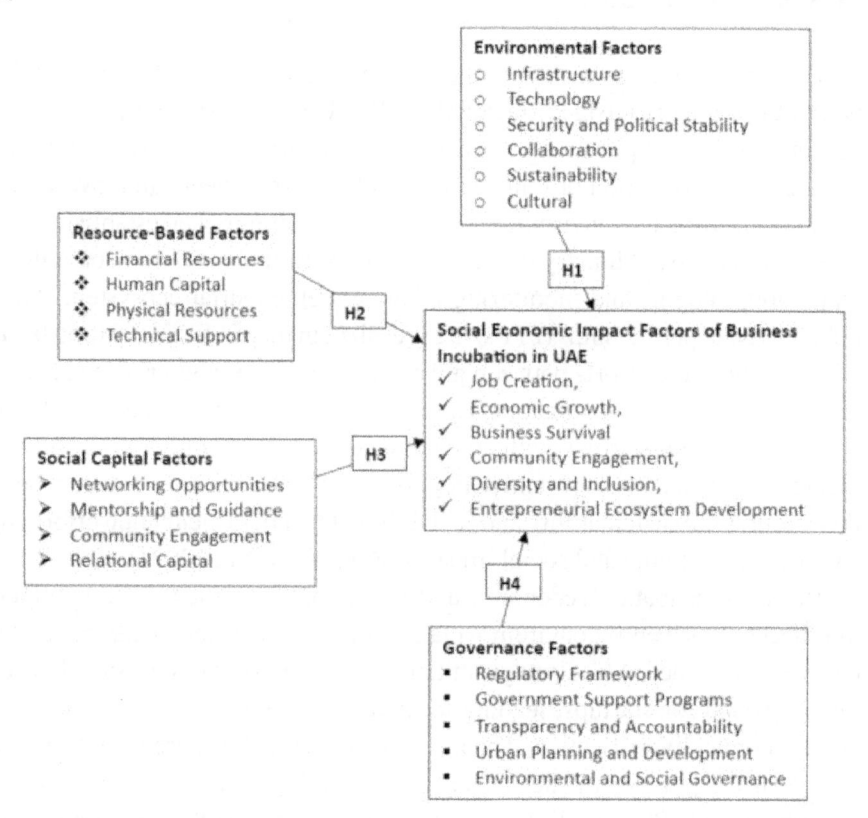

H1, H2, H3, H4

Hypotheses

H1: There is a significant relationship between the Environmental factors and Social Economic Impact Factors of Business Incubation in UAE

H2: The Social Economic Impact Factors of Business Incubation in the UAE is significantly influenced by the Resource-Based Factors

H3: The Social Capital Factors greatly influence the Social Economic Impact Factors of Business Incubation in the UAE

H4: There is a significant relationship between the Governance Factors and Social Economic Impact Factors of Business Incubation in UAE

METHODOLOGY

This study employs a qualitative research design to explore the economic and social impacts of business incubation services in the UAE, leveraging semi-structured interviews with 16 experts selected through purposive sampling based on their extensive experience in business incubation and economic development. The interviews, lasting between 30 to 35 minutes, covered topics such as the range of services provided by incubators, their impact on economic and social development, challenges faced, success factors, and suggestions for improvement. Specifically, the information collected included insights on environmental factors influencing incubation, resource-based factors such as financial, human, and technical support, social capital factors including networking opportunities and community engagement, governance factors related to the management and operational policies of incubators, and the overall socioeconomic impact of business incubation in the UAE (Terribile et al., 2023). The data were analyzed using thematic analysis, involving transcription, familiarization, coding, theme development, defining and naming themes, and reporting, to identify and interpret patterns within the data. Ethical considerations included informed consent, confidentiality, and secure data storage, while reliability and validity were ensured through triangulation, member checking, and maintaining an audit trail. This approach aims to provide a comprehensive understanding of the economic and social impacts of business incubation services in the UAE. The data collected from the interviews was analyzed using thematic analysis. The researcher transcribed and reviewed the responses to ensure accuracy. By coding the data and examining it for similarities, main themes and sub-themes were identified. These findings were presented in Table 2, which summarized the main themes and sub-themes discovered in the study along with the Interviewee profile (belonging to which sector and emirates). The Interview summary was efficiently presented in Table 2, which succinctly summarizes the identified main themes and sub-themes from the thematic analysis of the interviews conducted with 16 expertsacross the UAE and mentioned against each Interviewee in the summary table below (Man et al.,2024).

To validate the objectives using qualitative methodology, this research will focus on conducting interviews and performing thematic analysis. For all Objectives, interviews with incubated startup founders and incubator managers, a diverse group of incubated entrepreneurs, including women, minorities, and underrepresented groups, as well as community stakeholders such as investors and mentors will be conducted to gather detailed information on economic outcomes such as job creation, revenue growth, and business survival rates. These interviews will be transcribed and coded to identify key themes related to economic impact. Thematic analysis of these interviews will develop themes around social impact, such as community engagement and inclusivity to identify effective strategies and best practices for supporting startup growth and development. Thematic analysis will be used to identify key themes related to mentorship, access to funding, and infrastructure support. Data triangulation will ensure the reliability and validity of the findings by cross-verifying information from multiple sources and methods, ensuring a comprehensive and nuanced understanding of the economic and social impacts of business incubation programs in the UAE.

Table 2. Interview Summary

Interviewee no, (Experience in years), Designation, Location	Main Comments on "Economic and Social Impact of Business Incubation in UAE" (Other Interviewees agreeing to these comments)
1. (12) CEO, Gaming Software Company, Dubai, UAE.	- High-quality infrastructure provides startups with essential physical resources such as office spaces, laboratories, and advanced technological facilities, crucial for their operations and growth - Cutting-edge technological resources empower startups to innovate and compete globally. - A stable political environment and robust security measures create a safe and predictable operating environment for startups, attracting both local and international investors. - Stability fosters economic growth by providing a secure platform for business operations and investments, leading to job creation. - Security and political stability are crucial for the development of a resilient entrepreneurial ecosystem in the UAE. - Robust infrastructure enhances the entire entrepreneurial ecosystem. (Interviewee 3, 9, 11, 14, 16)(Mitra et al., 2023)
2. (13), Head, Economic Forum, Sharjah	- Reliable infrastructure supports business survival by reducing operational disruptions and costs. - Technology promotes diversity and inclusion by providing equal access to digital tools. - Collaboration fosters diversity and inclusion by enriching the entrepreneurial ecosystem. - Technical support drives economic growth by accelerating product development and commercialization. (Interviewee 5,8, 10, 15), (Nel-Sanders et al., 2022).
3. (12), Senior Vice President, Banking Sector, Abu Dhabi	- Well-developed infrastructure facilitates community engagement and job creation. - Technological support enhances business survival and economic growth. - Physical resources directly influence job creation and economic growth. (Interviewee 2, 5, 7, 12, 14) (Muturi, 2023); (Surya et al., 2021)
4. (11) Vice President, IT Sector Company, Abu Dhabi	- Integration of advanced technology fosters innovation and sustainable development. - Collaboration and sustainability practices drive economic growth and community engagement - Skilled mentors enhance economic growth and business survival. - The integration of sustainability into business incubation contributes to the development of a forward-thinking and resilient entrepreneurial ecosystem that prioritizes long-term social and environmental well-being.(Interviewee 1, 3, 6, 8,10, 12) (Aithal et al., 2023).

continued on following page

Table 2. Continued

Interviewee no, (Experience in years), Designation, Location	Main Comments on "Economic and Social Impact of Business Incubation in UAE" (Other Interviewees agreeing to these comments)
5. (14) HR Director Private Oil sector, Dubai	- UAE's multicultural environment fosters innovation and creativity. - Business incubators nurture human capital, fostering a competitive ecosystem. - Networking drives economic growth and innovation. (Interviewee 1, 4, 7, 9, 11, 13, 16), (Chaudhry et al., 2021); (Elia et al., 2021).
6. (13) Senior Manager, Aviation Administration, Ajman	- Cultural influences support diversity and inclusion. - Financial resources and networking promote job creation and economic growth. - Government programs drive economic growth and support diversity. (Interviewee 3, 6, 10, 15, 16), (Vîrjan et al., 2023)
7. (10) General Manager Cooperative Retail, Dubai	- Access to financial resources enables startups to scale and create jobs. - Networking fosters a dynamic entrepreneurial ecosystem. - Urban development drives economic growth (Interviewee 1, 5, 9, 11, 12), (Priyono et al., 2024)
8. (14) Head of Healthcare Organization, Dubai, UAE	- Financial support and relational capital enhance business survival and community engagement. - Transparency and sustainability practices drive socioeconomic development. - Mentorship drives economic growth by enhancing the capabilities of startups, enabling them to innovate and scale their businesses effectively. - Startups nurtured in incubators often introduce innovative products and services, contributing to the diversification of the UAE economy.(Interviewee 4, 6, 8, 12, 14, 16), (Almuharrami et al., 2021)
9. (15) International Consultant, Dubai, UAE	- Mentorship programs and regulatory frameworks support business survival and community engagement. - Government programs foster a resilient entrepreneurial ecosystem. - By fostering a supportive environment for startups, government programs play a vital role in developing a vibrant and resilient entrepreneurial ecosystem in the UAE. - Engaging the local community through events, workshops, and collaborative projects fosters a sense of belonging and mutual support among entrepreneurs. - ESG considerations also enhance business survival by encouraging startups to adopt sustainable practices that reduce risks and improve resilience.(Interviewee 1, 3, 6, 7, 14)(Haijun et al., 2024)
10. (12) Vice President Hospitality sector, Rasal Khaima	- Relational capital and community engagement drive innovation and economic growth. - Incubators act as catalysts for collaboration and investment. - Incubators provide essential resources, mentorship, and networking opportunities that help new businesses thrive. As these startups scale, they create new jobs, reducing unemployment rates and providing employment opportunities for a diverse workforce. - Incubators act as catalysts, bringing together various stakeholders, including entrepreneurs, investors, academia, and government agencies, to create a supportive and collaborative environment. - A well-developed entrepreneurial ecosystem attracts further investment, both domestic and international, and positions the UAE as a global hub for innovation and entrepreneurship. (Interviewee 1, 5, 8, 11, 13),(Aarstad et al., 2022); (Leal et al., 2023).

continued on following page

Table 2. Continued

Interviewee no, (Experience in years), Designation, Location	Main Comments on "Economic and Social Impact of Business Incubation in UAE" (Other Interviewees agreeing to these comments)
11. (14) Vice President, Environmental Agency, Umm Quain, UAE	- The Economic impact is to Attract foreign direct investment, create jobs, and boost GDP growth through State-of-the-art logistics and communication networks. - Community engagement is strengthened as businesses actively participate in environmental and social initiatives, fostering goodwill and support from the community. - More Free zones like Dubai Silicon Oasis, and Abu Dhabi's Masdar City offer tax exemptions, full foreign ownership, and streamlined business setup will boost the Business Incubators - Financial support from Government-backed programs like the Khalifa Fund and Dubai SME provide grants, loans, and equity investments to promote Entrepreneurship and Business startups. - The Strategic location advantage of UAE as it connects East and West, facilitates market access and attracts international investors. - Supportive governance includes a Proactive government role, regulatory reforms, and long-term visas for entrepreneurs. (Interviewee 1, 5, 7, 9, 15), (Behera et al., 2024); (Bernard de Saint Affrique, 2020).
12. (17) Senior President, Corporate Services, Abu Dhabi.	- Access to technologies and mentorship drives innovation and economic growth. - Sustainability practices and institutional support enhance business survival and community engagement - Sustainability ensures Robust governance and it ensures scalability and significant economic and social impacts. - Institutional support from Entities like the UAE Ministry of Economy and innovation councils. - Transparent operations and accountability mechanisms enhance the credibility of incubators, attracting more entrepreneurs and investors. (Interviewee 1, 6, 8, 13, 15, 16), (Madaleno et al., 2022); (Al Marri, 2021).
13. (11) Senior HR Director, Tourism Company, Abu Dhabi	- The Competitiveness spirit of Business Incubators enhances startup growth, promotes innovation, and leads to new industries and economic diversification. - This transparency leads to job creation as startups feel secure and supported in a trustworthy environment. - Public-private partnershipsinvolveCollaborative efforts to drive incubator growth and provide comprehensive support. - Competitiveness and transparency drive job creation and economic growth. - Public-private partnerships and political stability support community engagement. (Interviewee 2, 7, 10, 14), (Harlin et al., 2021)
14. (10) President, Healthcare Group, Fujirah	- Community engagement promotes diversity and supports local social initiatives. - Supportive governance enhances Proactive government role, regulatory reforms, and long-term visas for entrepreneurs. A multicultural environment ensures a Diverse and inclusive ecosystem that fosters creativity and innovation.(Interviewee 3, 5, 12, 13)(Eden et al., 2024); (Cavalcante, 2023); (Eden et al., 2024).

continued on following page

Table 2. Continued

Interviewee no, (Experience in years), Designation, Location	Main Comments on "Economic and Social Impact of Business Incubation in UAE" (Other Interviewees agreeing to these comments)
15. (10) Start-up Entrepreneur in Gaming, Abu Dhabi	- Entrepreneurial ecosystem ensures Supportive policies, programs, and networks sustain growth and success. - Overall impact drives sustainable economic and social development in the UAE. - Supportive entrepreneurial ecosystem and mentorship promote job creation and economic growth. - Knowledge exchange and urban planning support innovation and diversity. (Interviewee 2, 7, 11, 15),(Candeias et al., 2024); (Mitra et al., 2023); (Bednář et al., 2023)
16. (10), Community Head, Sharjah,	- Networking supports Incubators as hubs for entrepreneurs, investors, industry experts, and academia. - Networking and collaboration drive sustainable economic development. - Community engagement strengthens business survival and innovation. (Interviewee 4, 8, 9, 17),(Vaz et al., 2023); (DiBella et al., 2023)

Experts emphasize the importance of developing a comprehensive model to assess the economic and social impact of business incubation in the UAE. This model is crucial for preparing for future advancements and challenges. Technology plays a vital role in driving innovation, enhancing products and services, and optimizing operations. Therefore, businesses need to stay informed about technological advancements and actively explore new technologies to capitalize on their benefits. However, it is equally crucial for the industry to consider the ethical implications of using technology, ensuring that their practices align with core values. While technology presents numerous opportunities, it is essential to implement it thoughtfully, taking into account the potential risks and impacts. Additionally, collaboration, networking, industrial support through restructuring, and favorable government policies will enhance the progress and effectiveness of business incubation. These factors contribute to best practices and sustainable growth within the incubation ecosystem (Crupi et al., 2023).

FINDINGS AND DISCUSSIONS

In this section, we examine the hypotheses formulated to understand the relationship between various factors and the social-economic impact factors of business incubation in the UAE. The hypotheses are supported by the analysis of the benefits and challenges of generative AI, as well as a review of the most recent AI literature and from the summary table of the Interviewees ().

Hypothetical Decisions

H1: There is a significant relationship between Environmental factors and Social Economic Impact Factors of Business Incubation in the UAE. Environmental factors, such as technological advancements, regulatory frameworks, and market dynamics, play a critical role in shaping the social and economic impact of business incubation. The rapid advancements in generative AI technology (e.g., NLP models like GPT-4, and GANs) have created a fertile ground for innovation and entrepreneurship, providing incubated businesses with the tools to enhance productivity and creativity. The UAE's proactive stance in adopting advanced technologies and creating a supportive regulatory environment has fostered a conducive ecosystem for business incubation. The country's strategic investments in AI and its implementation in various sectors, including healthcare and education, have significantly contributed to the social and economic impact of business incubation. The correlation between a supportive technological environment and positive economic outcomes for incubated businesses is evident, reinforcing the importance of environmental factors in this context (Brandt et al., 2023).

H2: The Social Economic Impact Factors of Business Incubation in the UAE are significantly influenced by the Resource-Based Factors. Resource-based factors such as access to funding, infrastructure, mentorship, and skilled workforce are pivotal in determining the success and economic impact of business incubators. The availability of advanced AI tools and platforms has enhanced the resources available to startups, allowing them to innovate and scale efficiently. In the UAE, business incubators provide startups with essential resources, including state-of-the-art AI technologies, which help in reducing operational costs and improving product development. The significant influence of resource-based factors is evident in the enhanced operational efficiency and competitive advantage gained by incubated businesses. Access to these resources has enabled startups to leverage data-driven decision-making and achieve sustainable growth, underscoring the critical role of resource-based factors in driving the socioeconomic impact (Faccia et al., 2023).

H3: The Social Capital Factors greatly influence the Social Economic Impact Factors of Business Incubation in UAE. Social capital factors, including networks, partnerships, and community support, greatly influence the social and economic impact of business incubation. The collaborative ecosystem in the UAE, supported by both public and private sectors, enhances the social capital available to incubated businesses. The UAE's emphasis on building strong networks and fostering collaborations between startups, established companies, and research institutions has significantly boosted the social and economic impact of business incubation. The integration of generative AI into business processes has further facilitated networking and knowledge sharing, leading to innovative solutions and new business models.

The positive correlation between social capital factors and economic outcomes for incubated businesses highlights the importance of building robust networks and community support systems (Alnassai, 2023).

H4: There is a significant relationship between Governance Factors and Social Economic Impact Factors of Business Incubation in UAE. Governance factors, including policy frameworks, regulatory support, and institutional quality, have a significant relationship with the social and economic impact of business incubation. The UAE's governance framework, which promotes innovation and entrepreneurship through favorable policies and regulatory support, has been instrumental in driving the success of business incubators. The UAE's strategic governance initiatives, such as the establishment of AI ethics guidelines and supportive legal frameworks for startups, have created an enabling environment for business incubation. These governance factors ensure that incubated businesses operate within a well-regulated and supportive ecosystem, fostering trust and stability. The significant relationship between governance factors and socioeconomic impact is evident in the thriving startup ecosystem in the UAE, which is marked by increased innovation, job creation, and economic diversification (Alkaabi et al., 2023).

The findings and discussion underscore the importance of environmental, resource-based, social capital, and governance factors in influencing the social-economic impact of business incubation in the UAE. The integration of generative AI and other advanced technologies within the incubation ecosystem has further amplified these relationships, driving innovation and economic growth. By supporting start-ups with the necessary resources, networks, and regulatory frameworks, the UAE continues to enhance the social and economic impact of its business incubation initiatives (Potter et al., 2023).

Recent startup examples like Kitopi, a cloud kitchen platform, and Sarwa, a robo-advisory platform, demonstrate the economic potential of incubated businesses. Kitopi, incubated at IN5 in Dubai, has expanded rapidly and created numerous jobs, contributing significantly to the food tech industry. Similarly, Sarwa, which benefited from the DIFC FinTech Hive, has played a vital role in the financial technology sector, attracting substantial investment and creating highly skilled jobs. Research indicates that inclusive incubation programs lead to more equitable economic development (Nziku et al., 2024). For instance, a study by the Kauffman Foundation found that inclusive entrepreneurship initiatives result in higher innovation rates and more robust community development. In the UAE, organizations like the Sharjah Entrepreneurship Center (Sheraa) focus on inclusive entrepreneurship, providing tailored support to female entrepreneurs and young innovators (El Khatib et al., 2024). Startups such as Mums@Work, which connects mothers with flexible job opportunities, and Nabbesh, a freelance work platform, highlight the social benefits of incubation. Both startups have been supported by UAE-based incubators and have significantly impacted community engagement and social inclusion by creating platforms that empower diverse populations. Recent initiatives, such as the Abu Dhabi Global Market (ADGM) Tech Hub and Hub71, illustrate effective incubation strategies in the UAE. ADGM Tech Hub focuses on regulatory support and access to capital, while Hub71 offers a comprehensive ecosystem with office space, mentorship, and funding opportunities. Startups like Pure Harvest Smart Farms, which specialize in sustainable agriculture technology, have benefited from such ecosystems, showcasing the effectiveness of these strategies in promoting sustainable development (Ramadani et al., 2024).

Enhancing Business Incubation in the UAE

Objective a: To evaluate the economic impact of business incubation programs in the UAE, focusing on job creation and economic growth. To enhance the economic impact of business incubation programs in the UAE, it is crucial to provide strong policy and regulatory support. Streamlining regulations to simplify the process of starting and running a business will reduce bureaucratic hurdles, while policies protecting intellectual property rights can encourage innovation. Incentives such as tax breaks, grants, and subsidies for startups and incubators can further stimulate economic growth. Additionally, developing state-of-the-art incubation facilities across various emirates, particularly sector-specific incubators for fintech, healthtech, and agritech, will cater to specialized needs and foster economic diversification. Enhancing digital infrastructure with high-speed internet and robust cybersecurity measures will support the tech startup ecosystem, further driving job creation and economic growth (Erturk et al., 2024).

Objective b: To assess the social impact of business incubation, particularly in terms of community engagement, diversity, and inclusion within the entrepreneurial ecosystem. Assessing and enhancing the social impact of business incubation involves fostering a culture of inclusivity and community engagement. Establishing expert networks and mentorship programs will provide startups with the guidance needed to thrive, while educational programs and workshops can equip entrepreneurs with essential business and technical skills. Public awareness campaigns highlighting the role of incubators in economic and social development can inspire potential entrepreneurs from diverse backgrounds (Usman et al., 2024). Events such as hackathons, startup competitions, and innovation challenges can stimulate creative thinking and collaboration. By supporting initiatives like the Sharjah Entrepreneurship Center (Sheraa), which focuses on inclusive entrepreneurship, and startups that promote diversity and social inclusion, incubators can make significant strides in creating a more equitable and vibrant entrepreneurial ecosystem (Houssou et al., 2024).

Objective c: To identify effective strategies and best practices for business incubators in the UAE to enhance their contributions to sustainable economic and social development. To identify and implement effective strategies and best practices, business incubators in the UAE should focus on providing comprehensive support services, fostering strong networks, and ensuring access to funding. Encouraging the growth of venture capital firms and angel investors through favorable policies and tax incentives can increase funding opportunities for startups. Government grants and low-interest loans tailored to different stages of startup development can provide essential financial support (Bernardus et al., 2024). Facilitating partnerships between startups and established businesses, promoting cross-sector collaboration, and participating in global startup ecosystems will enhance resource sharing and innovation. Monitoring and evaluating incubator performance using clear metrics, and continuously identifying and adopting best practices from leading global incubators, will ensure continuous improvement and sustainable development (Sabiha et al., 2024).

Examples of Initiatives

Successful initiatives like Hub71 in Abu Dhabi, which offers a comprehensive ecosystem with office space, mentorship, and funding opportunities, demonstrate the effectiveness of these strategies. Similarly, Dubai Future Accelerators, which connects startups with government entities to work on innovative solutions, and the Sharjah Entrepreneurship Center (Sheraa), which supports inclusive entrepreneurship, highlight the potential of well-supported entrepreneurial ventures to drive both economic and social development. By implementing these strategies, the UAE can further enhance its business incubation landscape, fostering innovation, economic growth, and social development. Encouraging entrepreneurship through robust support systems and creating an enabling environment will help the UAE maintain its position as a global hub for innovation and startups, ultimately contributing to sustainable economic and social development (Uctu et al., 2024).

THE CONTRIBUTION AND ORIGINALITY (VALUE OF THE RESEARCH)

This research significantly contributes to the understanding of the economic and social impacts of business incubation in the UAE, offering valuable insights into the multifaceted influences of environmental, resource-based, social capital, and governance factors. By integrating the latest advancements in generative AI and other cutting-edge technologies into the analysis, the research provides a contemporary perspective on how these technologies can enhance the incubation process, fostering innovation, productivity, and competitive advantage for startups. This focus on AI, in particular, highlights the transformative potential of technological adoption in business incubation, making the findings highly relevant for modern entrepreneurial ecosystems. The originality of this research lies in its comprehensive examination of the interplay between various factors influencing business incubation in a specific regional context. Unlike previous studies that may have generalized findings across different regions, this research delves deeply into the unique socio-economic landscape of the UAE, providing a detailed analysis of how local policies, cultural attitudes, and technological advancements shape the incubation environment. This localized approach not only fills a gap in the existing literature but also offers practical insights for stakeholders in similar emerging markets looking to replicate the UAE's success. Furthermore, the research offers a robust theoretical framework that integrates multiple dimensions affecting business incubation, which can serve as a foundation for future studies. By exploring the interdependencies between environmental, resource-based, social capital, and governance factors, the research provides a nuanced understanding of the dynamics at play. This holistic perspective is valuable for policymakers, incubation managers, and entrepreneurs, as it highlights the critical areas where interventions and support can be most effective. The findings advocate for a balanced approach to incubation, emphasizing the importance of technological resources, robust networks, and supportive governance in driving sustainable economic and social impacts. Overall, this research not only advances academic knowledge but also offers actionable recommendations for enhancing business incubation programs. It underscores the importance of a supportive ecosystem that leverages advanced technologies, fosters strong social capital, and operates within a well-regulated governance framework, ultimately contributing to the broader discourse on innovation and entrepreneurship in emerging markets.

IMPLICATIONS OF THIS RESEARCH

Practical Implications

From a practical standpoint, the findings underscore the importance of providing startups with access to cutting-edge technologies and resources. Policymakers can leverage these insights to develop targeted policies that support business incubation, including financial incentives and reduced regulatory hurdles. Incubation programs should be tailored to address specific needs, such as incorporating AI training modules and securing expert mentorship. Effective resource allocation, and understanding the significance of social capital and governance factors, can further enhance the support provided to startups, ensuring robust networking opportunities and adherence to ethical standards.

Social Implications

The research on the economic and social impact of business incubation in the UAE reveals several critical implications for society. Business incubation fosters community empowerment by creating jobs and enhancing the standard of living. It promotes inclusive growth by providing resources and support to diverse groups, including women and minority entrepreneurs, thereby advancing social equity. Additionally, the emphasis on advanced technologies like generative AI contributes to skill development, equipping individuals with competencies essential for the modern economy. This cultural shift towards entrepreneurship and innovation results in a more dynamic and forward-thinking society.

Managerial Implications

Managerial implications emphasize the need for strategic planning, performance measurement, and risk management. Incubation center managers should integrate environmental and resource-based factors into their strategic planning to secure funding, attract skilled mentors, and build technology partnerships. Monitoring key performance indicators related to innovation and social capital development is crucial for continuous improvement. Additionally, managers must implement robust risk management frameworks to address potential challenges, such as data privacy concerns and job displacement. Fostering a culture of transparency, ethical behavior, and continuous learning will ensure sustainable growth and maximize the positive impact of business incubation on society.

LIMITATIONS AND FUTURE RESEARCH

Limitations

One significant limitation of the research is the focus on the UAE, which may limit the generalizability of the findings to other regions with different economic, cultural, and regulatory environments. The unique socio-economic landscape and government policies in the UAE might not be applicable elsewhere, which could affect the transferability of the results. Additionally, the research predominantly emphasizes the benefits and challenges of generative AI, potentially overlooking other critical factors that influence business incubation, such as market dynamics and sector-specific challenges. Another limitation is the reliance on existing literature and secondary data, which may not capture the most current trends and developments in AI and business incubation. The rapid pace of technological advancement means that the findings could quickly become outdated. Moreover, the research may have inherent biases due to the selection of sources and the interpretation of data, which could affect the validity and reliability of the conclusions drawn. Finally, the complexity and multifaceted nature of the socioeconomic impact factors makes it challenging to isolate and quantify the effects of specific variables. The interactions between environmental, resource-based, social capital, and governance factors are intricate, and disentangling these influences requires a more granular and longitudinal approach. This complexity could lead to an oversimplification of the relationships between these factors and the outcomes of business incubation.

Future Research Directions

Future research should aim to broaden the scope by including comparative studies across different regions and countries to enhance the generalizability of the findings. Investigating how varying economic, cultural, and regulatory environments impact the effectiveness of business incubation can provide more comprehensive insights. Additionally, exploring other emerging technologies beyond generative AI, such as blockchain, Internet of Things (IoT), and augmented reality (AR), could offer a more holistic understanding of the technological influences on business incubation. Conducting primary research, including surveys and interviews with stakeholders involved in business incubation, can provide more current and nuanced data. This approach would help capture real-time trends and address the limitations associated with secondary data. Longitudinal studies that track the progress and outcomes of incubated businesses over time would also be valuable in understanding the long-term impacts and sustainability of business incubation programs. Further research should delve into the interplay between different influencing factors and their collective impact on business incubation outcomes. Advanced analytical techniques, such as structural equation modeling (SEM), can be employed to better understand the relationships between environmental, resource-based, social capital, and governance factors. Additionally, exploring the role of policy interventions and how they can be optimized to support business incubation in different contexts would be beneficial. This would provide actionable insights for policymakers and practitioners aiming to enhance the economic and social impact of business incubation programs. An evaluation of the social return on investment (SROI) will be included to quantify the social impact of incubation programs in economic terms, bridging the gap between economic and social impact assessments. Fifth, the research will develop detailed policy recommendations and an implementation framework based on the findings, aimed at policymakers and stakeholders to provide actionable guidance. Finally, the study will align its objectives with the United Nations Sustainable Development Goals (SDGs), particularly those related to decent work, economic growth, and reduced inequalities. By linking the study to SDGs, it will be positioned within the global discourse on sustainable development, highlighting the broader societal relevance and impact of business incubation programs. These enhancements will provide comprehensive insights and practical implications, making the study a valuable contribution to entrepreneurship, economic development, and social innovation.

CONCLUSION

The research study on the economic and social impact of business incubation in the UAE highlights the significant roles played by environmental, resource-based, social capital, and governance factors in shaping the success and sustainability of incubated businesses. The UAE's proactive approach to integrating advanced technologies, such as generative AI, into its business incubation framework has proven to be a pivotal factor in enhancing productivity, fostering innovation, and gaining competitive advantages. This focus on technology adoption not only empowers startups but also contributes to the broader socio-economic development of the region.

The findings underscore the importance of a supportive incubation ecosystem that provides access to cutting-edge resources, robust networks, and conducive regulatory frameworks. These elements collectively drive the economic and social benefits of business incubation, including job creation, community empowerment, and skill development. The research also emphasizes the critical role of inclusive policies and strategic resource allocation in ensuring that diverse groups, including women and minority entrepreneurs, have the opportunity to thrive, thus promoting social equity and cohesion.

This study provides valuable insights and practical recommendations for stakeholders involved in business incubation. By acknowledging and addressing the interplay between various influencing factors, policymakers, incubation managers, and entrepreneurs can create a more effective and sustainable incubation environment. The UAE's experience serves as a model for other regions aiming to enhance their entrepreneurial ecosystems through strategic investments in technology, strong social capital, and supportive governance. Future research should continue to explore these dynamics, broadening the scope to include comparative studies and real-time data to further refine and validate the findings.Business incubation programs in the UAE have a significant economic and social impact. They drive job creation and economic growth, enhance community engagement, and promote diversity and inclusion within the entrepreneurial ecosystem. By adopting effective strategies and best practices, business incubators can further enhance their contributions to sustainable economic and social development. The success stories of startups like Kitopi, Sarwa, Mums@Work, Nabbesh, and Pure Harvest Smart Farms exemplify the potential of well-supported entrepreneurial ventures to transform economies and societies.

REFERENCES

Aarstad, J., Jakobsen, S. E., & Foss, L. (2022). Business incubator management and entrepreneur collaboration with R&D milieus: Does the regional context matter? *International Journal of Entrepreneurship and Innovation*, 23(1), 28–38. DOI: 10.1177/14657503211030808

Aithal, P. S., & Aithal, S. (2023). Super Innovation in Higher Education by Nurturing Business Leaders through Incubationship. *International Journal of Applied Engineering and Management Letters*, 7(3), 142–167. DOI: 10.47992/IJAEML.2581.7000.0192

Al Marri, S. M. K. (2021). *How can the UAE government best promote a successful national innovation ecosystem?* (Doctoral dissertation, University of Warwick). http://webcat.warwick.ac.uk/record=b3678194~S15

Alawad, M. (2023). Igniting Innovation: The Surge of Youth Entrepreneurship in the UAE. *International Journal of Entrepreneurship*, 28(1). https://zuscholars.zu.ac.ae/works/6413/

Alhajeri, G. (2022). Changing Behaviours and Its Theories to Achieve the Desire for Entrepreneurship in Future Generations in the UAE and Gulf Region. *International Business Research*, 15(11), 49. DOI: 10.5539/ibr.v15n11p49

Alkaabi, K., Ramadani, V., & Zeqiri, J. (2023). Universities, entrepreneurial ecosystem, and family business performance: Evidence from The United Arab Emirates. *Journal of the Knowledge Economy*, 15(2), 1–28. DOI: 10.1007/s13132-023-01384-9

Almuharrami, S. S. M. S., & Mohamad, N. B. (2021). The influence of relational and social capital on the infrastructure project performance in UAE. *Estudios de Economía Aplicada*, 39(10). Advance online publication. DOI: 10.25115/eea.v39i10.6290

Alnassai, J. M. I. A. (2023). A Study on the Barriers to Entrepreneurship in the UAE. *Journal of Risk and Financial Management*, 16(3), 146. DOI: 10.3390/jrfm16030146

Bednář, P., Danko, L., & Smékalová, L. (2023). Coworking spaces and creative communities: Making resilient coworking spaces through knowledge sharing and collective learning. *European Planning Studies*, 31(3), 490–507. DOI: 10.1080/09654313.2021.1944065

Behera, B., Haldar, A., & Sethi, N. (2024). Investigating the direct and indirect effects of Information and Communication Technology on economic growth in the emerging economies: Role of financial development, foreign direct investment, innovation, and institutional quality. *Information Technology for Development*, 30(1), 33–56. DOI: 10.1080/02681102.2023.2233463

Bergmann, T., & Utikal, H. (2021). How to support start-ups in developing a sustainable business model: The case of aeuropean social impact accelerator. *Sustainability (Basel)*, 13(6), 3337. DOI: 10.3390/su13063337

Bernard de Saint Affrique, L. A. H. A. (2020). *Insular urbanities*. https://resolver.tudelft.nl/uuid:40ed7979-1243-457e-a7f7-865fe809abc0

Bernardus, D., Sufa, S. A., & Suparwata, D. O. (2024). Supporting start-ups in Indonesia: Examining government policies, incubator business, and sustainable structure for entrepreneurial ecosystems and capital. *International Journal of Business, Law, and Education*, 5(1), 236–259. DOI: 10.56442/ijble.v5i1.372

Brandt, T., Sakkthivel, A. M., Abidi, N., Abudaqa, A., & Yanamandra, R. (2023). Does environment influence entrepreneurship? Empirical evidence from aspiring emirati women entrepreneurs in United Arab Emirates. https://www.theseus.fi/handle/10024/815018

Candeias, J. C., & Sarkar, S. (2024). Entrepreneurial Ecosystems Policy Formulation: A Conceptual Framework. *The Academy of Management Perspectives*, 38(1), 77–105. DOI: 10.5465/amp.2022.0047

Cavalcante, P. L. (2023). Innovation policy governance. In *Global Encyclopedia of Public Administration, Public Policy, and Governance* (pp. 6704–6709). Springer International Publishing. DOI: 10.1007/978-3-030-66252-3_4234

Chaudhry, I. S., Paquibut, R. Y., & Tunio, M. N. (2021). Do workforce diversity, inclusion practices, & organizational characteristics contribute to organizational innovation? Evidence from the UAE. *Cogent Business & Management*, 8(1), 1947549. DOI: 10.1080/23311975.2021.1947549

Clayton, P. (2024). Mentored without incubation: Start-up survival, funding, and the role of entrepreneurial support organization services. *Research Policy*, 53(4), 104975. DOI: 10.1016/j.respol.2024.104975

Crupi, A., & Schilirò, D. (2023). The UAE Economy and the Path to Diversification and Innovation. *International Journal of Business Management and Economic Research*, 2286–2300. https://ijbmer.com/docs/volumes/vol14issue5/ijbmer2023140507.pdf

Daskalopoulou, I., Karakitsiou, A., & Thomakis, Z. (2023). Social Entrepreneurship and Social Capital: A Review of Impact Research. *Sustainability (Basel)*, 15(6), 4787. DOI: 10.3390/su15064787

DiBella, J., Forrest, N., Burch, S., Rao-Williams, J., Ninomiya, S. M., Hermelingmeier, V., & Chisholm, K. (2023). Exploring the potential of SMEs to build individual, organizational, and community resilience through sustainability-oriented business practices. *Business Strategy and the Environment*, 32(1), 721–735. DOI: 10.1002/bse.3171

Eden, C. A., Chisom, O. N., & Adeniyi, I. S. (2024). Cultural competence in education: Strategies for fostering inclusivity and diversity awareness. *International Journal of Applied Research in Social Sciences*, 6(3), 383–392. DOI: 10.51594/ijarss.v6i3.895

Eden, C. A., Chisom, O. N., & Adeniyi, I. S. (2024). Parent and community involvement in education: Strengthening partnerships for social improvement. *International Journal of Applied Research in Social Sciences*, 6(3), 372–382. DOI: 10.51594/ijarss.v6i3.894

El Khatib, M., AlShibani, M., Almaeeni, A., & Almulla, A. (2024). Social, Economic, and Environmental Development factors (SEED) to foster collaborative sustainable development for SMART and digital initiatives. *International Journal of Business Analytics and Security*, 4(2), 107–122. https://journals.gaftim.com/index.php/ijbas/article/view/355

Elia, G., Margherita, A., Ciavolino, E., & Moustaghfir, K. (2021). Digital society incubator: Combining exponential technology and human potential to build resilient entrepreneurial ecosystems. *Administrative Sciences*, 11(3), 96. DOI: 10.3390/admsci11030096

Erturk, A., Colbran, S. E., Theofanidis, F., & Abidi, O. (Eds.). (2024). *Convergence of Digitalization, Innovation, and Sustainable Development in Business*. IGI Global. DOI: 10.4018/979-8-3693-0798-4

Faccia, A., Le Roux, C. L., & Pandey, V. (2023). Innovation and E-commerce models, the technology catalysts for sustainable development: The Emirate of Dubai case study. *Sustainability (Basel)*, 15(4), 3419. DOI: 10.3390/su15043419

Flanschger, A., Heinzelmann, R., & Messner, M. (2023). Between consultation and control: How incubators perform a governance function for entrepreneurial firms. *Accounting, Auditing & Accountability Journal*, 36(9), 86–107. DOI: 10.1108/AAAJ-09-2020-4950

Haijun, W., Shuaipeng, J., & Chao, M. (2024). The impact of ESG responsibility performance on corporate resilience. *International Review of Economics & Finance*. https://doi.org/DOI: 10.1016/j.iref.2024.05.033https://

Hamdan, A. M., Khamis, R., Al Hawaj, A. A., & Barone, E. (2020). The mediation role of public governance in the relationship between entrepreneurship and economic growth. *International Journal of Managerial Finance*, 16(3), 316–333. DOI: 10.1108/IJMF-04-2018-0111

Harlin, U., & Berglund, M. (2021). Designing for sustainable work during industrial startups—The case of a high-growth entrepreneurial firm. *Small Business Economics*, 57(2), 807–819. DOI: 10.1007/s11187-020-00383-3

Hasanov, M. (2024). The growth of entrepreneurial firms via business incubator initiatives. *Scientific Collection InterConf*, (194), 30-35. https://archive.interconf.center/index.php/conference-proceeding/article/view/5707

Hojeij, Z. (2024). An overview of university-industry collaboration in the Arab world. *Journal of Innovation and Entrepreneurship*, 13(1), 40. DOI: 10.1186/s13731-024-00400-9

Houssou, U., Schulz, K. P., Biga-Diambeidou, M., & Abihona, S. (2024). University incubators and entrepreneurial universities: A case study of the process of setting up a university incubator in a developing country. *International Journal of Technology Management*, 95(3/4), 434–455. DOI: 10.1504/IJTM.2024.138802

Kakabadse, N., Karatas-Ozkan, M., Theodorakopoulos, N., McGowan, C., & Nicolopoulou, K. (2020). Business incubator managers' perceptions of their role and performance success: Role demands, constraints, and choices. *European Management Review*, 17(2), 485–498. DOI: 10.1111/emre.12379

Klofsten, M., & Bienkowska, D. (2021). Business incubators within entrepreneurial ecosystems: sustainability aspects of new venture support and development. In *Handbook of Research on Business and Technology Incubation and Acceleration* (pp. 124–139). Edward Elgar Publishing. DOI: 10.4337/9781788974783.00015

Leal, M., Leal, C., & Silva, R. (2023). The Involvement of Universities, Incubators, Municipalities, and Business Associations in Fostering Entrepreneurial Ecosystems and Promoting Local Growth. *Administrative Sciences*, 13(12), 245. DOI: 10.3390/admsci13120245

Lose, T. (2021). Business incubators in South Africa: A resource-based view perspective. *Academy of Entrepreneurship Journal*, 27, 1–11. https://www.proquest.com/openview/83175b594ba2bd54d0435c16aad30e93/1?pq-origsite=gscholar&cbl=29726

Madaleno, M., Nathan, M., Overman, H., & Waights, S. (2022). Incubators, accelerators and urban economic development. *Urban Studies (Edinburgh, Scotland)*, 59(2), 281–300. DOI: 10.1177/00420980211004209

Man, T. W. Y., Berger, R., & Rachamim, M. (2024). A social constructivist perspective on novice entrepreneurial learning in business incubators. *International Journal of Emerging Markets*, 19(5), 1281–1305. DOI: 10.1108/IJOEM-11-2021-1784

Marsal, H., Hamdan, A., Awwad, B., & Mohamed, M. (2024). The Impact of Mentorship and Funding Support on Stimulating Entrepreneurship Motivation among Family Members. *European Journal of Family Business*, 14(1), 117–130. DOI: 10.24310/ejfb.14.1.2024.17011

Mishrif, A., Karolak, M., & Mirza, C. (2023). The Nexus Between Higher Education, Labour Market, and Industry 4.0 in the Context of the Arab Gulf States. In *Nationalization of Gulf Labour Markets: Higher Education and Skills Development in Industry 4.0* (pp. 1-23). Singapore: Springer Nature Singapore. DOI: 10.1007/978-981-19-8072-5_1

Mitra, S., Kumar, H., Gupta, M. P., & Bhattacharya, J. (2023). Entrepreneurship in smart cities: Elements of start-up ecosystem. *Journal of Science and Technology Policy Management*, 14(3), 592–611. DOI: 10.1108/JSTPM-06-2021-0078

Mitra, S., Kumar, H., Gupta, M. P., & Bhattacharya, J. (2023). Entrepreneurship in smart cities: Elements of start-up ecosystem. *Journal of Science and Technology Policy Management*, 14(3), 592–611. DOI: 10.1108/JSTPM-06-2021-0078

Muturi, D. (2023). Infrastructure investment and economic development. *Journal of Poverty. Investment and Development*, 8(2), 90–99. DOI: 10.47604/jpid.2074

Nafari, J., Honig, B., & Siqueira, A. C. O. (2024). Promoting academic social intrapreneurship: Developing an international virtual incubator and fostering social impact. *Technovation*, 133, 103024. DOI: 10.1016/j.technovation.2024.103024

Nel-Sanders, D., & Thomas, P. (2022). The role of government in promoting innovation-led entrepreneurial ecosystems. *Africa's Public Service Delivery & Performance Review*, 10(1), 13. DOI: 10.4102/apsdpr.v10i1.640

Neto, J. R., Figueiredo, C., Gabriel, B. C., & Valente, R. (2024). Factors for innovation ecosystem frameworks: Comprehensive organizational aspects for evolution. *Technological Forecasting and Social Change*, 203, 123383. DOI: 10.1016/j.techfore.2024.123383

Nicholls-Nixon, C. L., Singh, R. M., Hassannezhad Chavoushi, Z., & Valliere, D. (2024). How university business incubation supports entrepreneurs in technology-based and creative industries: A comparative study. *Journal of Small Business Management*, 62(2), 591–627. DOI: 10.1080/00472778.2022.2073360

Nziku, D. M., Mugione, F., & Salamzadeh, A. (2024). Women Entrepreneurship in the Middle East. In *Women Entrepreneurs in the Middle East* (pp. 23–52). Context, Ecosystems, and Future Perspectives for the Region. DOI: 10.1142/9789811283499_0003

Potter, J., Halabisky, D., Lavison, C., Boschmans, K., Shah, P., Shymanski, H., & Reid, A. (2023). Assessment of policies, programmes and regulations relating to MSME and start-up development in Abu Dhabi. https://www.oecd-ilibrary.org/content/paper/9b92546e-en

Priyono, A., & Hidayat, A. (2024). Fostering innovation through learning from digital business ecosystem: A dynamic capability perspective. *Journal of Open Innovation*, 10(1), 100196. DOI: 10.1016/j.joitmc.2023.100196

Ramadani, V., Alkaabi, K. A., & Zeqiri, J. (2024). Entrepreneurial mindset and family business performance: The United Arab Emirates perspectives. *Journal of Enterprising Communities: People and Places in the Global Economy*, 18(3), 682–700. DOI: 10.1108/JEC-08-2023-0153

Razavi Hajiagha, S. H., Ahmadzadeh Kandi, N., Amoozad Mahdiraji, H., Jafari-Sadeghi, V., & Hashemi, S. S. (2022). International entrepreneurial startups' location under uncertainty through a heterogeneous multi-layer decision-making approach: Evidence and application of an emerging economy. *International Journal of Entrepreneurial Behaviour & Research*, 28(3), 767–800. DOI: 10.1108/IJEBR-05-2021-0387

Sabiha, T., & Saida, S. (2024). The role of startups in promoting the development of smart cities–dubai as a model. *International Journal of Professional Business Review*, 9(5), 7. https://dialnet.unirioja.es/servlet/articulo?codigo=9570054

Shepherd, D. A., Souitaris, V., & Gruber, M. (2021). Creating new ventures: A review and research agenda. *Journal of Management*, 47(1), 11–42. DOI: 10.1177/0149206319900537

Surya, B., Menne, F., Sabhan, H., Suriani, S., Abubakar, H., & Idris, M. (2021). Economic growth, increasing productivity of SMEs, and open innovation. *Journal of Open Innovation*, 7(1), 20. DOI: 10.3390/joitmc7010020

Terribile, E., & Aquilina, R. (2023). The Impact of a Business Incubation Centre On Business Enterprises in Gozo. *MCAST Journal of Applied Research & Practice*, 7(2), 190–208. DOI: 10.5604/01.3001.0053.7301

Trethewey-Mould, R. L., & Moos, M. N. (2024). A stakeholder approach towards a consolidated framework for measuring business incubator efficacy. *The Southern African Journal of Entrepreneurship and Small Business Management*, 16(1), 776. DOI: 10.4102/sajesbm.v16i1.776

Uctu, R., & Al-Silefanee, R. (2024). Understanding Entrepreneurial Ecosystem in the MIDDLE EAST: Insights from Isenberg's Model. *International Journal of Entrepreneurial Knowledge*, 12(1), 86–109. https://www.ijek.org/index.php/IJEK/article/view/211. DOI: 10.37335/ijek.v12i1.211

Usman, F. O., Kess-Momoh, A. J., Ibeh, C. V., Elufioye, A. E., Ilojianya, V. I., & Oyeyemi, O. P. (2024). Entrepreneurial innovations and trends: A global review: Examining emerging trends, challenges, and opportunities in the field of entrepreneurship, with a focus on how technology and globalization are shaping new business ventures. *International Journal of Science and Research Archive*, 11(1), 552–569. DOI: 10.30574/ijsra.2024.11.1.0079

Vaz, R., de Carvalho, J. V., & Teixeira, S. F. (2023). Developing a digital business incubator model to foster entrepreneurship, business growth, and academia–industry connections. *Sustainability (Basel)*, 15(9), 7209. DOI: 10.3390/su15097209

Vîrjan, D., Manole, A. M., Stanef-Puică, M. R., Chenic, A. S., Papuc, C. M., Huru, D., & Bănacu, C. S. (2023). Competitiveness—The engine that boosts economic growth and revives the economy. *Frontiers in Environmental Science*, 11, 1130173. DOI: 10.3389/fenvs.2023.1130173

KEY TERMS AND DEFINITIONS

Business Incubation: A support process that helps startups and new businesses grow by providing resources like mentorship, access to funding, networking opportunities, and office space, to increase their chances of survival and success.

Community Engagement: Active participation and collaboration with community members to address local challenges, foster development, and create shared value, enhancing social cohesion and collective well-being.

Diversity and Inclusion: Strategies and practices to ensure that different identities, backgrounds, and perspectives are represented and valued within organizations and communities, promoting equity and reducing discrimination.

Economic Growth: The increase in the production of goods and services in an economy over time, often measured by the rise in Gross Domestic Product (GDP) and reflecting improvements in wealth, standards of living, and prosperity.

Economic Impact: The effect of an activity, policy, or program on the economy, measured in terms of job creation, revenue generation, economic growth, and wealth distribution within a particular area or community.

Entrepreneurial Ecosystems: The network of stakeholders, resources, and institutional support that enables entrepreneurship to thrive, including access to capital, mentorship, government policies, educational institutions, and industry connections.

Entrepreneurship: The process of identifying, developing, and bringing a unique idea or product to market, typically through the establishment of a new business or venture. It involves innovation, risk-taking, and the pursuit of profit.

Innovation: The creation and application of new ideas, products, or processes that improve performance, solve problems or meet new market needs, driving growth and competitive advantage.

Job Creation: The process of generating new employment opportunities, either through business expansion, the establishment of new businesses, or economic policies, often seen as a critical goal of economic development initiatives.

Social Impact: The effect of an activity or program on societal well-being, including improvements in quality of life, social equity, community welfare, and opportunities for underrepresented groups.

Social Ramifications: The wide-ranging effects or consequences of an action, decision, policy, or event on society. Social ramifications include changes in social behavior, cultural norms, quality of life, community dynamics, and societal values.

Chapter 7

Antecedents and Outcomes of Knowledge Sharing in Business Incubators From Social Capital Theory's Perspective

Masoumeh Zibarzani
Alzahra University, Iran

Mohd Zaidi Abd Rozan
https://orcid.org/0000-0003-1409-4522
Universiti Teknologi Malaysia, Malaysia

ABSTRACT

Knowledge sharing (KS) is referred to as an important strategy for improving innovation, productivity, efficiency, and competitiveness of organizations. The outcomes of KS are explained from different standpoints. However, previous studies significantly fail to explore the outcomes of KS from a relationship marketing (RM) perspective. This study examined the outcomes of KS on an organization's performance and relationship with customers in business incubators in Malaysia drawing on the social capital theory and RM concepts. The study used a quantitative PLS-SEM approach and using a cross-sectional survey method data was collected from 104 randomly selected respondents. Results reveal that the overall relationship between KS and the customer relationship is significant. The findings indicate that the KS has a positive effect on customer relationships and work performance. This

DOI: 10.4018/979-8-3693-4302-9.ch007

research expands the understanding of the effects of KS on organizations from the RM perspective in business incubators in Malaysia.

INTRODUCTION

Knowledge is recognized as a crucial resource within organizations, particularly in the contexts of competition and performance. The processes of creating, encoding, storing, managing, and disseminating knowledge attract considerable attention. Research has shown that knowledge management (KM) processes, especially Knowledge Sharing (KS), are definitelyrelated to the success of the organization in product success,financial and performance(Alharbi & Aloud, 2024). Explicitly, knowledge only uncovers its value when it is shared (Hsu & Wang, 2008).

Aslani et al. (2012) define KS as "the communication process in which one or two parts of an organization participate in knowledge transfer to develop new technologies, new products, etc." Evidently, KS impacts organizational performances at various levels (Wang & Noe, 2010). Different frameworks are developed to identify and assess the anticipated benefits of KS from diverse angles, pertaining to the context of study, type of organization, and numerous other factors. Although KS is crucial, its effectiveness is largely determined by the methods of knowledge retention and sharing. Additionally, the antecedents to KS play a significant role. Furthermore, the impact of KS on both the organization and its individuals is noteworthy. Therefore, to gain a comprehensive understanding of KS across various contexts, it is essential to consider three primary categories of factors: the antecedents of KS, the operationalization of KS, and the outcomes of KS.

Business incubators are one of the organizations that are in dire need of knowledge. They are specialized programs that provide a space for new businesses in their early days. The program supports new entrepreneurs and startups with services and support that help young businesses grow and reach their dependency on the market (Nicholls-Nixon et al., 2018). Such an organization is heavily dependent on the knowledge. They have to help startups to overcome initial challenges. Fostering collaboration between startups, mentors, and parent organizations is one way to help startups survive and grow. Moreover, informal communication networks among incubatees are essential. Startups, in nature, are often knowledge-intensive but are far from adequate communication and knowledge acquisition. KS can bridge this gap.

This motivates us to dive into the role of KS and how it can be strengthened in the incubators. Although KM in general and KS in specific are topics covered in academic literature, research on business incubators in Malaysia is scarce. Moreover, how social issues in the business incubator affect KS is not well understood. Furthermore, tenants are customers of a business incubator and business incubators rely on the resources gained from the relationship with their customers. Yet, the effects of KS have not been well examined from the perspective of the relationship between incubators and tenants. Therefore, there is a need for further research on KS within an incubator setting. Our systematic review of the literature discovered a significant gap in finding the outcomes of KS from the RM perspective. RM includes emotional and behavioral concepts such as reciprocity and trust (Yau et al., 2000), which are essential enablers for any sharing bond. On the other hand, it is typical to investigate the outcomes of KS and assess its success based on organizational metrics. Examining the outcomes of sharing from the RM perspective signifies a new approach, particularly in the context of the business incubators' performance.

This new approach is warranted for two following reasons. First, the previous studies examined the outcomes of KS in terms of performance from a management point of view which has been applied in a few studies of business incubators on (Adlešič & Slavec, 2012). Second, evolutionary approaches to the outcomes of KS in the form of the firm's performance have emphasized the organizations' success in reaching goals and objectives (Mendez-Duron & Garcia, 2009); however, not in terms of the firm's relationship with the customers. Therefore, our aim is to realize the following objectives: a) to identify the key internal factors affecting the KS in business incubators, b) to investigate the nature of KS among incubates, and c) to analyze the impacts of KS incubatees performance.

In the next section, the background and theoretical foundation of the arguments are presented. Next, the method of the study is explained in detail. Finally, the results are presented and discussed. The implication and the future directions are provided.

BACKGROUND

KS and Organizations

Providing access to pricelessknowledge and information is considered one of the most centralissues in the KM upon which most of the tiesare formed, and relations are established (Patnayakuni et al., 2006). Members of an organization engage in connections to access necessary information, expertise, and solutions to recurring problems, often obtaining this information more freely through informal interactions(Wang & Noe, 2010). Internal informal and mutual knowledge exchanges between individuals are free of charge, sustained over time, and beneficial. KS facilitates the development, innovation, and learning process (Kankanhalli et al., 2012) and contributes to operational effectiveness and competitive advantage (Cadima et al., 2012). A well-devised interaction framework that supports the transfer of internal knowledge will have gross benefits to the beholding organization (Wada et al., 2009). According to King and Marks (2008), KS cannot be fulfilled without the contribution of individuals to an informal sharing process or a communication system. According to (Widén-Wulff & Ginman, 2004)one of the challenges in KSis thesocial challenge related to forming communities that encourage KS. It requires the engagement of individuals and reasonable social interactions to effectively function as a channel of dissemination(Yan et al., 2023). Thus, it is vitalto learn about the role of people, their behaviors, and other social matters regarding KS (Wiig, 2002).

Business Incubators

Business incubators are one of the many but the most comprehensive programs, mainly designed to support business startupsin the first stages, which are highly critical (Nicholls-Nixon et al., 2018). A crucial component of the regional innovation system, they assist with technologydevelopment and lead to productivity and employment generation (Yang et al., 2024).

The early examples of business incubators provided early-stage companies with rental space and limited business consulting (Hackett & Dilts, 2004). Soon they shapeshifted into facilities that aimed at providing strategic, value-adding interventions (Jamil et al., 2015). Today, we define a business incubator as a process rather than a facility, that boosts the development of startups and provides an array of targeted resources and services to early-stage startups. They are entities that ensure business success for new technologicalendeavors with their understanding of the business environment, mentoring and legal services, as well as networking (Valliere & Nicholls-Nixon, 2024).

A startup needs to focus on innovation and entrepreneurship as much as the interaction with other innovators, researchers, and industries if they seek a sustainable business (Yang et al., 2024). Despite common belief, startups' success is not only dependent on innovation and high-technology products. It is widely knownthat new venture creation is "a multi-dimensional phenomenon" (Redondo & Camarero, 2020). Researchers have constantly arguedhow such programs be structured for better support and increased success rates. New businessesfunction within a social system embedded in business incubators (Li et al., 2020). As a result, among numerousvariables relating to the new firm in an incubator, their social contributions have been a primary focus by researchers to date(Yang et al., 2024).

While business assistance is a strategically crucial aspect of support, the relationship between a business incubator and its tenants as clients is also an important issue(Abduh et al., 2007). The satisfaction of tenants from a client's perspective with the assistance services provided by their incubators can determine the efficacy and efficiency of incubation programs (Allen & Bezan, 1990). The quality perception of managers is highly tied to their view of the performance of services (Abduh, 2003).

Nonetheless, it is critically important to identify the expectations perceived by clients and to acknowledge the potential discrepancies between these views(Vanderstraeten & Matthyssens, 2012). Meeting tenant expectations is the cornerstone of a good incubator performance evaluation, as reasonedby scholars(Vanderstraeten et al., 2014). Not only the consideration of tenants' perspective as clients is essential to the incubation services' success, but it also relates to incubators' reputation. Since only satisfied customers will provide word-of-mouth to potential clients (Abduh et al., 2007). Meanwhile, tenants depend on the incubator's reputation or credibility to enter the sector or secure external resources(Ferguson & Olofsson, 2004).

Incubators in Malaysia

Malaysia has joined international efforts in business incubation since the 90s when they joined the National Business Incubator Association (NBIA) in 1998. Malaysian initiatives to support entrepreneurial activities have developed vastly in the past decade. Digital Economy Corporation (MdeC) is one of the oldest governing bodies that ensures an enabling environment for small companies is developed, especially the ICT sector. One specifically designed technopreneurship agency, Multimedia Development Corporation (MdeC) kicked a flagship program of incubation in collaboration with the National Incubator Network Association (NINA) to support ICT SMEs (Indiran et al., 2021). They connect with various parties and government agencies to provide the required resources for the same cause. The findings of the MdeC impact survey affirm that MSC Malaysia has affected Malaysia's economy in a positive way (Ishak & Khairudin, 2020). In recent years, Malaysia has observed a growth inthe number of incubators all over the country. MdeC has expanded the eUsahawan (eU) Hub in a strategic collaboration with other partner organizations, as the touch points that increase digital entrepreneurship skills and business activities for communities. This network of hubs currently constitutes 199 centers throughout Malaysia that offer training, mentoring, and access to limited facilities such as stable Internet access. In addition, there are 117 MARA district offices and 14 MARA state offices that offer outreach programs and advisory services. Moreover, MTDC and major Universities and research centers run five Technology Incubator Centers that offer space rental for Startups and SMEs. In addition to this, nineteen private incubators are active in the country. The number of incubators is more than 20 times the number in 2015 (Jamil et al., 2015)which shows an exponential growth. Malaysia's third industrial master plan (2006-2020) emphasized the promotion of small enterprises. Due to strategies of the Malaysian government, a notable number of international incubators are currently performing in Malaysia and franchises or branches were not studied. The majority of Malaysian business incubators provide basic incubator facilities as well asadvisory and training services (Saffar, 2008).

Themajority of the incubators in Malaysia are set up by government-owned or government-related organizations,a trend that has been in place since 2014 when 94% of the incubators were still entrenched in the real-estate model with minimal business services(Khalid et al., 2014). The incubation process and services provided still are far from perfect and could be enhanced to become more effective. In addition, the viewpoint of 'incubator as a service provider' is missing from them.

Aim of the Study

This research aims to understand how KS practices influence organizational performance and to examine the impacts of KS within Malaysian business incubators. The study assesses the performance of these incubators through the lens of RM concepts, emphasizing the role of tenants as customers and the significance of customer-to-business relationships. Additionally, it explores social relationships and their configurations as key factors in KS. Currently, no existing model incorporates anRM perspective to delineate the outcomes of KS, nor does any model depict the role of social factors in KS practices in Malaysian business incubators. This project seeks to make a theoretical contribution to our understanding of KS and its effects on business incubators, viewed through an RM framework. There is also a pressing need, both in the academic literature and in practice, to explore the outcomes of KS from an RM standpoint. Viewing incubation as a service and tenants as service users will offer deeper insights into the current scenarios. While this study focuses on exploring KS and its outcomes in business incubators, discussions on the governance of business incubators and the success factors of incubation services are outside its scope. The study proposes using RM concepts to operationalize organizational performance. For this purpose, the type of organization chosen was business incubators in Malaysia, considering customer relationships at an individual level (employees of tenant startups).

Therefore, the basic research question that needs to be addressed is: How does KS improve organizational performance in Malaysia, and how it can be assessed?

This is dividedinto the following sub-questions:

What are the determinants and outcomes of KS intention, attitude, and extent among organization members?

How does a theoretical framework illustrate the relationship between KS and organizational performance at individual, team, and organizational in Malaysian incubators the best?

Which model is the best to explain the KS determinants and outcomes in this context and how to evaluate it?

The research questions arose from a systematic inspection and review of the literature onknowledge management and the incubator process. In this review, 173 published studies relevant to this research were analyzed. The review helped to identify the areas for further research. Key motivation theories were explored to determine the potential connection between KS, its determinants, and outcomes, and to formulate the theoretical framework. The research outcomes will enhance the understanding of how KS correlates with performance attributes in Malaysian business incubators. Additionally, this knowledge will assist managers, policymakers, and practitioners in making informed decisions about incubation strategies for business incubators in Malaysia.

Theoretical Framework

This study revolves around the social capital theory (Nahapiet & Ghoshal, 1998). Three basic interrelated dimensions of social capital are structural, cognitive, and relational (Lee et al., 2019) that formulated the antecedents of the KS. A notable number of scholars use this theory in the context of the relationship between organization and employee behavior, particularly in KS or integration (Chiu et al., 2006; Robert et al., 2008; van den Hooff & Huysman, 2009). KS is a multi-dimensional activity, a complex nature with social mechanisms behind it. The overall assumption is that KS occurs over the social relations that are informal and are created among the personnel of the organization. Hence, the social capital theory has also been utilized for explaining individual behavior, particularly in KS and organizational performance (Chiu et al., 2006). In addition, this theory facilitates the study of social resources, coordination, and cooperation for mutual benefit that enhances firm competencies and helps knowledge-intensive companies, suchas incubatees(Yan et al., 2023). The invaluable resources such as novel and refined knowledge could be channeled via social capital and social ties among the incubatees to the organizations. Thus, social capital dimensions are claimed to strongly influence KS due to the social nature of KS (Widén-Wulff & Ginman, 2004). However, one should differentiate between dimensions of social capital. Whereas the structural social capital principals' network and social relations via which the information travels within the incubators, the cognitive dimension involves the shared values on incubates that eventually make up the behavior of sharing. Finally, the relational dimension dictates the level of trust and normalization of mutual objectives that ease the interaction of information(Widén-Wulff & Ginman, 2004). The discussion so far leads to the following hypotheses:

H1: The structural social capital embedded in the community of incubatees has a positive impact on the members' KS (a) intention, (b) attitude, and (c) extent.

H2: The relational social capital embedded in the community of incubateeshas a positive impact on KS (a) intention, (b) attitude, and (c) extent.

H3: The cognitive social capital embedded in the community of incubateeshas a positive impact on KS (a) intention, (b) attitude, and (c) extent.

H4: The structural dimension of Social Capital (SC) has a positive effect on (a) relational SC and (b) cognitive SC.

H5: Cognitive SC has a positive effect on relational SC.

Scholars have highlighted the role that knowledge plays as a principal source for business firms to gain sustained competitive advantage (Cadima et al., 2012). A firm's ability to generate exchange and utilize its resources, which in this case is knowledge, into useful resources should lead to superior performance (Ngah & Ibrahim, 2008). Any organization, for example, can benefit from cost reduction or timely and detailed reporting, that enables timely response to customer needs, increasing firm performance (Wang & Noe, 2010). More specifically, knowledge-based firms such as incubatees need more than just value creation harvested from retaining knowledge. Their very livelihood depends on innovation and eventually increased performance(Valliere & Nicholls-Nixon, 2024).

Previous studies of KS literature have highlighted the idea that knowledge benefits the performance (Rustiarini et al., 2020). Management scholars emphasize the significance of KS for business performance(Reagans et al., 2004). However, the authors found considerable interest in studying the relationship between KS and RM's perspective of performance, and marketing performance for a few reasons. First, in a knowledge-intensive firm, both competitive advantage and organizational performance are often traced to knowledge and information (Nonaka et al., 2000). Second, the RM research literature indicates that collecting performance measures from both business performance and marketing views, separately, adds value toan understanding of performance (Farida et al., 2017). It is reasonable to assume that higher KS activities in the organization lead to higher relationship strength and relationship performance (Rustiarini et al., 2020). Performance from a traditional view (i.e., objective or subjective) and customer perspectives (i.e. subjective RM constructs) are equally important considerations and reflect the outcomes of KS on the firm. Based on these foundations, the authors proposed that KS influenced the firms' business performance as well as marketing performance. Business performance construct is identified in three levels individual, team, and organizational (Setini et al., 2020). Marketing performance, however, is operationalized by two general RM constructs that embody the four top-cited defining constructs of the RM discipline (Richard et al., 2007; Yanuarti & Murwatiningsih, 2019); relationship strength and relationship performance for parsimony purposes.

Therefore, the following hypotheses are formulated:

H6: KS intention of incubatee employees positively influences (a) individual, (b) team, (c) organizational work performance.

H7: KS attitude of incubatee employees positively influences (a) individual, (b) team, and (c) organizational work performance.

H8: KS extent of incubatee employees positively influences (a) individual, (b) team, and (c) organizational work performance.

H9: KS intention of incubatee employees positively influences (a) relationship strength and (b) relationship performance between the organization and customers.

H10: KS attitude of incubatee employees positively influences (a) relationship strength and (b) relationship performance between the organization and customers.

H11: KS extent of incubatee employees positively influences (a) relationship strength and (b) relationship performance between the organization and customers.

In addition, the relationship of components of KS and RM is considered:

H12: KS attitude positively influences KS intention

H13: KS intention positively influences KS extent

H14: Individual work performance positively affects teamwork performance.

H15: Teamwork performance positively affects organizational work performance.

H16: Relationship strength positively affects relationship performance.

Along with the aforementioned constructs, we examined the incubators' success in terms of their relationship with startups. Startups, here seen as customers to the incubators, have a relationship with their host, like any other organization that serves customers. Customers' behavior intentions to be willing to keep a sustainable relationship with the incubator appear to be of value for the incubator's sustainability (Zeithaml et al., 1996). Some behaviors depict the willingness of customers to keep a bond with the firm. Behavioral indicators offer some evidence that customer perceptions positively affect future intentions (Gieure et al., 2020). Future intentions may be illustrated in the forms of purchase, praising, spreading word-of-mouth, etc. (Zeithaml et al., 1996) and are considered as behavioral outcomes of RM constructs, such as commitment (Hennig-Thurau et al., 2002), satisfaction (Zeithaml et al., 1996), trust (Garbarino & Johnson, 1999), or loyalty (Gounaris, 2007). Customers' behavioral intention is a kind of emotional commitment to the firm. The higher the perception of determinants (relationship strength and relationship performance), the higher it is to accept customers to behave in favor of the firm and keep the relationship. Relationship strength and performance, therefore, impact the future intention of customers to keep their relationship with the organization. On these grounds:

H17: Relationship strength positively influences the future intention of customers to keep relationships.

H18: Relationship performance positively influences the future intention of customers to keep relationships.

METHODOLOGY

The hypotheses were tested relying on a PLS-SEM approach using the software SmartPLS. The summary of the design of the study is depicted in Figure 1. The measures (Table A in Appendix) were selected from previous studies except one of the items that were designed by the researcher ("I'll offer consulting to the new Startup in this incubator after we graduate"). For these measurements, a five-point Likert scale is employed in this thesis (5=Strongly agree, 1=Strongly disagree 5=Much Better, 1=Much Worse). In addition, two name-generator questions are used to help respondents identify their contact networks and answer a few questions about each of them. This data was applied to calculate three measures of the network data for each respondent. Measures used for measuring the structural dimension of social capital were network measures for individuals consisting of the standard and well-known measures in the network literature suggested by (Borgatti et al., 1998). The criteria for selecting the measures were that they should not necessitate additional data about the contacts beyond the connections themselves and should be calculated for each individual considering the characteristics of the entire network. Table 1 summarizes how three selected measures were operationalized and calculated in this study.

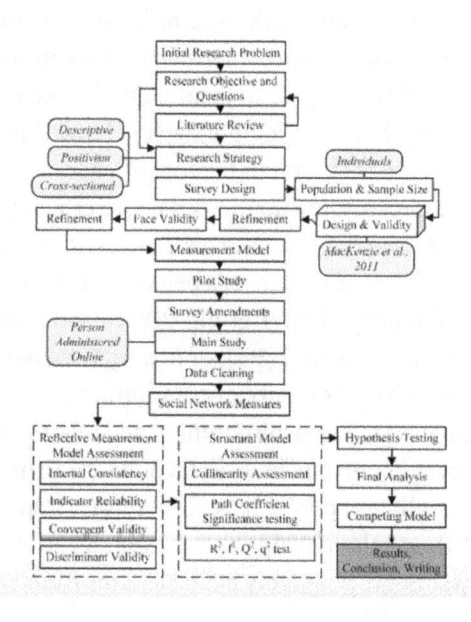

Table 1. Calculation of Network Measures

Name	Definition	Operationalization
Degree	The sum of the average of weights attached to any contact of an individual	$\sum \left(\dfrac{EC \times IF}{2} \right)$ Later normalized by the min-max method $x' = \dfrac{x - x_{min}}{x_{max} - x_{min}}$
Heterogeneity	The variety of contacts with respect to relevant dimensions (e.g., sex, age, knowledge and expertise).	The total number of knowledge and expertise seen in an individual's contacts
Compositional Quality	The number of contacts with high levels of needed characteristics (e.g., expertise in a specific field)	The number of contacts that received one of two higher rates in at least one expertise (more than 4)

Table 2 summarizes the minimum sample size required in this study using two methods. As the list of incubation programs in Malaysia was accessible, simple random sampling was feasible.

Table 2. Sample Size

	(Cohen, 1992)	**G*Power (Faul et al., 2007)**
Sample Size	59	77

Validity

A few steps were undertaken to develop and validate scales following MacKenzie et al. (2011) guidelines. An instrument was created that included a matrix of variables, and the items produced were organized for review. Raters were then asked to evaluate each item. Rates are captured from Information Systems Post-Graduate students, Universiti Teknologi Malaysia using a five-point Likert-type scale ranging from 1 (meaning the item doesn't capture the variable at all) to 5 (meaning the item captures the variable completely). Participants were asked to rate if each item belongs to the domain on a 5-point Likert-type scale ranging from 1 (Not at all) to 5 (Completely). A total of 30 responses were captured which is adequate to have a sound analysis (Yao et al., 2008). The total number of items for each segment is reported in Table 3. Note that the SC dimensions are not included in this process.

Table 3. Items and Constructs

	Number of domains	Number of items in total
KS Constructs	3	18
Performance Constructs	3	26
RM Constructs	4	18
Total	-	62

First, the mean rates of each item are compared to other items in terms of the construct it should represent. Later, the rates are analyzed by one-way repeated measures ANOVA for each item in order to make sure the item has the highest appropriateness score concerning the meant construct (Yao et al., 2008). The analysis is done using SPSS 23.0. Fourteen items out of 62 were deleted. Once the survey was prepared, it was sent to experts relevant to the field for 'face validity' including questions wording, sequence and layout, and further professional refinement. A total number of 30 emails were sent. A total number of five responses were received. The modifications suggested and applied were mainly about the wording or length of questions. A cross-sectional person-administered survey was used to collect the data (Cardona et al., 2017). In addition, before starting data collection and in accordance, a pilot test was conducted to test the questionnaire with 31 participants attending (Issac & Michael, 1981) using SmartPLS. Based on the results of Cronbach's alpha test, 16 items were removed in order to improve the predictive power of the measurement model in terms of reliability and validity of measures, the researcher removed problematic items.The validity of the measurement model was tested using criteria summarized in Table 4.

Table 4. Measurement Model Assessment Criteria

Assessment	Criterion	Value
Internal consistency reliability	Composite reliability	higher than 0.7
Convergent validity	Outer loading	higher than 0.4, preferably higher than 0.7
	AVE	higher than 0.5
Discriminant validity	Fornell-Larcker criterion	The square root of AVE is higher than the correlation among construct

Main Study

The main data collection phase was done using the survey for a duration of 7 months. The response rate was 93% percent, which is, higher than the acceptable limit (Table 5).Out of 104 respondents, 59 of them were male (56.7%). The majority of respondents surveyed were from the 31-39 age group (33.7%). The 25-30 age group came second (29.8%), which was closely followed by the below-25 age group (23.1%). The majority of respondents surveyed were having a bachelor's degree (41.3%), which was closely followed by the Certificate/Diploma group (32.7%). The respondents with a master's degree came third (13.5%). A small portion of respondents held an MBA degree (7.7%). The majority of respondents surveyed were incubator tenants for less than 1 month (41.9%). The second is the "2-6 months" group (32.3%). But, 80.7 percent of respondents were tenants for less than 1 year. Additionally, it was revealed that a notable portion of respondents (23.1%) had not started their business officially.

Table 5. Responses

Total number of observations	survey non-response	Non-Eligible responses	Valid responses
133	13	16	104

Values of composite reliability and AVE for all constructs are above 0.7 and 0.5, respectively.Moreover, all constructs meet the discriminant validity using the Fornell-Larcker approach (Fornell & Larcker, 1981). A PLS path modeling analysis was then used utilizing SmartPLS to validate the proposed model and test the stipulated hypotheses. The path model is depicted in Figure 2.

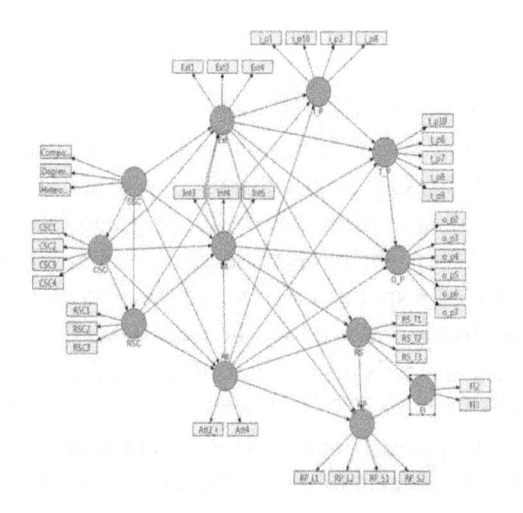

Results

The strength of the structural model was evaluated, t value(Table 6). Out of 34 paths, 16 paths are not statistically significant, and one path can be considered as 'partially significant'. Results are summarized in Table 7, and illustrated in Figure 3.

Table 6. Critical Values for Path Significance Testing

Critical value	Significance level			
	Not significant	1%	5%	10%
t value	Less than 1.65	>=1.65	>=1.96	>=2.57
Symbol	NS	*	**	***

Table 7. Summary of Results

		Att					CSC		
	Sig Level	path coefficient	f^2 Effect Size	q^2 Effect Size		Sig Level	path coefficient	f^2 Effect Size	q^2 Effect Size
CSC	***	0.4377	0.171	0.117	SSC	NS	0.0286	0.001	NA
RSC	NS	0.0383	-0.027	-0.028			Ext		
SSC	NS	0.0271	0.001	-0.004		Sig Level	path coefficient	f^2 Effect Size	q^2 Effect Size

continued on following page

Table 7. Continued

		Att					CSC		
	Sig Level	path coefficient	f² Effect Size	q² Effect Size		Sig Level	path coefficient	f² Effect Size	q² Effect Size
			FI		CSC	NS	0.1651	0.026	0.006
	Sig Level	path coefficient	f² Effect Size	q² Effect Size	Int	***	0.5108	0.334	0.188
RP	**	0.2285	0.051	0.036	RSC	NS	-0.0610	-0.002	-0.002
RS	***	0.4870	0.269	0.154	SSC	NS	0.0545	0.004	0.005
			I_P				Int		
	Sig Level	path coefficient	f² Effect Size	q² Effect Size		Sig Level	path coefficient	f² Effect Size	q² Effect Size
Att	NS	-0.2236	0.054	0.032	Att	***	0.5416	0.387	0.148
Ext	***	0.4924	0.265	0.11	CSC	NS	0.0701	0.001	-0.033
Int	***	0.3525	0.114	0.035	RSC	NS	0.1065	0.006	-0.002
			O_P		SSC	NS	0.0104	-0.00049	-0.026
	Sig Level	path coefficient	f² Effect Size	q² Effect Size			RP		
Att	**	0.0569	0.004	-0.003		Sig Level	path coefficient	f² Effect Size	q² Effect Size
Ext	***	0.3622	0.127	0.073	Att	**	0.2064	0.059	0.011
Int	*	0.1976	0.033	0.035	Ext	***	0.3071	0.124	0.061
T_p	NS	0.1799	0.037	0.017	Int	NS	0.1013	0.014	0.028
			RSC		RS	***	0.3369	0.157	0.06
	Sig Level	path coefficient	f² Effect Size	q² Effect Size			RS		
CSC	***	0.5283	0.411	0.204		Sig Level	path coefficient	f² Effect Size	q² Effect Size
SSC	**	0.2004	0.066	0.016	Att	NS	0.0445	0.002	0.198
			T_P		Ext	***	0.3791	0.129	0.294
	Sig Level	path coefficient	f² Effect Size	q² Effect Size	Int	NS	0.1641	0.019	0.232
Att	NS	0.0477	0.002	0.027					

CSC: cognitive social capital, RSC: relational social capital; SSC: structural social capital; Int: KS intention; Att: KS attitude; Ext: KS Extent; I_P: individual performance; T_P: team performance; O_P: organizational performance; FI: future intention; RS: relationship strength; RP: relationship performance

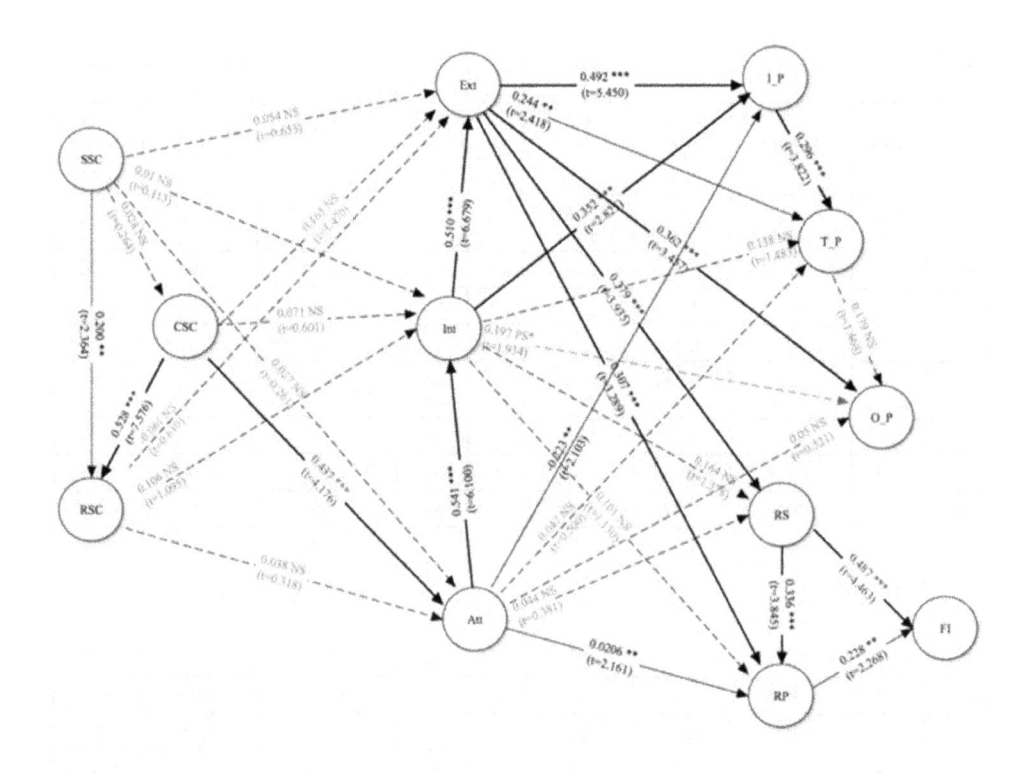

COMPETING MODEL

As explained earlier, almost half of the assumed hypotheses in this study were supported. Although there were no assumptions on the existence of full mediation effects, a mediation analysis was conducted. The results from this analysis and the results of the structural model assessment persuaded the author to provide the basis for a 'competing' model, which might better explain the effectiveness of constructs than the initial research model.

To put it briefly, 7 paths were omitted based on mediation analysis. On the other hand, SSC and RSC failed to explain any of the corresponding dependent variables. The attempt to have a second-order construct to remedy this issue has failed. Hence, both are deleted with the paths assigned to them.

The competing model is later analyzed through structural model assessment steps as shown in Figure 4. Table 8 summarizes the results of the structural model assessment for the competing model. Eliminating the effect of nonsignificant paths, three paths portray better statistical significance (Att →RP, Ext →TP, and T_P →O_P). The path Int →I_P, however, has a reduced significant value in the competing model.

That is due to omitting the mediating effect that affects the direct relationship. We can argue that this model is a better fit for the context of the study.

Table 8. Summary of Structural Model Assessment for Competing Model

	Path Coefficient	t value	Significance	P value	f²	q²
Att → Int	0.6038	7.8130	***	0.0000	0.574	NA
Att → RP	0.2483	3.2728	***	0.0014499	0.105	0.008
Att → RS	0.0424	0.3636	NS	0.716902	0.002	0.053
CSC → Att	0.4819	6.5058	***	0	0.302	NA
CSC → Ext	0.1385	1.4807	NS	0.1417391	0.024	0.009
Ext → I_P	0.4505	4.6675	***	0.0000092	0.216	0.079
Ext → O_P	0.4733	4.5948	***	0.0000123	0.263	0.116
Ext → RP	0.3389	3.7155	***	0.0003298	0.162	0.031
Ext → RS	0.3783	3.8628	***	0.0001961	0.13	0.146
Ext → T_P	0.3253	3.3852	***	0.0010076	0.104	0.06
I_P → T_P	0.3269	4.4639	***	0.0000206	0.107	0.044
Int → Ext	0.5052	6.5729	***	0	0.322	0.172
Int → I_P	0.2382	2.2623	**	0.0257785	0.063	0.011
Int → RS	0.1672	1.3736	NS	0.1725482	0.02	0.089
RP → FI	0.2286	2.2842	**	0.0244113	0.052	0.042
RS → FI	0.4868	4.5133	***	0.000017	0.269	0.178
RS → RP	0.3494	3.7760	***	0.0003	0.172	0.06
T_P → O_P	0.2292	1.9102	*	0.0588888	0.061	0.027

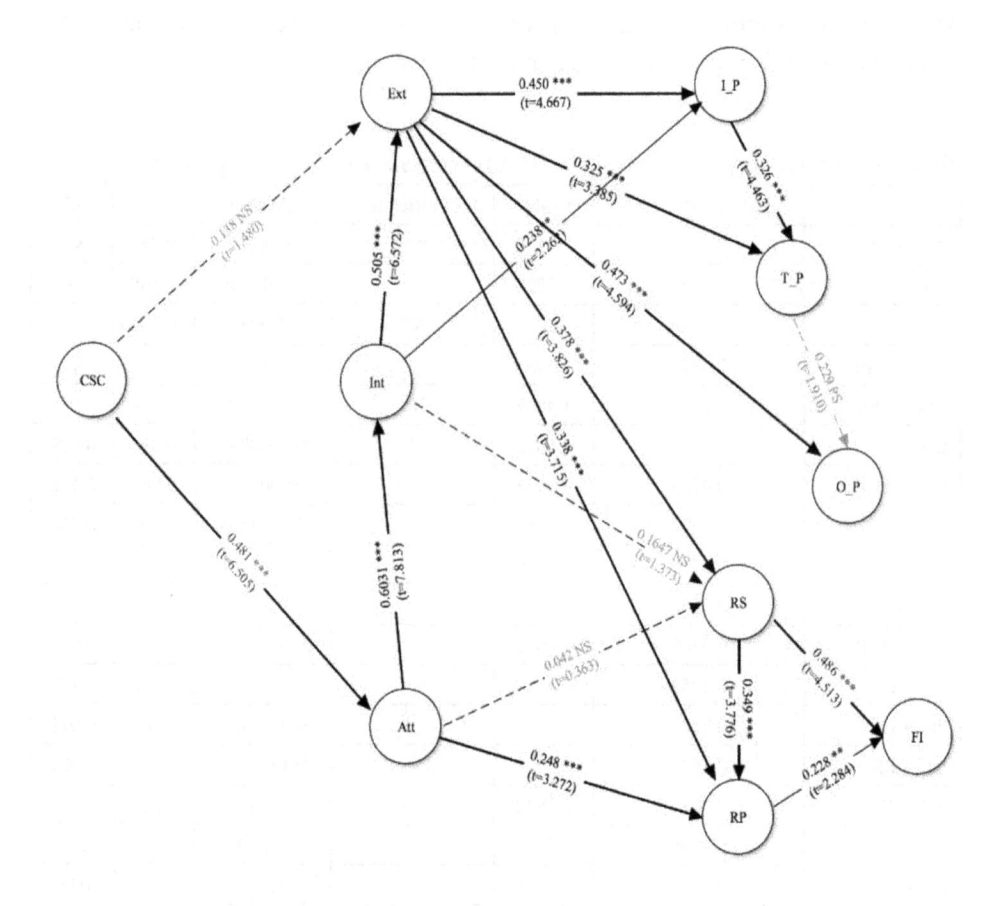

DISCUSSION

The current study suggests that incubators can be viewed as components of entrepreneurial ecosystems where the relational atmosphere among incubatees fosters beneficial connections that could enhance management efficiency. Reinforcing this idea, the primary objective of this study has been to investigate the social determinants and RM outcomes of KS in incubators in Malaysia. In doing so, this study has identified and tested SC dimensions as antecedents of KS. The outcomes of KS, on the other hand, have been investigated by the performance of work together in traditional operationalization together with RM concept constructs. The study has drawn upon the social capital theory and validated concepts in the RM context. This led to the conceptualization of the research model used in this study.

In answering research question one, it was found, directly contrary to expectation, that only cognitive of the dimensions of SC is affecting KS attitude, and results fail to support a meaningful relationship between relational and structural SC and any dimension of KS. This result indicates that, in the context of business incubators in Malaysia, the only determinant of KS components is shared understanding, norms, values, attitudes, beliefs, and common codes required for proper acting. A close network inside the incubator, where everyone is connected, does not provide relevant resources but facilitates access to other networks. While the pattern of interaction among individuals and access to other individuals or behavioral assets such as expectations and obligations don't affect KS.

The results contradict literature at the first glance, but they are consistent with a portion of previous studies that operationalized cognitive SC as the sole antecedent to KS (Rustiarini et al., 2020). One possible explanation should be found in the context of the study. Structural and relational dimensions of SC are best achieved and developed when the individuals share a longer history (Nahapiet & Ghoshal, 1998). Considering the fact that in specific contexts like business incubation, which is termed in nature, the majority of respondents (74.2%) have been incubator tenants for less than 6 months, it justifies the weak relationships. Cognitive SC, on the other hand, is a contextual factor of organizational climate promoted by organization management that reflects the caring of organization's members to help one another that is expected to lead individuals to go beyond the call of duty to share their work in the process (Bock et al., 2005).

This could be interpreted that sharing in business incubators does not strongly rely on the dense networks of connection or depth of connections (Redondo & Camarero, 2019). It rather is connected to the shared mindset of individuals and their shared feelings and actions. With respect to the effect of structural and cognitive SC, it is deducted that although the density of networks of connection does not affect KS, it strongly affectsthe depth of connections. So does the shared mindset of individuals and their shared feelings and actions. Although these effects could be of importance to managerial actions, the role of both structural and relational dimensions of SC had been overruled in creating any effect on KS and is not considered relevant, anymore.

In answer to question two, prior to interpreting findings on the role of KS in organizational performance at individual, team, and organizational levels or in the relationship between organization and customers, the interesting finding about the relationship between three constructs of KS is explained.

As expected, attitude towards KS strongly affects intention towards KS, which in turn affects the extent of sharing. Although it was expected because it accorded the literature (Bock & Kim, 2002), it was interesting when considering the answer to the previous question. Shared actions and mindsets among individuals in the organization (i.e. business incubator) are affecting only the attitude of individuals toward sharing, as an emotional construct, meaning individuals who are predisposed to higher cognitive SC tend to have a high level of positive attitudes toward sharing. A higher extent of KS does, however, appear to be contingent on individuals' intentions which are determined by positive attitudes, themselves.

In answer to question two, it was found that positive attitude and intentions and extent of KS were all significantly affecting individual performance. Nevertheless, when total effect and mediating effects were taken into consideration, this positive effect diminished and became insignificant for attitude. In the same fashion, organizational level work performance was explained by positive attitude and intentions and extent of KS, moderately, adequately, and strongly, respectively, which was reduced to the significant relationship of sharing extent solely. Team-level work performance, however, was explained only by sharing extent. To put it another way, sharing extent resulted in higher work performance at individual, team, and organizational levels. Intention towards KS only determined individual-level work performance. Finally, positive attitude did not directly affect any of the KS components and only had an indirect effect on them mediated via other KS components. It is confirmed in mediation analysis. These findings are consistent with previous studies that affirm the role of KS in performance (Christensen, 2007). However, these findings suggest that the influential nature attitude and intention towards KS in the Malaysian business incubator context are only through the mediation effect of sharing extent.

Not to mention, the relationship between work performance of each level was only affirmed in the case of individual level to the team level, suggesting that organizational performance is not related to later. It is reasonably correct in the study context, in which the organization is an incubator, while teams are Startups.

In answer to question three, the three components of KS did not explain the RM component similarly. Attitude only determined relationship performance, moderately. Intention, however, did not determine any. Sharing extent, on the other hand, strongly affected both relationship performance and relationship strength. The pattern is similar to the role of KS components in work performance. That is because of the relationship between KS components, itself. This suggests that the effects of KS components on work performance are not directly observable and must be examined through mediation of sharing extent. Mediator analysis and total effects proved that attitude and intention toward KS have strong indirect effects on relationship performance and relationship strength. The last but not the least, future intention (FI) is found to be related to other components of RM performance. It is worth mentioning that the relationship between relationship performance and relationship strength was affirmed, as expected.

These results approve the suggestion of this study that sharing outcomes could be studied through the RM lenses. That is the assessment results of the relationship between KS and the traditional view of performance accord with the results in the RM concepts. Higher KS activities in the organization led to higher relationship strength and relationship performance, and when the sharing is remarkable, the customers are likely to intend to keep a sustainable relationship with the organization.

IMPLICATIONS

Theoretical Implication

The primary theoretical contribution of our study to future research stems from achieving a deeper conceptual understanding of knowledge sharing through the lens of social capital theory in business incubators. More specifically, we contribute to the literature by firstly, employing marketing concepts in a business incubation context based on the idea that incubators provide service to tenants(Aernoudt, 2004), marketing models could be applicable to the relationship of tenants and incubators in this context.This study has. This is because incubators' aim to ensure the success of tenants and their sustainability relies on the attraction of more tenants to replace with graduated Startups, particularly, the private or semi-private incubators that do not rely on governmental funds. Moreover, incubators establish certain strategies to ensure the attraction of new investors, particularly the attraction of investors who are psychologically affected in their decisions by prior familiarity with the incubator. In any event, success in marketing requires a good enough solution for the incubators. In a traditional view, this solution is a good performance and public image. In RM, however, the solution is the relationship and how it functions and leads to need satisfaction for the customers. Therefore, incubators can employ certain strategies, which may ensure the best relationship with customers. This study has made substantial advancement in examining how internal relationships impact the decisions of tenant individuals regarding their future with the incubator.

Secondly, by applying the RM concepts, this study integrated the KS, work performance, and marketing issues. Clearly, by replacing commonly used work performance measures, this study identifies a new set of outcomes for KS, particularly in the business incubator context. This approach is in tandem with other studies (Abduh et al., 2007; Redondo et al., 2021), which are some of the few studies that have recognized incubators as service providers and have tried to investigate customer satisfaction with services. Having identified these specific outcomes of KS, this study assists future research in related areas, to test other RM variables and identify new ones. In addition, by having both work performance and RM outcomes, the research model has provided a comparable investigation by not relying upon one sole outcome.

Practical Implication

From a pragmatic perspective, the results of this study have several potential implications for business incubators. One implication of this finding is that a manager's task should be to encourage the internal networking of the incubatees in order to foster the links that might prove most profitable for them. To do so, managers should stimulate feelings of trust and reciprocity, since these relational ties portray the potential for encouraging the expansion of diverse and strong future relationships. Offering shared spaces and functions to promote interaction, activities for the incubator membersto network, and holding sharing meetings for sharing experiences, are some of the examples that help create a feeling of community among incubatees and collective social capital(Redondo & Camarero, 2019).

Moreover, the core foundation of this study is that the incubation process is a service provided for tenants. That being said, one must consider the role of service providers in business incubators for all stakeholders. Managers are the major providers that manage the whole process of service delivery. The consultants provide their expertise and skills as a service to the tenants. This schema applies to any other service and resource that is being provided to the tenants. Even the tenants, at some point, can be providers. Based on this view, it is no longer relevant to assume that the performance of the incubator should be evaluated based on actual outcomes, solely. Rather, the performance should be evaluated from the customers' point of view, as well.

The findings provide additional empirical support for the importance of KS in shaping performance and improving relationships with tenant firms in business incubators. Incubator managers might use these insights to reassess their strategies and introduce varied KS practices. Moreover, the results could be valuable to managers aiming to improve their relationships with tenant firms and establish strong client-organization connections.

Limitationsand Future Research Directions

The quantitative approach does not always provide comprehensive in-depth information and may pose a weakness in the description of the complex nature of human behavior. Moreover, KS can be seen from different levels of individual, team group, and organization levels. Thus, this complex process is influenced by a number of factors for each level. This work focused on only a few individual-level variables derived from the literature and theoretical principles. Future research may examine the effect by comparing it in different levels of individual, team group, and organization. Next, in the study of network status among tenant individuals that is used to measure the structural dimension of social capital for each of them, the researcher confined to individuals' attributes data in addition to relational data because none of the cases in Malaysia had acceptable numbers of member to fulfill required sample size.

CONCLUSION

This research has attempted to fill the void in the body of knowledge by investigating the role of KS in the relationship between business incubators and tenants. Drawing from a theory and combining the concepts from a different realm of studies, this study has conceptualized a research model that has been empirically validated using responses obtained from the online survey. However, the model was not fully supported, and a number of hypothesized relationships were not found to be significant in this specific context.

Based on these findings, this study has then discussed theoretical and practical implications for the business incubator context in Malaysia. Overall, the study results contribute to the body of knowledge by shedding light on the perceptual antecedents and consequences of KS in this specific context. Thus, the research model deepens the collective understanding of the relatively new concept of business incubation and also yields insights for practice. These insights can be used by managers of incubators in planning effective strategies toward better relationships with customers and attracting more resources in terms of expertise and finance.

REFERENCES

Abduh, M. (2003). *Exploring factors affecting perceived value added contributions of business incubation programs to tenants in Australia*. La Trobe University.

Abduh, M., D'Souza, C., Quazi, A., & Burley, H. T. (2007). Investigating and classifying clients' satisfaction with business incubator services. *Managing Service Quality*, 17(1), 74–91. DOI: 10.1108/09604520710720683

Adlešič, R. V., & Slavec, A. (2012). Social capital and business incubators performance: testing the structural model. *Economic and Business Review*, 14(3), 201-222. https://www.ebrjournal.net/ojs/index.php/ebr/article/view/145

Aernoudt, R. (2004). Incubators: Tool for entrepreneurship? *Small Business Economics*, 23(2), 127–135. DOI: 10.1023/B:SBEJ.0000027665.54173.23

Alharbi, G. L., & Aloud, M. E. (2024). The effects of knowledge management processes on service sector performance: Evidence from Saudi Arabia. *Humanities & Social Sciences Communications*, 11(1), 378. DOI: 10.1057/s41599-024-02876-y

Allen, D. N., & Bezan, E. J. (1990). *Value added contributions of Pennsylvania's business incubators to tenant firms and local economies*. Pennsylvania State University, Smeal College of Business Administration.

Aslani, F., Mousakhani, M., & Aslani, A. (2012). Knowledge Sharing: A Survey, Assessment and Directions for Future Research: Individual Behavior Perspective. *International Journal of Economics and Management Engineering*, 6(8), 2025–2029.

Bock, G. W., & Kim, Y. G. (2002). Determinants of the Individuals Knowledge Sharing Behavior: The Theory of Reasoned Action Perspective. *Proceedings of the Pacific-Asia Conference on Information System (PACIS)*. Meiji University.

Bock, G. W., Zmud, R. W., Kim, Y. G., & Lee, J. N. (2005). Behavioral intention formation in knowledge sharing: Examining the roles of extrinsic motivators, social-psychological forces, and organizational climate. *Management Information Systems Quarterly*, 29(1), 87–111. DOI: 10.2307/25148669

Borgatti, S. P., Jones, C., & Everett, M. G. (1998). Network measures of social capital. *Connections*, 21(2), 27–36.

Cadima, R., Ojeda, J., & Monguet, J. M. (2012). Social Networks and Performance in Distributed Learning Communities. *Educational Technology & Society*, 15(4), 296-304.

Cardona, A. R., Sun, Q., Li, F., & White, D. (2017). Assessing the effect of personal cultural orientation on brand equity and revisit intention: Exploring destination branding in Latin America. *Journal of Global Marketing*, 30(5), 282–296. DOI: 10.1080/08911762.2017.1336827

Chiu, C.-M., Hsu, M.-H., & Wang, E. T. (2006). Understanding knowledge sharing in virtual communities: An integration of social capital and social cognitive theories. *Decision Support Systems*, 42(3), 1872–1888. DOI: 10.1016/j.dss.2006.04.001

Chow, W. S., & Chan, L. S. (2008). Social network, social trust and shared goals in organizational knowledge sharing. *Information & Management*, 45(7), 458–465. DOI: 10.1016/j.im.2008.06.007

Christensen, P. H. (2007). Knowledge sharing: Moving away from the obsession with best practices. *Journal of Knowledge Management*, 11(1), 36–47. DOI: 10.1108/13673270710728222

Farida, N., Naryoso, A., & Yuniawan, A. (2017). Model of Relationship Marketing and E-Commerce in Improving Marketing Performance of Batik SMEs. *Journal of Database Management*, 8(1), 20–29.

Faul, F., Erdfelder, E., Lang, A.-G., & Buchner, A. (2007). G* Power 3: A flexible statistical power analysis program for the social, behavioral, and biomedical sciences. *Behavior Research Methods*, 39(2), 175–191. DOI: 10.3758/BF03193146 PMID: 17695343

Ferguson, R., & Olofsson, C. (2004). Science parks and the development of NTBFs—Location, survival and growth. *The Journal of Technology Transfer*, 29(1), 5–17. DOI: 10.1023/B:JOTT.0000011178.44095.cd

Fornell, C., & Larcker, D. F. (1981). Evaluating structural equation models with unobservable variables and measurement error. *JMR, Journal of Marketing Research*, 18(1), 39–50. DOI: 10.1177/002224378101800104

Gieure, C., del Mar Benavides-Espinosa, M., & Roig-Dobón, S. (2020). The entrepreneurial process: The link between intentions and behavior. *Journal of Business Research*, 112, 541–548. DOI: 10.1016/j.jbusres.2019.11.088

Gounaris, S. P. (2007). The relationships of customer-perceived value, satisfaction, loyalty and behavioral intentions. https://doi.org/DOI: 10.1300/J366v06n01

Hackett, S. M., & Dilts, D. M. (2004). A Systematic Review of Business Incubation Research. *The Journal of Technology Transfer*, 29(1), 55–82. DOI: 10.1023/B:JOTT.0000011181.11952.0f

Hausman, A. (2001). Variations in relationship strength and its impact on performance and satisfaction in business relationships. *Journal of Business and Industrial Marketing*, 16(7), 600–616. DOI: 10.1108/EUM0000000006194

Hennig-Thurau, T., Gwinner, K. P., & Gremler, D. D. (2002). Understanding relationship marketing outcomes: An integration of relational benefits and relationship quality. *Journal of Service Research*, 4(3), 230–247. DOI: 10.1177/1094670502004003006

Henttonen, K., Johanson, J. E., & Janhonen, M. (2013). Internal social networks in work teams: Structure, knowledge sharing and performance. *International Journal of Manpower*, 34(6), 616–634. DOI: 10.1108/IJM-06-2013-0148

Hsu, I. C., & Wang, Y. S. (2008). A model of intraorganizational knowledge sharing: Development and initial test [Review]. *Journal of Global Information Management*, 16(3), 45–73. DOI: 10.4018/jgim.2008070103

Indiran, L., Nallaluthan, K., Baskaran, S., & Dalayga, B. (2021). Business incubator: The genesis, evolution, and innovation invigoration. *International Journal of Academic Research in Business & Social Sciences*, 11(7), 342–354. DOI: 10.6007/IJARBSS/v11-i7/9940

Ishak, N., & Khairudin, F. N. (2020). Knowledge management and organisational performance of a department in Malaysia Digital Economy Corporation (MDEC). *Borneo Akademika*, 4(2), 29–41.

Issac, S., & Michael, W. B. (1981). *Handbook in research and evaluation*. EDITS.

Jamil, F., Ismail, K., & Mahmood, N. (2015). A review of commercialization tools: University incubators and technology parks. *International Journal of Economics and Financial Issues*, 5(1S).

Kankanhalli, A., Pee, L. G., Tan, G. W., & Chhatwal, S. (2012). Interaction of Individual and Social Antecedents of Learning Effectiveness: A Study in the IT Research Context. *IEEE Transactions on Engineering Management*, 59(1), 115–128. DOI: 10.1109/TEM.2011.2144988

Khalid, F. A., Gilbert, D., & Huq, A. (2014). The way forward for business incubation process in ICT incubators in Malaysia. *International Journal of Business and Society*, 15(3), 395.

King, W. R., & Marks, P. V. Jr. (2008). Motivating knowledge sharing through a knowledge management system. *Omega*, 36(1), 131–146. DOI: 10.1016/j.omega.2005.10.006

Lee, R., Tuselmann, H., Jayawarna, D., & Rouse, J. (2019). Effects of structural, relational and cognitive social capital on resource acquisition: A study of entrepreneurs residing in multiply deprived areas. *Entrepreneurship and Regional Development*, 31(5-6), 534–554. DOI: 10.1080/08985626.2018.1545873

Li, C., Ahmed, N., Khan, S. A. Q. A., & Naz, S. (2020). Role of business incubators as a tool for entrepreneurship development: The mediating and moderating role of business start-up and government regulations. *Sustainability (Basel)*, 12(5), 1822. DOI: 10.3390/su12051822

MacKenzie, S. B., Podsakoff, P. M., & Podsakoff, N. P. (2011). Construct measurement and validation procedures in MIS and behavioral research: Integrating new and existing techniques. *Management Information Systems Quarterly*, 35(2), 293–334. DOI: 10.2307/23044045

Martínez, A., Belso-Martínez, J. A., & Más-Verdú, F. (2012). Industrial clusters in Mexico and Spain: Comparing inter-organizational structures within context of change. *Journal of Organizational Change Management*, 25(5), 657–681. DOI: 10.1108/09534811211254563

Mendez-Duron, R., & Garcia, C. E. (2009). Returns from social capital in open source software networks. *Journal of Evolutionary Economics*, 19(2), 277–295. DOI: 10.1007/s00191-008-0125-5

Nahapiet, J., & Ghoshal, S. (1998). Social capital, intellectual capital, and the organizational advantage [Review]. *Academy of Management Review*, 23(2), 242–266. DOI: 10.2307/259373

Ngah, R., & Ibrahim, A. R. (2008). *The Impact of Intellectual Capital and Tacit Knowledge Sharing on Organizational Performance: A Preliminary Study of Malaysian SMEs.*

Nicholls-Nixon, C., Valliere, D., & Hassannezhad, Z. (2018). A typology of university business incubators: Implications for research and practice. International Conference on Innovation and Entrepreneurship.

Patnayakuni, R., Seth, N., & Rai, A. (2006). Building social capital with it and collaboration in supply chains: An empirical investigation.

Reagans, R., Zuckerman, E., & McEvily, B. (2004). How to make the team: Social networks vs. demography as criteria for designing effective teams. *Administrative Science Quarterly*, 49(1), 101-133.

Redondo, M., & Camarero, C. (2019). Social Capital in University Business Incubators: Dimensions, antecedents and outcomes. *The International Entrepreneurship and Management Journal*, 15(2), 599–624. DOI: 10.1007/s11365-018-0494-7

Redondo, M., & Camarero, C. (2020). Building the First Business Relationships: Incubatees in University Business Incubators (UBIs). *Entrepreneurship Research Journal*, 1.

Redondo, M., Camarero, C., & van der Sijde, P. (2021). Exchange of knowledge in protected environments. The case of university business incubators. *European Journal of Innovation Management*.

Richard, J. E., Thirkell, P. C., & Huff, S. L. (2007). An examination of customer relationship management (CRM) technology adoption and its impact on business-to-business customer relationships. *Total Quality Management & Business Excellence*, 18(8), 927–945. DOI: 10.1080/14783360701350961

Robert, L. P.Jr, Dennis, A. R., & Ahuja, M. K. (2008). Social capital and knowledge integration in digitally enabled teams. *Information Systems Research*, 19(3), 314–334. DOI: 10.1287/isre.1080.0177

Rustiarini, N. W., Arsawan, I. W. E., Rajiani, I., Supartha, W. G., Koval, V., & Suryantini, N. P. S. (2020). Leveraging knowledge sharing and innovation culture into SMEs sustainable competitive advantage. *International Journal of Productivity and Performance Management*. DOI: 10.1108/IJPPM-04-2020-0192

Saffar, A. (2008). Business incubation and support system in Asia-Pacific: Establishing international cooperation among Asian Incubators. Asia Pacific Conference on Business Incubation Asia-and Entrepreneurship Seoul, Korea.

Teigland, R., & Wasko, M. M. (2003). Integrating knowledge through information trading: Examining the relationship between boundary spanning communication and individual performance. *Decision Sciences*, 34(2), 261–286. DOI: 10.1111/1540-5915.02341

Tötterman, H., & Sten, J. (2005). Start-ups: Business incubation and social capital. *International Small Business Journal*, 23(5), 487–511. DOI: 10.1177/0266242605055909

Valliere, D., & Nicholls-Nixon, C. L. (2024). From business incubator to crucible: A new perspective on entrepreneurial support. *Journal of Small Business and Enterprise Development*, 31(2), 395–417. DOI: 10.1108/JSBED-04-2023-0181 van den Hooff, B., & Huysman, M. (2009). Managing knowledge sharing: Emergent and engineering approaches. *Information & Management*, 46(1), 1–8. DOI: 10.1016/j.im.2008.09.002

Vanderstraeten, J., & Matthyssens, P. (2012). Service-based differentiation strategies for business incubators: Exploring external and internal alignment. *Technovation*, 32(12), 656–670. DOI: 10.1016/j.technovation.2012.09.002

Vanderstraeten, J., Matthyssens, P., & Van Witteloostuijn, A. (2014). Toward a balanced framework to evaluate and improve the internal functioning of non-profit economic development business incubators. A study in Belgium. *International Journal of Entrepreneurship and Small Business*, 23(4), 478–508. DOI: 10.1504/IJESB.2014.065684

Wada, Y., Sakoda, M., Tsuji, H., Aoki, Y., & Seta, K. (2009). Designing Sticky Knowledge-Network SNS for Japanese Science Teachers. In M. J. Smith & G. Salvendy (Eds.), *Human Interface and the Management of Information: Designing Information Environments, Pt I* (Vol. 5617, pp. 447-456). DOI: 10.1007/978-3-642-02556-3_51

Wang, S., & Noe, R. A. (2010). Knowledge sharing: A review and directions for future research. *Human Resource Management Review*, 20(2), 115–131. DOI: 10.1016/j.hrmr.2009.10.001

Wasko, M. M., & Faraj, S. (2005). Why should I share? Examining social capital and knowledge contribution in electronic networks of practice. *MIS Quarterly*, 29(1), 35-57.

Widén-Wulff, G., & Ginman, M. (2004). Explaining knowledge sharing in organizations through the dimensions of social capital. *Journal of Information Science*, 30(5), 448–458. DOI: 10.1177/0165551504046997

Wiig, K. M. (2002). Knowledge management in public administration. *Journal of Knowledge Management*, 6(3), 224–239. DOI: 10.1108/13673270210434331

Yan, Y., Peng, Z., & Zha, X. (2023). Transactive memory system (TMS) and knowledge sharing: The effects of social capital and task visibility. *Library & Information Science Research*, 45(2), 101233. DOI: 10.1016/j.lisr.2023.101233

Yang, C., Jiang, B., & Zeng, S. (2024). An integrated multiple attribute decision-making framework for evaluation of incubation capability of science and technology business incubators. *Granular Computing*, 9(2), 31. DOI: 10.1007/s41066-024-00457-7

Yanuarti, D. W., & Murwatiningsih, M. (2019). Mediating Role of Competitive Strategy and Marketing Capability on The Relationship between EntrepreneurialOrientation and Market Performance. *Management Analysis Journal*, 8(2), 188–195.

Yao, G., Wu, C., & Yang, C. (2008). Examining the content validity of the WHOQOL-BREF from respondents' perspective by quantitative methods. *Social Indicators Research*, 85(3), 483–498. DOI: 10.1007/s11205-007-9112-8

Yau, O. H. M., McFetridge, P. R., Chow, R. P. M., Lee, J. S. Y., Sin, L. Y. M., & Tse, A. C. B. (2000). Is relationship marketing for everyone? *European Journal of Marketing*, 34(9/10), 1111–1127. DOI: 10.1108/03090560010342494

Zeithaml, V. A., Berry, L. L., & Parasuraman, A. (1996). The behavioral consequences of service quality. *the Journal of Marketing, 60*, 31-46. https://www.jstor.org/stable/1251929

KEY TERMS AND DEFINITIONS

Business Incubators: Business incubator are entities formed to help startups as a process rather than a facility, that boosts the development of startups and provides an array of targeted resources and services to early-stage startups.

Knowledge Sharing: The communication process in which one or two parts of an organization participate in knowledge transfer to develop new technologies, new products, etc.

Relationship Marketing: Relationship marketing is a strategy focused on building and maintaining long-term, mutually beneficial relationships with customers to foster loyalty and repeat business.

Social Capital: Social capital refers to the networks of relationships, trust, and norms that facilitate cooperation and support within a community.

Chapter 8
Shaping the Future:
Business Incubation and HRM Integration for Optimal Entrepreneurship and Innovation

Anjali Rai
ICFAI Business School (IBS), IFHE University, Hyderabad, India

ABSTRACT

Business incubation has become indispensable today as an activator of entrepreneurship and innovation, through which HRM's catalyst role is vital. Incubators offer a much-needed process of services and resources within which startups can be nurtured; HRM, on the other hand, looks into turning individuals into a world-class motivated workforce through effective management. This chapter also explains how bundling financial resources and physical tools with HRM increases the startup's success by incubating a strategic acceptance in the operation continuum to understand operational human capital. It lacks specific metrics, fails to name the market-driven reasons, and offers no insights into future-proofing a career or what technology may soon bring. Furthermore, more research on corporate culture, the role of regulatory frameworks, and the applications of HR policies are needed. This chapter aims to fill the gaps in our understanding with relevant research questions that describe how business incubation and HRM might foster innovation and growth performance.

INTRODUCTION

Today, entrepreneurship and innovation are the focus of global business that is progressing so rapidly that the role of the interface of business incubation with human resource management (HRM) has emerged as one of the critical determinants

DOI: 10.4018/979-8-3693-4302-9.ch008

in shaping entrepreneurship activities (Petrucci, 2018). While business incubation builds the necessary supportive ecosystem, resources, and networks on which nascent enterprises bank for growth, HRM ensures that dedicated high-performing teams manage these enterprises (Mukul & Saini, 2021). Integrating the two elements provides a robust enabling environment for an innovative startup to survive and be present in a situation that emulates creativity and strategic development (Aminova & Marchi, 2021).

Business incubation is an initiative by the most significant stakeholders to assist businesses they are backing with growth, as done by Silva et al., 2020. NBIA, the National Business Incubation Association, conducted a 2010 study that showed that, on average, incubated incorporations fared much better, reporting an 87% enhanced survival rate compared with non-NBIA incorporations, where only half are still around after four years. HRM see also Piwowar Sulej 2021. Good HRM practices are crucial in the initial years of a startup as they build a unique organizational culture and address any attrition rate or loss due to employees leaving early on, leading to better business growth. Huselid (1995) showed that strategic HR practices or "bundles" of Human Resource Management (HRM) practices affect financial performance through innovation and growth.

This integration compares to the startup seeing physical and monetary assets in a means that enables critical human source funding. Also, HRM supports incubators to help startups craft all human resource strategies, from talent attraction to leadership development and employee engagement. A contextual yet comprehensive methodology has much to offer for fostering an innovation culture where the business goals are consistent with the skills and motivations of employees. Different case studies illustrate the advantages of bringing business incubation close to HRM. For instance, Y Combinator, one of the startup accelerator industry veterans, will supply a wide range of mentorship and networking opportunities and clarify that team-building is essential. More impressively, Y Combinator (YC) alumni Airbnb and Dropbox have become great organizations of their time and enjoy both innovative and adaptive organizations.

Techstars is another top incubator that offers enterprise-grade support in HR, which allows companies to scale well without worrying about recruitment but being able to pay more attention and time to team dynamics and leadership development. Combining B-school incubators with HRM can be advantageous for future entrepreneurship and innovation in this distinctive business landscape. More lethal new ventures will be born out of this process while sprouting innovations that solve a few wicked problems organizations endure today. While beneficial results of the merging concept of business incubation and Human Resource Management (HRM) in fostering entrepreneurship and innovation have been reported, this chapter seeks to identify literature gaps that request a more profound investigation to understand better how they synergize. Consistent with the primary research questions, one of the most significant gaps in extant research is a consistent understanding and measurement approach for evaluating business incubation integration (HRM). Many studies have shown promising results, although the type and value of metrics vary from financial performance to innovation outputs or employee satisfaction.

Overall, with these findings, integrated business incubation and HRM practices may be successful in specific contexts or industry sectors, the facilitators of which are structured (Cirule & Uvarova, 2022). This is not a one-size-fits-all, but we see gaps in almost every rising startup. Just mention this offer from the next segment. Regarding technology startups, HR support abroad, a different kind for social enterprises and manufacturing startups, will be necessary (Arena et al., 2018). Therefore, further investigation of the design of business incubation and HRM synergy across specific contexts per industry sector is necessary to enhance their complementarities (Hughes et al., 2021). However, most research that has studied the combination of business incubation and HRM is relatively short-term in orientation, dealing with either the initial likelihood of survival by startups or early-stage innovation. There are fewer longitudinal studies of integrated practices on changes in startup growth and firm profitability or market success.

This technological progress also makes us realize the need for digital tools and platforms relevant to business incubation and HRM sensitivity. For how artificial intelligence and machine learning, as well as HR analytics, improve the talent management and development process in Incubation centers/ The use of technology to connect business support and HRM practices has not been thoroughly investigated, so exploration of this continuum could provide fresh options in merging the two processes. Regarding the success of HRM practices in incubators, the study cannot ignore cultural and organizational aspects. Nevertheless, the impact facets of these factors on business incubation and HRM integration have not been well researched. Future research in the field should explore how these factors influence the development of organizational culture, leadership styles, and intercultural dynamics within incubators at a deeper level to understand better what it takes for an environment that is innovation-friendly but where human capital management may be more effective.

An area that needs more investigation is the role of policy and institutional support in promoting business incubation HRM integration. A series of incubators, policies of the governments, funding mechanisms for them, and institutional framework could affect holistic HRM support in these themes. Research exploring the intersections of policy, institutional support, and integrated incubation can contribute to enhanced construction and execution of public policies. Theoretical frameworks propose the integration of business incubation and HRM, but practical implementation limitations significantly impede their effectiveness. Some challenges include resource constraints, scalability, the fast-growing nature of startups, and how HRM practices can adapt to them. This study implies substantial scope for integration between business incubation and HRM to contribute to improving entrepreneurship and innovation. However, at the same time, it also identifies multiple gaps in current knowledge that need resolution if this potential is realized. Consistent definitions and metrics, contextual differences, the long-term impact of the role of technology, cultural/ organizational factors, context policies on support, etc., future research in order to form more comprehensive insights for strategizing between business incubation and HRM can outline practical implementation hegemonic as healthy transparency about challenges correctly thus improve synergy overall to optimal level. The following research questions might address the above listing gap as a whole.

RQ1. How do business incubation-integrated HRM practices affect organizational success and startup innovation performance?

RQ 2: What are the specific HRM practices and their integration with business incubation that can improve startups' performance and growth orientation?

RQ3: What critical challenges are faced while incubators execute integrated HRM practices, and what best practices can be recommended to handle future paradigms?

The overarching purpose of this study is tied to its main underlying research question, i.e., what constitutes the composite relationship between business incubation and HRM, such that their integration can promote entrepreneurship.

Background

Business incubation and human resource management (HRM) converge at a point to be an essential research area due to the dynamic environment that modern startups rely on (Van Lancker et al., 2022; Hausberg & Korreck, 2021). Business Incubation is a collaborative program that encourages and facilitates entrepreneurship with early- or later-stage businesses to achieve growth, integrating HRM practices within a business incubation environment to strengthen startups. Businesses incubation is an organization created to support businesses and startups from the pre-seed stage to maturity, providing a network with resources and services like office space, capital investment opportunities, and access to mentorship and networking. Such incubators offer a secure setting for fledgling companies to critically develop their ideas and plan well before plunging into the cutthroat competition. The roots of business incubation can be traced back to the 1950s. However, it has evolved significantly and is now considered a core component in global entrepreneurship ecosystems. Business incubators are explicitly designed to lower a startup's failure risk by providing vital resources that would have been costly, difficult, or just plain impossible. This backing significantly boosts a new business's chances of making it through its ever-so-fragile early years, increasing the likelihood of success. Research demonstrates that firms engaging with incubation programs generally have higher survival rates than those who do not (Bruneel et al., 2012).Well-designed HRM practices can significantly impact how well a startup can hire, keep, and grow its employees, which is the most critical source of competitive advantage for many startups. Here are some challenges that startups may face regarding HRM due to its limited resources; they require employees who can be flexible and adapt according to requirements and the right culture from scratch.

In startups, HRM is not just about managing people; it focuses on leveraging human resources strategically concerning the overall business objectives, which would drive innovation and growth. Startups that engage in strategic HRM are anchored for long-term success. (Baron & Hannan, 2002). While integrating specific HRM practices within business incubation is a much newer literature base, this may have greater significance for improving success rates through increasing micro-business competitiveness. Significantly, this involves teaching HRM strategies within the incubation process to provide startups with tools and knowledge for team building, leadership development, and organizational culture creation right from day one. This could be implemented by offering HRM training and workshops specifically for the startups, establishing the availability of consultants who can provide specialist HR advice on best practices, and accepting an incubator based on their ability to demonstrate a certain level of awareness concerning handling staff matters. These programs are designed to enable startups to remain focused on the information and technology challenges that otherwise hinder their established growth phase. Why Innovation is at the Core of Entrepreneurship, key factors to win if one wants to be successful in our project, we have to make possible changes with an innovative approach—running Startups as the critical driver of innovation, introducing new high-tech and modern service/product models into the market. However, to make any of this possible here, startups must find a space that encourages creativity and experimentation; one becomes hard-pressed to squeeze the informal public square among them. This is where the role of business incubators and integration also matters. However, Startup incubators foster innovation by creating an enabling environment for startups to mature into full-fledged businesses. Reciprocally, integrating HRM strategies that promote a culture of innovation enables the startup to structure teams with motivated and skilled individuals who can also drive this agenda.

Finally, the merits of combining business incubation with HRM integration are acknowledged. Still, there needs to be more understanding of how these two aspects can best complement each other in fostering entrepreneurship. Further research could investigate the HRM practices that may be most meaningful for an incubation environment and how different types of incubators (e.g., university-based, private sector, government-supported introduce these in practice. There is also a need for more rigorous empirical investigation regarding the lasting effects on startup success and HRM integration.

This significant chapter explores successful startups of the modern era. Through examining examples of business incubation and HRM practices, this chapter offers insights regarding how these two components can be orchestrated together for entrepreneurship and innovation in the best possible manner. With the entrepreneurial field changing, new frontiers of research and practice may arise by combining HRM with business incubation.

This chapter focuses on business incubation and human resource management (HRM), a critical intersection crucial in steering entrepreneurship success through innovation. In other words, the main issues discussed in this chapter have been structured around several basic questions that need to be asked if human resource management practices are integrated into business incubation processes to improve financial and economic performance and sustainability and innovation potential for startups.

1. **The Role of Business Incubation in Startup Success:** The central theme of this chapter is how business incubation is used as a strategic means to help startups grow and develop. For startups still in the very early stages of business development, a structured environment to grow under can provide access to essential resources ranging from mentorship and networking opportunities to funding. The study showcases the capacity of business incubation to temporarily lessen failure rates, which hit many nascent ventures by developing an enabling environment that reduces risks and facilitates growth (Peters et al., 2004).

2. **The Role of HRM in the Incubation Process:** The chapter also focuses on integrating HRM practices into business incubation. The study discusses the importance of effective HRM in startups for the success of startups, particularly talent acquisition and leadership development, as well as other factors like organizational culture. With limited resources yet rapidly scaling demands, startups require HRM strategies that are just as agile and bespoke for addressing their specific requirements. The chapter describes how incubators can deploy HRM capabilities to help startups develop these competencies. This could look like HRM programs through incubators, access to expert advisory, and a hub for best practices between startups. The infusion of HRM into the incubation process aids entrepreneurial teams in developing a professionally competent team that is strategically focused at the organizational level and contributes effectively towards enhancing overall organizational performance (Cardon & Stevens, 2004).

3. **HRM Promotes Innovation via Incubation Synergy:** The chapter is centrally concerned with innovation, but new HRM practices create productive synergy for burgeoning business enterprises. According to the study, including HRM in the incubation process is essential to establishing an innovative environment. This

involves fostering a creative culture, allowing room for experimentation, and helping team members collaborate. HRM practices in recruitment, performance management, and employee development can be tied up with the innovation aspects for startups. For example, startups can build teams of greater variety in their skill sets than other firms by hiring individuals with technical skills and the mindset associated with starting a business, making them more likely to engage in innovative activities. For example, startups can be more entrepreneurial and innovative if they adopt performance management systems that reward creativity and exploration (Chen & Huang, 2009).

4. **Overcoming HRM and Incubation Integration Challenges:** The chapter also explores the difficulties of incorporating HRM into business incubation. These include the challenge that formal HRM practice imposes in terms of both its formality and speed compared to informal startup procedures, an absence of focus between incubators' support services vis-a-vis the specific human resource needs of startup firms, and a common entry barrier for startups as their lack financial resources are exercising it influence on investing residual funds into HRM. The chapter argues that incubators need to be more adaptable and individualized in their approach to HRM integration, from which there are two explicit dimensions. In the future, they may choose to create a menu of services that likely all startups need and that established businesses can provide (if not entirely, at least partially), as well as an environment where one startup helps other startups by sharing its service experience/challenges.

5. **Policy and Practice Implications:** This chapter outlines outcomes and broader considerations of HRM incubation integration for both policy and practice. These results support a more significant and vital role of HRM in shaping the success and innovation of startups, and they may also provide valuable insights to policy-makers and incubation managers. Supporting the integration of HRM in incubation programs will help to improve such programs and assist in building a more robust entrepreneurial ecosystem. This chapter also points to the necessity of additional research on those HRM practices that are most effective when used by an incubator. These key findings could be used to generate incubator best practices and guidelines for supporting HRM within startups, ultimately contributing towards increasing startup survivorship. To sum up, this chapter investigates how integrating quality HR practices into business incubator processes can promote startup success as part of an effort to encourage more innovation. The chapter offers a unique contribution in allowing for an informed discussion on the sustainability of entrepreneurship and the role played by incubation and HRM in shaping the future.

Literature Review

Recent academic and industry research has been particularly interested in the intersection of business incubation with Human Resource Management (HRM), highlighting its capabilities to boost entrepreneurship and innovation. A literature review illustrates the importance of start-up success, providing critical research and theoretical foundations for a composite understanding of how bridging these genres could facilitate growth in successful enterprises.

Business Incubation is considered one of the keys to supporting startups, including but not limited to funding, mentoring, and workspace. According to Hackett and Dilts (2004), business incubators are organizations that incubate start-up companies, helping them survive and grow through the demanding startup period when they are most vulnerable. The incubation process covers everything from setting up your business to everything in between, such as introductions, advice, and even part funding (van Rijnsoever et al., 2021).

Effective HRM practices are essential to new-stage start-ups. Baron and Hannan (2002) suggest that first HR practices significantly influence a startup's culture and seed performance over the long run. Strategic HRM goes beyond bringing in the right talent; developing and retaining employees internally is crucial to creating an environment where innovation can thrive (Altındağ & Bilaloğlu Aktürk, 2020). Studies by Delery and Doty (1996) showed that a selective staffing strategy, bundled training programs, and pay-for-performance plans were related to enhancing organizational outcomes. HRM and business incubation create a positive causal effect, increasing growth and innovative ideas for new start-ups. According to Clarysse, Wright, and Van Hove (2015), incubators significantly support startups in providing HR-related services, especially regarding talent management and leadership development programs. Integrating with startups makes such infrastructure accessible without ensuring they have enough resources and a disciplined management team for human capital development. Amezcua et al. (2013) found that support in HR had a positive effect on startup survival and innovation output for startups nested within incubators with robust HR systems; surprisingly, the same author also suggested lower qualities of performance due to living under such institutions when talking about governance transformation thanks likelihood and complexity from the other section attending interdependent workforces may provide new competitive advantages instead (Hambrick & Mason, 1984). The successes of startups from companies like Airbnb and Dropbox, founded using the Y Combinator methodology, are just some testaments to the positive implications of integrated incubation and HRM practices. They have created great company cultures and teams, thereby having a significant impact on their market success as well as innovation.

Theoretical Frameworks

The integration of business incubation and HRM is based on several theoretical frameworks. Barney (1991) argues that resources, including human capital, are fundamental to a firm's competitive advantage by highlighting this perspective in his study on the Resource-Based View (RBV) Of the Firm. This theory can help us understand business incubation, in this case, that the delivery of HRM resources provided by an incubator constitutes a strategic asset that subsequently influences mono duality options for firms to respond more adaptively and innovatively within markets. Dynamic Capabilities Theory (Teece et al., 1997) is another pertinent framework. This theory suggests that integrating and combining internal resources and external competencies is vital for firm flexibility and innovation. Business incubators with HRM support help startups develop dynamic capabilities since they instill a culture of learning and adapting.

Challenges and Prospects of Research

While tangible advantages of doing so are apparent, concurrent business incubation and HRM face integration challenges due to their typically different goals that need similar alignment(incubator vs. startup needs) and pace (HRM practices should be fit for fast-paced entrepreneurial ventures). Only further research can show the significance of these differences. It will allow incubators to know how they need better to support different types of start-ups with HR efforts. In addition to the conclusive proof of its positive impact, incubators can offer invaluable human resource management support vital for successful team building and leadership development and provide start-ups with the space and finance required for survival. This literature review emphasizes their importance and underscores the central requirement for additional research to identify optimal synergies between these components. The current chapter responded to the research question:

RQ1: How do business incubation-integrated HRM practices affect organizational success and startup innovation performance?

Incorporating business Incubator and human resource management (HRM) practices significantly impact start-ups' success rates and innovative outcomes (Guckenbiehl et al., 2021). Such an integration offers startups a comprehensive ecosystem comprising operational support and human capital to help them perform better, survive longer, and innovate. At the nascent stage of development, business incubators provide startups with essential resources, including funding and mentorship, which are indispensable to early-stage ventures but might not be available from other sources (Hackett & Dilts, 2004). This is where startup companies can gain a competitive advantage by leveraging best-in-class HRM practices to have an effective recruitment, onboarding, and performance management strategy in place, which ultimately helps them achieve high productivity from employees. When HRM is effective, it will attract, retain, and develop the right organizational talent, and creativity never grows without nurturing. Integration of HRM practices in incubation programs is vital in creating an excellent organizational culture and strengthening team dynamics. According to Delery and Doty (1996), more strategically oriented human resource management practices like extensive training programs, performance-based pay incentives, and selective staffing will lead to a motivated workforce with enhanced skills. Within a business incubation lens, this manifests in more cohesive collaboration, increased staff engagement, and improved innovation outcomes. A positive organizational culture inculcated by a practical HRM mind fosters a conducive setting for creativity and innovation. Startup survival increases, and there is more growth potential due to various empirical studies when startups are incubated with integrated HRM support. Amezcua et al. (2013) noted that startups experiencing strong HR support from their incubators demonstrated higher survival and produced more innovative outcomes than those without this type of assistance. This is because integrated HR practices help startups face such challenges with ease, as the key to scaling up is to handle higher demands of the workforce and, at the same time, keep coherence in place within the organization during rapid growth phases.

The firm's Resource-Based View (RBV) is predicated upon its resources, which include human capital and its role in maintaining a competitive advantage over time (Barney, 1991). The innovation literature stresses the importance of managing human resources effectively since startups must build their highly valued, often rare human capital as an asset or competitive advantage by incorporating HRM practices into business incubation. As Teece, Pisano, and Shuen (1997) suggested, this integration helps develop the dynamic capabilities necessary for achieving 1997 high-degree flexibility to remain agile towards ever-changing market parameters while preserving continuous innovation. A startup with a strong HRM foundation is at an advantage in growing and ensuring sustainability for the future. The embedding of HRM in business incubation thus includes practical challenges and identifying good practices. HRM supports those that successfully implement HRM and push for tailored, startup-specific solutions like easily changeable policies in different areas of HR; well-thought leadership development programs have adaptive designs and are flexible as the company grows. Incubators with extensive HRM integration not only provide more substantial support but also allow startups to focus on their core business operations as the management of a team is executed efficiently (Clarysse et al., 2015). By integrating business incubation with HRM practices, startups can receive a holistic package of support that impacts resource allocation and team dynamics, thus resulting in successful and innovative outcomes. This encompassing solution serves as an operational necessity for startups. It emphasizes creating and maintaining human capital, which is the key driver for innovation that ultimately leads to sustainable scales.

RQ 2: What are the specific HRM practices and their integration with business incubation that can result in improving performance, growth orientation, etc., of startups?

Combining some specific HRM practices and business incubation will significantly improve the performance and growth of startups. Critical HRM practices include talent acquisition, training, and employee development to improve performance and organizational culture. This practice enables startups with the resources they require and sets an environment of work to boost innovation and sustenance. Recruiting talent is crucial to startups because their initial team becomes a foundation for growth and success. Startups manage to solve the problem of attracting top-notch talent by working closely with incubators that support recruitment. According to Delery and Doty (1996), in their recognition of selective staffing, this is a good concept because it helps startups hire not just appropriate people from the technical side but also from cultural fit and value. These moral rubber-hitting-the-road obligations make or break a real team pursuing any objective.

In other words, it is through such training and development programs that the capabilities of your startup employees can be enhanced. Startup teams receive detailed education on evolving industry standards and practices from business incubators that provide or help to give them access to extensive training programs. For instance, Huselid (1995) found that firms investing in training their employees gained a slight improvement in productivity and performance. Startups need to have an environment that offers continuous learning, and this constant thirst for knowledge fuels innovation and agility, which are, on the other hand, very important in a changing business world.

It remains crucial for startup success to run performance management practices through frequent feedback, goal setting, and offering incentives based on individual performances. For example, when savvy incubators assist startups in placing effective performance management systems, the ability of founders to monitor their teams and guide progress is more straightforward. This will favor the startup because it ensures that employees are well-aligned with strategic objectives and driven by a high-performance culture. Performance management increases transparency and accountability in organizational performance (Delery & Doty, 1996).

Another critical HRM practice focusing on startup performance and growth is the extent to which 1the organization's culture encourages creativity, dedication, and competitiveness (Shehata et al., 2021). Incubators can help startups build an excellent organizational culture since they value collaboration, innovation, and agility (Gonçalves et al., 2022). Employee engagement and retention are instrumental in keeping a steady, motivated workforce together. Baron and Hannan (2002) illustrate how HR practices, specifically at the startup stage of entrepreneurship, can have long-term implications for organizational culture and success.

Given that startup founders and likely many early employees like to wear multiple hats at a time, such leadership development is essential. New business leaders (s) without experience can take advantage of incubators, which give training and mentorship to hone leadership skills for managing their teams effectively through the maze of business growth (Mvulirwenande & Wehn, 2020). According to Clarysse et al. (2015), startups' test on leadership is a determining factor for new ventures, implying that the right kind of leader leads strongly and distinctively behind the corporate potential direction and among employees.

Keeping an employee dedicated and satisfied can be a difficult task for startups. Hence, it is imperative to have specific strategies in place. Third-party incubators that help start-ups build engagement programs (think employee recognition, career development opportunities, and a supportive work environment) can decrease turnover while improving overall job satisfaction. Delighted employees are also more likely to focus on contributing efforts for the innovation and sustainability of startups (Huselid, 1995).

Effective use of technology for HRM practices, including HR analytics, Digital Performance Management tools, etc., makes the different functions within startups more efficient and productive (Varma & Dutta, 2023). Startups can digitize their HR activities and use technology for talent sourcing and onboarding processes to evolve from traditional practices; incubators helping provide more access to or training of these technologies will allow startups to improve the rationale of decision-making with analytics impacting in better overall outcome towards a new age form capabilities within existence (Teece et al., 1997). A set of HRM practices has been studied in this paper that, integrated with business incubation, has led to tremendous performance and growth for startups (Leitão et al., 2022). Instances are the recruitment process, training and development procedures, performance checking systems, and development of the organizational culture, among other practices such as how to direct newcomers successfully using technology tools in HRM. Integrating those HRM practices, incubator programs can deliver a fully-packed portfolio with activities that concurrently fulfill startups' operational and human capital demands within their ecosystems — critical success factors for innovation and sustainable growth.

RQ3. What critical challenges are faced while incubators execute integrated HRM practices, and what best practices can be recommended to handle future paradigms?

Implementing integrated Human Resource Management (HRM) practices faces numerous challenges in business incubators. Overcoming such challenges necessitates devising and providing the help of best practices to make it easier for startups. Below is a brief description of the critical challenges and best practices that can be adopted. Critical challenges are faced while incubators execute integrated HRM practices as resource constraints are significant for incubators, which usually have small financial and human resources to support bulky HRM (Vepo do Nascimento Welter et al., 2020). Build relationships with outsourced HR service providers or volunteer mentor networks that can provide low-cost support from skilled mentors (Hackett & Dilts, 2004). Diverse Needs of Startups are a significant challenge. Startups in an incubator are a diverse group, with differences that include the area of the industry they occupy, the general stage of development, and hence size when it comes to workforce needs, etc. Create an HRM framework that is malleable and can be tweaked to meet the specific needs of each growing startup. Clarysse, Wright, and Van Hove found that HR support must be periodically evaluated to accommodate shifts in the needs of startups.

The scalability of HRM Practices is a significant challenge. An HR practice that works well for small is unlikely to work as effectively when an organization starts scaling. Install scalable HRM systems and processes upfront. · Implement technology solutions like HR software to streamline and automate administrative tasks across different areas, scaling with the startup (Teece et al., 1997). Conserving Company Culture is a significant challenge. It is difficult to ensure startups preserve their strong and healthy organizational culture while growing. Develop an environment of continuous learning and flexibility. Running workshops around leadership and how organizational culture is developed to ensure startups retain their original core during the scale (Baron & Hannan, 2002). Talent acquisition and retention are significant challenges. Due to limited resources and high uncertainty, startups always scratch their heads for attracting good caliber on board. Provide career advancement and good benefits. Incubators can support through promoting networking and access to talent pools and assist in conducting workshops on influential people management processes (Huselid, 1995). Strategic and operational counsel is a challenge. Incubators must play that fine line between giving strategic HR advice and actively supporting startups in their daily operational needs. Resource both strategic HR planning and operational support. Why Use HR consultants for strategic guidance and internal staff or seasonal employees to take care of the day-to-day? (Delery & Doty, 1996)

Best practices implementation will enhance the performance. Develop training programs for startup founders and managers on core HRM competencies such as recruitment, performance management, and employee engagement. These programs can be applied through workshops, webinars, and one-on-one coaching. Use HR technology applications like ATS (Applicant et al.), Performance Management Software, Employee Engagement platforms, etc. These tools facilitate several HR function work streams that make them more efficient and effective designed for scale (Teece et al., 1997). Create a mentorship, guidance, and support network for the new-age HR professionals and experts ding them on all facets of Human

Resources. This network can encompass mentors, volunteer consultants, and partnerships with HR service providers (Hackett & Dilts, 2004). Setting up a Solution Feedback Loop, the companies where HR support will be provided should be able to provide startup them with routine feedback. Startups can use this feedback to refine the HRM services provided through incubation. Establish a peer-learning environment in your incubator where startups can post their HR-related queries and resolve them through others' shared experiences. A holistic practice that can catalyze community collaboration in sharing best practices and addressing common challenges (Clarysse et al., 2015). Offering leadership development programs that help new startup leaders hire and lead effectively. Leadership training covers team building, conflict resolution, and strategic HR planning (Baron & Hannan, 2002). Key to the successful implementation of integrated HRM practices is in part because business incubators encounter resource constraints, serve a range of needs – from early-stage through growth and scaling ventures, need to scale quickly, participate with scalability issues as tenants grow or move off-site, face challenges aligning economic incentives for all key stakeholders who operate rent-based businesses on site including office facilities management services which influence an environment encouraging collaboration among startups. Incubators overcome this challenge and substantially increase the startup's performance by following best practices such as leveraging process offerings, Maximum-panel of HR-expertise-platforms to prevent traps in congruence, implementing feedback methods, and designing collaborative communities focusing on leadership development.

Methodology

A detailed literature review research method was employed for the study to scrutinize the business incubation and the integrated human resource management (HRM) model for promoting entrepreneurship and innovation. It allows us to understand this integration's full impact and best practices. To frame the exploration theoretically and locate gaps in existing literature. It detailed a literature review of professional journals/field books/conference proceedings related to business incubation, HRM, and entrepreneurship. Search these databases with JSTOR, Google Scholar, and Web of Science for studies on the topic area. Identify findings to summarize, as well as research gaps. A comprehensive discourse overview that informs the research and underscores points from the literature. To consolidate results and provide recommendations for operationalizing HRM within business incubation. Evidence-based business and policy implications for improving the integration of HRM with business incubation towards more entrepreneurship and innovation.

Findings

Several significant findings have been developed from research integrating business incubation and Human Resource Management (HRM) to promote entrepreneurship and innovation. These results reveal the potential effect of cohesive HRM strategies on start-up outcomes, discuss common obstacles for incubators to execute these practices, and offer best practice recommendations. Startups with integrated HRM practices from incubators display higher documentation on performance variables such as revenue growth, survival rate, and market penetration. HRM practices such as selective staffing, training, and development were critical to achieving those outcomes (Huselid, 1995; Delery & Doty, 2001). For example, Clarysse, Wright, and Van Hove (2015) confirmed that firms with fuller HRM support within incubators exhibited better employee well-being, leading to organizational performance. Linking HRM practices in business incubation to innovation outcomes was significant among entrepreneurs. Baron and Hannan (2002) found that startups embedded within vital HRM programs received more well-built support for new product developments, filed patents at a considerably higher rate, and showed greater adaptability to consumer attitudes to market changes than other nascent organizations. Founders or employees of startups who were given training and development programs through incubators graduated with up-to-date knowledge about the industry, thus creating an innovation-friendly environment (Hackett & Dilts, 2004). There are several challenges that incubators have faced while implementing integrated human resource management (HRM) practices, such as limited resources, varied needs of startups, and scalability issues, which make it challenging to maintain organizational culture when a start-up grows large. Lack of resources presented a challenge, as many incubators lacked the financial and human resources to have in-house HRM capabilities. Incubators can establish relationships with external HR service providers and use volunteer mentors within the incubator who have specialist knowledge in HR to extend their human resource management support without leading to enormous costs (Hackett & Dilts, 2004).

In order to take care of so many essential needs all at once, I decided that devising a modular HRM framework was the best option for startups and my workload. The regular needs assessment would align HR support with changed startup needs (Clarysse et al., 2015). Teece, Pisano, and Shuen (1997) highlight that implementing scalable HRM systems and processes early in start-up development through technology solutions to support or automate classic HR functions ensured ongoing compliance with a growing practice. Organizations with a thriving organizational culture and influential leaders play significant roles in startup success. Many incubators did well at training founders on leadership and company culture, reinforcing startup priorities as the startups learned to evolve more quickly (Baron & Hannan,

2002). Start-up leaders had to attend leadership development programs that provided them with the necessary capabilities to lead and grow a successful team, setting the strategic direction of early-stage start-ups and directly impacting employee morale (Huselid, 1995).

Implementing HR technology tools like ATS, performance management software, and employee engagement platforms immensely contributed to the increased velocity and effectiveness of HR-related functions in startups. Startups were able to take advantage of streamlined HR processes through the use and implementation of advanced technologies — firms required either access or training in these new technological tools achieved by participating within incubators (Teece et al., 1997). HRM practices are also positively related to startups' performance and innovation results when integrated with business incubation. Incubators have many challenges, but by leading with the best practices of partnering with OSUs, establishing scalable HRM frameworks, and deploying technology solutions to address critical elements in all startups that need funding. Startups rely on a culture and leadership to help them succeed. Nonetheless, the results highlight that comprehensive HRM support as part of a holistic incubation strategy can contribute to more successful entrepreneurship and innovation.

CONCLUSION

Notably, embedding business incubation function and the mediating role of Human Resource Management (HRM) practices may contribute to higher performance gain and develop innovation orientation for startups. Important insights have emerged from this research that demonstrate the necessity of integration and provide a road map for future best practices and areas for further study. Incubators that apply a complete package of HRM practices perform better by way of higher turnover rates (e.g., earn higher revenue growth, encroach upon new markets at earlier points in their development) or survival than similar startups without such an incubation environment (Huselid, 1995; Delery & Doty, 1996). More importantly, integrated HRM practices positively enhance the ability to innovate regarding new product development, patent filings, and adaptability to market changes (Baron & Hannan, 2002), and different types of innovation spread among service companies. Incubators are also confronted with numerous challenges, including those related to resource constraints, the heterogeneity of startups supported under one roof, whether HRM practices can be scaled up, and ensuring a coherent organizational culture (Clarysse et al., 2015; Hackett & Dilts, 2004). These challenges can be met by long-term strategic planning and resource investment.

Partnering with external HR service providers, utilizing volunteer mentors, and leveraging HR technology tools are best practices for overcoming challenges driven by resource constraints (Hackett & Dilts, 2004). This can be aided by developing flexible HRM frameworks and conducting regular needs assessments that feed information in this format to ensure they have the wherewithal to make their support readily available before it worsens (Clarysse et al., 2015). Growth and a strong organizational culture are imperative for long-term success. For startups, this invariably leads to the best chances for a successful journey in the entrepreneurial ecosystem. Growing up, I received support from incubator programs encompassing training and development (Baron & Hannan, 2002). Leadership Development Gives a foundation of required skills to leaders of startups for better team handling and growing the business (Huselid, 1995).

The deployment and integration of HR technology tools help improve the efficiency and performance levels in various HR functions, helping start-ups automate critical processes and make data-driven decisions (Teece et al., 1997). A complete solution is needed: one that combines comprehensive HRM support with services (customized as required by the unique demands of startups) that can act sustainably and last. In this regard, invest in scalable HRM systems and take advantage of technology that can go a long way in better supporting startups. By encouraging collaborations between incubators and HR service providers to mitigate such resource constraints, the efficiency level of incubation programs can be further uplifted. Policy on building the HRM capabilities inside an incubator can bridge this gap and create a vibrant entrepreneurial ecosystem.

Future Directions

The research limitations include the fact that further exploration is needed to determine whether there are long-term effects of using integrated HRM practices for successful and growing startups. Comparative studies in different industries and locations are needed to generate further insights into the contextual moderating effects of HRM integration within business incubation. Therefore, to make entrepreneurship and innovation more robust HRM practices, incorporating business incubation formally or informally into an organization's value chain process becomes relevant. Addressing these challenges and following best practices will go a long way in increasing the performance and growth of startups through incubators. This synergistic approach helps individual startups and contributes to a live and innovative entrepreneur ecosystem.

REFERENCES

Altındağ, E., & Bilaloğlu Aktürk, H. (2020). The impact of new generation management approaches on the firm performance: The Moderating Role of Strategic Human Resource Management Applications. *SAGE Open*, 10(3), 2158244020948845. DOI: 10.1177/2158244020948845

Amezcua, A. S., Grimes, M. G., Bradley, S. W., & Wiklund, J. (2013). Organizational sponsorship and founding environments: A contingency view on the survival of business-incubated firms. *Academy of Management Journal*, 56(6), 1628–1654. DOI: 10.5465/amj.2011.0652

Aminova, M., & Marchi, E. (2021). The role of innovation on start-up failure vs. its success. *International Journal of Business Ethics and Governance*, 41-72.

Arena, M., Bengo, I., Calderini, M., & Chiodo, V. (2018). Unlocking finance for social tech start-ups: Is there a new opportunity space? *Technological Forecasting and Social Change*, 127, 154–165. DOI: 10.1016/j.techfore.2017.05.035

Barney, J. (1991). Firm resources and sustained competitive advantage. *Journal of Management*, 17(1), 99–120. DOI: 10.1177/014920639101700108

Baron, J. N., & Hannan, M. T. (2002). Organizational blueprints for success in high-tech start-ups: Lessons from the Stanford Project on Emerging Companies. *California Management Review*, 44(3), 8–36. DOI: 10.2307/41166130

Bruneel, J., Ratinho, T., Clarysse, B., & Groen, A. (2012). The evolution of business incubators: Comparing demand and supply of business incubation services across different incubator generations. *Technovation*, 32(2), 110–121. DOI: 10.1016/j.technovation.2011.11.003

Cardon, M. S., & Stevens, C. E. (2004). Managing human resources in small organizations: What do we know? *Human Resource Management Review*, 14(3), 295–323. DOI: 10.1016/j.hrmr.2004.06.001

Chen, C. J., & Huang, J. W. (2009). Strategic human resource practices and innovation performance, The mediating role of knowledge management capacity. *Journal of Business Research*, 62(1), 104–114. DOI: 10.1016/j.jbusres.2007.11.016

Cirule, I., & Uvarova, I. (2022). Open innovation and determinants of technology-driven sustainable value creation in incubated start-ups. *Journal of Open Innovation*, 8(3), 162. DOI: 10.3390/joitmc8030162

Clarysse, B., Wright, M., & Van Hove, J. (2015). A look inside accelerators: Building businesses. *Nature Biotechnology*, 33(4), 383–386.

Collings, D. G., & Mellahi, K. (2009). Strategic talent management: A review and research agenda. *Human Resource Management Review*, 19(4), 304–313. DOI: 10.1016/j.hrmr.2009.04.001

Combinator, Y. (n.d.). Retrieved from https://www.ycombinator.com/

Delery, J. E., & Doty, D. H. (1996). Modes of theorizing in strategic human resource management: Tests of universalistic, contingency, and configurational performance predictions. *Academy of Management Journal*, 39(4), 802–835. DOI: 10.2307/256713

Gonçalves, D., Bergquist, M., Alänge, S., & Bunk, R. (2022). How digital tools align with organizational agility and strengthen digital innovation in automotive startups. *Procedia Computer Science*, 196, 107–116. DOI: 10.1016/j.procs.2021.11.079

Guckenbiehl, P., de Zubielqui, G. C., & Lindsay, N. (2021). Knowledge and innovation in start-up ventures: A systematic literature review and research agenda. *Technological Forecasting and Social Change*, 172, 121026. DOI: 10.1016/j.techfore.2021.121026

Hackett, S. M., & Dilts, D. M. (2004). A systematic review of business incubation research. *The Journal of Technology Transfer*, 29(1), 55–82. DOI: 10.1023/B:-JOTT.0000011181.11952.0f

Hausberg, J. P., & Korreck, S. (2021). *Business incubators and accelerators: a co-citation analysis-based, systematic literature review*. Edward Elgar Publishing.

Hughes, M., Hughes, P., Morgan, R. E., Hodgkinson, I. R., & Lee, Y. (2021). Strategic entrepreneurship behaviour and the innovation ambidexterity of young technology-based firms in incubators. *International Small Business Journal*, 39(3), 202–227. DOI: 10.1177/0266242620943776

Huselid, M. A. (1995). The impact of human resource management practices on turnover, productivity, and corporate financial performance. *Academy of Management Journal*, 38(3), 635–672. DOI: 10.2307/256741

Isenberg, D. J. (2010). How to start an entrepreneurial revolution. *Harvard Business Review*, 88(6), 40–50.

Leitão, J., Pereira, D., & Gonçalves, Â. (2022). Business incubators, accelerators, and performance of technology-based ventures: A systematic literature review. *Journal of Open Innovation*, 8(1), 46. DOI: 10.3390/joitmc8010046

Madaleno, M., Nathan, M., Overman, H., & Waights, S. (2022). Incubators, accelerators and urban economic development. *Urban Studies (Edinburgh, Scotland)*, 59(2), 281–300. DOI: 10.1177/00420980211004209

Mukul, K., & Saini, G. K. (2021). Talent acquisition in startups in India: The role of social capital. *Journal of Entrepreneurship in Emerging Economies*, 13(5), 1235–1261. DOI: 10.1108/JEEE-04-2020-0086

Mvulirwenande, S., & Wehn, U. (2020). Opening the innovation incubation black box: A process perspective. *Environmental Science & Policy*, 114, 140–151. DOI: 10.1016/j.envsci.2020.07.023

National Business Incubation Association (NBIA). (2010). What is Business Incubation? https://www.inbia.org/

Nonaka, I. (1994). A dynamic theory of organizational knowledge creation. *Organization Science*, 5(1), 14–37. DOI: 10.1287/orsc.5.1.14

Peters, L., Rice, M., & Sundararajan, M. (2004). The role of incubators in the entrepreneurial process. *The Journal of Technology Transfer*, 29(1), 83–91. DOI: 10.1023/B:JOTT.0000011182.82350.df

Petrucci, F. (2018). The incubation process of mid-stage startup companies: A business network perspective. *IMP Journal*, 12(3), 544–566. DOI: 10.1108/IMP-07-2017-0043

Piwowar-Sulej, K. (2021). Human resources development as an element of sustainable HRM–with the focus on production engineers. *Journal of Cleaner Production*, 278, 124008. DOI: 10.1016/j.jclepro.2020.124008 PMID: 32901179

Schein, E. H. (2010). Organizational culture and leadership (Vol. 2). *John Wiley & Sons*.

Schumpeter, J. A. (1934). *The Theory of Economic Development: An Inquiry into Profits, Capital, Credit, Interest, and the Business Cycle*. Harvard University Press.

Shane, S., & Venkataraman, S. (2000). The promise of entrepreneurship as a field of research. *Academy of Management Review*, 25(1), 217–226. DOI: 10.5465/amr.2000.2791611

Shehata, G. M., Montash, M. A. H., & Areda, M. R. (2021). Examining the interrelatedness among human resources management practices, entrepreneurial traits and corporate entrepreneurship in emerging markets: An evidence from Egypt. *Journal of Entrepreneurship in Emerging Economies*, 13(3), 353–379. DOI: 10.1108/JEEE-08-2019-0117

Silva, D. S., Ghezzi, A., Aguiar, R. B. D., Cortimiglia, M. N., & ten Caten, C. S. (2020). Lean Startup, Agile Methodologies and Customer Development for business model innovation: A systematic review and research agenda. *International Journal of Entrepreneurial Behaviour & Research*, 26(4), 595–628. DOI: 10.1108/IJEBR-07-2019-0425

Techstars. (n.d.). Retrieved from https://www.techstars.com/

Teece, D. J., Pisano, G., & Shuen, A. (1997). Dynamic capabilities and strategic management. *Strategic Management Journal*, 18(7), 509–533. DOI: 10.1002/(SICI)1097-0266(199708)18:7<509::AID-SMJ882>3.0.CO;2-Z

Van Lancker, E., Knockaert, M., Audenaert, M., & Cardon, M. (2022). HRM in entrepreneurial firms: A systematic review and research agenda. *Human Resource Management Review*, 32(3), 100850. DOI: 10.1016/j.hrmr.2021.100850

van Rijnsoever, F. J., & Eveleens, C. P. (2021). Money Don't matter? How incubation experience affects start-up entrepreneurs' resource valuation. *Technovation*, 106, 102294. DOI: 10.1016/j.technovation.2021.102294

Varma, D., & Dutta, P. (2023). Empowering human resource functions with data-driven decision-making in start-ups: A narrative inquiry approach. *The International Journal of Organizational Analysis*, 31(4), 945–958. DOI: 10.1108/IJOA-08-2021-2888

Vepo do Nascimento Welter, C., Oneide Sausen, J., & Rossetto, C. R. (2020). The development of innovative capacity as a strategic resource in technology-based incubation activities. *Revista de Gestão*, 27(2), 169–188. DOI: 10.1108/REGE-02-2019-0034

Wright, P. M., & McMahan, G. C. (1992). Theoretical perspectives for strategic human resource management. *Journal of Management*, 18(2), 295–320. DOI: 10.1177/014920639201800205

KEY TERMS AND DEFINITIONS

Business Incubation: A startup company uses a business incubation process to foster the development and success of new companies through an array of support resources and services, developed with time over stages (translates) on scales more flexible than other schemes. Incubators seek to lower new ventures' risks and barriers by providing a structured environment during those critical stages of development.

Entrepreneurial Ecosystem: Ecosystem, in the context of this post, refers to a multi-faceted collective (comprising entrepreneurs, investors, institutions, etc.) that is systemic and aims to foster startup creation, growth, and sustainability. In a nutshell, an entrepreneurial ecosystem is called an environment that provides opportunities and challenges to entrepreneurs as they grow their businesses. It encapsulates all resources like capital, talent infrastructure, and policy frameworks.

Entrepreneurship: Entrepreneurship is creating a new entity following efforts to develop innovations that are expected to be perceived as new and have an orientation towards achieving some degree of growth through non-trivial improvements over existing practices and assumptions. Entrepreneurs see market gaps and move to fill them, often spurring economic growth and innovation.

HRM: Human Resource Management: Human Resource Management is a business function that implements strategies and methods for managing people in an organization. As HRM in startups, acquiring and retaining the right fit employees with proper development channeling the total potential workforce is a pivot to achieve the desired impact on business. These people's strategies are known as the bread and butter for startup success, bush fire machinery ahead.

Incubation Program: The process is an organized program typically run by business incubators and, as such, enables startups with the essentials to grow their idea into a company. Such programs frequently offer mentorship, workshops, access to networks, and occasionally some financial support during the inevitable early-stage struggles of startups.

Innovation: Basically, innovation is a new idea, product, service, etc, that has improved things and changed some industries. Startups see innovation as their lifeblood, essential for competing with established companies.

Knowledge Management: Creating, sharing, using, and managing knowledge and information within an organization. Proper knowledge management is essential for innovation (for startups: managing intellectual assets, not just the ones that generate revenue; learning from successes and failures.

Organizational Culture: The organizational culture is the collective values, beliefs, and practices that are followed by employees when executing their duties. One of the most critical aspects for startups is creating a tight bond and robust organizational culture that aligns employees with common goals, fosters team collaboration, and enhances innovation.

Strategic HRM: Human Resource Management (HRM) means proactively managing employees that fit an organization's business strategy or direction. For startups, strategic HRM means creating business-supporting and innovation-friendly HR practices that help them gain a competitive advantage.

Talent Acquisition: Talent acquisition identifies, attracts, and hires employees to meet an organization's needs. Initial talent acquisition is paramount, as competition for multi-skilled, forward-thinking employees who have what it takes to help scale companies can be fierce within a startup context.

Chapter 9

Green Business Incubation:
Fostering Green Entrepreneurship and Innovation

Amitab Bhattacharjee
https://orcid.org/0000-0003-3765-7412
Lincoln University College, Malaysia

ABSTRACT

Business incubators provide a business environment, where incubatee entrepreneurs can nurture their startup ventures successfully. By offering green infrastructural support, networking, green investors, and mentoring, business incubators can assist entrepreneurs in achieving enhanced business performance, successful market penetration, and financial success. Notwithstanding the emerging interest in the business incubation domain, the green incubation process for innovation and entrepreneurial success remains limited. The author therefore proposes the design of a green business incubation ecosystem and incubation process framework (initiative and context, green incubation facilities, and outcomes). Admittedly, establishing green incubation processes would enhance early-stage entrepreneurial success, foster green innovation, minimize startup challenges, and expand employment opportunities. Thus, the contribution of this chapter would broadly support the development of green business incubators, nascent entrepreneurial success, green innovation, and sustainable development worldwide.

DOI: 10.4018/979-8-3693-4302-9.ch009

INTRODUCTION

Business incubation provides crucial support and resources to nascent entrepreneurs at various stages of their journey, from idea conception to sustainable growth. Incubation programs are designed to nurture and accelerate the development of entrepreneurship, fostering innovation, job creation, and economic growth. Incubators offer supportive benefits such as infrastructure facilities, technological facilities, laboratory facilities, mentorship facilities and networking opportunities (Yang et al., 2024). Such facilities eliminate the need for early-stage entrepreneurs to invest heavily in setting up their own business infrastructure, while reducing operational costs, but all incubators may not have supportive facilities at sufficient level due to incubator size and policies (Awonuga et al., 2024).

The concept of business incubation process began to gain traction in between 1960s and 1970s after the establishment of the first business incubator in New York in 1959 (Capatina et al., 2023). One of the main objectives of incubators is to provide support to entrepreneurs and startups during their early stages, enhancing their prospects for survival opportunity and future growth (Iwu et al., 2024). As the number of business incubators around the world rapidly increases, it is crucial to comprehend the process that increases survival growth and knowledge spillover of green innovation and green entrepreneurship.

Entrepreneurship highly focuses on organizational goals while business incubators foster a sense of entrepreneurial community and collaboration among early-stage founders (Stephens and Lyons, 2023; Beyhan et al., 2024). Sharing experiences, potential challenge assessment, challenge overcoming strategies and entrepreneurial success routes with early-stage entrepreneurs creates a supportive ecosystem where entrepreneurs can learn from each other and celebrate achievements together (Bank et al., 2017; Nicholls-Nixon et al., 2024). Green business incubation processes can improve the nurturing of entrepreneurial talent, foster green innovation, and accelerate low-carbon economic development by providing entrepreneurs eco-friendly resources, green entrepreneurial guidance, and support needed to turn their ideas into successful businesses.

However, global climate concern and conflicting geographical issues have been gradually changing business incubation concepts (Anjaningrum et al., 2024). Day by day, green business incubation necessity is emerging more than ever (Bhattacharjee and Jahanshahi, 2021). Without any debate, it could be claimed that research interest has been growing in the business incubation domain, but no study yet introduced green business incubation for clear understanding of eco-friendly incubator development (Mian et al., 2016; Pepin et al., 2024). In this aspect, Games et al. (2021) and Nafari et al. (2024) mentioned that further study is needed for developing eco-friendly business incubation systems, which would encourage green entrepreneurship and entrepreneurial sustainability in the next generation industrial revolution. Therefore, this chapter introduces the green business incubation ecosystem to encourage green entrepreneurial initiatives and green innovations, while accelerating entrepreneurial performance, environmental and economic sustainability.

The green business incubation ecosystem demonstrates how to integrate zero and low-emission initiatives at different stages of business incubation processes for supporting early-stage green entrepreneurs and their startup ventures. This incubation ecosystem also defines how to establish cost-effective and eco-friendly incubators across the world. Additionally, the author explains how nascent entrepreneurs, early-stage startups can achieve sustainable benefits, innovation facilities, technological supports and higher entrepreneurial sustainability through using green business incubation facilities.

In addition, this chapter discusses the impact of business incubation support on entrepreneurial performance, green innovation scopes and easy market access. Essential strategies and techniques are included in a realistic manner, which would improve the readability and understanding of the green business incubation ecosystem and incubation process. The proposed eco-friendly incubation facilities discussed in this chapter would help early-stage green entrepreneurs and startups, including SMEs around the world, to achieve entrepreneurial success through ensuring climate-friendly economic and ecological development. Such contributions of this chapter broadly support the zero-emission policy of Paris and the Sustainable Development Goals (7th, 8th, 9th and 13th) of the United Nations. This chapter also encourages nascent entrepreneurs and early-stage startups across the globe to transition from emission friendly entrepreneurial practices to green entrepreneurship initiatives in the future, which would strengthen sustainable low-carbon economic and environmental development.

LITERATURE REVIEW

Business Incubation

Business incubation is a supportive process of institutional agreement aimed at fostering and aiding the development of early-stage start-ups and entrepreneurial initiatives. It ensures a nurturing business environment where nascent entrepreneurs can obtain facilities such as resources, advice, and mentorship to transform their ideas into thriving startups (Valliere and Nicholls-Nixon, 2024). Business incubation process differs greatly in their industry type, scope and on-demand support, but they generally provide a variety of services customized to meet the requirements of early-stage founders and nascent entrepreneurs.

Green Business Incubators

Green business incubators are designed by eco-friendly parameters for supporting the operational and financial growth of incubate entrepreneurs and their startups. Green business incubators integrate green policies to ensure a low or zero emission incubation process. They highly encourage nascent entrepreneurs for eco-friendly business practices. For instance, green incubators adopt clean energy and low-emission technologies to provide climate-friendly support to early-stage startups and nascent entrepreneurs.

Key Components of Business Incubation

- *Physical Infrastructure*: Business incubators provide different types of tangible infrastructural support to early-stage firms and Nascent entrepreneurs (Mátéet al., 2024), for example, laboratory equipment, engineering tests, communication networking devices, office space, logistics. These facilities foster operational efficiency while offering cost-effective benefit.
- *Business Operational Support:* Business incubators offer a wide range of new startup operational support to ensure entrepreneurial growth and efficient collaboration(Mhlongo and Mzyece, 2023). For instance, entrepreneurial mentorship and technological support can help early-stage firms to establish business networking opportunities with potential alliances and policies, which improves strategic planning, market research, and collaboration with financial investors & customers.
- *Funding Arrangement:* Nascent entrepreneurs and early-stage startups receive startup funding support from many business incubators (Dhiman and Arora, 2024). Under the commercial contracts, many business incubators arrange potential investors including external funding such as angel investors, government grants, venture capital, to ensure essential capital for early-stage firms.
- *Networking and Community Engagement:* New startup founders can obtain potential business networking contacts within the economic ecology through incubator networks (Secundo et al., 2023). Such contacts are imperative for early-stage entrepreneurs or nascent entrepreneurs to establish a successful business. Nascent entrepreneurs can make connections with business mentors, industry experts/professionals, and potential entrepreneurial collaborators through various entrepreneurial networking events, business workshops, and entrepreneurial community gatherings.
- *Mentorship and Training*: Business incubators offer entrepreneurial mentorship, and training sessions (Lindelöf and Hellberg, 2023) i.e., business

management, marketing and sales, product development, financial planning, and legal compliance to improve knowledge and skills of entrepreneurs that essential to overcome potential challenges of startup ventures successfully.

Green Energy

Green energy refers to clean energy collected from naturally replenishable resources available in the earth's ecology. Unlike fossil fuels or high-emission friendly alternatives, green energy sources are sustainable and emit little to no greenhouse gasses during operation.

Green Energy Sources

Green energy can be collected from many different sources such as sunlight, water, air, and the earth's ground (Brock et al., 2021; Luo et al., 2024). For example, photovoltaic solar panels are used to capture and store clean energy from sunlight, turbines are used to produce clean energy from wind, geothermal systems harness energy from the earth's ground, and biogas plants are used to produce carbon-neutral gas. Additionally, hydropower plants are utilized to generate clean electricity from water.

Business Incubation Process Framework

The incubation support, aimed at fostering innovation and economic growth, is structured to enhance the value of incubated firms, ultimately boosting their survival rates. Incubator facilities supporting entrepreneurs are integral to the incubation process (Van Erkelens et al., 2024). To encourage green entrepreneurial practices, many incubation facilities are now transitioning to eco-friendly environments (Bhattacharjee et al., 2024a). According to the recent study of Sohail et al. (2023), the conventional business incubation process consists of three segments: context, intervention, and output. Furthermore, studies of Al Ayyash et al. (2020) and Reid et al. (2024) emphasized that eco-friendly and social oriented business incubation process should be developed for promoting green entrepreneurship in the future. To fill this existing gap in the business incubation literature, this chapter therefore introduces a complete framework of the green business incubation process for improving incubator performance, green entrepreneurial performance and green innovation. For instance, Figure 1 illustrates a comprehensive framework of the green business incubation process with three segments: initiative and context, green incubation facilities, and outcomes. The significance of the green business incubation process is to ensure the emission-free operational environment for both incubators and incubatee entrepreneurs. Following the theory of planned behavior (Ajzen, 1991; Li et al., 2024), this chapter suggests that establishing green incubation facilities could encourage entrepreneurs to adopt eco-friendly and socially responsible business practices. The first segment of the green business incubation process is the *'initiative and context'*. It depicts that early-stage entrepreneurs collaborate with the green incubator for their specific business needs. Then the incubator identifies essential entrepreneurial programs for incubatee entrepreneurs through a dedicated selection and screening process.

In the second segment (green incubation facilities), incubatee entrepreneurs and their startups receive green incubation support such as networking assistance with green investors, green suppliers, green business partners based on industry and target market. Figure 1 shows that the green incubator has strong affiliation with various types of institutions such as educational institutions, financial institutions, governmental bodies, private organizations, businesses and industries. Support from incubator's affiliated institutions can magnificently aid incubatee entrepreneurs in obtaining essential facilities for increasing new firm growth. With the proper support of affiliated institutions, green incubators establish a green entrepreneurial friendly business environment, where early-stage entrepreneurs can firmly operate and grow their startups by accessing green capital support, green technological support, eco-friendly infrastructural facilities, governmental facilities and receiving necessary entrepreneurial training or mentorship.

Figure 1. Framework of the green business incubation process for ensuring eco-friendly incubation support to early-stage entrepreneurs and startups (Source: Developed by the author).

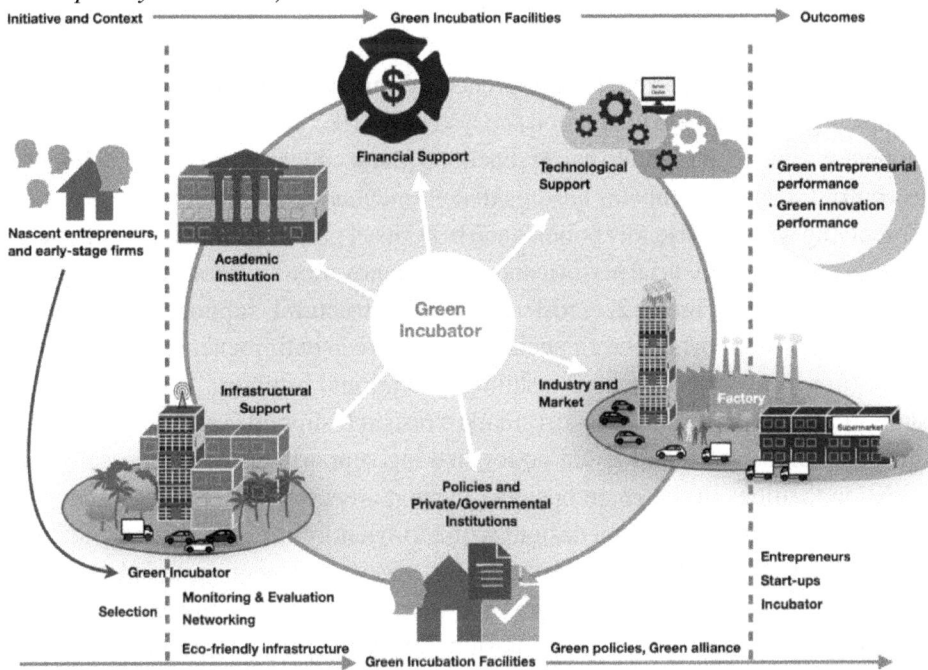

The green incubator's laboratory and its affiliated laboratories provide green innovation facilities for incubatee startups. Throughout the green incubation process, the green incubator monitors and evaluates the progress of incubatee firms, ensuring specific and tailored solutions based on the firm's growth condition. Compared to the conventional incubation process, the green incubation process could strengthen the competitive advantages for entrepreneurs' performance and green innovation scopes. Finally, in the third segment (outcomes), the incubator and entrepreneur evaluate two major outcomes such as entrepreneurial performance and innovation performance for further improvement and strategic development. Thus, the green business incubation process can enhance the sustainable growth of early-stage firms.

Developing Green Incubation Ecosystem

Despite the systematic literature on the conventional incubation process of incubators, insufficient synthesis and fragmented results strongly indicate an unclear understanding of the green business incubation ecosystem (Deyanova et al., 2022; Zane and Tribbitt, 2024). Consequently, previous studies highly recommended for further studies on the eco-friendly business incubation ecosystem (Kiran and Bose, 2020; Yang et al., 2024) because it is needed to develop green incubation facilities for green entrepreneurs and green innovation through ensuring economic and environmental sustainability (Hillemaneet al., 2019; Jahanshahi et al., 2023). Therefore, this chapter proposes a green business incubation ecosystem to accelerate environmentally friendly entrepreneurial initiatives. Figure 2 demonstrates a complete green business incubation ecosystem (GBIE). Generally, the conventional incubator provides support to entrepreneurs without concerning ecological impacts. In contrast, a green incubator ensures that all incubation facilities are eco-friendly. Complying with eco-friendly policies and benefits of green incubators, entrepreneurs can expand entrepreneurial performance, green innovation and product development.

According to Figure 2, eco-friendly infrastructural support, low-emission technological support, green financial support, green entrepreneurial management support, green entrepreneurial training/educational support, green innovation support, market accessing support, market research support, eco-friendly product development support, and green policy making support are the most essential incubation facilities in the green business incubation ecosystem. Figure 2 shows the architecture of green incubator designs with eco-friendly infrastructure and facilities. For example, the GBIE proposes that using renewable energy sourced electricity reduces the consumption of high-emission sourced electricity and reduces overhead costs of the incubator and incubate startups. With such competitive advantage, the green incubator can encourage early-stage entrepreneurs to adopt clean electricity and low-emission business practices.

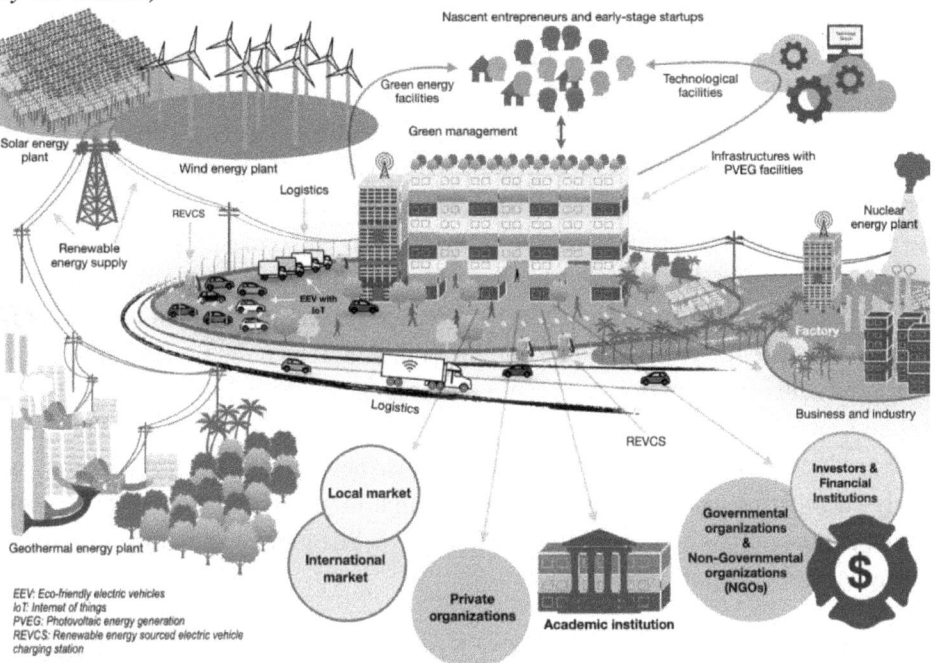

Figure 2. Design of the green business incubation ecosystem (Source: Developed by the author)

Next, the GBIE proposes that green incubator should implement green management, eco-friendly technology policies and green financing support (e.g., affiliate with green angel investors for collecting investment capitals for incubatee green entrepreneurs), which could ensure eco-friendly incubator management, low-emission technology transfer and startup venture capital management. These benefits accelerate socially responsible and eco-friendly entrepreneurial initiatives across the world.

Green incubator assists entrepreneurs to receive eco-friendly entrepreneurial facilities from incubator's affiliated institutions (Jahanshahi et al., 2023). Green policies would help incubators to affiliate with eco-friendly institutions and business partners (Torun et al., 2018; Cao et al., 2024) such as green investors, government organizations, financial institutions, academic institutions, external laboratories, established businesses, and factories. Such way entrepreneurs and startups can obtain green incubation facilities. Using the green incubator's laboratory, entrepreneurs can improve green innovation initiatives, testing/evaluating new measures, research & development. Besides, incubator's affiliated educational institutions could provide necessary training to incubate entrepreneurs to improve their entrepreneurial knowledge and startups development (Bernardus et al., 2024). Green incubator also assists nascent entrepreneurs and early-stage startups to manage seeds capital and access into markets (Rosado-Cubero et al., 2023). Additionally, the low-emission logistics of green incubators ensure eco-friendly distribution support to improve entrepreneur's operational efficiency and revenues (Bhattacharjee and Jahanshahi, 2024).

With low-emission strategy, the green business incubation ecosystem emphasizes five additional strategies: corporate strategy (Todorova, 2024), networking strategy (Bhattacharjee and Ghosh, 2024), innovation strategy (Lu and Wang, 2024), combustion emissions reduction strategy (Bhattacharjee et al., 2024a), and process emissions control strategy (Bhattacharjee et al., 2024a). Using networking strategy, entrepreneurs can make long-term alliances with industry partners through incubator's support. Both corporate strategy and innovation strategy help early-stage firms to access markets and increase competitive advantages, which really ensure sustainable revenue growth. Using combustion emissions reduction strategy, firms can limit emissions through eliminating emission friendly input resources. While process emissions control strategy helps firms to reduce emissions through business and product life cycle emission control systems. Thus, nascent entrepreneurs, and early-stage firms can grow successfully through improving revenue growth, sustainable innovations and operational efficiency, while green incubators can ensure sustainable incubation performance.

Green Business Incubation for Entrepreneurial Performance

The green business incubator emphasizes three major components: green policies, entrepreneurial performance and green innovation performance (Adelowo and Oladimeji, 2024). The philosophy of the green business incubation ecosystem depicts that entrepreneurs and startups should obtain incubation facilities from green incubators having low-emission technologies and renewable energy sourced electricity to reduce fixed costs and variable costs. Using networking strategy (Eldering et al., 2023; Bhattacharjee and Ghosh, 2024), entrepreneurs in SMEs can collect its seeds capital from angel investors or large firms through incubator's support that would reduce long-term debts and interest expenses of those entrepreneurs. In addition, firms applying networking strategy can ensure green technological and clean energy support from green incubators for developing low-emission business practices and ensuring survival growth (Jin et al., 2022; Fithri et al., 2024). Green incubation facilities, therefore, improve overall entrepreneurial performance by reducing costs and increasing competitive advantages. A recent study mentioned a positive connection between business incubation support and entrepreneurial performance (Almeida et al., 2021), signifying that green facilities of incubators can amplify profits and market share of early-stage firms.

Although *green business incubation support* imperatively influences the entrepreneurial performance of early-stage entrepreneurs, evidence is limited (Iyortsuun, 2017; Yang et al., 2024). Initially, green business incubation facilities can significantly eliminate investment costs required to implement green entrepreneurial initiatives in the long run, they can lead to significant cost savings and operational efficiencies (Fonseca and Jabbour, 2012; Jahanshahi et al., 2021). For example, using energy-efficient technologies and green infrastructure facilities, green business incubators and incubate entrepreneurs can reduce utility costs, office rent, transportation costs, technology costs, laboratory costs and minimize waste costs, while fostering revenue growth, operational efficiency and product development & innovation. Green incubators can assist early-stage startups and nascent entrepreneurs to escalate their revenue growth and socially responsible business practices in the post COVID-19 era (Bhattacharjee et al., 2021). Moreover, they would firmly foster competitive advantage, higher firm reputation, and long-term financial sustainability, and ecological sustainability (Sharda et al., 2015; Ushakov et al., 2023). Thus, green business incubation facilities can ensure higher entrepreneurial performance of early-stage entrepreneurs and low-carbon economic growth.

Role of Green Business Incubation in Green Innovation

To medicate today's global climate crisis, green innovation is indeed to resolve emission friendly business practices. As nascent entrepreneurs obtain early-stage incubation facilities from business incubators, green incubation support at the incubator is necessary to encourage early-stage firms and entrepreneurs for green innovation (Stephens and Lyons, 2023; Anjaningrum et al., 2024). The concept of green innovation is basically, developing or exploring solutions of products or service through eco-friendly measures such as developing products by eco-friendly resources, developing eco-friendly packaging, developing green manufacturing systems, developing low-emission technologies, and developing climate-friendly waste management systems (Cirule and Uvarova, 2022; Ordoñez de Pablos, 2023). The relationship between green business incubation facilities and green innovation has been a subject of varying viewpoints within the business incubation literature (Lu and Wang, 2024). Previous studies mentioned that eco-friendly incubation policies and facilities can encourage green innovation initiatives among entrepreneurs, which assist to minimize environmental impacts (Fichter and Hurrelmann, 2021; Bhattacharjee and Jahanshahi, 2024).

Scholars emphasized insights that establishing green incubators would be a realistic idea to increase the intention of green innovation among incubatee entrepreneurs over concentrating only profit oriented innovation (Qian et al., 2011; Pattanasak et al., 2022). For instance, developing laboratories with clean electricity and low-emission technologies can improve the socially and climate responsible innovation practices. In addition, providing training on green innovation to early-stage entrepreneurs at incubators would be beneficial for building eco-trust and social responsibility among new entrepreneurs (Bhattacharjee et al., 2024b), which then inspire them for green innovation and green entrepreneurial practices. According to the behavioral learning theory, entrepreneurs can learn through their interaction with the eco-friendly business environment (Singh et al., 2024). Hence, using eco-friendly facilities at incubators, the intention of green innovation among entrepreneurs would be increased. Therefore, green business incubation increases green innovation scope for early-stage entrepreneurs.

Role of Green Business Incubation in Market Access

New or early-stage entrepreneurs may face market entry challenges due to competitors or lack of market knowledge (Ssekiziyivu et al., 2023). Such challenges can be overcome through green business incubation support (Cao et al., 2024). Basically, green business incubators provide necessary eco-friendly entrepreneurial training to nascent and early-stage entrepreneurs about how to improve their market knowledge and how to gain sustainable market shares through developing eco-friendly initiatives, which are really essential for successful market penetration. Recent studies suggests that early-stage entrepreneurs could easily enter into the target market with the help of incubator's supervision (Jia et al., 2020; Bibeau et al., 2024). For instance, early-stage entrepreneurs can alliance with green business partners to increase eco-friendly business reputation, which leads to easy access into a matured market. In this situation, green incubators could assist entrepreneurs to find suitable green business alliances. Besides, early-stage startups especially SMEs are mostly required a significant amount of working capital for marketing purposes that could be minimized by using green business incubation facilities (Bhattacharjee and Juman, 2020; Nafari et al., 2024). For early-stage entrepreneurs, gaining market shares with new products or services significantly raises operating expenses and even it's time consuming, but green business incubation facilities could reduce those expenses and time. Therefore, green incubator's support ensures smooth market entry for early-stage entrepreneurs and startups.

Figure 3. Theoretical model with four constructs (Source: Developed by the author).

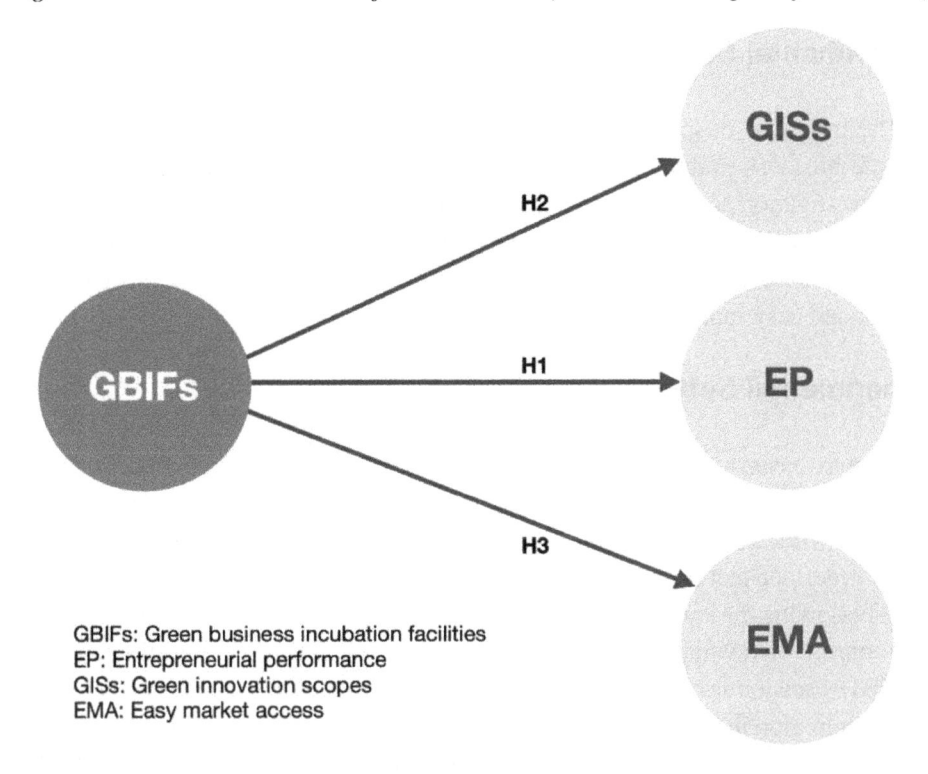

GBIFs: Green business incubation facilities
EP: Entrepreneurial performance
GISs: Green innovation scopes
EMA: Easy market access

Consistent with the aforementioned discussion and evidence, three prepositions (H1, H2 & H3) are hypothetically posited, see Figure 3 for a graphical indication of the theoretical model. In this model, four constructs i.e., green business incubation facilities, entrepreneurial performance, green innovation scopes and easy market access are included for empirical justification. Three hypothetical assumptions are the following: H1: Green business incubation facilities increase entrepreneurial performance of early-stage entrepreneurs. H2: Green business incubation facilities increase green innovation scopes for early-stage entrepreneurs. H3: Green business incubation facilities can increase the likelihood of easy market access for early-stage entrepreneurs.

METHODOLOGY

Experimental Scenario

The proposed business incubation techniques of this chapter have applied in real life business practices to establish their generalizability. Around 17 months long investigation conducted among incubate entrepreneurs in Malaysia. Data from close-ended questionnaire based online survey was used to examine the impact of green business incubation facilities on entrepreneurial performance, green innovation scopes, and easy market access.

Experimental Setting

Criteria-based investigation was conducted from October 2022 to February 2024 in Malaysia. The first of the two mandatory criteria was that entrepreneurs must have affiliated with the incubator for more than one fiscal year. The second mandatory criterion defined that firms must have undertaken eco-friendly entrepreneurial initiatives. Following the study of Jahanshahi et al. (2017), the survey questionnaire along with consent was available in both English and local language. The questionnaire was verified by academic experts for necessary corrections before conducting the survey. All participation in the survey was anonymous. During the data collection, a cluster random sampling technique was used, forming clusters based on male and female entrepreneurs. Around 179 early-stage entrepreneurs with eco-friendly initiatives participated in the first-round survey in the last quarter of 2022. All participants were provided feedback about green business incubation facilities, entrepreneurial performance, green innovation scopes and easy market access.

Approximately 10 months later, a second phase survey was conducted (from November 2023 to February 2024). In the 2nd phase survey, around 142 early-stage entrepreneurs were provided responses. Total 133 of 142 responses were accepted after screening all final feedback because 9 questionnaires were eliminated due to insufficient answers. However, the evaluation of all hypothetical assumptions was entirely based on online survey data. After data collection, factor analysis (Becker et al., 2023) was employed and then calculated compound-mean values. For example, the equation used to calculate compound-mean is $\frac{fr\,\bar{x}_1 + sr\,\bar{x}_2}{2}$, where $fr\,\bar{x}_1$ = mean values of first round survey data and $sr\,\bar{x}_2$ = mean values of second round survey data. Next, frequency analysis (Bhattacharjee et al., 2024a), Q^2 test and f^2 test were performed. To evaluate hypothetical associations between study constructs, *structural equation modeling (SEM)* was executed on the *statistical software 'R'*. All results with hypothetical decisions are demonstrated in the result and discussion section with graphical presentations.

Measurement of Constructs

Four constructs (green business incubation facilities, entrepreneurial performance, green innovation scopes and easy market access) and three controls were included to examine three hypothetical assumptions. Five questions asked for *green business incubation facilities* such as this incubator provides eco-friendly infrastructural, technological, financial, entrepreneurial connection, entrepreneurial training and legal facilities, which are essential for entrepreneurial and green innovation; this incubator has renewable energy sourced electricity supply and also encourage entrepreneurs to integrate renewable energy; this incubator assists early-stage entrepreneurs or startups with smooth market penetration; green incubation process of this incubator encourages green entrepreneurial initiatives; Overall incubation facilities of this incubator are eco-friendly and cost-effective, which improve entrepreneurial performance. These items were retrieved from (Ririh et al., 2020).

Four questions asked for *green innovation scopes* such as the eco-friendly incubator ensures sufficient green innovation facilities such as eco-friendly laboratory for early-stage entrepreneurs; the eco-friendly incubator increases green finance support to early-stage entrepreneurs for green innovation; the eco-friendly incubator provides eco-friendly resources to early-stage entrepreneurs for green innovation; green incubator encourages intention of green innovation among entrepreneurs. These items were retrieved from (Chien et al., 2022). Three questions asked about *easy market access* such as adopting incubator's support ensures easy market entry for early-stage entrepreneurs; using incubation facilities reduce market entry expenses and time; green incubation facilities help to gain market share even in the competitive business environment. These items were retrieved from (Scillitoe and Birasnav, 2022). All items of each construct were measured by a 5-Point Likert scale.

However, following the recent study of Bhattacharjee et al. (2024a), entrepreneurial performance was evaluated by the following equations:

Return on assets (ROA):

$$roa_1 = \left\{ \left(\frac{\partial nie_1}{\partial nas_1} \right) \times 100\% \right\} \quad (Eq.1)$$

$$roa_2 = \left\{ \left(\frac{\partial nie_2}{\partial nas_2} \right) \times 100\% \right\} \quad (Eq.2)$$

$$\overline{roa} = \frac{roa_1 + roa_2}{n} \quad (Eq.3)$$

Where,

∂nie_1 : *Net Income of* 2022 ; ∂nie_2 : *Net Income of* 2023

∂nas_1 : *Net Assets of* 2022; ∂nas_2 : *Net Assets of* 2023

Return on equity (ROE):

$$roe_1 = \left\{\left(\frac{\partial nie_1}{\partial seq_1}\right) \times 100\%\right\} (Eq.4)$$

$$roe_2 = \left\{\left(\frac{\partial ni_2}{\partial seq_2}\right) \times 100\%\right\} (Eq.5)$$

$$\overline{roe} = \frac{roe_1 + roe_2}{n} (Eq.6)$$

Where,

∂nie_1 : *Net Income of* 2022 ; ∂nie_2 : *Net Income of* 2023

∂seq_1 : *Shareholder's equity of* 2022; ∂seq_2 : *Shareholder's equity of* 2023

After the financial ratio analysis, results of ROA and ROE were adjusted with the Likert-Scale format (see Table 1 for details).

Table 1. Adjusting ratio results with Likert-Scale format (Source: Bhattacharjee et al., 2024a).

ROA and ROE		
Ratio range	**Scale**	**Likert-Scale Direction**
ROA or ROE < 0%	1	Low
0% < ROA or ROE < 0.5%	2	
0.5% < ROA or ROE < 1.25%	3	to
1.25% < ROA or ROE < 2%	4	
2% < ROA or ROE	5	High

RESULTS AND DISCUSSION

The influence of green business incubation facilities on entrepreneurial success is significant in Europe, and other continents, as they offer access to eco-friendly resources, mentorship, entrepreneurial networking opportunities, funding, skill development, and ensure long-term sustainability. By nurturing and empowering startups, these eco-friendly business incubation facilities play a crucial role in fostering green innovation, low-carbon economic growth, and green entrepreneurial sustainability (Jahanshahi et al., 2017; Vaz et al., 2023). In contrast to the conventional business incubation process, the green business incubation process could promote opportunities for green entrepreneurship and eco-friendly innovation, especially for SMEs (Fonseca and Jabbour, 2012; Tritoasmoro et al., 2024). Green incubators can further enhance environmentally friendly business practices and maximize emission control by expanding eco-friendly incubation facilities. However, based on the frequency analysis of survey data, it was found that 83% of respondents were male entrepreneurs, 89% were in the 20–35 age group, and 41% were social entrepreneurs.

Predictive Relevance and f^2 Assessment

Following the study of Bhattacharjee and Ghosh, (2024) Q^2 estimation was employed to examine the predictive relevance of the hypothetical model with four constructs. The satisfactory threshold for Q^2 values was initially used to evaluate the Q-square results of all constructs. For instance, Q-square values above zero ($Q^2>0$) is widely considered to indicate that the measuring model has sufficient predictive relevance (Becker et al., 2023). In contrast, it should be declined if Q-square values under zero ($Q^2< 0$) (Becker et al., 2023). A censorious evaluation shows that Q-square values of four constructs such as green business incubation facilities, entrepreneurial performance, green innovation scopes and easy market access are above the Q^2 threshold limit ($Q^2> 0$), see Figure 4.

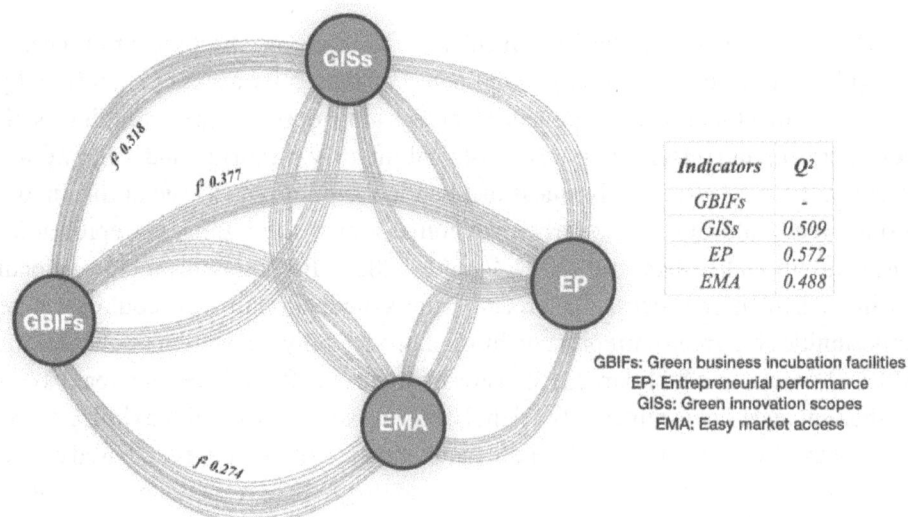

Figure 4. Networking diagram, f^2 values and Q^2 values (Source: Author's elaboration).

Indicators	Q^2
GBIFs	-
GISs	0.509
EP	0.572
EMA	0.488

GBIFs: Green business incubation facilities
EP: Entrepreneurial performance
GISs: Green innovation scopes
EMA: Easy market access

After the evaluation of predictive relevance, we employed f^2 test to find actual substantive impacts of green business incubation facilities on other latent variables. Referring to (Becker et al., 2023; Bhattacharjee et al., 2024a), f-square indicates minimum ($f^2 < 0.150$), moderate ($0.150 < f^2 < 0.350$) and large ($f^2 > 0.350$) effects sizes. Hence, a crucial look at Figure 4 shows that green business incubation facilities (GBIFs) have large impact on entrepreneurial performance ($f^2 = 0.377$). However, green business incubation facilities have moderate impact on green innovation scopes ($f^2 = 0.318$) and easy market access ($f^2 = 0.274$). Hence, the generalizability of the hypothetical model with four constructs is proven. It indicates that with the support of green incubators, early-stage entrepreneurs can achieve higher entrepreneurial performance and easily access target markets such as domestic markets.

Hypothetical Assessment and Explanation

The structural equation modeling (SEM) technique was employed to examine three hypothetical assumptions (H1, H2 & H3). Results derived from SEM analysis showed all green business incubation facilities are positively and significantly associated with other three constructs. For instance, see Figure 5 for graphical demonstration of SEM results.

Figure 5. Results of structural equation modeling (SEM) assessment (Source: Author's elaboration).

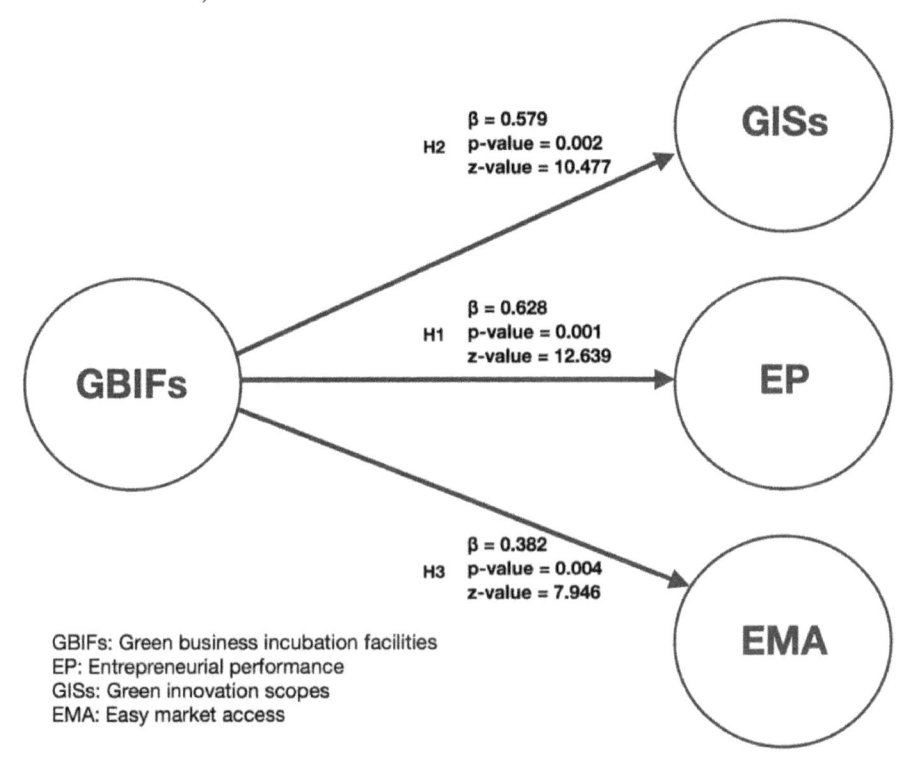

```
                    β = 0.579
                H2  p-value = 0.002        GISs
                    z-value = 10.477

                    β = 0.628
                H1  p-value = 0.001
      GBIFs         z-value = 12.639        EP

                    β = 0.382
                H3  p-value = 0.004
                    z-value = 7.946        EMA

GBIFs: Green business incubation facilities
EP: Entrepreneurial performance
GISs: Green innovation scopes
EMA: Easy market access
```

The first hypothetical assumption (H1) deals that green business incubation facilities increase entrepreneurial performance of early-stage entrepreneurs. The SEM results demonstrated in Figure 5 reveal that green business incubation facilities have a positive and significant influence on entrepreneurial performance ($\beta = 0.628$, $p = 0.001$). Similarly, the confidence ellipse in Figure 6 shows that the confidence ellipse area is positively distributed, and floated upward, which together firmly depict a positive correlation between entrepreneurial performance and green business incubation facilities.

Figure 6. Ellipse distribution shows a positive association between green business incubation facilities and entrepreneurial performance (Source: Author's elaboration).

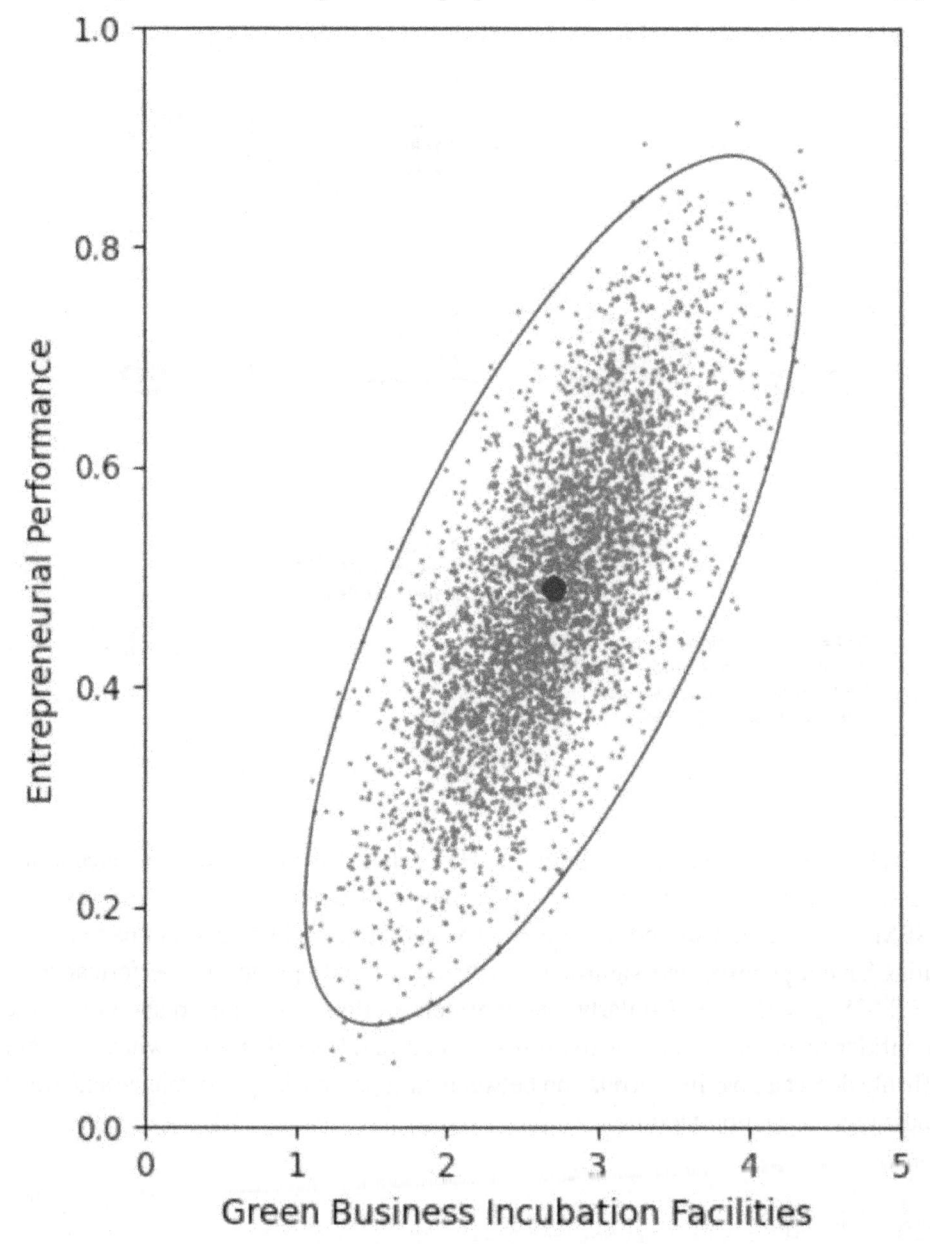

Consequently, confidence ellipses squeezed inside the oval-shaped outline in Figure 6 demonstrate that by using green incubation facilities, early-stage entrepreneurs and startups could ensure higher growth in entrepreneurial performance.

For instance, green incubators could assist early-stage entrepreneurs in redesigning low-emission procurement, manufacturing and distribution systems. These facilities would significantly reduce overall operating costs and production-level emissions. In addition, integrating clean energy limits dependency on high-emission electricity, strategically lowering utility costs as well as operating expenses. Hence, the first hypothetical assumption, H1, is supported.

The second hypothetical assumption (H2) deals that green business incubation facilities increase green innovation scopes for early-stage entrepreneurs. The SEM results demonstrated in Figure 5 indicate that green business incubation facilities have a positive and significant influence on green innovation scopes ($\beta = 0.579$, $p = 0.002$).

Figure 7. Curves indicate a positive association between green business incubation facilities and green innovation scopes (Source: Author's elaboration).

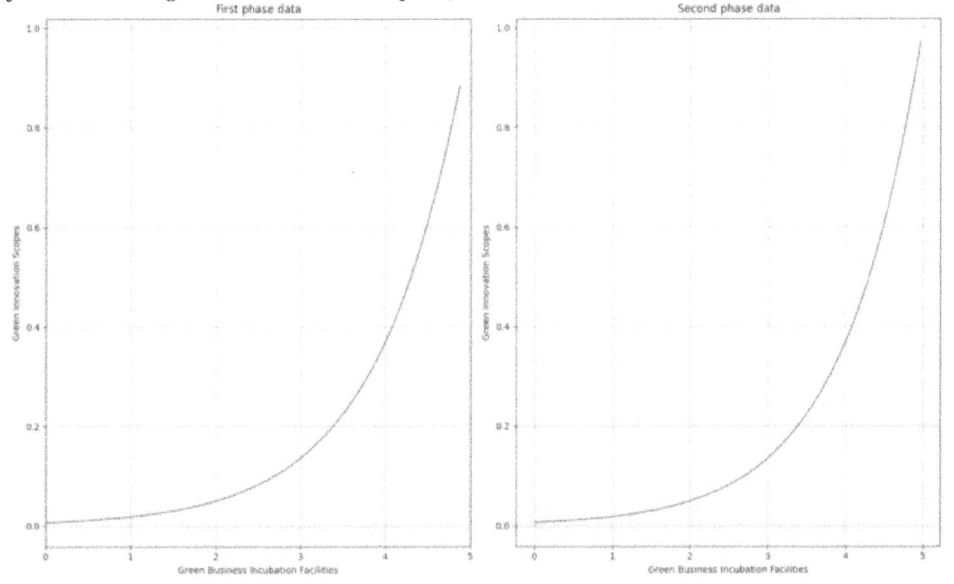

Similarly, the graphical representation of Figure 7 shows that both curves have an upward trend, strongly suggesting that green innovation scopes for early-stage entrepreneurs could be increased by implementing green business incubation facilities. Green incubators can provide eco-friendly resources and business alliance for nascent entrepreneurs and early-stage startups, magnificently expanding the range of opportunities for green innovations. Therefore, the hypothetical assumption, H2, is accepted.

The third hypothetical assumption (H3) proposes that green business incubation facilities can increase the likelihood of easy market access for early-stage entrepreneurs. The SEM results demonstrated in Figure 5 indicated that green business incubation facilities have positive and significant influence on easy market access for early-stage entrepreneurs ($\beta = 0.382, p = 0.004$). The curve with upward trend in Figure 8 robustly defines that early-stage entrepreneurs or startups could easily penetrate into local and international markets with the help of green business incubation facilities. For example, early-stage entrepreneurs can make alliances with large firms or other established firms through incubator's support, which would ensure obtaining target market share in a competitive market (Jahanshahi and Bhattacharjee, 2020). In addition, early-stage entrepreneurs can ensure on demand logistic support, marketing facilities and working capital facilities from green incubators that enormously improve market access potentiality for them. Consequently, the third hypothetical assumption, H3, is accepted.

Figure 8. The curve shows a positive correlation between green business incubation facilities and easy market access (Source: Author's elaboration).

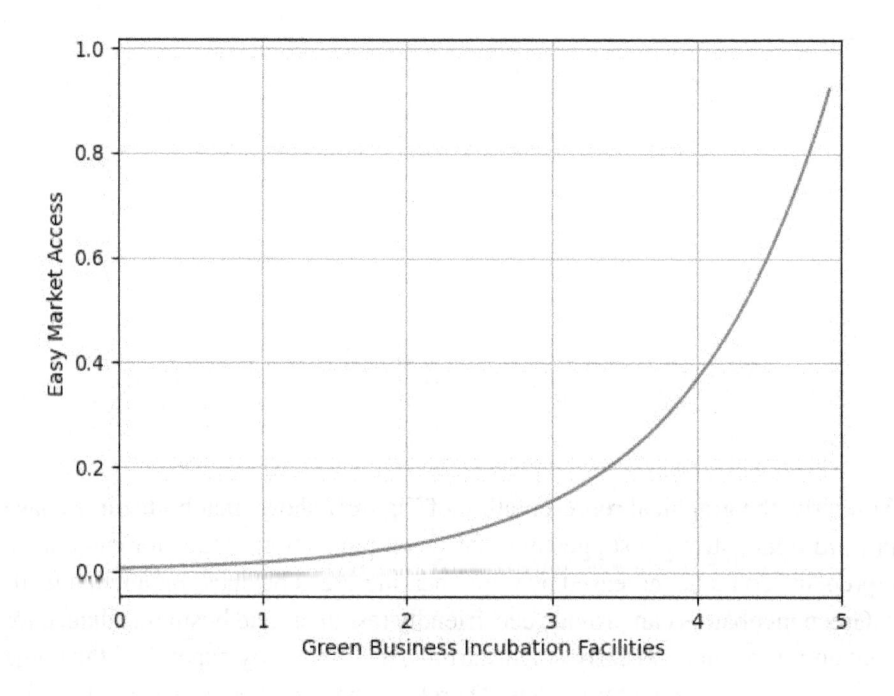

Green Business Incubation Towards Sustainability

Environmental Sustainability

Environmental sustainability refers to conserving natural components or resources and ensuring zero emission prospects to meet present and future economic needs while striving for an emission free world. Previous study emphasized that ecological disasters, such as numerous calamitous events causing irreversible destruction of the natural environment are highly associated with high-risk emission friendly business activities (Bhattacharjee et al., 2020; Zhang et al., 2024). Reducing *environmental risks* through integrating green policies into new business development is therefore imperative.

This chapter suggests that business incubators should implement environmental strategies and green management policies to promote green business practices. Adopting clean energy sourced electricity, green technologies and eco-friendly business incubation policies could encourage startup entrepreneurs and their businesses to integrate environmentally friendly business practices that would boost environmental sustainability. The theory of planned behavior (Ajzen, 1991; Li et al., 2024) defines that perceived behavioral control influences actual behavioral practices. This implies that implementing eco-friendly facilities at incubators can firmly foster the intention of eco-friendly business practices among incubatee entrepreneurs, while ensuring long-term environmental sustainability.

Economic Sustainability

Green incubator development around the world is an ideal way to ensure *global economic sustainability* in the future. Eco-friendly implementable measures in incubators can ensure green business incubation facilities for early-stage entrepreneurs and their startups (Paoloni and Modaffari, 2022). As economic sustainability is somewhat challenging due to high-risk emissions (Iwu et al., 2024), therefore, encouraging green entrepreneurial initiatives through green business incubation processes are essential to implement. Besides, green incubators could assist entrepreneurs to establish socially responsible business practices and widening green innovation scopes by providing green financing, green technologies, green entrepreneurial mentorship and other benefits, which enhance sustainable low-carbon economic development in the long run. Specifically, establishing green incubators in the developing and under-developed countries financed by developed countries would firmly expand the global economic market, increase entrepreneurial performance and green innovations that dramatically minimize global economic challenges.

Social Sustainability

Establishing green incubators could expand green entrepreneurial and employment opportunities, which in turn increases financial growth and sustainable development within society. Incubators support local communities for accelerating self-dependency programs that boosts green entrepreneurial intentions among young people (Paoloni and Modaffari, 2022; Jahanshahi et al., 2023). Consequently, increasing green entrepreneurial initiatives through green incubators would firmly expedite green innovations and open new employment opportunities. With the green innovation facilities provided by green incubators, entrepreneurs could develop green products that firmly improves individuals' eco-friendly lifestyles. Additionally, decreasing the unemployment rate in society could decrease potential community corruptions. As green business incubators employ green policies (Man et al., 2024), the impact of climate change on society due to industrial emissions will also be diminished. Consequently, the occurrence of climate disasters causing property damage would decrease that limits potential economic losses for individuals in society. Thus, green incubators can expedite long-term social sustainability.

Challenges of Green Business Incubators

Cyberthreat

The expansion of digital technological transformation in business increases the potential cyberthreat for entrepreneurs in many regions around the world. Potential business firms or aggressive regional agents are playing unethical cybercrime practices to collect confidential information about new innovation, product manufacturing blueprints, financial data and other highly confidential data of other entrepreneurs or startups to ensure competitive advantages and higher economic growth (Shandilya et al., 2024). Therefore, using shared technologies at incubators might be dangerous for innovation and sophisticated product manufacturing-oriented entrepreneurs/startups. In this aspect, ensuring sufficient cybersecurity by incubators for early-stage entrepreneurs and startups could be challenging against potential cyberthreat.

Worst Monopolistic Practices

In today's highly competitive market, complexity has reached unprecedented levels due to anti-alliance practices. Many giant companies have established monopolistic anti-alliance practices to gain more profits and significant control over local and international economic markets (Bhattacharjee et al., 2024b). Consequently, these types of companies always try to buy innovations of small firms to ensure monopolistic advantage in the target market (Liu, 2020). In some critical situations, aggressive giant firms apply destructive strategies in the market such as forced acquisition with unauthorized involvement of incubators, which could threaten the longevity of early-stage entrepreneurs/startups. Such practices may heighten barriers to the development of green innovation and green entrepreneur friendly green incubators, especially in the developing/under-developed regions.

Regional Crisis

Global regional crises such as war, pandemic effects and lack of democracy in economic policies significantly influences the equitable distribution of international economic and monetary flows, including climate finance for green economic development and green technologies (Stephens and Lyons, 2023). Developing green business incubators can be afforded by developed countries but establishing green business incubators might be difficult in developing and underdeveloped countries due to insufficient liquidity issues stemming from regional political conflicts and wars. If such complications continue to escalate, the development of the green business incubation ecosystem could become challenging in the future.

Inflation

Global inflation poses a significant challenge in the costs of development of the green incubation process (Cao et al., 2024). The costs associated with integrating renewable energy sourced electricity, eco-friendly infrastructure and low-emission technologies are continually increasing due to global inflation. As a result, expenses such as investment costs, interest on credit amounts, shipment costs, expense on technologies, and other operational expenses are soaring, which would increase potential expenses for incubators and early-stage entrepreneurs.

PRACTICAL IMPLICATIONS

The broad contribution of this chapter is to propose a green business incubation ecosystem and incubation process for improving early-stage green entrepreneurship practices and sustainable developments. This chapter emphasizes a positive impact of green business incubation facilities on entrepreneurial performance, green innovation scopes and easy market access, therefore the author suggests that nascent entrepreneurs and early-stage startups in the SMEs industry should use green incubator's support for long-term competitive advantages. The author encourages that governmental and non-governmental initiatives should increase to establish green business incubators in the developing and underdeveloped countries, so that early-stage entrepreneurs could achieve green entrepreneurial success and green innovation scopes, while minimizing high-leverage risks.

Additionally, establishing green business incubators can ensure sustainable growth of successful green entrepreneurial initiatives that can increase employment opportunities, low-carbon technological development, clean energy integration, and sustainable economic development. Thus, the contribution of this chapter would assist nascent entrepreneurs, early-stage green entrepreneurs/startups, industrial practitioners, incubator managers, governmental/non-governmental policymakers and similar bodies to understand, implement and practices of green incubation facilities and how to develop green business incubation ecosystem to ensure sustainable green economic growth and cleaner climate safety that makes the global zero emission target and sustainable development goals (7th, 8th, 9th and 13th) of the United Nations successful.

LIMITATIONS AND FUTURE RESEARCH DIRECTIONS

This chapter proposes the green business incubation ecosystem and green incubation facilities for fostering entrepreneurial performance, green innovation scopes and easy market access. These assumptions have been evaluated with empirical survey data from a country of Southeast Asia. Therefore, further research may examine the similar assumptions in multiple countries in Asia, Europe and other continents. all data in the case study survey collected from Malaysia. Considering this geographical limitation, the author suggests that further investigation should examine similar prospects in developing countries to increase generalizability of green business incubation. Such research will truly improve the green business incubation process in the future. Moreover, adopting green transformation in the manufacturing-oriented business will require more green investments. Therefore, future research should investigate how early-stage startups could accumulate green finance to integrate clean energy and low emission technologies in developing or underdeveloped countries. Thus, further studies could reveal interesting insights to ameliorate the green business incubation ecosystem and process.

CONCLUSION

Developing green incubators can improve green economic, environmental and social sustainability through increasing entrepreneurial performance and green innovations. In this chapter, the author proposes how to design and establish green business incubation processes to ensure sustainable entrepreneurial growth and green economic development in industry 5.0, which is the unique contribution of this chapter. The chapter findings suggest that business incubators should adopt low-carbon policies to encourage green entrepreneurial initiatives, and eco-friendly innovations among early-stage entrepreneurs. In terms of low emission prospects, low-carbon technologies and renewable energy sourced electricity would be prominent solutions for establishing green business incubators (Bhattacharjee and Bansal, 2023). With increasing the adoption of clean energy at incubators, dependency on coal or nuclear-sourced power will decrease.

Further, the cost-effective policies demonstrated in this chapter will help to design and execute green business incubation ecosystem, which will assist to decrease CO_2 emissions, high-emission energy consumption, incubator's expenses, and operating costs of early-stage startups, but increase efficiency, transparency, reliability, entrepreneurial performance, green innovation scopes and resilience. The benefits of developing the green business incubation ecosystem extend beyond environmental stewardship to include cost savings, regulatory compliance, and enhanced sustainable economic growth. By prioritizing sustainability through integrating renewable energy, green technologies and green policies, both green incubators and green entrepreneurs can achieve both ecological and economic advantages (Sun et al., 2020; Dlamini et al., 2023). Finally, establishing green business incubators can ensure promoting green entrepreneurial initiatives, low-carbon economic development, more employment opportunities, social development and environmental safety.

REFERENCES

Adelowo, C. M., & Oladimeji, O. O. (2024). How entrepreneurial characteristics and incubation facilities shape venture creation among technology business incubators in Nigeria. *International Journal of Technoentrepreneurship*, 5(1), 49–66. DOI: 10.1504/IJTE.2024.137530

Ajzen, I. (1991). The theory of planned behavior. *Organizational Behavior and Human Decision Processes*, 50(2), 179–211. DOI: 10.1016/0749-5978(91)90020-T

Al Ayyash, S., McAdam, M., & O'Gorman, C. (2020). Towards a new perspective on the heterogeneity of business incubator-incubation definitions. *IEEE Transactions on Engineering Management*, 69(4), 1738–1752. DOI: 10.1109/TEM.2020.2984169

Almeida, R. I. D. S., Pinto, A. P. S., & Henriques, C. M. R. (2021). The effect of incubation on business performance: A comparative study in the Centro region of Portugal. *Revista Brasileira de Gestão de Negócios*, 23, 127–140. DOI: 10.7819/rbgn.v23i1.4089

Anjaningrum, W. D., Yogatama, A. N., Sidi, A. P., Hermawati, A., & Suci, R. P. (2024). The impact of Penta-Helix Collaborative Business Incubation Process on the creative business strategic orientation and innovation capability. *International Journal of Learning and Intellectual Capital*, 21(1), 60–77. DOI: 10.1504/IJLIC.2024.136380

Awonuga, K. F., Mhlongo, N. Z., Olatoye, F. O., Ibeh, C. V., Elufioye, O. A., & Asuzu, O. F. (2024). Business incubators and their impact on startup success: A review in the USA. *International Journal of Science and Research Archive*, 11(1), 1418–1432. DOI: 10.30574/ijsra.2024.11.1.0234

Bank, N., Fichter, K., & Klofsten, M. (2017). Sustainability-profiled incubators and securing the inflow of tenants–The case of Green Garage Berlin. *Journal of Cleaner Production*, 157, 76–83. DOI: 10.1016/j.jclepro.2017.04.123

Becker, J. M., Cheah, J. H., Gholamzade, R., Ringle, C. M., & Sarstedt, M. (2023). PLS-SEM's most wanted guidance. *International Journal of Contemporary Hospitality Management*, 35(1), 321–346. DOI: 10.1108/IJCHM-04-2022-0474

Bernardus, D., Sufa, S. A., & Suparwata, D. O. (2024). Supporting Start-ups in Indonesia: Examining Government Policies, Incubator Business, and Sustainable Structure for Entrepreneurial Ecosystems and Capital. *International Journal of Business, Law, and Education*, 5(1), 236–259. DOI: 10.56442/ijble.v5i1.372

Beyhan, B., Akçomak, S., & Cetindamar, D. (2024). The startup selection process in accelerators: Qualitative evidence from Turkey. *Entrepreneurship Research Journal*, 14(1), 27–51. DOI: 10.1515/erj-2021-0122

Bhattacharjee, A., & Bansal, V. (2023). Sustainable Approaches of Blockchain Tech, Artificial Intelligence, and Climate Finance in the 4&5IR: Low Emission Technologies and Economy. In Trivedi, S., Aggarwal, R., & Singh, G. (Eds.), *Perspectives on Blockchain Technology and Responsible Investing* (pp. 85–116). IGI Global. DOI: 10.4018/978-1-6684-8361-9.ch004

Bhattacharjee, A., Bansal, V., & Juman, M. K. I. (2021). COVID-19 Emergency: Faux Healthcare Service Causes Distress and Life Dissatisfaction. *Asian Journal of Medicine and Health*, 18(12), 53–61. DOI: 10.9734/ajmah/2020/v18i1230290

Bhattacharjee, A., & Ghosh, A. (2024). Sustainable Green Supply Chain Management for Organizational Performance and Carbon Reduction. In Ramakrishna, Y., & Srivastava, B. (Eds.), *Strategies for Environmentally Responsible Supply Chain and Production Management* (pp. 128–155). IGI Global. DOI: 10.4018/979-8-3693-0669-7.ch007

Bhattacharjee, A., Ghosh, A., Juman, M. K., & Hossen, M. (2024b). Augmented Intelligence for Knowledge Management and Green Education in the Post-COVID-19 Era. In Doshi, R., Dadhich, M., Poddar, S., & Hiran, K. (Eds.), *Integrating Generative AI in Education to Achieve Sustainable Development Goals* (pp. 47–71). IGI Global. DOI: 10.4018/979-8-3693-2440-0.ch003

Bhattacharjee, A., & Jahanshahi, A. A. (2021). Artificial landscape strategy: A business growth recovery plan in the post pandemic world. *Academia Letters*, 2311. Advance online publication. DOI: 10.20935/AL2311

Bhattacharjee, A., & Jahanshahi, A. A. (2024). Simulation of Green Supply Chain Design With Renewable Energy and Green Technology for Intensifying Sustainability After COVID-19. In Martínez-Falcó, J., Marco-Lajara, B., Sánchez-García, E., & Millán-Tudela, L. (Eds.), *Green Supply Chain Management Practice and Principles* (pp. 219–248). IGI Global. DOI: 10.4018/979-8-3693-3486-7.ch011

Bhattacharjee, A., Jahanshahi, A. A., Bhuiyan, M., & Sultana, S. (2020). Mental health of cisgender and transgender during COVID-19 pandemic. *International Journal of Medical Research and Review*, 8(5), 344–351. DOI: 10.17511/ijmrr.2020.i05.02

Bhattacharjee, A., Jahanshahi, A. A., & Chakraborty, S. (2024a). Unlocking the link between low emission supply chains, blockchain adoption, and financial success: The payoff of socially responsible practices in supply chains. *Business Strategy & Development*, 7(1), e341. DOI: 10.1002/bsd2.341

Bhattacharjee, A., & Juman, M. K. I. (2020). Does delay or scarcity in working capital increase unexpected financial risk for women entrepreneurs in the developing country? *International Journal of Economics, Commerce and Management, 8*(8), 433-446. http://ijecm.co.uk/wp-content/uploads/2020/08/8827.pdf

Bibeau, J., Meilleur, R., & St-Jean, É. (2024). To formalize, or not to formalize, business incubators' networks: That is not the question. *Technovation*, 130, 102904. DOI: 10.1016/j.technovation.2023.102904

Brock, A., Sovacool, B. K., & Hook, A. (2021). Volatile photovoltaics: Green industrialization, sacrifice zones, and the political ecology of solar energy in Germany. *Annals of the American Association of Geographers*, 111(6), 1756–1778. DOI: 10.1080/24694452.2020.1856638

Cao, Z., Cunningham, L. F., Gao, W., & Liu, Y. (2024). The downsides of specialization: The impact of business incubator's specialization on startups' R&D efficiency and venture capital financing. *R & D Management*, 54(1), 39–59. DOI: 10.1111/radm.12635

Capatina, A., Cristea, D. S., Micu, A., Micu, A. E., Empoli, G., & Codignola, F. (2023). Exploring causal recipes of startup acceptance into business incubators: A cross-country study. *International Journal of Entrepreneurial Behaviour & Research*, 29(7), 1584–1612. DOI: 10.1108/IJEBR-06-2022-0527

Chien, F., Kamran, H. W., Nawaz, M. A., Thach, N. N., Long, P. D., & Baloch, Z. A. (2022). Assessing the prioritization of barriers toward green innovation: Small and medium enterprises Nexus. *Environment, Development and Sustainability*, 24(2), 1897–1927. DOI: 10.1007/s10668-021-01513-x

Cirule, I., & Uvarova, I. (2022). Open innovation and determinants of technology-driven sustainable value creation in incubated start-ups. *Journal of Open Innovation*, 8(3), 162. DOI: 10.3390/joitmc8030162

Deyanova, K., Brehmer, N., Lapidus, A., Tiberius, V., & Walsh, S. (2022). Hatching start-ups for sustainable growth: A bibliometric review on business incubators. *Review of Managerial Science*, 16(7), 2083–2109. DOI: 10.1007/s11846-022-00525-9

Dhiman, V., & Arora, M. (2024). Current State of Metaverse in Entrepreneurial Ecosystem: A Retrospective Analysis of Its Evolving Landscape. In Kumar, J., Arora, M., & Erkol Bayram, G. (Eds.), *Exploring the Use of Metaverse in Business and Education* (pp. 73–87). IGI Global. DOI: 10.4018/979-8-3693-5868-9.ch005

Dlamini, T. M., Iwu, C. G., & Ogunlela, G. O. (2023). Support Strategies of Government-Owned Business Incubators for SMEs' Sustainability. In *Leadership and Governance for Sustainability* (pp. 222–241). IGI Global. DOI: 10.4018/978-1-6684-9711-1.ch012

Eldering, C., van den Ende, J., & Hulsink, W. (2023). Why entrepreneur sourcing matters: The effects of entrepreneur sourcing on alternative types of business incubation performance. *R & D Management*, 53(3), 481–502. DOI: 10.1111/radm.12588

Fichter, K., & Hurrelmann, K. (2021). Sustainability-oriented business incubation: framing and supporting sustainable entrepreneurship. In *Handbook of Research on Business and Technology Incubation and Acceleration* (pp. 478–495). Edward Elgar Publishing. DOI: 10.4337/9781788974783.00038

Fithri, P., Hasan, A., Syafrizal, S., & Games, D. (2024). Validation Studies a Questionnaire Developed to Measure Incubator Business Technology Performance Using PLS-SEM Approach. *Andalasian International Journal of Applied Science. Engineering and Technology*, 4(1), 64–78. DOI: 10.25077/aijaset.v4i1.132

Fonseca, S. A., & Jabbour, C. J. C. (2012). Assessment of business incubators' green performance: A framework and its application to Brazilian cases. *Technovation*, 32(2), 122–132. DOI: 10.1016/j.technovation.2011.10.006

Games, D., Kartika, R., Sari, D. K., & Assariy, A. (2021). Business incubator effectiveness and commercialization strategy: A thematic analysis. *Journal of Science and Technology Policy Management*, 12(2), 176–192. DOI: 10.1108/JSTPM-03-2020-0067

Hillemane, B. S. M., Satyanarayana, K., & Chandrashekar, D. (2019). Technology business incubation for start-up generation: A literature review toward a conceptual framework. *International Journal of Entrepreneurial Behaviour & Research*, 25(7), 1471–1493. DOI: 10.1108/IJEBR-02-2019-0087

Iwu, C. G., Malawu, N., Ndlovu, E. N., Makwara, T., & Sibanda, L. (2024). Sustaining Family Businesses through Business Incubation: An Africa-Focused Review. *Journal of Risk and Financial Management*, 17(5), 178. DOI: 10.3390/jrfm17050178

Iyortsuun, A. S. (2017). An empirical analysis of the effect of business incubation process on firm performance in Nigeria. *Journal of Small Business and Entrepreneurship*, 29(6), 433–459. DOI: 10.1080/08276331.2017.1376265

Jahanshahi, A. A., & Bhattacharjee, A. (2020). Competitiveness improvement in public sector organizations: What they need? *Journal of Public Affairs*, 20(2), e2011. DOI: 10.1002/pa.2011

Jahanshahi, A. A., Bhattacharjee, A., & Maghsoudi, T. (2021). Internal capabilities as the source of achieving competitive advantage in small-sized businesses. *International Journal of Business Innovation and Research*, 26(2), 141–162. DOI: 10.1504/IJBIR.2021.118446

Jahanshahi, A. A., Bhattacharjee, A., & Polas, M. R. H. (2023). The micro-foundations of sustainable entrepreneurship: The role of individuals' pro-social identity and organisational pro-social identity. *International Journal of Productivity and Quality Management*, 40(2), 149–170. DOI: 10.1504/IJPQM.2023.134270

Jahanshahi, A. A., Brem, A., & Bhattacharjee, A. (2017). Who takes more sustainability-oriented entrepreneurial actions? The role of entrepreneurs' values, beliefs and orientations. *Sustainability (Basel)*, 9(10), 1636. Advance online publication. DOI: 10.3390/su9101636

Jia, J., Yan, J., Jahanshahi, A. A., Lin, W., & Bhattacharjee, A. (2020). What makes employees more proactive? Roles of job embeddedness, the perceived strength of the HRM system and empowering leadership. *Asia Pacific Journal of Human Resources*, 58(1), 107–127. DOI: 10.1111/1744-7941.12249

Jin, W., Ding, W., & Yang, J. (2022). Impact of financial incentives on green manufacturing: Loan guarantee vs. interest subsidy. *European Journal of Operational Research*, 300(3), 1067–1080. DOI: 10.1016/j.ejor.2021.09.011

Kiran, R., & Bose, S. C. (2020). Stimulating business incubation performance: Role of networking, university linkage and facilities. *Technology Analysis and Strategic Management*, 32(12), 1407–1421. DOI: 10.1080/09537325.2020.1772967

Li, H., Kinoshita, T., Chen, J., Xie, J., Luo, S., & Su, D. (2024). What promotes residents' donation behavior for adaptive reuse of cultural heritage projects? An application of the extended theory of planned behavior. *Sustainable Cities and Society*, 102, 105213. DOI: 10.1016/j.scs.2024.105213

Lindelöf, P., & Hellberg, R. (2023). Incubation-An evolutionary process. *Technovation*, 124, 102755. DOI: 10.1016/j.technovation.2023.102755

Liu, Y. (2020). The micro-foundations of global business incubation: Stakeholder engagement and strategic entrepreneurial partnerships. *Technological Forecasting and Social Change*, 161, 120294. DOI: 10.1016/j.techfore.2020.120294 PMID: 32921840

Lu, X., & Wang, J. (2024). Is innovation strategy a catalyst to solve social problems? The impact of R&D and non-R&D innovation strategies on the performance of social innovation-oriented firms. *Technological Forecasting and Social Change*, 199, 123020. DOI: 10.1016/j.techfore.2023.123020

Luo, S., Chishti, M. Z., Beata, S., & Xie, P. (2024). Digital sparks for a greener future: Unleashing the potential of information and communication technologies in green energy transition. *Renewable Energy*, 221, 119754. DOI: 10.1016/j.renene.2023.119754

Man, T. W. Y., Berger, R., & Rachamim, M. (2024). A social constructivist perspective on novice entrepreneurial learning in business incubators. *International Journal of Emerging Markets*, 19(5), 1281–1305. DOI: 10.1108/IJOEM-11-2021-1784

Máté, D., Estiyanti, N. M., & Novotny, A. (2024). How to support innovative small firms? Bibliometric analysis and visualization of start-up incubation. *Journal of Innovation and Entrepreneurship*, 13(1), 5. DOI: 10.1186/s13731-024-00361-z

Mhlongo, S. D., & Mzyece, M. (2023). The business of business incubation: How stakeholders measure value and investment returns in South African fintech incubators. *African Journal of Science, Technology, Innovation and Development*, 15(2), 236–249. DOI: 10.1080/20421338.2022.2069215

Mian, S., Lamine, W., & Fayolle, A. (2016). Technology Business Incubation: An overview of the state of knowledge. *Technovation*, 50, 1–12. DOI: 10.1016/j.technovation.2016.02.005

Nafari, J., Honig, B., & Siqueira, A. C. O. (2024). Promoting academic social intrapreneurship: Developing an international virtual incubator and fostering social impact. *Technovation*, 133, 103024. DOI: 10.1016/j.technovation.2024.103024

Nicholls-Nixon, C. L., Singh, R. M., Hassannezhad Chavoushi, Z., & Valliere, D. (2024). How university business incubation supports entrepreneurs in technology-based and creative industries: A comparative study. *Journal of Small Business Management*, 62(2), 591–627. DOI: 10.1080/00472778.2022.2073360

Ordoñez de Pablos, P. (2023). Digital innovation and green economy for more resilient and inclusive societies: Understanding challenges ahead for the green growth. *Journal of Science and Technology Policy Management*, 14(3), 461–466. DOI: 10.1108/JSTPM-05-2023-193

Paoloni, P., & Modaffari, G. (2022). Business incubators vs start-ups: A sustainable way of sharing knowledge. *Journal of Knowledge Management*, 26(5), 1235–1261. DOI: 10.1108/JKM-12-2020-0923

Pattanasak, P., Anantana, T., Paphawasit, B., & Wudhikarn, R. (2022). Critical factors and performance measurement of business incubators: A systematic literature review. *Sustainability (Basel)*, 14(8), 4610. DOI: 10.3390/su14084610

Pepin, M., Tremblay, M., Audebrand, L. K., & Chassé, S. (2024). The responsible business model canvas: Designing and assessing a sustainable business modeling tool for students and start-up entrepreneurs. *International Journal of Sustainability in Higher Education*, 25(3), 514–538. DOI: 10.1108/IJSHE-01-2023-0008

Qian, H., Haynes, K. E., & Riggle, J. D. (2011). Incubation push or business pull? Investigating the geography of US business incubators. *Economic Development Quarterly*, 25(1), 79–90. DOI: 10.1177/0891242410383275

Reid, A. E., Crump, M. E., & Singh, R. P. (2024). Improving Black Entrepreneurship through Cannabis-Related Education. *Education Sciences*, 14(2), 135. DOI: 10.3390/educsci14020135

Ririh, K. R., Wicaksono, A., Laili, N., & Tsurayya, S. (2020). Incubation scheme in among incubators: A comparative study. *International Journal on Management of Innovation & Technology*, 17(07), 2050052. DOI: 10.1142/S0219877020500522

Rosado-Cubero, A., Hernández, A., Jiménez, F. J. B., & Freire-Rubio, T. (2023). Promotion of entrepreneurship through business incubators: Regional analysis in Spain. *Technological Forecasting and Social Change*, 190, 122419. DOI: 10.1016/j.techfore.2023.122419

Scillitoe, J. L., & Birasnav, M. (2022). Ease of market entry of Indian startups: Formal and informal institutional influences. *South Asian Journal of Business Studies*, 11(2), 195–215. DOI: 10.1108/SAJBS-07-2019-0131

Secundo, G., Mele, G., Passiante, G., & Albergo, F. (2023). University business idea incubation and stakeholders' engagement: Closing the gap between theory and practice. *European Journal of Innovation Management*, 26(4), 1005–1033. DOI: 10.1108/EJIM-08-2021-0435

Shandilya, S. K., Datta, A., Kartik, Y., & Nagar, A. (2024). Achieving Digital Resilience with Cybersecurity. In *Digital Resilience: Navigating Disruption and Safeguarding Data Privacy* (pp. 43–123). Springer. DOI: 10.1007/978-3-031-53290-0_2

Sharda, A., Goel, A., Mishra, A., & Chandra, S. (2015). Green Entrepreneurship in India: Global Evaluation, Needs Analysis, and Drivers for Growth. In Manimala, M., & Wasdani, K. (Eds.), *Entrepreneurial Ecosystem* (pp. 261–282). Springer. DOI: 10.1007/978-81-322-2086-2_11

Singh, J., Singh, C. D., & Deepak, D. (2024). Effectiveness of green manufacturing in resolving environmental issues: A review. *International Journal of Materials & Product Technology*, 68(1/2), 122–157. DOI: 10.1504/IJMPT.2024.136813

Sohail, K., Belitski, M., & Christiansen, L. C. (2023). Developing business incubation process frameworks: A systematic literature review. *Journal of Business Research*, 162, 113902. DOI: 10.1016/j.jbusres.2023.113902

Ssekiziyivu, B., Mwesigwa, R., Kabahinda, E., Lakareber, S., & Nakajubi, F. (2023). Strengthening business incubation practices among startup firms. Evidence from Ugandan communities. *Journal of Enterprising Communities: People and Places in the Global Economy*, 17(2), 498–518. DOI: 10.1108/JEC-08-2021-0131

Stephens, S., & Lyons, R. M. (2023). The changing activities of business incubation clients: An Irish case study. *Journal of Science and Technology Policy Management*, 14(3), 612–625. DOI: 10.1108/JSTPM-01-2021-0016

Sun, L., Cao, X., Alharthi, M., Zhang, J., Taghizadeh-Hesary, F., & Mohsin, M. (2020). Carbon emission transfer strategies in supply chain with lag time of emission reduction technologies and low-carbon preference of consumers. *Journal of Cleaner Production*, 264, 121664. DOI: 10.1016/j.jclepro.2020.121664

Todorova, T. (2024). Corporate culture and corporate strategy: Some economic aspects of the modern organisation. *International Journal of Business Performance Management*, 25(1), 147–158. DOI: 10.1504/IJBPM.2024.135136

Torun, M., Peconick, L., Sobreiro, V., Kimura, H., & Pique, J. (2018). Assessing business incubation: A review on benchmarking. *International Journal of Innovation Studies*, 2(3), 91–100. DOI: 10.1016/j.ijis.2018.08.002

Tritoasmoro, I. I., Ciptomulyono, U., Dhewanto, W., & Taufik, T. A. (2024). Determinant factors of lean start-up-based incubation metrics on post-incubation start-up viability: Case-based study. *Journal of Science and Technology Policy Management*, 15(1), 178–199. DOI: 10.1108/JSTPM-12-2021-0187

Ushakov, D. S., Ivanova, D. G., Rubinskaya, E. D., & Shatila, K. (2023). The mediating impact of innovation on green entrepreneurship practices and sustainability. In *Climate-Smart Innovation* (pp. 3–18). Social Entrepreneurship and Sustainable Development in the Environmental Economy. DOI: 10.1142/9789811264252_0001

Valliere, D., & Nicholls-Nixon, C. L. (2024). From business incubator to crucible: A new perspective on entrepreneurial support. *Journal of Small Business and Enterprise Development*, 31(2), 395–417. DOI: 10.1108/JSBED-04-2023-0181

Van Erkelens, A. M., Thompson, N. A., & Chalmers, D. (2024). The dynamic construction of an incubation context: A practice theory perspective. *Small Business Economics*, 62(2), 583–605. DOI: 10.1007/s11187-023-00771-5

Vaz, R., De Carvalho, J. V., & Teixeira, S. F. (2023). Developing a digital business incubator model to foster entrepreneurship, business growth, and academia–industry connections. *Sustainability (Basel)*, 15(9), 7209. DOI: 10.3390/su15097209

Yang, C., Jiang, B., & Zeng, S. (2024). An integrated multiple attribute decision-making framework for evaluation of incubation capability of science and technology business incubators. *Granular Computing*, 9(2), 1–14. DOI: 10.1007/s41066-024-00457-7

Zane, L. J., & Tribbitt, M. A. (2024). Examining the influence of specific IC elements on alliance formation of new ventures. *Journal of Intellectual Capital*, 25(1), 38–59. DOI: 10.1108/JIC-07-2022-0155

Zhang, Y., Lan, M., Zhao, Y., Su, Z., Hao, Y., & Du, H. (2024). Regional carbon emission pressure and corporate green innovation. *Applied Energy*, 360, 122625. DOI: 10.1016/j.apenergy.2024.122625

KEY TERMS AND DEFINITIONS

Green Angel Investor: A green angel investor is an individual who finances eco-friendly entrepreneurial initiatives.

Green Entrepreneurship: Green entrepreneurship refers to socially responsible and eco-friendly entrepreneurial principles that integrate environmental awareness, and eco-friendly business practices towards low-carbon economic sustainability.

Green Incubator: The green incubator is designed with eco-friendly infrastructure and resources, ensuring that the business incubation process emits minimal or zero environmental emissions.

Green Technologies: Green technologies refer to advanced technologies in industries and businesses that improve climate protection through reducing high-risk emissions.

Low-Carbon Economy: A low-carbon economy refers to developing an economy by establishing zero or low-emission industrial processes and adopting eco-friendly business practices, ensuring sustainable economic growth with environmental sustainability.

Nascent Entrepreneurs: Nascent entrepreneurs are individuals having entrepreneurial intentions, actively engaging in identifying opportunities and transforming ideas into real startup ventures.

SMEs: The small and medium enterprises (SMEs) are firms having not more than 250 employees.

Chapter 10

Get–Set–Go–Blockchain Startup:
Innovative Business Incubation

Satya Sekhar Venkata Gudimetla
https://orcid.org/0000-0001-5171-065X
GITAM University (Deemed), India

ABSTRACT

'Blockchain Startup' is an innovative business idea which works with the decentralized financial (Defi) transactions through an encrypted system with the help of initial coin offering (ICO). The ICO is a way for startups and organizations within the crypto market to raise funds through unregulated crowdfunding. Blockchain is technology is used for cryptocurrency as an open-source currency – functioning through a central distribution agency or state lead control. Cryptocurrency helps in reducing intermediation of banking sector. Hence, protecting the Defi-transactions from hacking depends on the incentive-compatible proof-of-work (PoW). However, investors are crazy about digital currency/ crypto currency trading irrespective of risks involved. This chapter addresses the issues 1) to make aware of the status, progress of blockchain startup ventures and 2) to understand the threats and challenges involved in blockchain-startup business.

INTRODUCTION

'Blockchain Startup' is an innovative business idea that works with decentralized financial (Defi) transactions through an encrypted system with the help of the 'Initial Coin Offering' (ICO). Blockchain startup ventures are expected to be established with the help of cryptocurrency as an open-source currency that functions through a

DOI: 10.4018/979-8-3693-4302-9.ch010

central distribution agency or state lead control. Thus, cryptocurrency helps reduce the intermediation of the banking sector. However, there is a need to protect decentralized finance (De-Fi) transactions from hacking, which depends on incentive-compatible proof of work (Pow). This chapter aims to find issues and challenges involved in the blockchain startup business along with the research survey results.

Purpose of the Study

1. To make aware of the status and progress of blockchain startup ventures.
2. To understand the threats and challenges involved in blockchain-startup business.

BLOCKCHAIN- DEFINITION

"Blockchain is a professional database that records and stores transactions and flows occasionally, agreeing to be responsible for one unit of profit at a given time. An irrefutable copy of the blockchain is placed on each side of the ''Digital Financial Assets, a decentralized server farm network managed by cryptocurrency miners who continue registering and validating the cryptocurrency exchange''- Goundar, 2020.

Blockchain is a chain of files containing whatever needs to be permanently recorded. A primary blockchain connects files to form a simple string of chains. A more sophisticated Blockchain connects files to create a net-like structure" -YANO Makoto et al., 2019.

DECENTRALIZED FINANCE (DEFI)

Decentralized Finance (DeFi) eliminates the regulation of banks and financial institutions, financial products, and financial services. DeFi is an open global financial market designed for the internet age, an alternative to the opaque, tightly controlled system of decades-old systems and processes. It gives control and visibility over investor money. It offers investors an alternative to local funds, bank options, and the global market. DeFi products open financial services to anyone with an internet connection and are primarily owned and controlled by users. So far, tens of billions of dollars worth of crypto money have flowed through DeFi applications, increasing daily. DeFi is an umbrella for financial products and services, open to owners of a network organization with access to Ethereum. In DeFi, work is always written, and an expert can let investors connect or access certain content. Governments that were once slow and prone to human error are now programmed and more secure because they are run by code that anyone can review and control. There is an exciting crypto-economics where investors can borrow, buy, long/short, and earn interest, and that is just the beginning. Crypto-savvy Argentines are using DeFi to prevent massive expansion. Organizations began to pay agents regularly. Some even take out and hold large sums of loans without needing personal proof.

Research Gap

There are very few studies based on primary data relating to blockchain startups. A sample survey is conducted to elicit the opinions of startup business investors regarding their promises and performance, as well as problems and prospects. It analyses investors' views on various issues like investment purpose, returns from business, understanding the investment techniques, and proposals for future investments relating to blockchain startups.

Contribution of the Study

This paper provides data analysis with the statistical significance test using 'F' distribution and ANOVA. The following issues are examined:

1. There is a relation between the objectives of investing in a startup business and an entrepreneur's income level.
2. There is a relation between the expected term and the withdrawal of funds from the startup business.
3. A significant relationship exists between the returns level and the expected goal period to reach the financial goal of the entity.

REVIEW OF LITERATURE

A systematic literature review is conducted through search engines using keywords such as blockchain, blockchain startup, ICO, business models for startup, etc.

There are differences between how blockchain startups and investors in blockchain startups weigh investment criteria. These differences can be anticipated by blockchain startups to better correspond to the investment criteria investors in blockchain find important, and investors can use this information to analyze the investment criteria that blockchain startups lack in general to save time in the screening process. The focus will be set, and the conclusion will be based on whether the jockey or the horse is the most essential factor in the blockchain space, that is, respectively, whether the management team or the business is the most crucial factor for investors to invest.

The results give reason to assume that investors think different investment criteria are essential regarding the phase in which the startups find themselves (Wierik, 2019).

Crowdfunding as a means of alternative financing is growing globally. Donation and reward-based entities remain the largest group. However, equity-based platforms also raise funds in some European countries and Australia. Equity crowdfunding is illegal in Canada and is sought to be legalized in the U.S. under the JOBS Act (Mitra, 2012).

The regulatory framework for blockchain startups varies according to various countries' government rules and regulatory authorities. For instance, the European securities regulations can be compared with their U.S. counterparts and focus on prospectus exemptions, highlighting the significant differences between Europe and the U.S. Europe needs to be more amicable to blockchain startups (Boreiko et al., 2019). In Germany, about 177 blockchain startups have to deal with a lack of blockchain knowledge of decision-makers, a missing regulatory framework, and a negative public reputation. The German government has recognized these issues and announced a blockchain strategy in September 2019 (Hendrik Petersen, 2022).

Shneor and Flåten (2015) suggest "a framework highlighting ways entrepreneurs can tap into resources available through online communities. In particular, the framework addresses online community-enabled product development, marketing, and crowdfunding activities concerning the three core attributes of entrepreneurial processes – opportunity recognition, marshaling of resources, and capacity development".

Albrecht et al. (2019) investigate how different social media channels are linked to the capitalization of blockchain startups. The study presented empirical evidence from online search trends, financial data, and a corpus of 231,758 tweets related to 524 ICOs. The results suggest that higher search volume, positive sentiment, and the increased use of emotive language on Twitter are linked to high capitalization.

Boreiko et al. (2019) state, "Initial coin offerings are a new way for blockchain startups to finance project development by issuing coins or tokens in exchange for fiat money or other cryptocurrencies. In this article, we start from the current distinction between different types of tokens and argue that it can create confusion and should be at least partially abandoned. The conceptual difference between a currency token and a tradable utility token is just the dimension of the crypto environment in which the token is spent. More specifically, 'utility tokens' combine the customer payment mechanism with the utility component and, when tradable on a secondary market, the investment one".

Bryan, Kevin A., Hovenkamp, and Erik (2020) mention, "A typical startup is both new and small, providing little data for estimating competitive effects. Despite this uncertainty, it is unlikely that a policy of near-universal inaction best serves society."

Viktoriia Semenova (2021) states that "the early success of the Blockchain Technology-based startups' entry and growth related to the supportive entrepreneurial environments, a greater degree of regulatory clarity, the formation of strategic associations, entrepreneur's active engagement in sharing expertise and shaping the regulations and standards, a profound business model, and experienced management. It is recommended that policymakers should support the creation of new ventures and the transfer of knowledge about Blockchain Technology."

Schückes & Gutmann (2020) investigate the economic and behavioral factors that motivate entrepreneurs to fund their startup operations with ICOs. They suggest that the entrepreneur's social identity, in conjunction with the enabling mechanisms of blockchain technology, shapes entrepreneurial pursuits and funding choices.

Reichenbach & Walther's (2021) study investigates signal validity in equity-based crowdfunding by examining whether signals that increase crowd participation are associated with higher post-offering success. Post-offering success is measured as the probability of survival. They used a hand-collected data set of 88 campaigns with over 64,000 investments and 742 updates from a well-established and leading German equity-based crowdfunding platform, Companisto. They find that indicating that the chief executive officer holds a university degree and a higher number of business-related updates is associated with a lower risk of failure, which aligns with recent research on offering success.

Szczukiewicz(2021) states, "The Blockchain has been one of the leading technology breakthroughs in recent years. It has enabled the creation of multiple cryptocurrencies and tokens, which, amongst others, financed the activities of various startup projects. The last few years have seen the emergence of another blockchain-enabled product – Non-Fungible Tokens (NFT)- a digital certificate of ownership".

Ahluwalia, S., Mahto, R. V., & Guerrero, M. (2020) reveal that "Cryptocurrencies (e.g., Bitcoin, EOS, Ethereum, Litecoin, and others) are disrupting the traditional banking and financial systems. Cryptocurrencies are based on a set of technologies called blockchain technology. The potential effect of blockchain technology on institutional economics is profound. Blockchain technology-based applications in supply chain management, marketing, and finance are already decentralizing and streamlining vital institutional functions".

Jaladati and Chitsaz (2023) state that "securing adequate financial resources is the primary challenge of entrepreneurial ventures' establishment and growth. Initial coin offering, an innovative entrepreneurial fundraising method, caters to this critical need, but its success depends on acceptance by the public, similar to crowdfunding. They also reveal that 'extensive information disclosure by the businesses and 'adequate investor knowledge of the initial coin offerings' are the most legitimizing cognitive legitimacy sources."

Taherdoost and Madanchian (2023) state, "A blockchain-based business model is decentralized, runs on a secure network, and relies on peer-to-peer transactions, the three main characteristics of blockchain technology. Adopting blockchain-based technology may cause businesses to reevaluate their current business models, which could boost their profitability, productivity, and efficiency".

Ala et al. (2023) focus on the advantages and drawbacks of blockchain, a distributed ledger technology (DLT) that relies on a network of peers to achieve consensus. They suggest the 'Hashgraph' is a better alternative to blockchain failures.

Antonio Briola et al. (2023) state, "In one of his public declarations, Terra project's co-founder, Do Kwon, stated that 95% of the companies entering the crypto market were going to *die*. Indeed, he further affirmed that there was entertainment in watching companies die (Quiroz-Gutierrez, 2022)."

Pollman (2023) provides an original theory of startup failure: how law and culture have shaped a system for dealing with many startups that cannot reach an exit that will produce a financial return for all participants.

THEORETICAL BACKGROUND

Financing Startup Business: Venture Capital

Venture capital is money investors provide to startups and small businesses with perceived long-term growth potential. It is a significant funding source for startups that need access to capital markets. It typically entails high risk for the investor but has the potential for above-average returns.

Venture capital funds invest in companies in exchange for equity in the companies they invest in, which usually have a novel technology or business model in high-technology industries, such as biotechnology and I.T. In addition to angel investing, equity crowdfunding, and other seed funding options, venture capital is attractive for new companies with a limited operating history that are too small to raise capital in the public markets and have not reached the point where they are able to secure a bank loan or complete a debt offering—in exchange for the high-risk venture capitalists assuming that by investing in smaller and less mature companies, venture capitalists usually get significant control over company decisions and a substantial portion of the companies' ownership.

Venture capital is also a way in which the private and public sectors can construct an institution that systematically creates networks for new firms and industries so that they can progress. This institution helps identify and combine business functions such as finance, technical expertise, marketing know-how, and business models. Startup companies with the potential to grow need a certain amount of investment.

Wealthy investors like to invest their capital in such businesses with a long-term growth perspective. This capital is known as venture capital, and the investors are called venture capitalists. Such investments are risky as they are illiquid but can give impressive returns if invested in the right venture. Returns to venture capitalists depend on the growth of the company.

The Elements of Startup: Business Plan

The various elements of a typical business plan should consist of different elements, which are briefly explained below.

1. **Executive summary**: This is the most critical aspect of a business plan, often written at the end . It should be written like a robust sales talk to persuade and convince the venture capitalist to consider the proposal.
2. **Background on the venture**: The business plan should summarize the fundamental nature of the proposed venture and its activities, as well as an outline of its objectives.
3. **The product or service**: The plan should explain the venture's proposed product or service. This is especially important if the product or service is technically oriented.
4. **Market analysis**: The business plan should be able to convince the venture capital firm that there is a real commercial opportunity for the business and its products and services. It should offer the analyst a clear description and analysis of the SWOT(strengths, weaknesses, opportunities, and strengths).
5. **Marketing**: After analyzing the market position and the opportunities, it is necessary to address how the prospective business will exploit them.
6. **Business opportunities**: The Business plan should explain how the business practically operates. It should make clear the process of making the product or providing the proposed service.
7. **The management team**: The plan should articulate that the business entity has the quality of management to turn the business plan into reality. The management team should be capable and reasonably experienced in management strategy, finance, and marketing, and their roles should be specified.
8. **Financial projections**: The business plan should make precise financial projections realistically. The plan should forecast cash flows, fixed costs, variable costs, working capital requirements, etc. The proforma income statement and the Balance sheet should also be projected.
9. **The amount of finance required and the exit opportunities**: The business plan should state how much finance is needed for the business and from what sources and explain the purposes for which the funds will be applied. In the

end, the venture capitalist has to look for a clear exit route for their investment through means such as public listing or the third-party acquisition of the company financed.

Private and Public: ICO

A private ICO is restricted to some private institutions and service providers for participation. Only trusted investors can participate in a private ICO. Generally, only accredited investors like financial institutions and service providers can participate in private ICOs. The largest ICO belonged to messaging service Telegram, a UK-based company that raised more than $1.7 billion from a private ICO. A Public IPO is a free investment, and any investor can participate.

Digital Payment System

Technology has improved the efficiency of payment processes for various financial transactions and customers. This has increased the adoption of different financial services amongst individuals, micro-small-and-medium-sized enterprises (MSMEs), and more giant corporations. Products and services facilitated by digital payments include loans, insurance, savings, and investments. The digital payment ecosystem is highly complex, and to understand the effectiveness of each system employed, you will need first to understand the role of various parties and participants.

Types of Digital Payment Systems

Digital payment systems involving individuals paying each other are called peer-to-peer (P2P) payment systems. Those that involve financial transactions between businesses and consumers can be referred to as peer-to-business (P2B) payments, consumer-to-business (C2B), or business-to-consumer (B2C). Financial transactions involving large and small companies are called business-to-business (B2B).

The term peer-to-peer (P2P) will be used frequently later in this book about financial services, such as investment and lending, that involve individual consumers or investors and their peers rather than individual consumers and businesses. There are several ways to categorize how consumers and businesses pay for goods and services. Categories could be based on the underlying infrastructure and systems often referred to as the 'payment rails' or 'payment schemes' that power payments. Alternatively, they could reflect the method of payment used by the payee, e.g., a credit card, cash, cheque, or a mobile banking application.

Regulatory Framework of ICOs and Crypto Assets

Marian (2015) proposes a regulatory system that imposes costs on anonymity to curtail potential illicit uses of cryptocurrency, such as tax evasion, money laundering, or financing terrorism, without disincentivizing the innovation that cryptocurrency could bring. Angela et al. (2019) explain how various governments have approached regulating cryptocurrency and blockchain technology.

The evolution of the terminology used by regulators for cryptocurrencies from 2013 to 2019 is explained in the Global Cryptoasset Regulatory Landscape Study. It states that various terminologies used are- Bitcoin, Virtual Currency, Electronic Currency, Cryptocurrency, Digital Currency, Virtual Asset, Crypto Asset, Digital Financial Asset, Intangible Asset, and Digital Asset.

In the United States, crypto assets are regulated by the Federal Government and State governments. Nearly 35 bills relating to crypt and CBDCs have been introduced by the U.S. Congress. The European Union has a regulatory system and published guidelines in MiCA, MiFID II, and ESMA. Further, the European Banking Authority issued more regulations for cryptocurrency. Venezuela is treated as heaven for cryptocurrency because it has its own CBDC. Spain and Switzerland issued separate guidelines for payment, security, and utility tokens according to the nature of the transactions.

The Institute of Digital Money is established by the People's Bank of China (PBOC) to frame regulations on cryptocurrency. China is considered one of the most critical countries in blockchain governance besides the U.S. (Coleman, 2016).

ADBI working paper, 2019, states, "135 economies allow the free use of cryptocurrency, 61 economies regulate its use, and 22 economies ban it." The index of cryptocurrency regulation is also published in this paper. The regulatory mechanism varies according to government policy, categorized into (i) Ban on Cryptocurrency, (ii) Completely Regulated Policy, and (iii) Fully liberalized policy.

Table 1. an overview of the status of cryptocurrency regulations in East Asia and the Pacific.

Ban on Crypto currency	Completely Regulated Policy	Fully Liberalized Policy
Indonesia	Australia	Brunel Darusslam
Vietnam	Srilanka	Cambodia
Nepal	Afganisthan	Fiji
Bangladesh	Thailand	Hongkong
	Papua New Guinea	China
	Philippines	Pakistan
	Japan	India
	Republic of korea	Maldives
	Myanmar	Singapore
	Bhutan	Newzealand

Source: Asian Development Bank Institute, ADB working papers 978. -Cryptocurrency Regulations: Institutions and Financial Openness.

Taxation for Income on Startup Business: Crypto Asset

The transactions of blockchain startup companies are quite different from traditional systems because they do not involve intermediation by banking institutions. Cryptocurrency service providers should follow the 'Common Reporting Standard' to achieve global tax transparency according to the amendments to the First Report 2014, published by OECD in 2022.

Table 2. the definition of digital currencies and crypto assets for global tax purposes.

Intangible assets other than Goodwill	Financial Instruments or Asset	Commodity or virtual commodity	Currency	Not specified
Australia	Argentina	Austria	Belgium	USA
Franc	Brazil	Canada	Cote	
Chile	Croatia,	China	d'Ivoire	
Czech Republic	Denmark	Indonesia	Italy	
Luxembourg,	Israel		Poland	
Nigeria	Japan			
Spain	Slovak			
Sweden	Republic			
Switzerland	and South			
The United Kingdom	Africa			

Source: Author

Crypto Wallet

Cryptocurrency users have a "crypto wallet" with a special request to own their home temporarily. Private keys can verify the validity of cryptocurrency transactions, while wallets reduce the risk of stolen electronic devices. Wallets used by cryptocurrency exchanges can easily be hacked. Having at least one backup is recommended, regardless of the wallet stored on the cloud. The wallet can be stored in the cloud, on an internal hard drive, or an external device. Irrespective of how the investor wallet is stored, having at least one backup is recommended. Backup wallets do not publish actual cryptocurrencies, only information about their assets and current holders.

Paper Wallets

The wallet is created using the key pair generated on a computer without an internet connection. The private key is written or printed on paper and removed from the computer. The paper wallet can be stored in a safe place for later retrieval. The physical wallet contains metal tokens; Special keys are available in the security hologram engraved on the back of the park. Now available applications are Bitcoin X.T., Bitcoin Unlimited, and Bitcoin Core.

Software Wallets

Software wallets are accessible through desktops, laptops, or smartphones. It is offered free of charge, unlike hardware wallets. It stores private keys through the encrypted system at a remote server.

Hardware wallets

Hardware wallets are computer peripherals that sign transactions at the user's request. These protect users by storing their private keys in the devices and encrypting them internally. Hence, private keys cannot be stolen by malware because passwords can protect the devices.

Non-Fungible Token

A non-fungible token (NFT) is a non-interchangeable data unit stored in a digital ledger or blockchain. NFTs can be associated with easily reproducible items such as photos, videos, audio, and other types of digital files as unique items. Copies of the original file are not restricted to the owner of the NFT and can be copied and shared like any file. The lack of interchangeability distinguishes NFTs from blockchain-based cryptocurrencies, such as Bitcoin.

CLASSIFICATION OF BLOCKCHAIN STARTUPS

Blockchain startups can be classified into crowdfunding, crypto exchanges, startups for smartcard technology, crypto wallets, non-fungible tokens, crypto games, and startups relating to financial services.

Crowdfunding

Crowdfunding is an innovative platform that emerged after the global financial crisis in 2008. It is a model where many investors come together to raise debt or equity capital through an internet-based platform. Many investors raise small amounts of money to invest in new businesses. It is a platform that matches crowdfund raisers with savers or investors. This platform provides a wide range of information about potential borrowers/lenders, from credit scores to business models and portfolios. Some known crowdfunding platforms are- British Rock Group, Crowdcube, Crowdfunder, Kickstarter, Indiegogo, Medstart, Pledge Music, Razoo, Ouya, and Peblle.

Lending Based Platform

In this model, funds are raised in the form of loans from funders with a condition to repay the principal along with interest as per agreement conditions—examples: Crowdo, Fundedhere, Moolahsense, Lendingclub, Kiva, Propser, Zidisha, etc. The following are the essential categories of this model.

- Customer-to-Business Lending Model (C2B): In this model, investors acquire bonds issued by the company for a specified period. Bonds are also known as Debentures to raise loans from individual investors.
- Peer-to-Peer Consumer Lending Model (P2P-C): In this case, the money is borrowed among individuals through an online platform.
- Peer-to-Peer Business Lending Model (P2P-B): In this model, money is borrowed by institutional and individual lending to business entities.
- Peer-Business Lending Model (P2B): In this case, the lending process is initiated from individuals to business entities.
- Business-to-Business Lending Model (B2B): In this case, the money is borrowed among business entities through an online platform.

STARTUPS FOR CRYPTO EXCHANGES

A Crypto Exchange function can be compared to a Stock Exchange, where securities are traded. The trading function for digital assets or cryptocurrencies will occur through crypto exchanges. These exchanges may function on centralized or decentralized platforms and charge necessary fees. There are two types of online trading concerning crypto-currency. Investors may trade to hold or sell cryptocurrencies. There are three types of crypto-trading- i) day trading, ii) swing trading, and iii) position trading (Mark et al., 2024).

Startup for Smart Card Technology

Credit cards, debit cards, and other card products can also be intelligent cards that utilize microprocessors to store more data than a traditional magnetic strip. Data is stored in a chip, typically called an EMV chip. The chip embedded in a smart card can currently store approximately three times more information than a magnetic field. This type of payment system is known as a wallet or e-wallet system. The money is stored electronically in the I.C. chips built into the card. Anyone who makes a purchase pays through an electronic device, i.e., Mobile Phone or Laptop. Innovative card systems were first introduced in Europe in the late 1990s and are widely used in countries like France, Germany, and Japan to pay for public phone calls, transportation, and purchases through reliable services. It took a while for the idea to take off in the U.S., where reliable and low-cost communications made it easier to use credit and debit cards. There are two main types of smart cards: social-based intelligent cards and electronic wallets.

Smart card readers must communicate with the chip on smart cards and can support multiple control methods. Some smartcard readers can be used with the help of various devices like personal computers, point-of-sale terminals, and phones, allowing customers to quickly conduct business without leaving home.

Crypto Game

Crypto-gaming companies target people who own multiple mobile devices, making them a good target audience for blockchain games capable of engaging players for extended periods. However, an investor participating in this crypto game should remember that it may or may not give returns to fiat money. However, the result of a winning or losing game is revealed in a fraction of a second. There are about 1,400 blockchain games, with about 100 new ones added monthly, according to 'DappRadar.'

Play-to-Earn Games

In the play-to-earn model, players earn tokens by winning a battle with their Axies against other players or selling them on Axie's marketplace. These tokens can then be sold for fiat money. They need SLP and AXS tokens to breed their Axies, which can be later sold or generated again. As more developers are making such games available for mobile gamers, the blockchain gaming industry is tapping into a new market with huge potential. More people own and use smartphones regularly than desktop computers.

Predictive Markets-Startups

Predictive Markets Startups use statistical and machine learning techniques to analyze historical data to predict future outcomes. In this competitive age, predictive analytics not only helps in making informed decisions and solving business problems but also to have an edge over the competitors.

BASIC STEPS FOR FINANCING

The venture capital financing process outlines basic steps taken from initial contact with potential startup companies through the first financing round.

1) Startup companies looking for financing make initial contact with CVCs. CVCs can also seek out potential startups looking for funding.
2) The startup management team presents a 'Business plan' to the CVC. If the reviewed business plan generates interest, the CVC will ask the startup for more information, including a product demonstration. Investors will also conduct due diligence to investigate and better understand the product, technology, market, and related issues.
3) If the CVCs are interested in the proposed startup's product or service, they will look to determine the startup's value. They communicate this valuation to the startup, often via a term sheet. If the startup is happy with the offer, a purchase price and investor equity are agreed upon. Negotiations can take place during this stage of investment valuation.
4) Legal counsels from both sides agree to a finalized term sheet where business terms for the investment are specified. A closed period, a lock-up period, is also established during which the startup company cannot discuss investing opportunities with other investment groups. This indicates that a pending deal is in

the process of completion. Once a term sheet is finalized, both sides negotiate and finalize financing terms.

5) Negotiations are conducted between the legal counsels from the CVC and the startup company. The startup legal team typically creates transaction documents that the CVC counsel reviews. Negotiations continue until all legal and business issues are addressed. During this time, the CVC conducts a more thorough investigation of the startup company, understanding its books and records, financial statements, projected performance, employees and suppliers, and even its customer base.

6) Closing of financing is the final step. This can occur immediately upon execution of the definitive agreements or after a few weeks. The additional time may be necessary if the CVC needs time to complete their due diligence or based on the startup company's financial needs.

BLOCKCHAIN STARTUP BUSINESS MODELS

1. **P2P Blockchain Business Model:** This model provides competitive services to competitors. It allows end users to interact directly with each other. Monetization can be made in various ways, including tokens, BaaS, or exchange rates.
2. **Blockchain As A Service Business Model (Baas):** It provides an ecosystem for other businesses to manage their blockchain systems. In this ecosystem, companies can experiment, test, and research. For example, Microsoft (Azure), Amazon (AWS), IBM (BlueMix), and others all offer blockchain as a service (BaaS). End users do not have to worry about how blockchain works and whether they need to set it up before using it. BaaS also eliminates the need for hardware, allowing the startup, company, or organization to focus on growth. The service has the most up-to-date blockchain solutions, including Bitcoin and Ethereal.
3. **Token Economy – Utility Token Business Model:** This model is prevalent in the industry. Many startups, businesses, and e-commerce sites now use blockchain-based utility models. Ripple is a utility because it strengthens the network and facilitates its functioning. Businesses retain some power and release the rest to support network performance. They benefit when the price of energy products changes. Token utilities must have three main characteristics: appropriate role, function, and purpose.
4. **Blockchain-Based Software Products:** This has led blockchain companies to develop and sell solutions to many established companies. Prove to other organizations that blockchain technology can be beneficial because they do not just take upfront payments. They also need to provide support after use. Another important reason to purchase a blockchain-based software solution is that the

business needs more intelligence. Companies want to avoid going through the skill development process. Therefore, it is easier for them to purchase a blockchain solution that suits their needs.

5. **Development Platforms:** This leads us to our next decentralized business model, development platforms. Companies nowadays focus on developing apps that can result in a blockchain infrastructure. Those apps can be served to the end-user using blockchain and the cloud, providing rapid development. Hyperledger is one of those examples that provide tools, frameworks, and guidelines for blockchain development. The key here is rapid development; they are trying to do just that.

6. **Network Fee Charge:** This model will include the network costs associated with the blockchain. This type of blockchain business applies to blockchain solutions such as Ethereum or dApps, which charge a small fee for different activities on the network. For example, the Ethereum network charges developers an Ethereum fee to register their dApps.

7. **Blockchain Professional Services:** These services are provided by business professionals to startups or other businesses to help them become blockchain-ready. For example, companies want someone to create their customized blockchain projects. In this case, they may contract with Deloitte, IBM, or other companies to complete the project. The important thing here is to refrain from investing in hardware, software, or design teams but to accept the services of companies that have directly achieved the image of blockchain development.

Examples of Successful NFT Startups

1. A NFT marketplace: NBA Top ShotOpenSea, Rarible
2. A blockchain services business: Block Gemini Technologies, Enterprise Grade
3. A cryptocurrency exchange service: BinanceOKEX, Kraken
4. An influencer marketing business: Angel Broking, Afluencer, InfluencerSoft
5. A NFT album: Photobucket, RAC, DAVE CAHILL
6. A Bitcoin vending machine: CoinDesk, Lamassu Bitcoin ATMs
7. A NFT online course: Sorare
8. An online courses business: Course Hero, edX, Thinkific
9. A decentralized app: Uni Swap, Dapp.com, LBRY
10. A NFT cryptocurrency: NiceHash, CryptoKitties, Bibox
11. A NFT blog: Overblog, DigiFinex, ONE37pm
12. A NFT community: Mintable.app, Abbreviations, and acronyms dictionary
13. A charity that accepts cryptocurrencies: Cryptocurrency News, Coinsfera
14. A cryptocurrency business: CoinMarketCap, Coinbase

15. A cybersecurity system: Compuquip Cybersecurity, Cybersecurity, Fidelis Cybersecurity
16. A bitcoin broker: Poloniex, ByBit, BitMEX
17. A NFT artist: Nifty Gateway, CoinPost, Hashmasks
18. A DeFi company: FTX, Zerion
19. A NFT loan platform: coingape.com, DeFi For You.
20. A Bitcoin crowdfunding website: BitBay, MintMe, MicroVentures
21. A NFT creator: IPFS, Enjin, Degoo Cloud
22. A NFT news site: WND, Phys.org
23. A NFT broker: ethereum.org, The Block, Crypto Briefing
24. A NFT book: CryptoSlam, BFI, Dendy Cinemas

Startups Relating to Financial Services

Financial services are "activities, benefits, and satisfaction connected with the sale of money that offers to users and customers, the financial related value."

1. **Banking Services** – This includes all the operations provided by the banks, including the simple deposit and withdrawal of money to issue loans, credit cards, etc.
2. **Foreign Exchange service**s include currency exchange, foreign exchange banking, or the wire transfer.
3. **Investment Services** generally include asset management, hedge fund management, and custody service.
4. **Insurance Services** sells insurance policies, brokerages, insurance underwriting, and reinsurance.
5. Other services include advisory services, venture capital, angel investment, etc.

Global Blockchain Startup Hubs

Table 3. the status of regional blockchain startup hubs. Blockchain startup hubs are growing globally: Europe- 1176, North America- 1098, Asia-602, Australia-184, Africa-68, and South America-86.

Name of the region	No. of Startups
Amsterdam	70
Austin	25
Boston	41
Barcelona	24
Bangalore, India	55
Chicago	34
Hongkong	63
Madrid	23
Melbourne, Australia	22
Moscow	26
Los angels	114
London	269
NYC	212
New Delhi, India	59
Pune-Mumbai, India	45
Silicon valley	275
Sydney, Australia	44
Toronto	74
Vancouver	34
Zug	100

Source: https://www.startus-insights.com/innovators-guide/blockchain-a-global-startup-hub-analysis/

The blockchain startup is an innovative incubation in the form of an initial Coin Offering (ICO),[1] where a company sells a new cryptocurrency to raise money. ICO is a way for startups and organizations within the crypto market to raise funds through unregulated crowdfunding. These ICOs help raise corporate entities' funds without issuing shares or debentures. There is no central control for ICOs or government intervention in raising such funds. The investor can enter the project in exchange for the coins as a tool for the payment system (Schueffel, 2017). ICOs are becoming increasingly popular, and blockchain projects raised more money in 2018 through ICOs than they had over the previous year (Flyod, 2018).

Thus, a certain amount of cryptocurrency is sold as "coins" to investors or sponsors in exchange for legal or other higher and more stable digital currencies such as Bitcoin or Ethereum. These tokens will be paid in cash as future income if the funding goals of the ICO are met and the market is successfully deployed.

Successful Startups With ICOs

Table 4. the blockchain startups with ICOs, categorized into 15 groups according to their business objective.

Classification	Successful companies with ICOs
1. Asset Management	DimCoin, iconomi,, mybit.io
2. Browsers and Social	matchpool, bitbounce, crypviser
3. Crowdfunding and lending	suretly, salt, cofoundit, wetrust, everex
4. Computing storage	Filecoin, Sonm, iexec, dfinity
5. Digital Payments and banking	blockpay, mminexcoin, polybis, monetha
6. DAO and Token launch	Aragon, Adel
7. Exchanges and Wallets	omisego, corion-platform, mothership
8. Financial Services	Veritaseum, Hive, equibit
9. Gambling and Gaming	Gnosis, augun, wings
10. Health care and Insurance	patientory, insurex, encrypgen
11. Media and Advertising	voise, opus, viberate, po.et, synereo
12. Identity and Internet of Things	Civi, IOTA
13. Infrastructure and Development	lisk, stratis, blockpool, cosmos, nebelio, bacor
14. Prediction markets	betking, kibo, skincoin, monsterbyte, wagerr
15. Trading	lykke, sentiment, investfeed, cryptoping

Source: https://www.cbinsights.com/research/blockchain-startups-most-well-funded/

CHALLENGES TO BLOCKCHAIN STARTUPS

1. **Regulatory Uncertainty:** Regulatory uncertainty is one of blockchain startups' most significant legal challenges. Due to the decentralized nature of blockchain technology, it is often difficult to determine which laws and regulations apply to a particular project. This can be a significant problem for startups looking to raise funds through an initial coin offering (ICO) or NFTs. In many jurisdictions, there still needs to be clear guidance on how ICOs should be regulated, or certain issued coins may come attached with different meanings. For example, in one country, the phrase "coin" may refer to money, whereas in another, it may refer

to a "virtual asset." As a result, many startups have been forced to either delay their ICO plans or move to a more favorable regulatory environment.

2. **Intellectual Property:** Blockchain startups face another legal challenge: protecting their intellectual property (I.P.). Due to the global nature of the blockchain industry, enforcing I.P. rights in multiple jurisdictions can be challenging. This is a huge problem for startups looking to protect their software code. Unlike traditional software companies, blockchain startups often cannot rely on copyright law to protect their code. This is because the distributed nature of the blockchain means that anyone can copy and use the code without permission. NFTs have also been a source of I.P. challenges for startups. In many jurisdictions, whether NFTs are being determined to be protected by copyright or trademark law still needs to be determined. As a result, many startups have had to get creative in protecting their NFTs, such as using smart contracts or other technological measures. One way to overcome this challenge is to use open-source licenses that allow others to use your code but require them to give credit where it is due. Alternatively, you can use a combination of copyright and trademark law to protect your brand and logos.

3. **Data Protection:** Another legal challenge blockchain startups face is data protection. Due to the decentralized nature of blockchain technology, it cannot be easy to control how personal data is collected, used, and stored. This is a huge problem for startups gathering data from multiple sources. In many jurisdictions, data protection laws require companies to get explicit consent from individuals before collecting and using their data.

4. **Taxation:** Another legal challenge faced by blockchain startups is taxation. Due to the global nature of the blockchain industry, it can be challenging to determine which tax laws apply to a particular project. This is a huge problem for startups looking to raise funds through an ICO. In many jurisdictions, there still needs to be clear guidance on how ICOs should be taxed. As a result, many startups have been forced to either delay their ICO plans or move to a more favorable tax environment. Understanding the tax implications of your blockchain project is critical to its success.

5. **Insurance:** Insurance may be required for crypto businesses to manage legal risks. Traditional insurance policies may cover some cryptocurrency-related risks depending on how a particular cryptocurrency (like Bitcoin or Ethereum) is classified, such as "money" or "securities." For blockchain startups, it is critical to work with an experienced insurance broker who understands the unique risks associated with the industry. They can help you find the right policy to protect your business from legal liabilities.

SURVEY ON BLOCKCHAIN STARTUPS

The convenience sampling method is used to select sample investors for this study. The questionnaires are given to only those individuals who have invested in startup businesses. The survey was conducted during the four months from April 2023 to July 2023. Hence, the results are only representative but have yet to be exhaustive.

Table 5. opinions about 'dealing in blockchain startups is easy to understand.'

Classification	Semi-Urban		Urban		Metrocities		Total		Total
OPINION	Male	Female	Male	Female	Male	Female	Male	Female	
Strongly Disagree	31 (20)	8 (11)	21 (17)	7 (15)	13 (15)	3 (21)	65(18)	18(13)	83 (15)
Disagree	44(28)	21 (29)	38 (31)	10 (21)	23 (26)	2 (14)	105(28)	33(26)	138 (30)
Neither Agree or Disagree	23 (15)	14 (19)	23 (19)	9 (19)	16 (18)	3 (21)	62(17)	26(19)	88 (19)
Agree	23 (15)	12 (16)	27 (22)	6 (13)	11 (13)	4 (29)	61(17)	22(16)	83 (16)
Strongly Agree	35 (22)	18 (25)	13 (11)	15 (32)	25 (28)	2 (15)	73(20)	35(26)	108 (22)
Total	156 (100)	73(100)	122(100)	47(100)	88(100)	14(100)	366(100)	134(100)	500(100)

Note: Figures in parentheses are column-wise percentages.

The results reveal interesting insights. Forty-five percent of respondents (both strongly disagree and disagree) are against this statement. This indicates that most investors (55 percent) need to be aware of the technical aspects of blockchain startups. Only 22 percent of investors opined that it is straightforward to deal with.

Investment Objectives and Goals: It is essential to know the objective of investors when investing in blockchain startups.

Table 6.

Classification	Semi-Urban		Urban		Metrocities		Total		Total
OPINION ↓	Male	Female	Male	Female	Male	Female	Male	Female	
To maintain purchasing power	28(18)	13(18)	21(17)	9(19)	11(13)	2(14)	60(16)	24(18)	84(18)
Generate regular cash flows	27(18)	12(18)	24(20)	7(15)	12(13)	3(21)	63(17)	22(16)	85(18)
To make speculation	44(28)	22(30)	37(30)	12(26)	27(31)	3(21)	108(30)	3(28)	145(28)
To have a long term investment	31(20)	19(25)	22(17)	14(30)	29(33)	2(14)	82(23)	35(26)	117(20)
For post-retirement benefits	26(16)	7(9)	18(16)	5(10)	9(10)	4(29)	53(14)	16(12)	69(16)
Total	156(100)	73(100)	122(100)	47(100)	88(100)	14(100)	366(100)	134(100)	500(100)

Table 6 shows that 28 percent of respondents have a speculative attitude towards their investment. Twenty percent of investors would like to have a long-term investment. Only 9 percent of females and 16 percent of males are interested in investing in blockchain startups for post-retirement benefits, which are in the income group in Semi-urban. Table 7 provides the statistical results for the significance test in this regard.

Table 7.

Anova: Two-Factor

SUMMARY	Count	Sum	Average	Variance
Row 1	6	84	14	84.8
Row 2	6	85	14.16667	89.36667
Row 3	6	145	24.16667	233.3667
Row 4	6	117	19.5	113.1
Row 5	6	69	11.5	75.5
Column 1	5	156	31.2	54.7
Column 2	5	73	14.6	35.3
Column 3	5	122	24.4	54.3
Column 4	5	47	9.4	13.3
Column 5	5	88	17.6	91.8
Column 6	5	14	2.8	0.7

ANOVA

Source of Variation	SS	df	MS	F	P-value	F crit
Rows	626	4	156.5	8.360043	0.000391	2.866081
Columns	2606.267	5	521.2533	27.84473	2.31E-08	2.71089
Error	374.4	20	18.72			
Total	3606.667	29				

* Calculated Vale of 'F' > Critical Value of 'F'. They are statistically significant. Hence, there is no relation between objective of investment and level of income.

Investor's attitude: Table 8 provides data on the investor's attitude towards withdrawing income from the proposed investment.

Table 8.

Classification	Semi-Urban		Urban		Metrocities		Total		Total
OPINION	Male	Female	Male	Female	Male	Female	Male	Female	
Within one year	79 (51)	26(36)	24(20)	8(17)	25(28)	3(21)	128(35)	37(28)	165(33)
Within 3 years	31(20)	17(23)	36(30)	11(23)	14(16)	2(14)	81(22)	30(22)	111(22)
3 to 5 years	28(18)	8(11)	29(24)	9(19)	17(19)	3(21)	74(20)	20(15)	94(19)
After 5 years	18(11)	22(30)	33(27)	19(40)	32(34)	6(44)	83(23)	47(35)	130(26)
Total	156(100)	73(100)	122(100)	47(100)	88(100)	14(100)	366(100)	134(100)	500(100)

Table 9.

	6027.33	
Total	3	23

* Rows: Calculated 'F' < Critical value of 'F' and

* Columns: Calculated 'F' > Critical value of 'F'.

Table 9 gives an analysis of the statistical results. This data will help analyze investors' requirements, as this reflects redemptions and repurchases of various schemes. Fifty-one percent of males and 36 percent of females in the income group 'Semi-urban' were shown interest in withdrawing funds within one year. Meanwhile, investors- 34 percent of males and 44 percent of females- from the group -Metrocities showed interest in retaining the funds for more than five years. Hence, there is a relation between expected tenure and withdrawal of proposed income. However, there is no significant relation between the opinions of the male and female respondents.

Investors' Expectations: Table 10 depicts investors' expectations to reach their financial goals. Thirty-six percent of respondents opined they could achieve their goal after ten years only. However, 45 percent of female respondents (in the Urban group) have opined that they can reach their financial goal within three years. By observing the results, investors may be underestimating or overestimating their financial goals. There is a significant relationship between the level of income and the expected target period for reaching the goal. The same opinion was obtained from male and female respondents, and the statistical values are insignificant.

Table 10.

Column 5	4	88	22	60.66667
Column 6	4	14	3.5	1.666667

ANOVA

Source of Variation	SS	df	MS	F	P-value	F crit
Rows	1067.125	3	355.7083	1.634626	0.223502	3.287382
Columns	2965.708	5	593.1417	2.725737	0.060403	2.901295
Error	3264.125	15	217.6083			
Total	7296.958	23				

* Rows: Calculated 'F' < Critical value of 'F' and

* Columns: Calculated 'F' < Critical value of 'F'.

CONCLUSION

This chapter presents an overview of blockchain startup business models. This chapter provides information on global startup hubs and successful startup companies with their ICOs. The reasons for the failure of blockchain startups are also analyzed. It is stated that 95% of blockchain startups relating to cryptocurrencies or stable coins are dying. The regulatory mechanism and tax treatment on crypto-assets or cryptocurrencies are also examined. Blockchain startups face several challenges: regulatory restrictions, intellectual property rules, data protection, and taxation systems.

The survey reveals that although investors are disinterested in risky investments, they are even less enthusiastic about blockchain startups being able to provide a superior alternative to their investment judgment. It is interesting to note that most investors are interested in having short-term investments rather than long-term ones. Only some of them are interested in speculation through blockchain startups. The survey also found that 'self-motivation' towards decision-making for investing in blockchain startups dominates all other motivating factors like parents, spouses, children, friends, agents, and advertisement through media.

Future Research Implications

Further, there is a need to protect blockchain startups with insurance for unprecedented financial losses. The survey shows a need for technological literacy for entrepreneurs who want to venture into blockchain startups.

REFERENCES

Ahluwalia, S., Mahto, R. V., & Guerrero, M. (2020). Blockchain Technology and Startup Financing: A Transaction COST Economics Perspective. *Technological Forecasting and Social Change*, 151, 119854. DOI: 10.1016/j.techfore.2019.119854

Albrecht, S., Lutz, B., & Neumann, D. (2019). How Sentiment Impacts the Success of Blockchain Startups - An Analysis of Social Media Data and Initial Coin Offerings. Conference: Proceedings of the 52nd Hawaii International Conference on System Sciences.

Boreiko, D., Ferrarini, G., & Giudici, P. (2019). Blockchain Startups and Prospectus Regulation. *European Business Organization Law Review*, 20(4), 665–694. Advance online publication. DOI: 10.1007/s40804-019-00168-6

Briola, A. (2023). 'Anatomy of a Stablecoin's Failure: The Terra-Luna Case.' *Finance Research Letters*, 51. https://www.sciencedirect.com/science/article/pii/S1544612322005359

Bryan, K. A. & Hovenkamp, E. (2020). Startup Acquisitions, Error Costs, and Antitrust Policy. *The University of Chicago Law Review. University of Chicago. Law School*, 87(2), 3.

Coleman, L. (2016). China's mining dominance: Good or bad for Bitcoin? *Cryptocoins News*. Retrieved August 23, 2017, from www.cryptocoinsnews.com/chinas-mining dominance-good-or-bad-for-bitcoin.

Goundar, S. (2020). Introduction to Blockchains and Cryptocurrencies. .DOI: 10.1142/9789811205279_0001

Jaladati, H., & Chitsaz, E. (2023). Unraveling the Secrets to Startup Crowdfunding: Cognitive Legitimacy in Initial Coin Offerings. *Journal of Entrepreneurship Research*, 2(3), 1–22.

Makoto, Y., Chris, D., Kenichi, M., & Yoshio, K. (2019). *Creation of a Blockchain and a New Ecosystem. Policy Discussion Papers 19029, Research Institute of Economy, Trade and Industry*. RIETI.

Marian, O. (2015). A Conceptual Framework for the Regulation of Cryptocurrencies. University of Chicago Law Review, 82, 53–68.

Mark Hooson and Nikita Tambe. (2024). How to Trade Cryptocurrency. https://www.forbes.com/advisor/in/investing/cryptocurrency/how-to-trade-cryptocurrency/

Mitra, D. (2012). The Role of Crowdfunding in Entrepreneurial Finance. *Delhi Business Review.*, 13(2), 67–72. DOI: 10.51768/dbr.v13i2.132201218

OECD. (2022). Crypto-Asset Reporting Framework and Amendments to the Common Reporting Standard, OECD, Paris. https://www.oecd.org/tax/exchange-of-tax-information/crypto-asset-reporting-framework-and-amendments-to-the-common-reporting-standard.htm

Petersen, H. (.2022). An evaluation of the German blockchain startup environment. FSBC Working Paper. Frankfurt School Blockchain Centre. https://fsblockchain.medium.com/an-evaluation-of-the-german-blockchain-startup-environment-e42aeb394677

Pollman, E. (2023). Startup Failure. *Duke Law Journal,* 73.

Schückes, M., & Gutmann, T. (2021). Why do startups pursue initial coin offerings (ICOs)? The role of economic drivers and social identity on funding choice. *Small Bus Econ,57*, 1027–1052. .DOI: 10.1007/s11187-020-00337-9

Schueffel, P. (2017). *The Concise fintech compendium.* School of Management Fribourg.

Semenova, V. (2021). Entry Dynamics of Startup Companies and the Drivers of Their Growth in the Nascent Blockchain Industry. New Horizons in Business and Management Studies: Conference Proceedings, 136-148. DOI: 10.14267/978-963-503-867-1_13

Shneor, R., & Flåten, B.-T. (2015). *Opportunities for Entrepreneurial Development and Growth through Online Communities, Collaboration, and Co-Creation. In Entrepreneurial Challenges in the 21st Century.* Palgrave Macmillan.

Szczukiewicz K. (2021). NFT Metaverse Startups and A Possibility of Fundraising Through Token Issuance. *Seria: Administracja i Zarządzanie* (57).

Taherdoost, H., & Madanchian, M. (2023). Blockchain-Based New Business Models: A Systematic Review. *Electronics (Basel)*, 12(6), 1479. DOI: 10.3390/electronics12061479

Wierik, T. M. (2019). Analyzing Investment Decision Criteria for Blockchain Startups. http://essay.utwente.nl/78563/

KEY TERMS AND DEFINITIONS

Blockchain: It is an immutable, cryptographic, distributed, consensus-driven ledger. It is a software protocol for the instantaneous transfer of money and other forms of value via the Internet. It is a system of linking blocks in a chain format that stores data and is chronologically consistent. Because one cannot delete or modify the chain without consensus from the network.

Crowdfunding: Crowdfunding is a way of raising debt and equity with a collective effort of multiple investors through an internet-based platform.

Crypto-Wallet: It stores the private key needed to unlock funds from the investor's wallet address on the blockchain.

Cryptocurrency: It is an encrypted, decentralized digital currency transferred between peers and confirmed in a public ledger via a process known as mining. This is also known as Digital currency.

Decentralized Financial Transactions (DeFi): DeFi is an economic paradigm that leverages a distributed ledger. Technologies to offer services such as lending, investing, or exchanging crypto assets like cryptocurrency, smart contracts, bitcoin, etc., without relying on a traditional centralized intermediary.

Digital Currency: It is also known as Crypto Currency. It is an encrypted, decentralized digital currency transferred between peers and confirmed in a public ledger via a process known as mining. Digital currencies are issued by private developers and denominated in their unit of account. They are obtained, stored, accessed, and transacted electronically, neither denominated in any sovereign currency nor issued or backed by any government or central bank.

Mobile Wallets: Mobile wallet applications like GooglePay, AndroidPay, ApplePay, Alipay, and PayPal are used for electronic payments. One has to download the particular mobile wallet app on their phone and add information about their debit/credit card details, which will be stored securely.

Proof of Elapsed Time: This is a consensus mechanism often used on permissioned blockchain networks to decide the mining rights or the block winners on the network.

Proof of Service: This document functions like a legal "receipt" confirming the delivery of documents from one party to another in a legal matter. It is a written version of a sworn statement attesting to the completion of the service process.

Proof-of-Concept: This demonstrates the feasibility and practical potential of any blockchain project in any field, such as Energy, Communication, Services, Insurance, etc. It determines whether a new product or business idea is feasible and likely to be successful in the market before a company continues its development.

Proof-of-Work (PoW): enables cryptocurrency transactions to be confirmed and recorded without a central authority. Each block of transactions has a specific hash. For the block to be confirmed, a crypto miner must generate a target hash that's less than or equal to that of the block. Miners use mining devices that quickly generate computations to accomplish this.

Smart Contract: Smart contracts defined. Smart contracts are simply programs stored on a blockchain that run when predetermined conditions are met. They are typically used to automate the execution of an agreement so that all participants can be immediately sure of the outcome without any intermediary's involvement or time loss.

Stablecoin: Stablecoin is a fixed-price cryptocurrency whose market value is attached to another stable asset. Unlike average cryptocurrencies, stablecoin can be pegged to assets such as certain fiat currencies that can be traded on exchanges, including the U.S. dollar or the Euro.

Chapter 11
Touchdowns to Take-Off:
Sporting Ventures on the Incubation Runway

Amitava Pal
https://orcid.org/0009-0007-8934-2718
ICFAI University, Jharkhand, India

Kavita Mathad
https://orcid.org/0000-0002-0058-9084
Presidency University, India

ABSTRACT

This study investigates the field of sports entrepreneurship, specifically examining the process of incubation and its impact on innovation. Sports companies have a significant role in fostering economic growth and community development. However, achieving success in this field necessitates strategic support and access to resources. Business incubation offers a well-organized setting for ambitious sports entrepreneurs to enhance their ideas, develop robust strategies, and attain sustainable success. Conducting qualitative research with sports entrepreneurs offered valuable insights for entrepreneurs and incubation practitioners, shedding light on effective strategies and the typical obstacles.

INTRODUCTION

The chapter explores the dynamic sphere of promoting entrepreneurship and encouraging innovation within the thrilling world of sports through the avenue of business incubation. The objective is to dissect the unique challenges and opportunities presented by sporting ventures, highlighting how incubation can serve as a catalyst

DOI: 10.4018/979-8-3693-4302-9.ch011

Copyright © 2025, IGI Global. Copying or distributing in print or electronic forms without written permission of IGI Global is prohibited.

for their growth and success. Sports ventures hold a special place in both the hearts of enthusiasts and the landscape of the global economy. Beyond the thrill of competition, they embody a nexus of passion, creativity, and commerce (Hammerschmidt et al., 2023). From cutting-edge sports technologies to innovative fan engagement platforms (Litwin, 2023), these ventures not only entertain but also drive significant economic activity, creating jobs and fostering community development. However, navigating the competitive and rapidly evolving sports industry requires more than just talent and ambition. It demands strategic guidance, resources, and a nurturing environment conducive to innovation. This is where business incubation steps in, offering a structured framework for fledgling sports startups to refine their ideas, develop viable business models, and ultimately, soar to new heights of success. By focusing on promoting entrepreneurship and innovation through business incubation, aspire to unlock the full potential of sports ventures, harnessing their power to drive positive societal change and economic growth. Through this exploration, we aim to inspire and empower aspiring sports entrepreneurs and incubation practitioners alike to embark on an exhilarating journey of discovery and achievement in the dynamic world of sports innovation.

UNDERSTANDING SPORTING VENTURES

Understanding sporting ventures involves recognizing the distinctive nature of businesses operating within the sports industry. These ventures encompass a wide array of activities, ranging from professional sports teams and leagues to sports technology startups and fitness-focused enterprises. What sets sporting ventures apart are their inherent ties to the world of sports, whether through product offerings, services, or experiences (Hammerschmidt et al., 2022). Sporting ventures often leverage the universal appeal of sports to connect with consumers on a deeply emotional level, tapping into their passion, loyalty, and sense of identity. This unique characteristic allows sporting ventures to transcend traditional market boundaries, reaching diverse audiences across geographical and cultural divides (Adgully Bureau, 2023). Examples of successful sporting ventures abound, each making its mark on the industry in distinct ways. From iconic sports franchises like Manchester United and the New York Yankees to innovative startups like Strava and Peloton, these ventures have not only redefined the way we engage with sports but have also contributed significantly to the evolution of the industry (Ostsieker, 2019). Beyond entertainment, sporting ventures play a vital role in driving technological innovation, promoting health and wellness, and fostering social inclusion. For instance, wearable fitness trackers and virtual reality training platforms have revolutionized the way athletes train and compete, while community-based sports initiatives have empowered underserved populations to access sports and recreation opportunities (Pelin Avcı et al., 2023). Sporting ventures represent a diverse and dynamic ecosystem that spans across sectors and industries, united by a common passion for sports and a shared commitment to pushing the boundaries of innovation. Their unique characteristics and contributions, bring in valuable insights into the transformative potential of sports entrepreneurship and the opportunities it presents for driving positive change on a global scale.

THE ROLE OF BUSINESS INCUBATION

Business incubation plays a vital role in nurturing and propelling the growth of startups in the sports industry, offering a structured support system to tackle the unique challenges they face. Essentially, it provides early-stage ventures with the necessary resources, guidance, and networking opportunities to navigate the complexities of the sports market and thrive (Awonuga et al., 2024). For instance, consider the role of organizations like leAD Sports Accelerator, founded by Klaus, Horst, and Stefan Bente, the grandsons of Adidas Founder Adi Dassler, the program aims to commemorate their grandfather's legacy while fostering sports entrepreneurship and innovation (Glover, 2017). It offers startups in the sports sector access to funding, mentorship, and industry connections, enabling them to refine their products, validate their ideas, and gain traction in the market. One of the primary benefits of incubating sports startups is the tailored support and expertise they receive. Incubators specializing in sports entrepreneurship understand the intricacies of the industry, allowing them to offer targeted advice on product development, market entry strategies, and partnership opportunities. For example, the Nike Accelerator program provides startups working on innovative fitness and sports-related technologies with access to Nike's resources, expertise, and global network and have been developed to promote equality (Lynch, 2023). Business incubation nurtures a collaborative ecosystem where startups can connect with like-minded entrepreneurs, investors, and industry insiders. This network effect can lead to valuable partnerships, strategic alliances, and knowledge exchange, accelerating the growth trajectory of sports ventures. Take, for instance, Techstars Sports Accelerator Powered by Indy (*Techstars Sports Accelerator Powered by Indy*, n.d.), which brings together startups, sports organizations, and corporate partners to drive innovation and disruption in the sports industry through mentorship, investment, and collaboration. Compared to traditional startups, sports ventures incubated within specialized programs benefit from industry-specific resources and opportunities, giving them a competitive edge in a fast-paced and competitive market. By leveraging the support of business incubators, sports entrepreneurs can effectively navigate the unique challenges of the sports industry and position themselves for long-term success and impact.

OBJECTIVE OF THE STUDY

The objective of this study is

- To comprehensively explore the role of incubation programs in supporting sports startups.

This includes identifying the positives and areas for growth within current incubation practices, understanding the expectations of sports start-ups from these programs, and outlining key recommendations for enhancing incubation support in the sports entrepreneurship ecosystem.

METHODOLOGY

The study utilised a qualitative methodology, employing targeted interviews with the founders of sports start-ups. The purpose of these interviews was to collect comprehensive information about the founders' experiences, difficulties, and thoughts on the assistance offered by incubators. The study aimed to understand the special challenges that sports start-ups confront and how incubation programmes might help them overcome these obstacles. By examining the unique circumstances of the sports industry, the study hoped to provide a comprehensive understanding of the complexities involved in establishing and growing a sports firm. The qualitative data generated valuable, context-specific information about the several aspects of the startup experience. It revealed the most advantageous forms of aid and highlighted areas that require further support. The study sought to emphasise the merits and drawbacks of existing incubation programmes by directly capturing the insights of these entrepreneurs who have experience with them. The objective of this qualitative study is to offer a thorough comprehension of how incubators may enhance their support for sports entrepreneurs throughout the process of developing ideas and entering the market. The comprehensive narratives and qualitative observations provide a rigorous examination of the incubation process, highlighting the significance of customised assistance and the tangible effects of incubator programmes. The study's findings will help to cultivate a more dynamic and inventive sports entrepreneurial environment. The study seeks to generate beneficial effects on both economic growth and societal well-being through sports innovation by identifying effective tactics and emphasising areas that need improvement. The results will assist incubators in improving their support mechanisms, guaranteeing that they are well prepared to foster the upcoming cohort of sports entrepreneurs and innovators.

INSIGHTS FROM THE START UP FOUNDERS

Critical Role of Seed Funding

Insight: Start-ups emphasized on the reach to seed funding provided by incubators, which is crucial for initiating operations, developing prototypes, conducting market research, and validating business models. This initial financial support is got allows start-ups to focus on product development without the immediate pressure of generating revenue.

Impact: It accelerates the timeline from ideation to market entry, enabling startups to iterate on their concepts and refine their value propositions based on early feedback.

Access to Prototyping Facilities

Insight: Founders highlighted the importance of access to high-quality prototyping facilities and technology resources within incubators. This access facilitates rapid prototyping, testing, and refinement of products or services, which is critical in enhancing product functionality and market readiness.

Impact: It reduces costs associated with outsourcing prototyping, accelerates time-to-market, and enhances the quality and scalability of the startup's offerings.

Mentorship as a Cornerstone

Insight: Mentorship programs offered by incubators were universally valued for providing startups with strategic guidance and expertise. Mentors support founders in areas such as business strategy formulation, market entry strategies, navigating industry-specific challenges, and personal development.

Impact: Effective mentorship enhances decision-making, mitigates risks, and fosters professional growth and leadership skills among founders, ultimately contributing to the long-term success of the startup.

Network and Partnership Opportunities

Insight: Startups benefited significantly from the extensive networks and strategic partnerships facilitated by incubators. These networks provide access to investors, industry experts, potential customers, and collaboration opportunities with other startups and established companies.

Impact: Networking opportunities accelerate market penetration, validate business models through partnerships, and open doors to funding rounds and distribution channels essential for scaling operations.

Navigating Regulatory Challenges

Insight: Founders identified regulatory compliance as a major challenge, particularly in sectors involving health data privacy, intellectual property rights, and adherence to industry standards in sports technology and equipment.

Impact: Incubators that offer regulatory guidance and access to legal expertise help startups navigate complex legal frameworks, mitigate risks, and ensure compliance, thereby safeguarding their operations and innovations.

Sustainability and Innovation

Insight: There is a growing demand for incubators to support startups in integrating sustainable practices into their business models. Startups recognize the importance of aligning with consumer preferences for eco-friendly products and practices.

Impact: Incubators fostering sustainability initiatives enable startups to differentiate themselves in the market, attract environmentally conscious consumers, and contribute positively to societal and environmental goals.

Technology Adoption

Insight: Startups expressed a keen interest in incubators supporting the adoption of emerging technologies such as artificial intelligence (AI), virtual reality (VR), augmented reality (AR), and Internet of Things (IoT) in sports applications.

Impact: Incubators that provide access to technology experts, development resources, and innovation labs empower startups to enhance product offerings, improve user experiences, and gain a competitive edge in the evolving sports tech landscape.

Market Access and International Expansion

Insight: Founders highlighted the need for incubators to facilitate market access strategies and international expansion opportunities. This includes understanding global market dynamics, cultural nuances, and regulatory requirements.

Impact: Effective internationalization support enables startups to explore new markets, forge strategic alliances, and diversify revenue streams, ultimately fostering sustainable growth and market resilience.

Challenges in Funding Continuity

Insight: Securing follow-on funding beyond the initial incubation phase remains a significant challenge for startups. Founders seek ongoing support in investor relations, fundraising strategies, and maintaining financial stability post-incubation.

Impact: Incubators that provide continuous investor networking opportunities, pitch preparation support, and access to funding sources help startups navigate funding challenges and sustain growth momentum beyond the startup phase.

Adapting to Market Dynamics

Insight: Startups recognize the importance of adapting to evolving market dynamics, consumer behaviours, and technological advancements to maintain competitive advantage and relevance.

Impact: Incubators that offer market trend analysis, consumer insights, and strategic advisory services empower startups to pivot effectively, innovate proactively, and capitalize on emerging opportunities in the dynamic sports industry landscape.

CHALLENGES IN SPORTS ENTREPRENEURSHIP

As per the sports start up founders, they encounter a variety of challenges unique to the industry that can hinder their progress and success. These challenges include navigating complex regulatory frameworks, accessing specialized facilities and equipment, securing partnerships with established sports organizations, and breaking into a fiercely competitive market dominated by well-established players. However, business incubation presents a compelling solution to address these challenges and empower sports entrepreneurs to overcome barriers to entry and thrive in the industry. By providing tailored support, resources, and networking opportunities, incubators play a crucial role in mitigating the challenges faced by startups in the sports sector. Few references got discussed in the discussion. Like, Sports Tech

Tokyo accelerator program offers startups in the sports technology space access to mentors, investors, and industry experts, helping them navigate regulatory hurdles and gain insights into market dynamics (*SPORTS TECH TOKYO - Connecting the World to Sports Innovation*, n.d.). By leveraging the expertise and networks of the accelerator, startups can streamline their operations and accelerate their growth trajectory. It has been highlighted that business incubators provide sports entrepreneurs with access to specialized facilities, equipment, and testing environments that may otherwise be inaccessible. The founders mentioned the Green Sports Alliance incubator, which provides startups developing sustainable sports solutions with access to advanced facilities for prototyping and product testing. This enables them to refine their offerings and showcase their value to potential partners and investors (*Green Sports Alliance: Driving Sustainability in Sports*, n.d.). Another critical point that came during discussion is that business incubation nurtures collaboration and partnerships within the sports ecosystem, enabling startups to leverage the resources and expertise of established players in the industry. People talked about the LA Dodgers Accelerator program brings together startups, investors, and sports organizations to drive innovation and disruption in the sports industry through mentorship, investment, and collaboration (Staff & Staff, 2022). By addressing the common challenges faced by entrepreneurs in the sports industry and providing them with the support and resources they need to succeed, business incubation plays a crucial role in unlocking the full potential of sports entrepreneurship and driving positive change in the industry.

GLOBAL REFERENCES

Incubated Entities

Zwift

Zwift is a virtual training platform that combines the fun of video games with serious training for cyclists and runners. Participating in the Launchpad LA incubator, Zwift received essential mentorship, funding, and networking opportunities. The platform launched its beta version in 2014 and quickly gained traction among cycling enthusiasts. Today, Zwift boasts millions of users worldwide and has secured significant venture capital to expand its offerings (*The at Home Cycling & Running Virtual Training App*, n.d.)

WHOOP

WHOOP (*Whoop*, n.d.), founded by Harvard College students in 2012, has recently raised $100 million in a Series E funding round, valuing the company at over $1 billion. Known for its wearable technology focused on health monitoring and optimization, WHOOP offers a subscription service that includes the WHOOP Strap 3.0 and a coaching platform. The company has expanded significantly, with over 330 employees and notable partnerships in sports, including the PGA Tour and NFLPA. WHOOP credits its early success to support from Harvard's Innovation Lab, (*Billion-Dollar Valuations and Exits for Harvard-born Startups*, 2020) which connected founders with resources and a collaborative environment. The company continues to innovate in health technology and plans to further grow its workforce, primarily in Boston.

Stryd

Stryd is a pioneer in wearable technology for runners, providing a foot pod that measures running power to optimize performance and reduce injury risk (*Stryd | Run With Power | Stryd (Global)*, n.d.). Through the Techstars Boulder accelerator program, Stryd received seed funding and mentorship. The company launched its first product via a successful crowdfunding campaign. Stryd has grown significantly, becoming a key player in the running technology market with ongoing product innovations.

Nix Biosensors

Nix Biosensors founded by Meridith Cass a graduate from Harvard Business School, a collegiate athlete and marathoner, develops hydration biosensors for athletes, offering real-time sweat analysis to optimize hydration strategies. Incubated at MassChallenge (Yannone, 2019), Nix developed its prototype with access to labs, mentorship, and funding opportunities. The company launched its first product targeting elite athletes and sports teams. Nix Biosensors continues to innovate and plans to expand its technology into consumer and military markets, supported by continued investment and strategic partnerships (Yannone, 2019b). They are known for their electronic pods that weigh less than 0.5 ounces and are yet durable and reusable.

PlaySight Interactive

PlaySight Interactive (Bernardob, 2023) provides smart sports technology solutions, including AI-powered video and analytics platforms for athletes and coaches. As part of the Plug and Play Tech Center, PlaySight refined its product with the help of technology experts, mentors, and investors (Wikipedia contributors, 2024). The company launched its SmartCourt system, initially targeting tennis, and has since expanded to other sports. Today, PlaySight's technology cover over 24 plus variety of sports across 20 plus countries and is used by top sports facilities and teams globally, supported by substantial funding to fuel further expansion.

Table 1. Summary table

Company	Overview	Incubation Program	Key Points
Zwift	Virtual training platform merging video games with serious training for cyclists and runners	Launchpad LA	Launched beta in 2014, millions of users, significant venture capital backing
Whoop	Wearable technology providing performance data and analytics for athletes	Harvard Innovation Lab (i-lab)	Launched in 2015, leader in wearable fitness, over $200 million in funding
Stryd	Wearable tech for runners, measuring running power to optimize performance	Techstars Boulder	Launched via crowdfunding, key player in running technology, continuous innovation
Nix Biosensors	Hydration biosensors for real-time sweat analysis	MassChallenge	Targeting elite athletes, plans to expand to consumer and military markets, ongoing investment
PlaySight Interactive	Smart sports technology solutions with AI-powered video and analytics platforms	Plug and Play Tech Center	Launched SmartCourt system, technology used globally by sports facilities and teams, substantial funding
Arena	High-performance swimwear brand founded by Horst Dassler, son of Adidas founder	Adidas internal resources	Launched in 1973, top swimwear brand, sponsorships with elite athletes, continuous product innovation

Sports Business Incubators Global References

Below is a comprehensive list of some of the best sports accelerators (Failory, 2024)

Data Pitch (United Kingdom, London): Data Pitch is a startup accelerator focused on leveraging data to solve industry challenges. Established in 2017, it fosters collaborations between startups and established businesses, offering substantial investment opportunities and strategic support to the corporate and the public enterprises to use shared data and hence build sustainable business that positively impact the three Ps- People, Planet and Profits.

RSE Ventures (United States, New York): A private investment firm, founded in 2012 by Matt Higgins and Stephen M. Ross, RSE Ventures invests in sports, entertainment, media, consumer, and technology sectors. With a portfolio spanning diverse industries, it provides significant resources and expertise to its portfolio companies. The speciality of RSE Ventures that is liked by the founders is they are both the investors and incubators. They happen to be one stop solution for the founders and entreprenures.

Global Sports Venture Studio (United States, New York): Collaborating with the LA Dodgers and R/GA, Global Sports Venture Studio aims to innovate within the sports industry. Founded in 2015, it supports startups through strategic partnerships, investment opportunities, and industry mentorship. The Global Sports Venture Studio expertise in world-class research that bring in actionable insights to the table.

Startupbootcamp Australia (Australia, Melbourne): Launched in 2018, Startupbootcamp Australia focuses on solving global challenges through innovation. It offers a 13-week accelerator program, providing startups with mentorship, funding opportunities, and access to a global network of investors and corporations.

ideaTree Inc. (United States, West Hollywood): Founded in 2012 by Siddharth Arora, ideaTree Inc. provides comprehensive resources for tech startups. It supports entrepreneurs through a 26-week accelerator program, fostering growth and innovation in the competitive startup ecosystem.

Paris&Co Incubateurs (France, Paris): As Paris' economic development agency, Paris&Co Incubateurs supports early-stage startups across various sectors. With a strong focus on innovation, it offers incubation programs designed to accelerate growth and facilitate market entry.

Blue Star Innovation Partners (United States, Frisco): Established in 2017, Blue Star Innovation Partners specializes in growth-stage investments. It focuses on software and payments sectors, providing strategic support and funding to drive innovation and market expansion.

DT Mentoring Program (Hungary, Budapest): The DT Mentoring Program is a robust incubation ecosystem that assists startups in business growth and employee management. With a 12-week program duration, it offers mentorship, resources, and networking opportunities crucial for startup success.

Retail Hub (Italy, Milan): Founded in 2020 by Massimo Volpe, Retail Hub facilitates networking and market entry for startups in the retail sector. It supports entrepreneurs in navigating industry challenges and exploring new market opportunities through specialized programs.

Berkeley Blockchain Xcelerator (United States, Berkeley): Launched in 2019, Berkeley Blockchain Xcelerator is a collaborative initiative between UC Berkeley and industry partners. It accelerates blockchain startups through mentorship, resources, and access to a vibrant entrepreneurial ecosystem.

Venturr (United Kingdom, London): Venturr provides a platform for data and analytics startups to thrive. Founded by Kam Rafique, it supports startups in scaling their operations and achieving market success through tailored mentorship and strategic guidance.

Nexes (Spain, Girona): Established in 2008, Nexes offers affordable services and resources to early-stage businesses. It serves as a launchpad for small enterprises, providing essential support during the critical early years of operation.

Florida-Israel Business Accelerator (United States, Tampa): FIBA focuses on accelerating tech companies from Israel looking to establish a presence in the U.S. market. It provides access to resources, technology validation, and seed funding opportunities.

leAD Lake Nona Sports & Health Academy (United States, Orlando): leAD Sports & Health Tech Partners identifies and supports early-stage sports and health tech startups globally. It offers a 21-week accelerator program aimed at fostering innovation and growth in the sports industry.

Sports Tech Acceleration Program (India, Mumbai): Based in Mumbai, the Sports Tech Acceleration Program supports startups disrupting the sports technology landscape. It empowers entrepreneurs with mentorship, market insights, and funding opportunities to drive innovation.

Creatribe (Argentina, La Plata): Founded in 2018, Creatribe accelerates tech companies' growth in Argentina. It offers a 17-week program that equips startups with the tools and resources needed to scale their operations and succeed in competitive markets.

IIT Madras: IIT-Madras is launching a significant initiative to fund sports-tech startups focusing on AI and IoT products through its Pravartak Technologies Foundation and CESSA. This effort aims to bridge technology with the sports industry, enhancing sporting performance through innovative products and applications. Startups can receive up to Rs 5 crore in funding and will be supported in developing

AI and IoT-based solutions such as sensors, networks, actuators, and controllers. The initiative includes establishing a sports tech incubator fund and hosting India's first 'IIT Madras Sports Technology Start-up Conclave' to foster innovation in sectors like media, entertainment, player engagement, performance measurement, esports, analytics, commerce, and communities. Evaluation by expert panels will determine funding amounts ranging from Rs 10 lakh to Rs 50 lakh per startup, with equity stake and incubation support provided. This initiative underscores IIT-Madras's commitment to fostering entrepreneurial spirit and technological innovation in sports tech, potentially impacting India's sports landscape significantly (Somadder & Somadder, 2024)

BEST PRACTICES AND STRATEGIES

Focus on User-Centric Innovation

Innovation that directly addresses the needs and pain points of users is crucial for success in the sporting industry. Especially in the usage of sports equipment's it is seen that the users do certain changes or adjustments in order to make the best of the product. These are the users who tend to bring in the changes in the overall design and features of the product.

Example: **Whoop** Whoop's focus on providing athletes with actionable performance insights demonstrates the importance of user-centric innovation. By addressing the specific needs of athletes for better training and recovery data, Whoop developed a product that became essential for many professional sports teams and individual athletes (Staff & Staff, 2022)

Best Practice: Conduct thorough market research and engage with potential users early in the development process to ensure the product or service meets their needs and preferences.

Leverage Technology and Data

Utilizing advanced technology and data analytics can set a sporting venture apart by offering unique value propositions and improving user experience.

Example: **Stryd** Stryd introduced running power as a new metric, going beyond traditional metrics like pace and heart rate. Their foot pod uses sophisticated sensors and data analysis to provide runners with insights that help optimize performance and reduce injury risk.

Best Practice: Invest in cutting-edge technology and data analytics capabilities to offer innovative solutions that provide tangible benefits to users (*Stryd | Run With Power | Stryd (Global)*, n.d.)

Foster Community and Engagement

Creating a community around the product can drive engagement and brand loyalty. Social features that allow users to share their progress and compete with others can significantly enhance user experience.

Example: **Zwift** Zwift successfully merged the fun of video games with serious training, creating a virtual community where cyclists and runners can train together and compete in a social, engaging environment. Zwift, had the gamification phenomenon incorporate to a larger extent. This community aspect has been a key driver of Zwift's popularity and growth (*The at Home Cycling & Running Virtual Training App*, n.d.-b)

Best Practice: Integrate social features that allow users to connect, share, and compete with each other, fostering a sense of community and enhancing engagement without any constraints of distance to be travelled.

Provide Comprehensive Support and Resources

Access to mentorship, funding, and networking opportunities is critical for early-stage ventures. Business incubators should offer a comprehensive support system to help startups navigate the challenges of the early stages and hence continue to do so until the business shows all signs of sustaining the business competition.

Example: **Nix Biosensors** Participating in MassChallenge provided Nix Biosensors with the necessary infrastructure, mentorship, and funding opportunities to develop their hydration biosensor technology. The incubator's network was instrumental in helping Nix secure initial users and endorsements. The uniqueness of the product with a customised feedback and feedforward for the user has what made the biosensors succeed in the market.

Best Practice: Entrepreneurs should seek incubators that offer a broad range of support services, while incubators should strive to provide holistic support tailored to the unique needs of sporting ventures (*Nix Biosensors | Hydration Monitor | Revolutionary Sweat Science*, n.d.)

Continuous Innovation and Adaptation

The sporting industry is dynamic, with evolving trends and technologies. Continuous innovation and the ability to adapt to changing market conditions are vital to have ever green products on the product line for sustained success.

Example: **PlaySight Interactive** PlaySight started with its SmartCourt system for tennis but has continuously expanded its technology to other sports. The company's commitment to innovation and adaptation has allowed it to remain relevant and grow in a competitive market.

Best Practice: Foster a culture of continuous improvement and be open to pivoting or expanding the product offering in response to market feedback and technological advancements (Awonuga et al., 2024)

RECOMMENDATIONS FOR ENTREPRENEURS AND INCUBATORS

For Entrepreneurs

For Entrepreneurs, navigating the competitive landscape of sports entrepreneurship requires strategic planning and leveraging available resources. Engaging with potential users early in the product development phase ensures that products features align closely with market demands, fostering customer satisfaction and loyalty. Furthermore, utilizing advanced technology and data analytics not only enhances product offerings but also position the startups as innovators in their respective fields with an added advantage of first mover's profits. Building a community around the product strengthens brand identity and provides valuable feedback channels, essential for continuous improvement. Strategic partnerships and comprehensive support from incubators are instrumental in scaling operations and gaining market traction, underscoring the importance of choosing the right incubation programs. For Entrepreneurs, these recommendations have been documented from insights gathered through discussions with founders who have successfully navigated the challenges of sports entrepreneurship.

1. **Engage with Users Early**: Involving the hard core users of the related products in the development process to ensure the product designed meets their needs and preferences.

2. **Leverage Technology**: With the current pace at which the products are getting advanced in all sense and the rate at which the competition gets thicker it is a must that the Entrepreneurs have to utilize advanced technology and data analytics to provide unique and valuable solutions.
3. **Build a Community**: Creating a platform that encourages user interaction and community building is crucial to enhance engagement and loyalty.
4. **Seek Comprehensive Support**: Choose incubators that offer a wide range of support services, including mentorship, funding, and networking opportunities.
5. **Form Strategic Partnerships**: Network is net worth, entrepreneurs need to be smart to identify the right partnerships that can enhance resources, credibility, and market access.
6. **Innovate Continuously**: Stay ahead of industry trends and continuously improve and adapt your offerings. Companies invest on innovation with the hope of a breakthrough outcome that would make them the pioneers and become the monopoly in the market.

For Incubators

For Incubators, providing holistic support is crucial in nurturing the growth of sports ventures operating in the dynamic business environment. This includes offering a wide array of services such as mentorship, funding opportunities, and networking platforms. Creating an environment that fosters innovation encourages startups to leverage cutting-edge technology and data analytics, thereby staying competitive. Additionally, facilitating community building initiatives within startups enhances user engagement and loyalty, contributing to long-term success. Promoting strategic partnerships and sponsorships through established networks can significantly boost startups' market visibility and credibility. Finally, promoting continuous learning ensures that startups remain agile and responsive to evolving industry trends, positioning them for sustained growth and impact in the sports sector. For Incubators, the recommendations are informed by insights from successful incubation programs in the sports industry.

1. **Provide Holistic Support**: Offer comprehensive services that address the various needs of sporting ventures, right from product modification, funding to mentorship and networking. Entrepreneurs look up to the incubators for their continuous support, not just from ideation to commercialisation but then to face the challenges through the competition.
2. **Foster Innovation**: Create an environment that encourages startups to leverage cutting-edge technology and data analytics. The sudden growth in the digitalisation and internationalisation of various sectors especially post COVID-19

has made it more important for the firms to adapt and adopt newer technologies and master the skills to deal with the data generated in a much more efficient and effectively.
3. **Encourage Community Building**: Support startups in developing features and strategies that foster user engagement and community. This becomes more crucial as the markets keep developing day by day coming up with a good number of newer and better products being launched in the market. Community building is a must to be connected to all the stakeholders in the value chain.
4. **Facilitate Strategic Partnerships**: Use of network to help startups form strategic partnerships and sponsorships. As there is *no one size fits all* concept witnessed in the business problems, connecting and collaborating becomes more important to survive the competition.
5. **Promote Continuous Learning**: Encourage startups to stay informed about industry trends and continuously innovate and adapt. The incubators to support the founders or the entrepreneurs to help them understand and sty in tune with the changes that happen and impact the said business.

COLLABORATION AND PARTNERSHIPS

For incubators focused on nurturing sports startups, fostering collaboration between sports organizations, investors, and startups is paramount to their success and growth. Here's why collaboration is crucial from an incubator's point of view:

Access to Expertise and Resources: Collaborating with established sports organizations and seasoned investors provides startups with access to specialized expertise, industry insights, and resources that are essential for their development and scaling. Collaborating with the firms that complement in expertise is bound to bring in positive by bring in newer perspective towards growth and progress of the firm.

Validation and Credibility: Partnering with reputable sports organizations validates the startup's concept and enhances its credibility in the market. This validation is crucial for attracting further investment and gaining customer trust as it endorses the quality of the product.

Network Expansion: Collaborations broaden the startup's network, opening doors to potential customers, strategic partners, and distribution channels that can accelerate market penetration and growth.

Risk Mitigation: By sharing risks with partners, startups can undertake more ambitious projects and initiatives, knowing they have the support and backing of experienced entities in the sports industry.

Innovation Acceleration: Joint efforts often lead to synergistic innovations that leverage technological advancements, market trends, and consumer insights, propelling startups ahead of competitors.

EXAMPLES OF SUCCESSFUL PARTNERSHIPS

Collaborations between big brands and tech businesses are changing the face of sports innovation in today's quickly changing sports market. These collaborations expand sustainable practices and cutting-edge technology in sports gear, content creation, and performance analytics, as well as improve athletic performance and fan engagement. These partnerships are motivational examples of how incorporating technology may transform the sports industry for prospective companies. In turn, incubators are essential but crucial for supporting and advising entrepreneurs as they pursue related lines of inquiry by providing them with the tools and know-how needed to prosper in this ever-changing ecosystem. This brings in aspects different dimensions to be considered as in case of the skills to be acquired for sustaining in the business. The table that follows highlights important partnerships and the possible roles that incubators may play in supporting these kinds of developments(Hatherill, 2023) (*The NBA Launches a First-of-its-kind New App Experience for Fans, Driven by the Power of Data - Source*, 2024) (*Nike and Apple Partnership*, 2022) (*GOPRO AND RED BULL FORM EXCLUSIVE GLOBAL PARTNERSHIP*, 2016) (*Under Armour and IBM to Transform Personal Health and Fitness, Powered by IBM Watson*, n.d.) (Baum & Baum, 2016)

Table 2.

Collaboration	Description	Incubator's Role
Adidas and Parley for the Oceans	Collaboration focused on creating eco-friendly sportswear using recycled ocean plastics.	Incubators facilitated introductions and provided support to startups looking to integrate sustainable practices into their products, similar to Adidas and Parley's collaboration.
NBA and Microsoft	Partnership aimed at enhancing fan engagement and viewer experiences through technology like augmented reality (AR) and data analytics.	Incubators encouraged startups to explore opportunities in sports technology and fan engagement, inspired by the NBA's collaboration with Microsoft.
Nike and Apple	Collaboration resulted in the development of fitness tracking products like Nike+ using Apple's technology.	Incubators advised startups on integrating wearable technology into sports apparel, similar to Nike's collaboration with Apple.

continued on following page

Table 2. Continued

Collaboration	Description	Incubator's Role
Red Bull and GoPro	Partnership to use GoPro cameras for capturing extreme sports content, showcasing athletes' perspectives.	Incubators supported startups in leveraging action cameras for sports content creation, drawing inspiration from Red Bull's partnership with GoPro.
Under Armour and IBM Watson	Collaboration focused on using IBM Watson's artificial intelligence for analysing and improving sports performance data.	Incubators guided startups in utilizing artificial intelligence for sports performance analytics, reflecting Under Armour's collaboration with IBM Watson.

KEY CONSIDERATIONS FOR INCUBATORS

These important factors for incubators are the result of in-depth interviews with founders, entrepreneurs and other key players in the sports innovation and entrepreneurship space. Startups emphasised on how important strategic matchmaking is to forming alliances that support their business goals and improve their market placement. They underlined the need of resource alignment, pointing out that partnerships ought to give access to vital resources like capital, coaching, and state-of-the-art technology to support expansion and advancement. A recurrent issue that emerged was long-term sustainability, with startups emphasising the importance of forming alliances that support their continued relevance and influence in the sports sector. In order to create and nurture the ground-breaking ideas and keep a competitive edge in the market, incubators should cultivate an innovation ecosystem where a variety of expertise and disciplines come together. This was highlighted in the last insights. These ideas provide a shared understanding of how incubators might best assist entrepreneurs in overcoming obstacles and grasping possibilities in the ever-changing field of sports innovation.

Strategic Matchmaking: Identify and facilitate partnerships that align with startups' goals, values, and growth strategies of the firms. The strategic matchmaking could be in terms of various other benefits like international market access, technology transfer or resource sharing.

Resource Alignment: Ensure that collaborations provide startups with access to the necessary resources, such as funding, know-how skills, mentorship, and technology.

Long-term Sustainability: Foster collaborations that nurture organically to contribute to the long-term goals and ensure sustainability and market relevance of startups in the sports industry.

Innovation Ecosystem: Cultivate an ecosystem where cross-disciplinary collaborations thrive, fostering innovation and competitive advantage. In such a way that the firms within the ecosystem would collaborate to complement each other in terms of production expertise, and/or resource sharing and compete for markets and profits.

Collaboration and partnerships are instrumental in driving the success of sports startups incubated within an incubator's environment. By facilitating strategic collaborations with sports organizations, investors, and industry leaders, incubators can significantly enhance the growth trajectory and market impact of startups, ultimately contributing to a vibrant and innovative sports ecosystem.

FUTURE TRENDS IN SPORTS ENTREPRENEURSHIP AND INNOVATION

Exploration of Emerging Trends

Sports entrepreneurship and innovation are evolving rapidly, driven by technological advancements, changing consumer behaviours, and societal trends. Several emerging trends are shaping the future landscape of sporting ventures:

Wearable Technology and Data Analytics

Trend: Continued advancements in wearable devices and data analytics are enhancing athletes' performance monitoring, injury prevention, and overall health monitoring and management.

Example: Companies like WHOOP and Stryd are pioneering wearable technologies that provide athletes with real-time insights into their physical metrics, optimizing training and recovery strategies.

Virtual and Augmented Reality (VR/AR)

Trend: VR and AR technologies are transforming fan engagement and athlete training experiences by creating immersive virtual environments. The customer engagement or the fan engagement or the sport enthusiast engagement as applicable has gone way beyond gamification.

Example: Zwift utilizes VR to create virtual training worlds where cyclists and runners can compete and train together, enhancing the social and interactive aspects of indoor training.

Sustainability and Eco-Friendly Practices

Trend: Increasing consumer demand for sustainable products is pushing sports brands to adopt eco-friendly practices and materials. Many companies and the gen z associate sports not just as a leisure but as for fitness and quality longevity, on same lines they do want to see the sports products be greener in nature and the firms producing them be more sustainable.

Example: Adidas' partnership with Parley for the Oceans to create sportswear from recycled ocean plastic illustrates how sustainability can drive innovation and consumer loyalty.

E-Sports and Gaming Integration

Trend: The convergence of sports and gaming is blurring traditional boundaries, creating new opportunities for fan engagement and revenue generation. The presence and application of AR and VR make it much more authentic with enhancing the experience or the feel factor for the customers.

Example: NBA 2K League, an e-sports league operated by the NBA, showcases professional gamers competing in virtual basketball tournaments, attracting a global audience. This increased the reach of the league across taking its brand image to greater heights.

Personalized Fitness and Health Solutions

Trend: There is a growing demand for personalized fitness programs and health solutions tailored to individual needs and preferences. Due to the increased purchasing power from the customers and the applications of advanced technology specially in case of biosensors, products focusing on the tailored requirement of individuals are more promising for the firms in terms of profit generation.

Example: Companies like Peloton offer personalized fitness experiences through interactive streaming of live and on-demand fitness classes, revolutionizing home fitness routines. These are sunrise products as they are likely to be in demand from most of the ancillary industries or sectors like the healthcare, fashion industry, hospitality industry and alike.

Predictions for the Future of Sporting Ventures and Their Impact on Society

The future of sports entrepreneurship and innovation holds immense potential for transformation across various facets of sports, from athlete performance and fan engagement to societal impact. By embracing emerging trends and leveraging technological advancements, sporting ventures can not only enhance their competitive edge but also contribute positively to global sports culture and community well-being. As these trends continue to evolve, they will shape a dynamic and inclusive future for sports entrepreneurship in the years to come.

Integration of AI and Machine Learning: AI-powered technologies will continue to play a pivotal role in sports analytics, coaching, and fan engagement, enhancing performance prediction and athlete development.

Expansion of Virtual Sports Experiences: Virtual sports events and experiences will become more immersive and widespread, offering fans globally accessible ways to engage with their favourite sports and athletes. This specially adds to the new age generation preferences hence has a greater reach as a product.

Rise of Health and Wellness Tech: Innovations in health monitoring devices and technologies will empower individuals to take greater control over their fitness, health, and well-being, contributing to a healthier society. This dimension of sports industry is more promising as the segment of these products is not just the sports aspirants or professionals but includes anybody with a focus on fitness.

Inclusivity and Diversity: Sports entrepreneurship to increasingly focus on promoting inclusivity and diversity, addressing societal issues such as gender equality and accessibility in sports participation and leadership. In addition, the affordability of the aspirants to get the training, and related facilitation is a challenge and needs to be addressed.

Globalization of Sports Business: With an increased globalisation and liberalised media broadcasting, the sports industry across the world is gaining attention with all kinds of games coverage and viewership from various parts of the world. The growth in the sports industry has facilitated growth in various other ancillary industry like the tourism, hospitality, aviation industry, healthcare industry and alike. The sport industry continues to expand globally, driven by digital platforms, international partnerships, and the growing popularity of sports beyond traditional markets.

CONCLUSION

This chapter, explores the complex relationship between entrepreneurship, innovation, incubation and the sports business, acknowledging the potential for transformation and the tremendous opportunities that arise from these factors. Entrepreneurship in sports involves more than just establishing new enterprises; it entails questioning established norms, pushing limits, and effecting significant transformations. It is examined how entrepreneurial endeavours in the field of sports not only improve athlete performance through state-of-the-art technologies and training methods but also transform fan involvement and operational effectiveness inside sports organisations. These advancements, which include wearable technology for analysing performance and immersive virtual experiences for spectators, highlight the industry's ability to constantly evolve and adapt. Nevertheless, among these prospects exist obstacles that entrepreneurs in the sports sector must successfully have overcome. The presence of regulations, high starting costs, and the specific requirements of sports-related technologies create considerable obstacles for entering and expanding in this industry. The role of business incubators is crucial in this context. They play a role of catalyst. Incubators enable companies by offering essential resources such as Know-how skills, Funding, Subject matter experts, mentorship, access to networks, navigate the firm through compliance including the regulatory aspects and provide strategic assistance in sustaining the business developed. This support helps startups overcome problems, speed up their development, and improve their business strategies. In the future, anyone with a business interest in the sports sector, such as investors, policymakers, industry executives, and athletes, have an important responsibility to create a favourable environment that promotes entrepreneurial development and innovation. The imperative is evident: there must be collaborative endorsement and advancement of entrepreneurship in sports through vigorous business incubation techniques. Inclination to investing in business incubators that focus on sports is crucial for the development of sport industry. These investments guarantee that businesses obtain the necessary financial support and required infrastructure facilities to succeed. In addition to providing financial assistance, stakeholders could enhance their contribution by promoting collaboration and mentorship between well established firms and the budding or aspiring entrepreneurs. This will facilitate the exchange of crucial knowledge, networks, and expertise necessary for achieving success. It is essential to support policies that promote innovation, such as regulatory frameworks that can adapt to new technology and tax incentives for investment. To fully harness the power of sports entrepreneurship in generating economic growth, job creation, and global competitiveness within the sports industry, it is essential to provide a supportive regulatory framework and foster an innovative culture inside sports organisations. One such would be to have a dedicated special economic zone for setting up manufacturing units of sports equipment. These special economic zones could carry the tax holiday as an incentive to attract potential entrepreneurs to take up sports products manufacturing as their business. By adopting these ideas and allocating resources optimally to foster the growth of sports entrepreneurship through efficient incubation and assistance, one can create a sector that is dynamic and able to withstand challenges, while still captivating and inspiring global audiences. The corporate, the public sector units, the think tanks and the policy makers can work together to create a future in which sports not only provide entertainment but also drive technical progress and have a significant impact on society and the country as a whole.

REFERENCES

Adgully Bureau. (2023, August 25). *Leveraging sports marketing to build a stronger consumer connection*. Adgully.com. https://adgully.com/leveraging-sports-marketing-to-build-a-stronger-consumer-connection-135782.html

Avcı, P., Bayrakdar, A., Meriçelli, M., & Panoutsakopoulos, V. (2023). The use of developing technology in sports:. In I. Bayraktar (Ed.), *Özgür Publications*. Özgür Yayın-Dağıtım Co. Ltd. DOI: 10.58830/ozgur.pub315

Awonuga, N. K. F., Mhlongo, N. N. Z., Olatoye, N. F. O., Ibeh, N. C. V., Elufioye, N. O. A., & Asuzu, N. O. F. (2024). Business incubators and their impact on start-up success: A review in the USA. *International Journal of Science and Research Archive*, 11(1), 1418–1432. DOI: 10.30574/ijsra.2024.11.1.0234

Baum, S., & Baum, S. (2016, January 7). Under Armour's collaboration with IBM Watson provides big data insights to advance connected fitness approach. *MedCity News*. https://medcitynews.com/2016/01/under-armours-collaboration-with-ibm-watson/

Bernardob. (2023, December 14). *Sports AI and automated production technology*. Playsight. https://playsight.com/

Billion-Dollar valuations and exits for Harvard-born startups. (2020, October 30). Harvard Business School. https://www.hbs.edu/news/articles/Pages/billion-dollar-valuations-exits-harvard-born-startups.aspx

Failory. (2024, February 11). Top 16 sports Accelerators and incubators in 2024. *Failory*. https://www.failory.com/startups/sports-accelerators-incubators

Glover, Z. (2017, August 22). Meet the 16 startups selected for the LEAD Sports Accelerator. *Forbes*. https://www.forbes.com/sites/zacglover/2017/08/22/meet-the-16-startups-selected-for-the-lead-sports-accelerator/#:~:text=The%20program%20was%20founded%20by,Founder%20Adi%20Dassler%20with%20grandchildren

Gopro And Red Bull Form Exclusive Global Partnership. (2016, May 23). Go Pro. https://gopro.com/en/gr/news/gopro-and-red-bull-form-exclusive-global-partnership

Green Sports Alliance: Driving Sustainability in sports. (n.d.). https://www.greensportsalliance.org/

Hammerschmidt, J., González Huertas, M., Puumalainen, K., & Calabuig, F. (2023). Sport entrepreneurship: the role of innovation and creativity in sport management. *Review of Managerial Science,* 1–3. DOI: 10.1007/s11846-023-00711-3

Hammerschmidt, J., Kraus, S., & Jones, P. (2022). Sport Entrepreneurship: Definition and Conceptualization. *Journal of Small Business Strategy*, 32(2). Advance online publication. DOI: 10.53703/001c.31718

Hatherill, C. (2023, June 15). *Adidas x Parley — Parley*. Parley. https://parley.tv/initiatives/adidasxparley

Litwin, D. (2023, December 13). *The future of fan engagement in Sports: Trends and Innovations*. MarketScale. https://marketscale.com/industries/sports-and-entertainment/the-future-of-fan-engagment-in-sports/

Lynch, J. (2023, August 17). Nike launches its 'Accelerator Program' to drive equality in sports. *Hypebeast*. https://hypebeast.com/2023/8/nike-fc-launch-new-accelerator-program-football

Nike and apple partnership. (2022, February 7). [Slide show]. SlideShare. https://www.slideshare.net/slideshow/nike-and-apple-partnership/251126995

Nix Biosensors | Hydration Monitor | Revolutionary Sweat Science. (n.d.). Nix Biosensors. https://nixbiosensors.com/

Ostsieker, P. (2019, September 17). *(Sports) Entrepreneurship: Problem first!* https://www.linkedin.com/pulse/sports-entrepreneurship-problem-first-philipp-ostsieker/

Somadder, E., & Somadder, E. (2024, May 27). *IIT-Madras set to provide funds to incubate Sports-Tech startups*. Equitypandit. https://www.equitypandit.com/iit-madras-set-to-provide-funds-to-incubate-sports-tech-startups/

Sports Tech Tokyo - Connecting the world to sports innovation. (n.d.). https://sportstech.tokyo

Staff., & Associates. (2022, July 27). LA Dodgers seeking innovating startups and growth stage companies for global sports Venture Studio. *American Entrepreneurship Today®*. https://americanentrepreneurship.com/news/startup-news/la-dodgers-seeking-innovating-startups-and-growth-stage-companies-for-global-sports-venture-studio

Stryd | Run with Power | Stryd (Global). (n.d.). Stryd (Global). https://www.stryd.com/gl/en

Techstars Sports accelerator powered by Indy. (n.d.). Techstars. https://www.techstars.com/accelerators/indy-sports

The At Home Cycling & Running virtual training app. (n.d.). Zwift. https://www.zwift.com/news/102-the-early-days

The NBA launches a first-of-its-kind new app experience for fans, driven by the power of data. (2024, April 16). https://news.microsoft.com/source/features/digital-transformation/the-nba-launches-a-first-of-its-kind-new-app-experience-for-fans-driven-by-the-power-of-data/

Under Armour and IBM to transform personal health and fitness, powered by IBM Watson. (n.d.). IBM UK Newsroom. https://uk.newsroom.ibm.com/2016-Jan-06-Under-Armour-And-IBM-To-Transform-Personal-Health-And-Fitness-Powered-By-IBM-Watson

Whoop. (n.d.). https://www.whoop.com/in/en/

Wikipedia contributors. (2024, April 6). *PlaySight Interactive*. Wikipedia. https://en.wikipedia.org/wiki/PlaySight_Interactive

Yannone, T. (2019, January 31). Five fitness wearables created in Boston. *Boston Magazine*. https://www.bostonmagazine.com/health/2019/01/31/futuristic-fitness-wearables/

KEY TERMS AND DEFINITIONS

Adaptation to Market Dynamics: The ability of startups to adjust strategies in response to market changes.

AI (Artificial Intelligence): Technology used in sports tech to create smart, responsive products and analyze data for performance insights.

AR (Augmented Reality): Technology enhancing fan experiences and athlete training by overlaying digital elements onto real-world environments.

Business Incubation: Programs that support startups with resources like mentorship, funding, and networking opportunities to foster growth.

Seed Funding: Initial capital provided to startups to kickstart their business operations.

Compilation of References

Aarstad, J., Jakobsen, S. E., & Foss, L. (2022). Business incubator management and entrepreneur collaboration with R&D milieus: Does the regional context matter? *International Journal of Entrepreneurship and Innovation*, 23(1), 28–38. DOI: 10.1177/14657503211030808

Abduh, M. (2003). *Exploring factors affecting perceived value added contributions of business incubation programs to tenants in Australia*. La Trobe University.

Abduh, M., D'Souza, C., Quazi, A., & Burley, H. T. (2007). Investigating and classifying clients' satisfaction with business incubator services. *Managing Service Quality*, 17(1), 74–91. DOI: 10.1108/09604520710720683

Adelowo, C. M., & Oladimeji, O. O. (2024). How entrepreneurial characteristics and incubation facilities shape venture creation among technology business incubators in Nigeria. *International Journal of Technoentrepreneurship*, 5(1), 49–66. DOI: 10.1504/IJTE.2024.137530

Adgully Bureau. (2023, August 25). *Leveraging sports marketing to build a stronger consumer connection*. Adgully.com. https://adgully.com/leveraging-sports-marketing-to-build-a-stronger-consumer-connection-135782.html

Adlešič, R. V., & Slavec, A. (2012). Social capital and business incubators performance: testing the structural model. *Economic and Business Review*, 14(3), 201-222. https://www.ebrjournal.net/ojs/index.php/ebr/article/view/145

Aernoudt, R. (2004). Incubators: Tool for Entrepreneurship? *Small Business Economics*, 23(2), 127–135. DOI: 10.1023/B:SBEJ.0000027665.54173.23

Aerts, K., Matthyssens, P., & Vandenbempt, K. (2007). Critical role and screening practices of European business incubators. *Technovation*, 27(5), 254–267. DOI: 10.1016/j.technovation.2006.12.002

Ahluwalia, S., Mahto, R. V., & Guerrero, M. (2020). Blockchain Technology and Startup Financing: A Transaction COST Economics Perspective. *Technological Forecasting and Social Change*, 151, 119854. DOI: 10.1016/j.techfore.2019.119854

Ahmad, N., & Seymour, R. G. (2008). Defining Entrepreneurial Activity: Definitions Supporting Frameworks for Data Collection, *OECD Statistics Working Papers, 2008/1, OECD Publishing*. DOI: 10.1787/18152031

Aithal, P. S., & Aithal, S. (2023). Super Innovation in Higher Education by Nurturing Business Leaders through Incubationship. *International Journal of Applied Engineering and Management Letters*, 7(3), 142–167. DOI: 10.47992/IJAEML.2581.7000.0192

Akpoviroro, K. S., Oba-Adenuga, O. A., & Akanmu, P. M. (2021). The role of business incubation in promoting entrepreneurship and SMEs development. *Management and Entrepreneurship: Trends of Development*, 2(16), 82–100. DOI: 10.26661/2522-1566/2021-1/16-07

Akpuokwe, C. U., Chikwe, C. F., & Eneh, N. E. (2024). Innovating business practices: The impact of social media on fostering gender equality and empowering women entrepreneurs. Magna Scientia Advanced Research and Reviews, 10(2), 032-043.

Al Ayyash, S., McAdam, M., & O'Gorman, C. (2020). Towards a new perspective on the heterogeneity of business incubator-incubation definitions. *IEEE Transactions on Engineering Management*, 69(4), 1738–1752. DOI: 10.1109/TEM.2020.2984169

Al Marri, S. M. K. (2021). *How can the UAE government best promote a successful national innovation ecosystem?* (Doctoral dissertation, University of Warwick). http://webcat.warwick.ac.uk/record=b3678194~S15

Alavi, M., & Leidner, D. E. (2001). Review: Knowledge Management and Knowledge Management Systems: Conceptual Foundations and Research Issues. *Management Information Systems Quarterly*, 25(1), 107. DOI: 10.2307/3250961

Alawad, M. (2023). Igniting Innovation: The Surge of Youth Entrepreneurship in the UAE. *International Journal of Entrepreneurship*, 28(1). https://zuscholars.zu.ac.ae/works/6413/

Alayoubi, M. M., Shobaki, M. J. A., & Abu-Naser, S. S. (2020). *Requirements for Applying the Strategic Entrepreneurship as an Entry Point to Enhance Technical Innovation: Case Study - Palestine Technical College- Deir al-Balah*. http://dstore.alazhar.edu.ps/xmlui/handle/123456789/580

Alayoubi, M. M., Shobaki, M. J. A., & Abu-Naser, S. S. (2020b). *Requirements for Applying the Strategic Entrepreneurship as an Entry Point to Enhance Technical Innovation: Case Study - Palestine Technical College- Deir al-Balah.* http://dstore.alazhar.edu.ps/xmlui/handle/123456789/580

Albort-Morant, G., & Ribeiro-Soriano, D. (2016). A bibliometric analysis of international impact of business incubators. *Journal of Business Research*, 69(5), 1775–1779. DOI: 10.1016/j.jbusres.2015.10.054

Albrecht, S., Lutz, B., & Neumann, D. (2019). How Sentiment Impacts the Success of Blockchain Startups - An Analysis of Social Media Data and Initial Coin Offerings. Conference: Proceedings of the 52nd Hawaii International Conference on System Sciences.

Alhajeri, G. (2022). Changing Behaviours and Its Theories to Achieve the Desire for Entrepreneurship in Future Generations in the UAE and Gulf Region. *International Business Research*, 15(11), 49. DOI: 10.5539/ibr.v15n11p49

Alharbi, G. L., & Aloud, M. E. (2024). The effects of knowledge management processes on service sector performance: Evidence from Saudi Arabia. *Humanities & Social Sciences Communications*, 11(1), 378. DOI: 10.1057/s41599-024-02876-y

Alkaabi, K., Ramadani, V., & Zeqiri, J. (2023). Universities, entrepreneurial ecosystem, and family business performance: Evidence from The United Arab Emirates. *Journal of the Knowledge Economy*, 15(2), 1–28. DOI: 10.1007/s13132-023-01384-9

Allahar, H., & Brathwaite, C. (2016). Business Incubation as an Instrument of Innovation: The Experience of South America and the Caribbean. *International Journal of Innovation*, 4(2), 71–85. DOI: 10.5585/iji.v4i2.107

Allen, D. N., & Bezan, E. J. (1990). *Value added contributions of Pennsylvania's business incubators to tenant firms and local economies.* Pennsylvania State University, Smeal College of Business Administration.

Allen, D. N., & Rahman, S. (1985). Small business incubators: A positive environment for Entrepreneurship. *Journal of Small Business Management*, 23(3), 12–22.

Almeida, R. I. D. S., Pinto, A. P. S., & Henriques, C. M. R. (2021). The effect of incubation on business performance: A comparative study in the Centro region of Portugal. *Revista Brasileira de Gestão de Negócios*, 23, 127–140. DOI: 10.7819/rbgn.v23i1.4089

Al-Mubaraki, H. M., & Busler, M. (2017). Challenges and opportunities of innovation and incubators as a tool for knowledge-based economy. *Journal of Innovation and Entrepreneurship*, 6(1), 15. DOI: 10.1186/s13731-017-0075-y

Al-Mubaraki, H., & Busler, M. (2010). Business incubators models of the USA and UK: A SWOT analysis. *World Journal of Entrepreneurship, Management and Sustainable Development*, 6(4), 335–354. DOI: 10.1108/20425961201000025

Almuharrami, S. S. M. S., & Mohamad, N. B. (2021). The influence of relational and social capital on the infrastructure project performance in UAE. *Estudios de Economía Aplicada*, 39(10). Advance online publication. DOI: 10.25115/eea.v39i10.6290

Alnassai, J. M. I. A. (2023). A Study on the Barriers to Entrepreneurship in the UAE. *Journal of Risk and Financial Management*, 16(3), 146. DOI: 10.3390/jrfm16030146

Alpenidze, O., Pauceanu, R. M., & Sanyal, S. (2019). Key success factors for business incubators in Europe: an empirical study. *Academy of Entrepreneurship Journal*, 25(1), 1. https://www.abacademies.org/articles/Key-success-factors-for-business-incubators-in-europe-an-empirical-1528-2686-25-1-211.pdf

Altındağ, E., & Bilaloğlu Aktürk, H. (2020). The impact of new generation management approaches on the firm performance: The Moderating Role of Strategic Human Resource Management Applications. *SAGE Open*, 10(3), 2158244020948845. DOI: 10.1177/2158244020948845

Amezcua, A. S., Grimes, M. G., Bradley, S. W., & Wiklund, J. (2013). Organizational sponsorship and founding environments: A contingency view on the survival of business-incubated firms. *Academy of Management Journal*, 56(6), 1628–1654. DOI: 10.5465/amj.2011.0652

Aminova, M., & Marchi, E. (2021). The role of innovation on start-up failure vs. its success. *International Journal of Business Ethics and Governance*, 41-72.

Amit, R., MacCrimmon, K., Zietsma, C., & Oesch, J. M. (2001). Does money matter? Wealth attainment as the motive for initiating growth-orientated technology businesses. *Journal of Business Venturing*, 16(2), 119–143. DOI: 10.1016/S0883-9026(99)00044-0

Amit, R., & Muller, E. (1994). *Push and pull entrepreneurship, Frontiers in Entrepreneurship Research*. Babson College.

Amit, R., & Muller, E. (1995). Push and Pull Entrepreneurship. *Journal of Small Business and Entrepreneurship*, 12(4), 64–80. DOI: 10.1080/08276331.1995.10600505

Anjaningrum, W. D., Yogatama, A. N., Sidi, A. P., Hermawati, A., & Suci, R. P. (2024). The impact of Penta-Helix Collaborative Business Incubation Process on the creative business strategic orientation and innovation capability. *International Journal of Learning and Intellectual Capital*, 21(1), 60–77. DOI: 10.1504/IJLIC.2024.136380

Arafat, M. Y., Saleem, I., Dwivedi, A. K., & Khan, A. (2018). Determinants of agricultural entrepreneurship: A GEM data based study. *The International Entrepreneurship and Management Journal*, 16(1), 345–370. DOI: 10.1007/s11365-018-0536-1

Arena, M., Bengo, I., Calderini, M., & Chiodo, V. (2018). Unlocking finance for social tech start-ups: Is there a new opportunity space? *Technological Forecasting and Social Change*, 127, 154–165. DOI: 10.1016/j.techfore.2017.05.035

Arogundade, B. B. (2011). Entrepreneurship education: An imperative for sustainable development in Nigeria. *Journal of Emerging Trends in Educational Research and Policy Studies*, 2(1), 26–29.

Arokiasamy, A. R. (2012). The Influence of Globalization in Promoting Entrepreneurship in Malaysia. *South East European Journal of Economics and Business*, 7(2), 149–157. DOI: 10.2478/v10033-012-0021-7

Aslani, F., Mousakhani, M., & Aslani, A. (2012). Knowledge Sharing: A Survey, Assessment and Directions for Future Research: Individual Behavior Perspective. *International Journal of Economics and Management Engineering*, 6(8), 2025–2029.

Assenova, V. A. (2020). Early-stage venture incubation and mentoring promote learning, scaling, and profitability among disadvantaged entrepreneurs. Organization Science, 31(6), 1560-1578.

Astebro, T. B., Bazzazian, N., & Braguinsky, S. (2012). Startups by recent university graduates and their faculty: Implications for university entrepreneurship policy. *Research Policy*, 41(4), 663–677. DOI: 10.1016/j.respol.2012.01.004

Audretsch, D., Colombelli, A., Grilli, L., Minola, T., & Rasmussen, E. (2020). Innovative start-ups and policy initiatives. *Research Policy*, 49(10), 104027. DOI: 10.1016/j.respol.2020.104027

Autio, E., Keeley, R. H., Klofsten, M., & Ulfstedt, T. (1997). Entrepreneurial intent among students: Testing an intent model in Asia, Scandinavia, and USA. *Frontiers of Entrepreneurship Research*, 17(5), 95–109.

Autio, E., Sapienza, H. J., & Almeida, J. G. (2000). Effects of age at entry, knowledge intensity, and imitability on international growth. *Academy of Management Journal*, 43(5), 909–924. DOI: 10.2307/1556419

Avcı, P., Bayrakdar, A., Meriçelli, M., & Panoutsakopoulos, V. (2023). The use of developing technology in sports:. In I. Bayraktar (Ed.), *Özgür Publications*. Özgür Yayın-Dağıtım Co. Ltd. DOI: 10.58830/ozgur.pub315

Awonuga, K. F., Mhlongo, N. Z., Olatoye, F. O., Ibeh, C. V., Elufioye, O. A., & Asuzu, O. F. (2024). Business incubators and their impact on startup success: A review in the USA. *International Journal of Science and Research Archive*, 11(1), 1418–1432. DOI: 10.30574/ijsra.2024.11.1.0234

Ayatse, F. A., Kwahar, N., & Iyortsuun, A. S. (2017). Business Incubation Process and Firm Performance: An Empirical Review. *Journal of Global Entrepreneurship Research*, 7(1), 2. DOI: 10.1186/s40497-016-0059-6

Azih, E., & Inanga, E. L. (2014). Performance Effectiveness of Technology Incubation in Nigeria. Business and Economics Journal. https://www.semanticscholar.org/paper/Performance-Effectiveness-of-Technology-Incubation-Azih-Inanga/46f293fc34a532194097484f2ec1cb718992cb6a

Bakar, R., Islam, M. A., & Lee, J. (2014). Entrepreneurship Education: Experiences in Selected Countries. *International Education Studies*, 8(1), 80–88. DOI: 10.5539/ies.v8n1p88

Banerji, D., & Reimer, T. (2019). Startup founders and their LinkedIn connections: Are well-connected entrepreneurs more successful? *Computers in Human Behavior*, 90, 46–52. DOI: 10.1016/j.chb.2018.08.033

Bank, N., Fichter, K., & Klofsten, M. (2017). Sustainability-profiled incubators and securing the inflow of tenants–The case of Green Garage Berlin. *Journal of Cleaner Production*, 157, 76–83. DOI: 10.1016/j.jclepro.2017.04.123

Baporikar, N. (2018a). Entrepreneurship Development and Project Management (Text & Cases). Himalaya Publishing House.

Baporikar, N. (2015). Drivers of Innovation. In Ordoñez de Pablos, P., Turró, L., Tennyson, R., & Zhao, J. (Eds.), *Knowledge Management for Competitive Advantage During Economic Crisis* (pp. 250–270). IGI Global. DOI: 10.4018/978-1-4666-6457-9.ch014

Baporikar, N. (2016). *Handbook of Research on Entrepreneurship in the Contemporary Knowledge-Based Global Economy*. IGI Global. DOI: 10.4018/978-1-4666-8798-1

Baporikar, N. (2020). *Handbook of Research on Entrepreneurship Development and Opportunities in Circular Economy*. IGI Global. DOI: 10.4018/978-1-7998-5116-5

Baporikar, N. (Ed.). (2018b). *Knowledge Integration Strategies for Entrepreneurship and Sustainability*. IGI Global. DOI: 10.4018/978-1-5225-5115-7

Baporikar, N. (Ed.). (2024). *Ecosystem Dynamics and Strategies for Startups Scalability*. IGI Global. DOI: 10.4018/979-8-3693-0527-0

Barbero, J. L., Casillas, J. C., Wright, M., & Garcia, A. R. (2013). Do different types of incubators produce different types of innovations? *The Journal of Technology Transfer*, 39(2), 151–168. DOI: 10.1007/s10961-013-9308-9

Barney, J. (1991). Firm Resources and Sustained Competitive Advantage. *Journal of Management*, 17(1), 99–120. DOI: 10.1177/014920639101700108

Baron, J. N., & Hannan, M. T. (2002). Organizational blueprints for success in high-tech start-ups: Lessons from the Stanford Project on Emerging Companies. *California Management Review*, 44(3), 8–36. DOI: 10.2307/41166130

Barrow, C. (2001). *Incubators, A Realist's Guide to the World's New Business Accelerators*. Wiley.

Baum, S., & Baum, S. (2016, January 7). Under Armour's collaboration with IBM Watson provides big data insights to advance connected fitness approach. *MedCity News*. https://medcitynews.com/2016/01/under-armours-collaboration-with-ibm-watson/

Becker, J. M., Cheah, J. H., Gholamzade, R., Ringle, C. M., & Sarstedt, M. (2023). PLS-SEM's most wanted guidance. *International Journal of Contemporary Hospitality Management*, 35(1), 321–346. DOI: 10.1108/IJCHM-04-2022-0474

Bednář, P., Danko, L., & Smékalová, L. (2023). Coworking spaces and creative communities: Making resilient coworking spaces through knowledge sharing and collective learning. *European Planning Studies*, 31(3), 490–507. DOI: 10.1080/09654313.2021.1944065

Behera, B., Haldar, A., & Sethi, N. (2024). Investigating the direct and indirect effects of Information and Communication Technology on economic growth in the emerging economies: Role of financial development, foreign direct investment, innovation, and institutional quality. *Information Technology for Development*, 30(1), 33–56. DOI: 10.1080/02681102.2023.2233463

Belitski, M., & Heron, K. (2017). Expanding entrepreneurship education ecosystems. *Journal of Management Development*, 36(2), 163–177. DOI: 10.1108/JMD-06-2016-0121

Bergek, A., & Norrman, C. (2008). Incubator Best Practice: A Framework. *Technovation*, 28(1–2), 20–28. DOI: 10.1016/j.technovation.2007.07.008

Bergmann, T., & Utikal, H. (2021). How to support start-ups in developing a sustainable business model: The case of aeuropean social impact accelerator. *Sustainability (Basel)*, 13(6), 3337. DOI: 10.3390/su13063337

Bernard de Saint Affrique, L. A. H. A. (2020). *Insular urbanities*. https://resolver.tudelft.nl/uuid:40ed7979-1243-457e-a7f7-865fe809abc0

Bernardob. (2023, December 14). *Sports AI and automated production technology*. Playsight. https://playsight.com/

Bernardus, D., Sufa, S. A., & Suparwata, D. O. (2024). Supporting start-ups in Indonesia: Examining government policies, incubator business, and sustainable structure for entrepreneurial ecosystems and capital. *International Journal of Business, Law, and Education*, 5(1), 236–259. DOI: 10.56442/ijble.v5i1.372

Beyhan, B., Akçomak, S., & Cetindamar, D. (2024). The startup selection process in accelerators: Qualitative evidence from Turkey. *Entrepreneurship Research Journal*, 14(1), 27–51. DOI: 10.1515/erj-2021-0122

Bhattacharjee, A., & Juman, M. K. I. (2020). Does delay or scarcity in working capital increase unexpected financial risk for women entrepreneurs in the developing country? *International Journal of Economics, Commerce and Management*, 8(8), 433-446. http://ijecm.co.uk/wp-content/uploads/2020/08/8827.pdf

Bhattacharjee, A., & Bansal, V. (2023). Sustainable Approaches of Blockchain Tech, Artificial Intelligence, and Climate Finance in the 4&5IR: Low Emission Technologies and Economy. In Trivedi, S., Aggarwal, R., & Singh, G. (Eds.), *Perspectives on Blockchain Technology and Responsible Investing* (pp. 85–116). IGI Global. DOI: 10.4018/978-1-6684-8361-9.ch004

Bhattacharjee, A., Bansal, V., & Juman, M. K. I. (2021). COVID-19 Emergency: Faux Healthcare Service Causes Distress and Life Dissatisfaction. *Asian Journal of Medicine and Health*, 18(12), 53–61. DOI: 10.9734/ajmah/2020/v18i1230290

Bhattacharjee, A., & Ghosh, A. (2024). Sustainable Green Supply Chain Management for Organizational Performance and Carbon Reduction. In Ramakrishna, Y., & Srivastava, B. (Eds.), *Strategies for Environmentally Responsible Supply Chain and Production Management* (pp. 128–155). IGI Global. DOI: 10.4018/979-8-3693-0669-7.ch007

Bhattacharjee, A., Ghosh, A., Juman, M. K., & Hossen, M. (2024b). Augmented Intelligence for Knowledge Management and Green Education in the Post-COVID-19 Era. In Doshi, R., Dadhich, M., Poddar, S., & Hiran, K. (Eds.), *Integrating Generative AI in Education to Achieve Sustainable Development Goals* (pp. 47–71). IGI Global. DOI: 10.4018/979-8-3693-2440-0.ch003

Bhattacharjee, A., & Jahanshahi, A. A. (2021). Artificial landscape strategy: A business growth recovery plan in the post pandemic world. *Academia Letters*, 2311. Advance online publication. DOI: 10.20935/AL2311

Bhattacharjee, A., & Jahanshahi, A. A. (2024). Simulation of Green Supply Chain Design With Renewable Energy and Green Technology for Intensifying Sustainability After COVID-19. In Martínez-Falcó, J., Marco-Lajara, B., Sánchez-García, E., & Millán-Tudela, L. (Eds.), *Green Supply Chain Management Practice and Principles* (pp. 219–248). IGI Global. DOI: 10.4018/979-8-3693-3486-7.ch011

Bhattacharjee, A., Jahanshahi, A. A., Bhuiyan, M., & Sultana, S. (2020). Mental health of cisgender and transgender during COVID-19 pandemic. *International Journal of Medical Research and Review*, 8(5), 344–351. DOI: 10.17511/ijmrr.2020.i05.02

Bhattacharjee, A., Jahanshahi, A. A., & Chakraborty, S. (2024a). Unlocking the link between low emission supply chains, blockchain adoption, and financial success: The payoff of socially responsible practices in supply chains. *Business Strategy & Development*, 7(1), e341. DOI: 10.1002/bsd2.341

Bibeau, J., Meilleur, R., & St-Jean, É. (2024). To formalize, or not to formalize, business incubators' networks: That is not the question. *Technovation*, 130, 102904. DOI: 10.1016/j.technovation.2023.102904

Billion-Dollar valuations and exits for Harvard-born startups. (2020, October 30). Harvard Business School. https://www.hbs.edu/news/articles/Pages/billion-dollar-valuations-exits-harvard-born-startups.aspx

Bitzer, V., Francken, M., & Glasbergen, P. (2008). Intersectoral Partnerships for A Sustainable Coffee Chain: Really Addressing Sustainability or Just Picking (Coffee) Cherries? *Global Environmental Change*, 18(2), 271–284. DOI: 10.1016/j.gloenvcha.2008.01.002

Blank, T. H. (2021). When Incubator Resources are Crucial: Survival Chances of Student Startups Operating in an Academic Incubator. *The Journal of Technology Transfer*, 46(6), 1845–1868. DOI: 10.1007/s10961-020-09831-4

Bock, G. W., & Kim, Y. G. (2002). Determinants of the Individuals Knowledge Sharing Behavior: The Theory of Reasoned Action Perspective. *Proceedings of the Pacific-Asia Conference on Information System (PACIS)*. Meiji University.

Bock, G. W., Zmud, R. W., Kim, Y. G., & Lee, J. N. (2005). Behavioral intention formation in knowledge sharing: Examining the roles of extrinsic motivators, social-psychological forces, and organizational climate. *Management Information Systems Quarterly*, 29(1), 87–111. DOI: 10.2307/25148669

Bøllingtoft, A. (2012). The bottom-up business incubator: Leverage to networking and cooperation practices in a self-generated, entrepreneurial-enabled environment. *Technovation*, 32(5), 304–315. DOI: 10.1016/j.technovation.2011.11.005

Bøllingtoft, A., & Ulhøi, J. P. (2005). The Networked Business Incubator—Leveraging Entrepreneurial Agency? *Journal of Business Venturing*, 20(2), 265–290. DOI: 10.1016/j.jbusvent.2003.12.005

Booth-Jones, L. (2012). *Assessing small business training programme effectiveness in an incubator setting and beyond*. Masters dissertation, Nelson Mandela Metropolitan University.

Boreiko, D., Ferrarini, G., & Giudici, P. (2019). Blockchain Startups and Prospectus Regulation. *European Business Organization Law Review*, 20(4), 665–694. Advance online publication. DOI: 10.1007/s40804-019-00168-6

Borgatti, S. P., Jones, C., & Everett, M. G. (1998). Network measures of social capital. *Connections*, 21(2), 27–36.

Borooah, V. K., Collins, G., Hart, M., & MacNabb, A. (1997). Women in business. In Deakins, D., Jennings, P., & Mason, C. (Eds.), *Small Firms: Entrepreneurship in the Nineties*. Paul Chapman Publishing.

Boyd, N. G., & Vozikis, G. S. (1994). The influence of self-efficacy on the development of entrepreneurial intentions and actions. *Entrepreneurship Theory and Practice,* 18(4), 63-77. *Business Review (Federal Reserve Bank of Philadelphia)*, 6, 273–295. DOI: 10.1007/s40821-016-0065-1

Brandt, T., Sakkthivel, A. M., Abidi, N., Abudaqa, A., & Yanamandra, R. (2023). Does environment influence entrepreneurship? Empirical evidence from aspiring emirati women entrepreneurs in United Arab Emirates. https://www.theseus.fi/handle/10024/815018

Braun, G., & Hentschel, R. (2011). Incubators. In Kramme, R., Hoffmann, K.-P., & Pozos, R. S. (Eds.), *Springer Handbook of Medical Technology* (pp. 1285–1290). Springer. DOI: 10.1007/978-3-540-74658-4_71

Breznitz, S. M., & Feldman, M. P. (2010). The engaged university. *The Journal of Technology Transfer*, 37(2), 139–157. DOI: 10.1007/s10961-010-9183-6

Briola, A. (2023). 'Anatomy of a Stablecoin's Failure: The Terra-Luna Case.' *Finance Research Letters*, 51. https://www.sciencedirect.com/science/article/pii/S1544612322005359

Brock, A., Sovacool, B. K., & Hook, A. (2021). Volatile photovoltaics: Green industrialization, sacrifice zones, and the political ecology of solar energy in Germany. *Annals of the American Association of Geographers*, 111(6), 1756–1778. DOI: 10.1080/24694452.2020.1856638

Browne, E. (2021). Social and commercial enterprise interactions: Insights from UK business incubators (Doctoral dissertation, University of Plymouth).

Bruneel, J., Ratinho, T., Clarysse, B., & Groen, A. (2012). The Evolution of Business Incubators: Comparing demand and supply of business incubation services across different incubator generations. *Technovation*, 32(2), 110–121. DOI: 10.1016/j.technovation.2011.11.003

Bryan, K. A. & Hovenkamp, E. (2020). Startup Acquisitions, Error Costs, and Antitrust Policy. *The University of Chicago Law Review. University of Chicago. Law School*, 87(2), 3.

Cadima, R., Ojeda, J., & Monguet, J. M. (2012). Social Networks and Performance in Distributed Learning Communities. *Educational Technology & Society*, 15(4), 296-304.

Caliendo, M., & Kritikos, A. (2010). Start-Ups by the Unemployed: Characteristics, Survival and Direct Employment Effects. *Small Business Economics*, 35(1), 71–92. DOI: 10.1007/s11187-009-9208-4

Campbell, C., Kendrick, R. C., & Samuelson, D. S. (1985). Stalking the Latent Entrepreneur: Business Incubators and Economic Development. *Economic Development Review (Schiller Park, Ill.)*, 3(2), 43–49.

Candeias, J. C., & Sarkar, S. (2024). Entrepreneurial Ecosystems Policy Formulation: A Conceptual Framework. *The Academy of Management Perspectives*, 38(1), 77–105. DOI: 10.5465/amp.2022.0047

Cao, Z., Cunningham, L. F., Gao, W., & Liu, Y. (2024). The downsides of specialization: The impact of business incubator's specialization on startups' R&D efficiency and venture capital financing. *R & D Management*, 54(1), 39–59. DOI: 10.1111/radm.12635

Capatina, A., Cristea, D. S., Micu, A., Micu, A. E., Empoli, G., & Codignola, F. (2023). Exploring causal recipes of startup acceptance into business incubators: A cross-country study. *International Journal of Entrepreneurial Behaviour & Research*, 29(7), 1584–1612. DOI: 10.1108/IJEBR-06-2022-0527

Cardona, A. R., Sun, Q., Li, F., & White, D. (2017). Assessing the effect of personal cultural orientation on brand equity and revisit intention: Exploring destination branding in Latin America. *Journal of Global Marketing*, 30(5), 282–296. DOI: 10.1080/08911762.2017.1336827

Cardon, M. S., & Stevens, C. E. (2004). Managing human resources in small organizations: What do we know? *Human Resource Management Review*, 14(3), 295–323. DOI: 10.1016/j.hrmr.2004.06.001

Carling, J., & Collins, F. (2018). Aspiration, Desire and Drivers of Migration. *Journal of Ethnic and Migration Studies*, 44(6), 909–926. DOI: 10.1080/1369183X.2017.1384134

Castles, S., & Miller, M. J. (2009). *The Age of Migration: International Population Movements in the Modern World*. Guilford Press.

Cavalcante, P. L. (2023). Innovation policy governance. In *Global Encyclopedia of Public Administration, Public Policy, and Governance* (pp. 6704–6709). Springer International Publishing. DOI: 10.1007/978-3-030-66252-3_4234

Chandra, A., & Medrano Silva, M. A. (2012). Business Incubation in Chile: Development, Financing and Financial Services. *Journal of Technology Management & Innovation*, 7(2), 1–13. DOI: 10.4067/S0718-27242012000200001

Chaudhry, I. S., Paquibut, R. Y., & Tunio, M. N. (2021). Do workforce diversity, inclusion practices, & organizational characteristics contribute to organizational innovation? Evidence from the UAE. *Cogent Business & Management*, 8(1), 1947549. DOI: 10.1080/23311975.2021.1947549

Chen, C. J., & Huang, J. W. (2009). Strategic human resource practices and innovation performance, The mediating role of knowledge management capacity. *Journal of Business Research*, 62(1), 104–114. DOI: 10.1016/j.jbusres.2007.11.016

Chen, C.-J. (2009). Technology Commercialization, Incubator and Venture Capital, and New Venture Performance. *Journal of Business Research*, 62(1), 93–103. DOI: 10.1016/j.jbusres.2008.01.003

Chen, N., Chiang, N., & Storey, N. (2012). Business Intelligence and Analytics: From Big Data to Big Impact. *Management Information Systems Quarterly*, 36(4), 1165. DOI: 10.2307/41703503

Chen, X. (2009). *Students Who Study Science, Technology, Engineering, and Mathematics (STEM) in Postsecondary Education. Stats in Brief. NCES 2009-161*. National Center for Education Statistics.

Chien, F., Kamran, H. W., Nawaz, M. A., Thach, N. N., Long, P. D., & Baloch, Z. A. (2022). Assessing the prioritization of barriers toward green innovation: Small and medium enterprises Nexus. *Environment, Development and Sustainability*, 24(2), 1897–1927. DOI: 10.1007/s10668-021-01513-x

Chiu, C.-M., Hsu, M.-H., & Wang, E. T. (2006). Understanding knowledge sharing in virtual communities: An integration of social capital and social cognitive theories. *Decision Support Systems*, 42(3), 1872–1888. DOI: 10.1016/j.dss.2006.04.001

Chow, W. S., & Chan, L. S. (2008). Social network, social trust and shared goals in organizational knowledge sharing. *Information & Management*, 45(7), 458–465. DOI: 10.1016/j.im.2008.06.007

Christensen, P. H. (2007). Knowledge sharing: Moving away from the obsession with best practices. *Journal of Knowledge Management*, 11(1), 36–47. DOI: 10.1108/13673270710728222

Cirule, I., & Uvarova, I. (2022). Open innovation and determinants of technology-driven sustainable value creation in incubated start-ups. *Journal of Open Innovation*, 8(3), 162. DOI: 10.3390/joitmc8030162

Clark, K., & Drinkwater, S. (2000). Pushed out or pulled in? Self-employment amongst Britain's ethnic minorities. *Labour Economics*, 7(5), 603–628. DOI: 10.1016/S0927-5371(00)00015-4

Clarysse, B., Wright, M., & Van Hove, J. (2015). A look inside accelerators: Building businesses. *Nature Biotechnology*, 33(4), 383–386.

Clayton, P. (2024). Mentored without incubation: Start-up survival, funding, and the role of entrepreneurial support organization services. *Research Policy*, 53(4), 104975. DOI: 10.1016/j.respol.2024.104975

Coleman, L. (2016). China's mining dominance: Good or bad for Bitcoin? *Cryptocoins News*. Retrieved August 23, 2017, from www.cryptocoinsnews.com/chinas-mining dominance-good-or-bad-for-bitcoin.

Collings, D. G., & Mellahi, K. (2009). Strategic talent management: A review and research agenda. *Human Resource Management Review*, 19(4), 304–313. DOI: 10.1016/j.hrmr.2009.04.001

Collins, C., Hanges, P., & Locke, E. A. (2004). The Relationship of Achievement Motivation to Entrepreneurial Behaviour: A Meta-Analysis. *Human Performance*, 17(1), 95–117. DOI: 10.1207/S15327043HUP1701_5

Combinator, Y. (n.d.). Retrieved from https://www.ycombinator.com/

Cooper, S. Y., & Park, J. S. (2008). The Impact of 'Incubator' Organizations on Opportunity Recognition and Technology Innovation in New, Entrepreneurial High-Technology Ventures. *International Small Business Journal*, 26(1), 27–56. DOI: 10.1177/0266242607084658

Corsi, C., & Prencipe, A. (2016). Improving Innovation in University Spin-Offs: The Fostering Role of University and Region. *Journal of Technology Management & Innovation*, 11(2), 13–21. DOI: 10.4067/S0718-27242016000200002

Cromie, S. (1987a). Motivations of aspiring male and female entrepreneurs. *Journal of Organizational Behavior*, 8(3), 251–261. DOI: 10.1002/job.4030080306

Crupi, A., & Schilirò, D. (2023). The UAE Economy and the Path to Diversification and Innovation. *International Journal of Business Management and Economic Research*, 2286–2300. https://ijbmer.com/docs/volumes/vol14issue5/ijbmer2023140507.pdf

Czaika, M., & Reinprecht, C. (2020). Drivers of Migration: A Synthesis of Knowledge. *Regional Studies*, 54(1), 10–18.

Daraojimba, C., Abioye, K. M., Bakare, A. D., Mhlongo, N. Z., Onunka, O., & Daraojimba, D. O. (2023). Technology and innovation to growth of entrepreneurship and financial boost: A decade in review (2013-2023). *International Journal of Management & Entrepreneurship Research*, 5(10), 769–792. DOI: 10.51594/ijmer.v5i10.593

Dasgupta, T. (2022). Analysis of Strategies followed by New-Age Indian Entrepreneurs for seeking Business Opportunities and Competitive Advantage (Doctoral dissertation, ICFAI University Jharkhand).

Daskalopoulou, I., Karakitsiou, A., & Thomakis, Z. (2023). Social Entrepreneurship and Social Capital: A Review of Impact Research. *Sustainability (Basel)*, 15(6), 4787. DOI: 10.3390/su15064787

Davidsson, P. (2006). *Nascent Entrepreneurship: Empirical Studies and Developments*. Springer.

Dawson, C., & Henley, A. (2012). Push versus pull entrepreneurship: An ambiguous distinction? *International Journal of Entrepreneurial Behaviour & Research*, 18(6), 697–719. DOI: 10.1108/13552551211268139

Delery, J. E., & Doty, D. H. (1996). Modes of theorizing in strategic human resource management: Tests of universalistic, contingency, and configurational performance predictions. *Academy of Management Journal*, 39(4), 802–835. DOI: 10.2307/256713

DeMartino, R., & Barbato, R. (2003). Differences between women and men MBA entrepreneurs: Exploring family flexibility and wealth creation as career motivators. *Journal of Business Venturing*, 18(6), 815–832. DOI: 10.1016/S0883-9026(03)00003-X

Denktas-Sakar, G., & Karatas-Cetin, C. (2012). Port Sustainability and Stakeholder Management in Supply Chains: A Framework on Resource Dependence Theory. *The Asian Journal of Shipping and Logistics*, 28(3), 301–319. DOI: 10.1016/j.ajsl.2013.01.002

Dent, B. (2008). The Potential for Kitchen Incubators to Assist Food-Processing Enterprises. *International Journal of Entrepreneurship and Small Business*, 6(3), 496. DOI: 10.1504/IJESB.2008.019141

Deyanova, K., Brehmer, N., Lapidus, A., Tiberius, V., & Walsh, S. (2022). Hatching start-ups for sustainable growth: A bibliometric review on business incubators. *Review of Managerial Science*, 16(7), 2083–2109. DOI: 10.1007/s11846-022-00525-9

Dhanabagiyam, S., Doe, M. B., Thamizhselvi, M., Irfan, M., Thalari, S. K., & Libeesh, P. (2024). Factors influencing growth of micro-entrepreneurship in the hospitality industry: An empirical study in India. *Cogent Business & Management*, 11(1), 2285260. Advance online publication. DOI: 10.1080/23311975.2023.2285260

Dhiman, V., & Arora, M. (2024). Exploring the Linkage between Business Incubation and Entrepreneurship: Understanding Trends, Themes and Future Research Agenda. LBS Journal of Management & Research. DOI: 10.1108/LBSJMR-06-2023-0021

Dhiman, V., & Arora, M. (2024). Current State of Metaverse in Entrepreneurial Ecosystem: A Retrospective Analysis of Its Evolving Landscape. In Kumar, J., Arora, M., & Erkol Bayram, G. (Eds.), *Exploring the Use of Metaverse in Business and Education* (pp. 73–87). IGI Global. DOI: 10.4018/979-8-3693-5868-9.ch005

Dhochak, M., Acharya, S. R., & Sareen, S. B. (2019). Assessing the effectiveness of business incubators. *International Journal of Innovation and Learning*, 26(2), 177–194. DOI: 10.1504/IJIL.2019.10022108

DiBella, J., Forrest, N., Burch, S., Rao-Williams, J., Ninomiya, S. M., Hermelingmeier, V., & Chisholm, K. (2023). Exploring the potential of SMEs to build individual, organizational, and community resilience through sustainability-oriented business practices. *Business Strategy and the Environment*, 32(1), 721–735. DOI: 10.1002/bse.3171

Dlamini, T. M., Iwu, C. G., & Ogunlela, G. O. (2023). Support Strategies of Government-Owned Business Incubators for SMEs' Sustainability. In *Leadership and Governance for Sustainability* (pp. 222–241). IGI Global. DOI: 10.4018/978-1-6684-9711-1.ch012

Dobrev, S., & Barnett, W. (2005). Organizational roles and transition to entrepreneurship. *Academy of Management Journal*, 48(3), 433–449. DOI: 10.5465/amj.2005.17407910

Earle, J. S., & Sakova, Z. (2000). Business start-ups or disguised unemployment? Evidence on the character of self-employment from transition economies, *Labour Economics*.

Eden, C. A., Chisom, O. N., & Adeniyi, I. S. (2024). Cultural competence in education: Strategies for fostering inclusivity and diversity awareness. *International Journal of Applied Research in Social Sciences*, 6(3), 383–392. DOI: 10.51594/ijarss.v6i3.895

Eden, C. A., Chisom, O. N., & Adeniyi, I. S. (2024). Parent and community involvement in education: Strengthening partnerships for social improvement. *International Journal of Applied Research in Social Sciences*, 6(3), 372–382. DOI: 10.51594/ijarss.v6i3.894

Eesley, C. E., & Lee, Y. S. (2020). Do university entrepreneurship programs promote entrepreneurship? *Strategic Management Journal*, 42(4), 833–861. DOI: 10.1002/smj.3246

Egbetokun, A. (2023). Business Incubators in Africa: A Review of the Literature. *Innovation and Development*, 1–28. DOI: 10.1080/2157930X.2023.2295090

El Khatib, M., AlShibani, M., Almaeeni, A., & Almulla, A. (2024). Social, Economic, and Environmental Development factors (SEED) to foster collaborative sustainable development for SMART and digital initiatives. *International Journal of Business Analytics and Security*, 4(2), 107–122. https://journals.gaftim.com/index.php/ijbas/article/view/355

Eldering, C., van den Ende, J., & Hulsink, W. (2023). Why entrepreneur sourcing matters: The effects of entrepreneur sourcing on alternative types of business incubation performance. *R & D Management*, 53(3), 481–502. DOI: 10.1111/radm.12588

Elia, G., Margherita, A., Ciavolino, E., & Moustaghfir, K. (2021). Digital society incubator: Combining exponential technology and human potential to build resilient entrepreneurial ecosystems. *Administrative Sciences*, 11(3), 96. DOI: 10.3390/admsci11030096

Erturk, A., Colbran, S. E., Theofanidis, F., & Abidi, O. (Eds.). (2024). *Convergence of Digitalization, Innovation, and Sustainable Development in Business*. IGI Global. DOI: 10.4018/979-8-3693-0798-4

Eveleens, C. P., Van Rijnsoever, F. J., & Niesten, E. M. M. I. (2016). How network-based incubation helps start-up performance: A systematic review against the background of management theories. *The Journal of Technology Transfer*, 42(3), 676–713. DOI: 10.1007/s10961-016-9510-7

Faccia, A., Le Roux, C. L., & Pandey, V. (2023). Innovation and E-commerce models, the technology catalysts for sustainable development: The Emirate of Dubai case study. *Sustainability (Basel)*, 15(4), 3419. DOI: 10.3390/su15043419

Failory. (2024, February 11). Top 16 sports Accelerators and incubators in 2024. *Failory*. https://www.failory.com/startups/sports-accelerators-incubators

Farida, N., Naryoso, A., & Yuniawan, A. (2017). Model of Relationship Marketing and E-Commerce in Improving Marketing Performance of Batik SMEs. *Journal of Database Management*, 8(1), 20–29.

Faul, F., Erdfelder, E., Lang, A.-G., & Buchner, A. (2007). G* Power 3: A flexible statistical power analysis program for the social, behavioral, and biomedical sciences. *Behavior Research Methods*, 39(2), 175–191. DOI: 10.3758/BF03193146 PMID: 17695343

Ferguson, R., & Olofsson, C. (2004). Science parks and the development of NTBFs—Location, survival and growth. *The Journal of Technology Transfer*, 29(1), 5–17. DOI: 10.1023/B:JOTT.0000011178.44095.cd

Fernández-Alles, M., Camelo-Ordaz, C., & Franco-Leal, N. (2014). Key resources and actors for the evolution of academic spin-offs. *The Journal of Technology Transfer*, 40(6), 976–1002. DOI: 10.1007/s10961-014-9387-2

Fini, R., Grimaldi, R., Santoni, S., & Sobrero, M. (2011). Complements or substitutes? The role of universities and local context in supporting the creation of academic spin-offs. *Research Policy*, 40(8), 1113–1127. DOI: 10.1016/j.respol.2011.05.013

Fini, R., Rasmussen, E., Siegel, D., & Wiklund, J. (2018). Rethinking the Commercialization of Public Science: From Entrepreneurial Outcomes to Societal Impacts. *The Academy of Management Perspectives*, 32(1), 4–20. DOI: 10.5465/amp.2017.0206

Fithri, P., Hasan, A., Syafrizal, S., & Games, D. (2024). Validation Studies a Questionnaire Developed to Measure Incubator Business Technology Performance Using PLS-SEM Approach. *Andalasian International Journal of Applied Science. Engineering and Technology*, 4(1), 64–78. DOI: 10.25077/aijaset.v4i1.132

Flanschger, A., Heinzelmann, R., & Messner, M. (2023). Between consultation and control: How incubators perform a governance function for entrepreneurial firms. *Accounting, Auditing & Accountability Journal*, 36(9), 86–107. DOI: 10.1108/AAAJ-09-2020-4950

Fonseca, S. A., & Jabbour, C. J. C. (2012). Assessment of business incubators' green performance: A framework and its application to Brazilian cases. *Technovation*, 32(2), 122–132. DOI: 10.1016/j.technovation.2011.10.006

Fornell, C., & Larcker, D. F. (1981). Evaluating structural equation models with unobservable variables and measurement error. *JMR, Journal of Marketing Research*, 18(1), 39–50. DOI: 10.1177/002224378101800104

Freiling, J., Marquardt, L., & Reit, T. (2022). Virtual Business Incubators: A Support for Entrepreneurship in Rural Areas? In Hornuf, L. (Ed.), *Diginomics Research Perspectives: The Role of Digitalization in Business and Society* (pp. 65–88). Springer International Publishing. DOI: 10.1007/978-3-031-04063-4_4

Galbraith, B., McAdam, R., & Cross, S. E. (2019). The evolution of the incubator: Past, present, and future. *IEEE Transactions on Engineering Management*, 68(1), 265–271. DOI: 10.1109/TEM.2019.2905297

Games, D., Kartika, R., Sari, D. K., & Assariy, A. (2021). Business incubator effectiveness and commercialization strategy: A thematic analysis. *Journal of Science and Technology Policy Management*, 12(2), 176–192. DOI: 10.1108/JSTPM-03-2020-0067

Gandhi, V., Syed, A. A., & Kumar, S. (2022). A study of performance indicators of technology business incubators (Tbis) in india. *Management Dynamics*, 21(1), 14–23. DOI: 10.57198/2583-4932.1006

Gao, Y., Tsai, S. B., Du, X., & Xin, C. (2020). *Sustainability in the Entrepreneurial Ecosystem: Operating Mechanisms and Enterprise Growth*. IGI Global. http://books.google.ie/books?id=6kjmDwAAQBAJ&pg=PA316&dq=A+gateway+to+an+entrepreneurial+society.+J.+Econ.+Sustain.+Dev.+2015,+6,+153%E2%80%93160.&hl=&cd=1&source=gbs_api

Giacomin, O., Guyot, J. L., Janssen, F., & Lohest, O. (2007, June). Novice creators: personal identity and push pull dynamics. In 52th *International Council for Small Business (ICSB)World conference* (pp. 1-30).

Giacomin, O., Janssen, F., Pruett, M., Shinnar, R. S., Llopis, F., & Toney, B. (2011). Entrepreneurial intentions, motivations and barriers: Differences among American, Asian and European Students. *The International Entrepreneurship and Management Journal*, 7(2), 219–238. DOI: 10.1007/s11365-010-0155-y

Gieure, C., del Mar Benavides-Espinosa, M., & Roig-Dobón, S. (2020). The entrepreneurial process: The link between intentions and behavior. *Journal of Business Research*, 112, 541–548. DOI: 10.1016/j.jbusres.2019.11.088

Gilad, B., & Levine, P. (1986). A behavioural model of entrepreneurial supply. *Journal of Small Business Management*, 24(4), 45–53.

Gill, A. M. (1988). Choice of employment status and the wages of employees and the self-employed: Some further evidence. *Journal of Applied Econometrics*, 3(3), 229–234. DOI: 10.1002/jae.3950030306

Giordano Martínez, K., Fernández-Laviada, A., & Herrero Crespo, Á. (2018). Influence of Business Incubators Performance on Entrepreneurial Intentions and Its Antecedents during the Pre-incubation Stage. *Entrepreneurship Research Journal*, 8(2), 20160095. DOI: 10.1515/erj-2016-0095

Global Startup Accelerator Map and List of Startup Accelerators. (n.d.). StartupBlink; StartupBlink. Retrieved 20 July 2024, from https://www.startupblink.com/accelerators

Glover, Z. (2017, August 22). Meet the 16 startups selected for the LEAD Sports Accelerator. *Forbes*. https://www.forbes.com/sites/zacglover/2017/08/22/meet-the-16-startups-selected-for-the-lead-sports-accelerator/#:~:text=The%20program%20was%20founded%20by,Founder%20Adi%20Dassler%20with%20grandchildren

Gnyawali, D. R., & Fogel, D. S. (1994). Environments for Entrepreneurship Development: Key Dimensions and Research Implications. *Entrepreneurship Theory and Practice*, 18(4), 43–62. DOI: 10.1177/104225879401800403

Gonçalves, D., Bergquist, M., Alänge, S., & Bunk, R. (2022). How digital tools align with organizational agility and strengthen digital innovation in automotive startups. *Procedia Computer Science*, 196, 107–116. DOI: 10.1016/j.procs.2021.11.079

Gonthier, J., & Chirita, G. M. (2019). The Role of Corporate Incubators as Invigorators of Innovation Capabilities in Parent Companies. *Journal of Innovation and Entrepreneurship*, 8(1), 8. DOI: 10.1186/s13731-019-0104-0

Gopro And Red Bull Form Exclusive Global Partnership. (2016, May 23). Go Pro. https://gopro.com/en/gr/news/gopro-and-red-bull-form-exclusive-global-partnership

Gounaris, S. P. (2007). The relationships of customer-perceived value, satisfaction, loyalty and behavioral intentions. https://doi.org/DOI: 10.1300/J366v06n01

Goundar, S. (2020). Introduction to Blockchains and Cryptocurrencies. .DOI: 10.1142/9789811205279_0001

Green Sports Alliance: Driving Sustainability in sports. (n.d.). https://www.greensportsalliance.org/

Grimaldi, R., & Grandi, A. (2005). Business incubators and new venture creation: An assessment of incubating models. *Technovation*, 25(2), 111–121. DOI: 10.1016/S0166-4972(03)00076-2

Guckenbiehl, P., De Zubielqui, G. C., & Lindsay, N. (2021). Knowledge and innovation in start-up ventures: A systematic literature review and research agenda. *Technological Forecasting and Social Change*, 172, 121026. DOI: 10.1016/j.techfore.2021.121026

Hackett, S. M. (2004). Real Options and the Option to Incubate: An Exploratory Study of the Process of Business Incubation. *SSRN*. DOI: 10.2139/ssrn.1260438

Hackett, S. M., & Dilts, D. M. (2004). A real options-driven theory of business incubation. *The Journal of Technology Transfer*, 29(1), 41–54. DOI: 10.1023/B:JOTT.0000011180.19370.36

Hackett, S. M., & Dilts, D. M. (2004). A Systematic Review of Business Incubation Research. *The Journal of Technology Transfer*, 29(1), 55–82. DOI: 10.1023/B:JOTT.0000011181.11952.0f

Hagen-Zanker, J. (2020). Why Do People Migrate? A Review of the Theoretical Literature. *Migration Studies*, 8(3), 314–330.

Haijun, W., Shuaipeng, J., & Chao, M. (2024). The impact of ESG responsibility performance on corporate resilience. *International Review of Economics & Finance*. https://doi.org/DOI: 10.1016/j.iref.2024.05.033https://

Hakim, C. (1989). New recruits to self-employment in the 1980s. *Employment Gazette*, (June), 286–297.

Hamdan, A. M., Khamis, R., Al Hawaj, A. A., & Barone, E. (2020). The mediation role of public governance in the relationship between entrepreneurship and economic growth. *International Journal of Managerial Finance*, 16(3), 316–333. DOI: 10.1108/IJMF-04-2018-0111

Hammerschmidt, J., González Huertas, M., Puumalainen, K., & Calabuig, F. (2023). Sport entrepreneurship: the role of innovation and creativity in sport management. *Review of Managerial Science*, 1–3. DOI: 10.1007/s11846-023-00711-3

Hammerschmidt, J., Kraus, S., & Jones, P. (2022). Sport Entrepreneurship: Definition and Conceptualization. *Journal of Small Business Strategy*, 32(2). Advance online publication. DOI: 10.53703/001c.31718

Hannon, P. D., & Chaplin, P. (2003). Are Incubators Good for Business? Understanding Incubation Practice—The Challenges for Policy. *Environment and Planning. C, Government & Policy*, 21(6), 861–881. DOI: 10.1068/c0215

Harlin, U., & Berglund, M. (2021). Designing for sustainable work during industrial startups—The case of a high-growth entrepreneurial firm. *Small Business Economics*, 57(2), 807–819. DOI: 10.1007/s11187-020-00383-3

Harrison, R., & Hart, M. (1983). Factors influencing new business formation: A case study of Northern Ireland. *Environment & Planning A*, 15(10), 1395–1412. DOI: 10.1068/a151395

Hasanov, M. (2024). The growth of entrepreneurial firms via business incubator initiatives. *Scientific Collection InterConf*, (194), 30-35. https://archive.interconf.center/index.php/conference-proceeding/article/view/5707

Hassan, N. A. (2020). University Business Incubators as a tool for Accelerating Entrepreneurship: Theoretical Perspective. Review of Economics and Political Science. DOI: 10.1108/REPS-10-2019-0142

Hatherill, C. (2023, June 15). *Adidas x Parley — Parley*. Parley. https://parley.tv/initiatives/adidasxparley

Hausberg, J. P., & Korreck, S. (2021). *Business incubators and accelerators: a co-citation analysis-based, systematic literature review*. Edward Elgar Publishing.

Hausman, A. (2001). Variations in relationship strength and its impact on performance and satisfaction in business relationships. *Journal of Business and Industrial Marketing*, 16(7), 600–616. DOI: 10.1108/EUM0000000006194

Hennig-Thurau, T., Gwinner, K. P., & Gremler, D. D. (2002). Understanding relationship marketing outcomes: An integration of relational benefits and relationship quality. *Journal of Service Research*, 4(3), 230–247. DOI: 10.1177/1094670502004003006

Henttonen, K., Johanson, J. E., & Janhonen, M. (2013). Internal social networks in work teams: Structure, knowledge sharing and performance. *International Journal of Manpower*, 34(6), 616–634. DOI: 10.1108/IJM-06-2013-0148

Hernandez-Gantes, V. M., & Others, A. (n.d.). *Fostering Entrepreneurship through Business Incubation: The Role and Prospects of Postsecondary Vocational-Technical Education. Report 2: Case Studies.*https://eric.ed.gov/?id=ED399396

Hernández, R., & Carrà, G. (2016). A Conceptual Approach for Business Incubator Interdependencies and Sustainable Development. *Agriculture and Agricultural Science Procedia*, 8, 718–724. DOI: 10.1016/j.aaspro.2016.02.054

Hervieux, C., & Voltan, A. (2018). Framing social problems in social entrepreneurship. *Journal of Business Ethics*, 151(2), 279–293. DOI: 10.1007/s10551-016-3252-1

Hessels, J., van Gelderen, M., & Thurik, A. R. (2008). Entrepreneurial aspirations, motivations and their drivers. *Small Business Economics*, 31(3), 323–339. DOI: 10.1007/s11187-008-9134-x

Hillemane, B. S. M., Satyanarayana, K., & Chandrashekar, D. (2019). Technology business incubation for start-up generation: A literature review toward a conceptual framework. *International Journal of Entrepreneurial Behaviour & Research*, 25(7), 1471–1493. DOI: 10.1108/IJEBR-02-2019-0087

Himanen, P., Au, A., & Margulies, P. (2011). The new incubators. *World Policy Journal*, 28(3), 22–34. DOI: 10.1177/0740277511425351

Hisrich, R. D., Peters, M. P., & Shepherd, D. (2005). Entrepreneurship 6ed. *Tata McGraw-Hill Publishing Company Limited.*

Hitt, M. A., Ireland, R. D., & Lee, H. (2000). Technological learning, knowledge management, firm growth and performance: An introductory essay. *Journal of Engineering and Technology Management*, 17(3-4), 231–246. DOI: 10.1016/S0923-4748(00)00024-2

Hofstede Center. (2010). Geert hofstede cultural dimensions. Available at https://geerthofstede.com/

Hojeij, Z. (2024). An overview of university-industry collaboration in the Arab world. *Journal of Innovation and Entrepreneurship*, 13(1), 40. DOI: 10.1186/s13731-024-00400-9

Horne, J., & Fichter, K. (2022). Growing for sustainability: Enablers for the growth of impact startups – A conceptual framework, taxonomy, and systematic literature review. *Journal of Cleaner Production*, 349, 131163. DOI: 10.1016/j.jclepro.2022.131163

Houssou, U., Schulz, K. P., Biga-Diambeidou, M., & Abihona, S. (2024). University incubators and entrepreneurial universities: A case study of the process of setting up a university incubator in a developing country. *International Journal of Technology Management*, 95(3/4), 434–455. DOI: 10.1504/IJTM.2024.138802

Hsieh, R. M., & Kelley, D. J. (2016). The Role of cognition and information access in the recognition of innovative opportunities. *Journal of Small Business Management*, 54(S1), 297–311. DOI: 10.1111/jsbm.12300

Hsu, I. C., & Wang, Y. S. (2008). A model of intraorganizational knowledge sharing: Development and initial test [Review]. *Journal of Global Information Management*, 16(3), 45–73. DOI: 10.4018/jgim.2008070103

Hughes, M., Hughes, P., Morgan, R. E., Hodgkinson, I. R., & Lee, Y. (2021). Strategic entrepreneurship behaviour and the innovation ambidexterity of young technology-based firms in incubators. *International Small Business Journal*, 39(3), 202–227. DOI: 10.1177/0266242620943776

Huisman, D., & De Ridder, W. J. (1984). *Vernieuwend Ondernemen* [Innovative Business]. SMO.

Huselid, M. A. (1995). The impact of human resource management practices on turnover, productivity, and corporate financial performance. *Academy of Management Journal*, 38(3), 635–672. DOI: 10.2307/256741

Hwang, V. (2019). *Access to Capital for Entrepreneurs*. http://books.google.ie/books?id=b9gBzwEACAAJ&dq=Access+to+Capital+for+Entrepreneurs:+Removing+Barriers%3B+Elsevier:+Amsterdam,+The+Netherlands,+2019&hl=&cd=1&source=gbs_api

Indiran, L., Nallaluthan, K., Baskaran, S., & Dalayga, B. (2021). Business incubator: The genesis, evolution, and innovation invigoration. *International Journal of Academic Research in Business & Social Sciences*, 11(7), 342–354. DOI: 10.6007/IJARBSS/v11-i7/9940

Isenberg, D. J. (2010). How to start an entrepreneurial revolution. *Harvard Business Review*, 88(6), 40–50.

Ishak, N., & Khairudin, F. N. (2020). Knowledge management and organisational performance of a department in Malaysia Digital Economy Corporation (MDEC). *Borneo Akademika*, 4(2), 29–41.

Isher, A. K. (2024). Driving Innovation and Economic Development: The Role of Business Incubators in Agri-Tech Start-Up Ecosystems. *Economic Affairs*, 69(2). Advance online publication. DOI: 10.46852/0424-2513.3.2024.7

Issac, S., & Michael, W. B. (1981). *Handbook in research and evaluation*. EDITS.

Iwu, C. G., Malawu, N., Ndlovu, E. N., Makwara, T., & Sibanda, L. (2024). Sustaining Family Businesses through Business Incubation: An Africa-Focused Review. *Journal of Risk and Financial Management*, 17(5), 178. DOI: 10.3390/jrfm17050178

Iyortsuun, A. S. (2017). An empirical analysis of the effect of business incubation process on firm performance in Nigeria. *Journal of Small Business and Entrepreneurship*, 29(6), 433–459. DOI: 10.1080/08276331.2017.1376265

Jahanshahi, A. A., & Bhattacharjee, A. (2020). Competitiveness improvement in public sector organizations: What they need? *Journal of Public Affairs*, 20(2), e2011. DOI: 10.1002/pa.2011

Jahanshahi, A. A., Bhattacharjee, A., & Maghsoudi, T. (2021). Internal capabilities as the source of achieving competitive advantage in small-sized businesses. *International Journal of Business Innovation and Research*, 26(2), 141–162. DOI: 10.1504/IJBIR.2021.118446

Jahanshahi, A. A., Bhattacharjee, A., & Polas, M. R. H. (2023). The micro-foundations of sustainable entrepreneurship: The role of individuals' pro-social identity and organisational pro-social identity. *International Journal of Productivity and Quality Management*, 40(2), 149–170. DOI: 10.1504/IJPQM.2023.134270

Jahanshahi, A. A., Brem, A., & Bhattacharjee, A. (2017). Who takes more sustainability-oriented entrepreneurial actions? The role of entrepreneurs' values, beliefs and orientations. *Sustainability (Basel)*, 9(10), 1636. Advance online publication. DOI: 10.3390/su9101636

Jaladati, H., & Chitsaz, E. (2023). Unraveling the Secrets to Startup Crowdfunding: Cognitive Legitimacy in Initial Coin Offerings. *Journal of Entrepreneurship Research*, 2(3), 1–22.

Jamil, F., Ismail, K., & Mahmood, N. (2015). A review of commercialization tools: University incubators and technology parks. *International Journal of Economics and Financial Issues*, 5(1S).

Jha, S. K., & A, T. R. (2024). The Future of Incubation. *IIMB Management Review*, 36(1), 48–55. DOI: 10.1016/j.iimb.2024.03.003

Jia, J., Yan, J., Jahanshahi, A. A., Lin, W., & Bhattacharjee, A. (2020). What makes employees more proactive? Roles of job embeddedness, the perceived strength of the HRM system and empowering leadership. *Asia Pacific Journal of Human Resources*, 58(1), 107–127. DOI: 10.1111/1744-7941.12249

Jin, W., Ding, W., & Yang, J. (2022). Impact of financial incentives on green manufacturing: Loan guarantee vs. interest subsidy. *European Journal of Operational Research*, 300(3), 1067–1080. DOI: 10.1016/j.ejor.2021.09.011

Kakabadse, N., Karatas-Ozkan, M., Theodorakopoulos, N., McGowan, C., & Nicolopoulou, K. (2020). Business incubator managers' perceptions of their role and performance success: Role demands, constraints, and choices. *European Management Review*, 17(2), 485–498. DOI: 10.1111/emre.12379

Kankanhalli, A., Pee, L. G., Tan, G. W., & Chhatwal, S. (2012). Interaction of Individual and Social Antecedents of Learning Effectiveness: A Study in the IT Research Context. *IEEE Transactions on Engineering Management*, 59(1), 115–128. DOI: 10.1109/TEM.2011.2144988

Kareem, Q., & Adman, M. (2006). The Role of Incubators for Small and Medium Enterprises, International Forum: Requirements for the Qualification of Small and Medium Enterprises in the Arab Countries, 17-18 / 4/2006, Hassiba Ben Ali University, Chlef, Algeria.

Keenan, J., Wein, J., & Willis, T. (2018). Economic Assessment of Startup Accelerators.

Ketchen, D. J. Jr, Thomas, J. B., & Snow, C. C. (1993). Organizational configurations and performance: A comparison of theoretical approaches. *Academy of Management Journal*, 36(6), 1278–1313. DOI: 10.2307/256812

Khalid, F. A., Gilbert, D., & Huq, A. (2014). The way forward for business incubation process in ICT incubators in Malaysia. *International Journal of Business and Society*, 15(3), 395.

Khan, A. M., Arafat, M. Y., Raushan, M. A., Saleem, I., Khan, N. A., & Khan, M. M. (2019). Does intellectual capital affect the venture creation decision in India? *Journal of Innovation and Entrepreneurship*, 8(1), 10. Advance online publication. DOI: 10.1186/s13731-019-0106-y

Khan, M. R. (2013). Mapping entrepreneurship ecosystem of Saudi Arabia. *World Journal of Entrepreneurship, Management and Sustainable Development*, 9(1), 28–54. DOI: 10.1108/20425961311315700

Khorsheed, M. S., Alhargan, A., & Qasim, S. M. (2012). A Three-Tier service model for national ICT incubator in Saudi Arabia. Paper presented at the Proceedings of IEEE International Conference on Management and Service Science.

Kilcrease, K. (2012). The Batavia industrial center: The hatching of the world's first business incubator. *New York History*, 93(1), 71–93.

King, W. R., & Marks, P. V.Jr. (2008). Motivating knowledge sharing through a knowledge management system. *Omega*, 36(1), 131–146. DOI: 10.1016/j.omega.2005.10.006

Kiran, R., & Bose, S. C. (2020). Stimulating business incubation performance: Role of networking, university linkage and facilities. *Technology Analysis and Strategic Management*, 32(12), 1407–1421. DOI: 10.1080/09537325.2020.1772967

Klofsten, M., & Bienkowska, D. (2021). Business incubators within entrepreneurial ecosystems: sustainability aspects of new venture support and development. In *Handbook of Research on Business and Technology Incubation and Acceleration* (pp. 124–139). Edward Elgar Publishing. DOI: 10.4337/9781788974783.00015

Kolvereid, L., & Isaksen, E. (2006). New business start-up and subsequent entry into self-employment. *Journal of Business Venturing*, 21(6), 866–885. DOI: 10.1016/j.jbusvent.2005.06.008

Kolympiris, C., & Klein, P. G. (2017). The Effects of Academic Incubators on University Innovation. *Strategic Entrepreneurship Journal*, 11(2), 145–170. DOI: 10.1002/sej.1242

Korang, V. (2024). Establishing a Network for Promoting and Developing Entrepreneurship Education. *Convergence Chronicles*, 5(1), 343–353.

Krueger, N. F.Jr. (1993). The impact of prior entrepreneurial exposure on perceptions of new venture feasibility and desirability. *Entrepreneurship Theory and Practice*, 18(1), 5–21. DOI: 10.1177/104225879301800101

Krueger, N. F.Jr, & Carsrud, A. L. (1993). Entrepreneurial intentions: Applying the theory of planned behavior. *Entrepreneurship and Regional Development*, 5(4), 315–330. DOI: 10.1080/08985629300000020

Kulal, A. (2022). Business Incubator: Seeding Start-ups Awareness among Post Graduation students with reference to CEOL, Mangalore.

Kurode, T., Kurode, A. V., & Moitra, K. (2016). A Study of Critical Challenges in Startup Management. *SSRN*. DOI: 10.2139/ssrn.3348534

Lalkaka, R. (2003). Business Incubators in Developing Countries: Characteristics and Performance. *International Journal of Entrepreneurship and Innovation Management*, 3(1/2), 31. DOI: 10.1504/IJEIM.2003.002217

Leal, M., Leal, C., & Silva, R. (2023). The Involvement of Universities, Incubators, Municipalities, and Business Associations in Fostering Entrepreneurial Ecosystems and Promoting Local Growth. *Administrative Sciences*, 13(12), 245. DOI: 10.3390/admsci13120245

Lee, R., Tuselmann, H., Jayawarna, D., & Rouse, J. (2019). Effects of structural, relational and cognitive social capital on resource acquisition: A study of entrepreneurs residing in multiply deprived areas. *Entrepreneurship and Regional Development*, 31(5-6), 534–554. DOI: 10.1080/08985626.2018.1545873

Leitão, J., Pereira, D., & Gonçalves, Â. (2022). Business incubators, accelerators, and performance of technology-based ventures: A systematic literature review. *Journal of Open Innovation*, 8(1), 46. DOI: 10.3390/joitmc8010046

Lesakova, L. (2012). The role of business incubators in supporting the SME start-up. *Acta Polytechnica Hungarica*, 9(3), 85–95.

Lewis, D., Harper-Anderson, E., & Molnar, L. A. (2011). *Incubating Success: Incubation Best Practices That Lead to Successful New Ventures*. https://doi.org/ DOI: 10.13140/RG.2.1.2732.6881

Li, C., Ahmed, N., Qalati, S. A., Khan, A., & Naz, S. (2020). Role of Business Incubators as a Tool for Entrepreneurship Development: The Mediating and Moderating Role of Business Start-Up and Government Regulations. *Sustainability (Basel)*, 12(5), 1822. DOI: 10.3390/su12051822

Li, H., Kinoshita, T., Chen, J., Xie, J., Luo, S., & Su, D. (2024). What promotes residents' donation behavior for adaptive reuse of cultural heritage projects? An application of the extended theory of planned behavior. *Sustainable Cities and Society*, 102, 105213. DOI: 10.1016/j.scs.2024.105213

Liñán, F., & Chen, Y. W. (2009). Development and cross-cultural application of a specific instrument to measure entrepreneurial intentions. *Entrepreneurship Theory and Practice*, 33(3), 593–617. DOI: 10.1111/j.1540-6520.2009.00318.x

Lindelöf, P., & Hellberg, R. (2023). Incubation-An evolutionary process. *Technovation*, 124, 102755. DOI: 10.1016/j.technovation.2023.102755

Litwin, D. (2023, December 13). *The future of fan engagement in Sports: Trends and Innovations*. MarketScale. https://marketscale.com/industries/sports-and-entertainment/the-future-of-fan-engagment-in-sports/

Liu, Y. (2020). The micro-foundations of global business incubation: Stakeholder engagement and strategic entrepreneurial partnerships. *Technological Forecasting and Social Change*, 161, 120294. DOI: 10.1016/j.techfore.2020.120294 PMID: 32921840

Lose, T. (2021). Business incubators in South Africa: A resource-based view perspective. *Academy of Entrepreneurship Journal*, 27, 1–11. https://www.proquest.com/openview/83175b594ba2bd54d0435c16aad30e93/1?pq-origsite=gscholar&cbl=29726

Luo, S., Chishti, M. Z., Beata, S., & Xie, P. (2024). Digital sparks for a greener future: Unleashing the potential of information and communication technologies in green energy transition. *Renewable Energy*, 221, 119754. DOI: 10.1016/j.renene.2023.119754

Lüthje, C., & Franke, N. (2003). The 'making 'of an entrepreneur: Testing a model of entrepreneurial intent among engineering students at MIT. *R & D Management*, 33(2), 135–147. DOI: 10.1111/1467-9310.00288

Lu, X., & Wang, J. (2024). Is innovation strategy a catalyst to solve social problems? The impact of R&D and non-R&D innovation strategies on the performance of social innovation-oriented firms. *Technological Forecasting and Social Change*, 199, 123020. DOI: 10.1016/j.techfore.2023.123020

Lynch, J. (2023, August 17). Nike launches its 'Accelerator Program' to drive equality in sports. *Hypebeast*. https://hypebeast.com/2023/8/nike-fc-launch-new-accelerator-program-football

MacKenzie, S. B., Podsakoff, P. M., & Podsakoff, N. P. (2011). Construct measurement and validation procedures in MIS and behavioral research: Integrating new and existing techniques. *Management Information Systems Quarterly*, 35(2), 293–334. DOI: 10.2307/23044045

Madaleno, M., Nathan, M., Overman, H., & Waights, S. (2022). Incubators, Accelerators and Urban Economic Development. *Urban Studies (Edinburgh, Scotland)*, 59(2), 281–300. DOI: 10.1177/00420980211004209

Madichie, N. O. (2010). Business incubation in the UAE: Prospects for enterprise development. *International Journal of Entrepreneurship and Innovation Management*, 12(3/4), 291. DOI: 10.1504/IJEIM.2010.035085

Mair, J., Robinson, J., & Hockerts, K. (Eds.). (2006). *Social Entrepreneurship.*, DOI: 10.1057/9780230625655

Majid, H. I., & Arif, M. T. (2006) The Role of Productive Incubators in the Development of Small Enterprises, International Forum: Requirements for the Qualification of Small and Medium Enterprises in the Arab Countries.. *Hassiba Ben Ali University, Chlef, Algeria, 1.*

Makoto, Y., Chris, D., Kenichi, M., & Yoshio, K. (2019). *Creation of a Blockchain and a New Ecosystem. Policy Discussion Papers 19029, Research Institute of Economy, Trade and Industry.* RIETI.

Man, T. W. Y., Berger, R., & Rachamim, M. (2024). A social constructivist perspective on novice entrepreneurial learning in business incubators. *International Journal of Emerging Markets*, 19(5), 1281–1305. DOI: 10.1108/IJOEM-11-2021-1784

Marian, O. (2015). A Conceptual Framework for the Regulation of Cryptocurrencies. University of Chicago Law Review, 82, 53–68.

Mark Hooson and Nikita Tambe. (2024). How to Trade Cryptocurrency. https://www.forbes.com/advisor/in/investing/cryptocurrency/how-to-trade-cryptocurrency/

Markley, D. M., & McNamara, K. T. (1995). Economic and Fiscal Impacts of a Business Incubator. *Economic Development Quarterly*, 9(3), 273–278. DOI: 10.1177/089124249500900307

Marsal, H., Hamdan, A., Awwad, B., & Mohamed, M. (2024). The Impact of Mentorship and Funding Support on Stimulating Entrepreneurship Motivation among Family Members. *European Journal of Family Business*, 14(1), 117–130. DOI: 10.24310/ejfb.14.1.2024.17011

Martínez, A., Belso-Martínez, J. A., & Más-Verdú, F. (2012). Industrial clusters in Mexico and Spain: Comparing inter-organizational structures within context of change. *Journal of Organizational Change Management*, 25(5), 657–681. DOI: 10.1108/09534811211254563

Masutha, M., & Rogers, C. M. (2014). *Small enterprise development in South Africa: role of Business Incubators. Bulletin of Geography, Social –Economic Series No. 26.* Nicholas Copernicus University.

Máté, D., Estiyanti, N. M., & Novotny, A. (2024). How to support innovative small firms? Bibliometric analysis and visualization of start-up incubation. *Journal of Innovation and Entrepreneurship*, 13(1), 5. DOI: 10.1186/s13731-024-00361-z

Matuluko, M. (2015). Nigeria's Communications Minister to release new ICT Blueprint in January. Available at: https://techpoint.ng

McDonald, R. M., & Eisenhardt, K. M. (2019). Parallel Play: Startups, Nascent Markets, and Effective Business-model Design. *Administrative Science Quarterly*, 65(2), 483–523. DOI: 10.1177/0001839219852349

McIver-Harris, K., & Tatum, A. (2020). Measuring Incubator Success During a Global Pandemic: A Rapid Evidence Assessment. SSRN *Electronic Journal*. https://doi.org/DOI: 10.2139/ssrn.3687712

Mecke, P. (2014). *The role of business incubators in developing entrepreneurship*. Centre for Enterprise Manchester Metropolitan University Business School.

Mendez-Duron, R., & Garcia, C. E. (2009). Returns from social capital in open source software networks. *Journal of Evolutionary Economics*, 19(2), 277–295. DOI: 10.1007/s00191-008-0125-5

Mhlongo, S. D., & Mzyece, M. (2023). The business of business incubation: How stakeholders measure value and investment returns in South African fintech incubators. *African Journal of Science, Technology, Innovation and Development*, 15(2), 236–249. DOI: 10.1080/20421338.2022.2069215

Mian, S. A. (1996). The University Business Incubator: A Strategy for Developing New Research/Technology-Based Firms. *The Journal of High Technology Management Research*, 7(2), 191–208. DOI: 10.1016/S1047-8310(96)90004-8

Mian, S. A. (1997). Assessing and managing the university technology business incubator: An integrative framework. *Journal of Business Venturing*, 12(4), 251–285. DOI: 10.1016/S0883-9026(96)00063-8

Mian, S. A. (2021). Whither modern business incubation? Definitions, evolution, theory, and evaluation. In *Handbook of research on business and technology incubation and acceleration* (pp. 17–38). Edward Elgar Publishing. DOI: 10.4337/9781788974783.00008

Mian, S., Lamine, W., & Fayolle, A. (2016). Technology Business Incubation: An overview of the state of knowledge. *Technovation*, 50, 1–12. DOI: 10.1016/j.technovation.2016.02.005

Mishrif, A., Karolak, M., & Mirza, C. (2023). The Nexus Between Higher Education, Labour Market, and Industry 4.0 in the Context of the Arab Gulf States. In *Nationalization of Gulf Labour Markets: Higher Education and Skills Development in Industry 4.0* (pp. 1-23). Singapore: Springer Nature Singapore. DOI: 10.1007/978-981-19-8072-5_1

Mitra, D. (2012). The Role of Crowdfunding in Entrepreneurial Finance. *Delhi Business Review.*, 13(2), 67–72. DOI: 10.51768/dbr.v13i2.132201218

Mitra, S., Kumar, H., Gupta, M. P., & Bhattacharya, J. (2023). Entrepreneurship in smart cities: Elements of start-up ecosystem. *Journal of Science and Technology Policy Management*, 14(3), 592–611. DOI: 10.1108/JSTPM-06-2021-0078

Moses, Ch., Ola-David, O., Steven, O., Olumuyiwa, O., Mosunmola, A., Mayowa, A., & Achugamonu, U. (2015). Entrepreneurship Education and Poverty Alleviation: Impact Analysis of Covenant University Graduate between 2006- 2013, *2nd Covenant University Conference on African Development Issues (CU-ICADI)*, 11th - 13th May, 2015, Africa Leadership Development Center, Covenant University, Ota, Nigeria.

Mrkajic, B. (2017). Business Incubation Models and Institutionally Void Environments. *Technovation*, 68, 44–55. DOI: 10.1016/j.technovation.2017.09.001

Mubaraki, H. M. A., & Busler, M. (2015). The Importance of Business Incubation in Developing Countries: Case Study Approach. *International Journal of Foresight and Innovation Policy*, 10(1), 17. DOI: 10.1504/IJFIP.2015.070054

Mukul, K., & Saini, G. K. (2021). Talent acquisition in startups in India: The role of social capital. *Journal of Entrepreneurship in Emerging Economies*, 13(5), 1235–1261. DOI: 10.1108/JEEE-04-2020-0086

Murad, M., Othman, S. B., & Kamarudin, M. a. I. B. (2024). Entrepreneurial university support and entrepreneurial career: the directions for university policy to influence students' entrepreneurial intention and behavior. *Journal of Entrepreneurship and Public Policy*. DOI: 10.1108/JEPP-08-2023-0082

Muturi, D. (2023). Infrastructure investment and economic development. *Journal of Poverty. Investment and Development*, 8(2), 90–99. DOI: 10.47604/jpid.2074

Mvulirwenande, S., & Wehn, U. (2020). Opening the innovation incubation black box: A process perspective. *Environmental Science & Policy*, 114, 140–151. DOI: 10.1016/j.envsci.2020.07.023

Nafari, J., Honig, B., & Siqueira, A. C. O. (2024). Promoting academic social intrapreneurship: Developing an international virtual incubator and fostering social impact. *Technovation*, 133, 103024. DOI: 10.1016/j.technovation.2024.103024

Nahapiet, J., & Ghoshal, S. (1998). Social capital, intellectual capital, and the organizational advantage [Review]. *Academy of Management Review*, 23(2), 242–266. DOI: 10.2307/259373

Narayanan, V. K., & Shin, J. (2019). The Institutional Context of Incubation: The Case of Academic Incubators in India. *Management and Organization Review*, 15(3), 563–593. DOI: 10.1017/mor.2018.52

National Bureau of Statistics. (2014). *Measuring Better: Presentation of Preliminary Results of the Rebased Nominal Gross Domestic Product (GDP) Estimates for Nigeria 2010 to 2013*. National Bureau of Statistics.

National Business Incubation Association (NBIA). (2010). What is Business Incubation? https://www.inbia.org/

National Business Incubation Association. (2014). *The History of Business Incubation: What is Business Incubation?* National Business Incubation Association.

Naudé, W. (2011). Entrepreneurship and Economic Development: An Introduction. *Entrepreneurship and Economic Development*, 3-17.

Nel-Sanders, D., & Thomas, P. (2022). The role of government in promoting innovation-led entrepreneurial ecosystems. *Africa's Public Service Delivery & Performance Review*, 10(1), 13. DOI: 10.4102/apsdpr.v10i1.640

Neto, J. R., Figueiredo, C., Gabriel, B. C., & Valente, R. (2024). Factors for innovation ecosystem frameworks: Comprehensive organizational aspects for evolution. *Technological Forecasting and Social Change*, 203, 123383. DOI: 10.1016/j.techfore.2024.123383

Ngah, R., & Ibrahim, A. R. (2008). *The Impact of Intellectual Capital and Tacit Knowledge Sharing on Organizational Performance: A Preliminary Study of Malaysian SMEs*.

Nicholls-Nixon, C. L., Singh, R. M., Hassannezhad Chavoushi, Z., & Valliere, D. (2024). How university business incubation supports entrepreneurs in technology-based and creative industries: A comparative study. *Journal of Small Business Management*, 62(2), 591–627. DOI: 10.1080/00472778.2022.2073360

Nicholls-Nixon, C., Valliere, D., & Hassannezhad, Z. (2018). A typology of university business incubators: Implications for research and practice. International Conference on Innovation and Entrepreneurship.

Nike and apple partnership. (2022, February 7). [Slide show]. SlideShare. https://www.slideshare.net/slideshow/nike-and-apple-partnership/251126995

Nix Biosensors | Hydration Monitor | Revolutionary Sweat Science. (n.d.). Nix Biosensors. https://nixbiosensors.com/

Nonaka, I. (1994). A dynamic theory of organizational knowledge creation. *Organization Science*, 5(1), 14–37. DOI: 10.1287/orsc.5.1.14

Nwabueze, A. U., & Ozioko, R. E. (2011). Information and communication technology for sustainable development in Nigeria. *Library Philosophy and Practice*, (1), 92.

Nwekeaku, C. (2013). Entrepreneurship education and challenges to Nigerian universities. *Journal of Education and Practice*, 4(3), 51–56.

Nziku, D. M., Mugione, F., & Salamzadeh, A. (2024). Women Entrepreneurship in the Middle East. In *Women Entrepreneurs in the Middle East* (pp. 23–52). Context, Ecosystems, and Future Perspectives for the Region. DOI: 10.1142/9789811283499_0003

Odeyemi, O., Oyewole, A. T., Adeoye, O. B., Ofodile, O. C., Addy, W. A., Okoye, C. C., & Ololade, Y. J. (2024). Entrepreneurship in Africa: A review of growth and challenges. *International Journal of Management & Entrepreneurship Research*, 6(3), 608–622. DOI: 10.51594/ijmer.v6i3.874

OECD. (2022). Crypto-Asset Reporting Framework and Amendments to the Common Reporting Standard, OECD, Paris. https://www.oecd.org/tax/exchange-of-tax-information/crypto-asset-reporting-framework-and-amendments-to-the-common-reporting-standard.htm

Okpara, J. O., Halkias, D., Nwajiuba, C., Harkiolakis, N., & Caracatsanis, S. M. (2011). Challenges facing women entrepreneurs in Nigeria. *Management Research Review*, 34(2), 221–235. DOI: 10.1108/01409171111102821

Omoh, G. (2015). *Youth unemployment in Nigeria up to 50% - Mckinsey & Co.* Vanguard.

Ordoñez de Pablos, P. (2023). Digital innovation and green economy for more resilient and inclusive societies: Understanding challenges ahead for the green growth. *Journal of Science and Technology Policy Management*, 14(3), 461–466. DOI: 10.1108/JSTPM-05-2023-193

Oshewolo, S. (2010). Galloping poverty in Nigeria: An appraisal of government interventionist Policies. *Journal of Sustainable Development in Africa*, 12(6), 264–274.

Ostsieker, P. (2019, September 17). *(Sports) Entrepreneurship: Problem first!* https://www.linkedin.com/pulse/sports-entrepreneurship-problem-first-philipp-ostsieker/

Paoloni, P., & Modaffari, G. (2022). Business incubators vs start-ups: A sustainable way of sharing knowledge. *Journal of Knowledge Management*, 26(5), 1235–1261. DOI: 10.1108/JKM-12-2020-0923

Patil, P., & Deshpande, Y. (2019). Why women enter into entrepreneurship? An exploratory study. *Journal of Organizational studies and Innovation*, 6(2), 30-40.

Patil, K. (2020). Indo-US S&T cooperation and the role of innovation diplomacy. *Science & Diplomacy*, 15.

Patil, P. A., & Deshpande, Y. M. (2021). Women entrepreneurship: a journey begins. In *Research Anthology on Challenges for Women in Leadership Roles* (pp. 36–56). IGI Global. DOI: 10.4018/978-1-7998-8592-4.ch003

Patil, P., & Deshpande, Y. (2018). Women entrepreneurship: A road ahead. *International Journal of Economics, Business, and Entrepreneurship*, 1(1). Advance online publication. DOI: 10.31023/ijebe.101.0004

Patil, P., & Deshpande, Y. (2021). Understanding perception of women entrepreneurs toward employees with reference to quality of work life balance (QWLB). *Journal of Small Business and Entrepreneurship*, 33(4), 475–488. DOI: 10.1080/08276331.2021.1949831

Patnayakuni, R., Seth, N., & Rai, A. (2006). Building social capital with it and collaboration in supply chains: An empirical investigation.

Pattanasak, P., Anantana, T., Paphawasit, B., & Wudhikarn, R. (2022). Critical Factors and Performance Measurement of Business Incubators: A Systematic Literature Review. *Sustainability (Basel)*, 14(8), 4610. DOI: 10.3390/su14084610

Pearce, J., Grafman, L., Colledge, T., & Legg, R. (2019b, May 6). *Leveraging Information Technology, Social Entrepreneurship, and Global Collaboration for Just Sustainable Development.* https://hal.archives-ouvertes.fr/hal-02120513/

Pepin, M., Tremblay, M., Audebrand, L. K., & Chassé, S. (2024). The responsible business model canvas: Designing and assessing a sustainable business modeling tool for students and start-up entrepreneurs. *International Journal of Sustainability in Higher Education*, 25(3), 514–538. DOI: 10.1108/IJSHE-01-2023-0008

Petersen, H. (.2022). An evaluation of the German blockchain startup environment. FSBC Working Paper. Frankfurt School Blockchain Centre. https://fsblockchain.medium.com/an-evaluation-of-the-german-blockchain-startup-environment-e42aeb394677

Peters, L., Rice, M., & Sundararajan, M. (2004). The role of incubators in the entrepreneurial process. *The Journal of Technology Transfer*, 29(1), 83–91. DOI: 10.1023/B:JOTT.0000011182.82350.df

Petrucci, F. (2018). The incubation process of mid-stage startup companies: A business network perspective. *IMP Journal*, 12(3), 544–566. DOI: 10.1108/IMP-07-2017-0043

Pettersen, I. B., Aarstad, J., Høvig, Ø. S., & Tobiassen, A. E. (2015). Business Incubation and the Network Resources of Start-Ups. *Journal of Innovation and Entrepreneurship*, 5(1), 7. DOI: 10.1186/s13731-016-0038-8

Phani, B. V., & Khandekar, S. (2017). *Innovation, Incubation and Entrepreneurship.* Springer. DOI: 10.1007/978-981-10-3334-6

Piwowar-Sulej, K. (2021). Human resources development as an element of sustainable HRM–with the focus on production engineers. *Journal of Cleaner Production*, 278, 124008. DOI: 10.1016/j.jclepro.2020.124008 PMID: 32901179

Pollman, E. (2023). Startup Failure. *Duke Law Journal,* 73.

Pompa, C. (2013). Literature review on the impact of business incubation, mentoring, investment and training on start-up companies. EPS PEAKS--Economic and Private Sector Professional Evidence and Applied Knowledge Services.

Potter, J., Halabisky, D., Lavison, C., Boschmans, K., Shah, P., Shymanski, H., & Reid, A. (2023). Assessment of policies, programmes and regulations relating to MSME and start-up development in Abu Dhabi. https://www.oecd-ilibrary.org/content/paper/9b92546e-en

Priyono, A., & Hidayat, A. (2024). Fostering innovation through learning from digital business ecosystem: A dynamic capability perspective. *Journal of Open Innovation*, 10(1), 100196. DOI: 10.1016/j.joitmc.2023.100196

Qian, H., Haynes, K. E., & Riggle, J. D. (2011). Incubation push or business pull? Investigating the geography of US business incubators. *Economic Development Quarterly*, 25(1), 79–90. DOI: 10.1177/0891242410383275

Ramadani, V., Alkaabi, K. A., & Zeqiri, J. (2024). Entrepreneurial mindset and family business performance: The United Arab Emirates perspectives. *Journal of Enterprising Communities: People and Places in the Global Economy*, 18(3), 682–700. DOI: 10.1108/JEC-08-2023-0153

Ramchandani, P. H. (2017). A Descriptive Study of Opportunities and Challenges of Startup India Mission. *International Journal of Advanced Research and Innovative Ideas in Education*, 3, 61–65.

Razavi Hajiagha, S. H., Ahmadzadeh Kandi, N., Amoozad Mahdiraji, H., Jafari-Sadeghi, V., & Hashemi, S. S. (2022). International entrepreneurial startups' location under uncertainty through a heterogeneous multi-layer decision-making approach: Evidence and application of an emerging economy. *International Journal of Entrepreneurial Behaviour & Research*, 28(3), 767–800. DOI: 10.1108/IJEBR-05-2021-0387

Reagans, R., Zuckerman, E., & McEvily, B. (2004). How to make the team: Social networks vs. demography as criteria for designing effective teams. *Administrative Science Quarterly, 49*(1), 101-133.

Redondo, M., & Camarero, C. (2019). Social Capital in University Business Incubators: Dimensions, antecedents and outcomes. *The International Entrepreneurship and Management Journal*, 15(2), 599–624. DOI: 10.1007/s11365-018-0494-7

Redondo, M., & Camarero, C. (2020). Building the First Business Relationships: Incubatees in University Business Incubators (UBIs). *Entrepreneurship Research Journal*, 1.

Redondo, M., Camarero, C., & van der Sijde, P. (2021). Exchange of knowledge in protected environments. The case of university business incubators. *European Journal of Innovation Management*.

Reid, A. E., Crump, M. E., & Singh, R. P. (2024). Improving Black Entrepreneurship through Cannabis-Related Education. *Education Sciences*, 14(2), 135. DOI: 10.3390/educsci14020135

Reynolds, P. D., Camp, S. M., Bygrave, W. D., Autio, E., & Hay, M. (2001). *Global Entrepreneurship Monitor 2001* Executive Report, Babson College.

Reynolds, P. D., Camp, S. M., Bygrave, W. D., Autio, E., & Hay, M. (2001). *Global Entrepreneurship Monitor 2001 Executive Report*. Kauffman Centre for Entrepreneurial Leadership.

Rice, M. P. (2002). Co-production of Business Assistance In Business Incubators: An Exploratory Study. Journal of Business Venturing, 17(2), 163–187. https://doi .org/ (00)00055-0DOI: 10.1016/S0883-9026

Richard, J. E., Thirkell, P. C., & Huff, S. L. (2007). An examination of customer relationship management (CRM) technology adoption and its impact on business-to-business customer relationships. *Total Quality Management & Business Excellence*, 18(8), 927–945. DOI: 10.1080/14783360701350961

Ririh, K. R., Wicaksono, A., Laili, N., & Tsurayya, S. (2020). Incubation scheme in among incubators: A comparative study. *International Journal on Management of Innovation & Technology*, 17(07), 2050052. DOI: 10.1142/S0219877020500522

Ritsilä. (2002). Effects of Unemployment on New Firm Formation: Micro-level Panel Data Evidence from Finland. *Small Business Economics*, (19), 31–40.

Rizzi, D. I., Wescinski, J. V., Poli, O., & Jacoski, C. A.Universidade Comunitária da Região de Chapecó. (2017). The Importance of Incubation Processes from the Perspective of Incubated and Graduated Companies. *Journal of Information Systems and Technology Management*, 14(2), 263–279. DOI: 10.4301/S1807-17752017000200007

Robert, L. P.Jr, Dennis, A. R., & Ahuja, M. K. (2008). Social capital and knowledge integration in digitally enabled teams. *Information Systems Research*, 19(3), 314–334. DOI: 10.1287/isre.1080.0177

Robinson, S., & Stubberud, H. A. (2014). Business incubators: What services do business owners really use? *International Journal of Entrepreneurship*, 18, 29.

Rosado-Cubero, A., Hernández, A., Jiménez, F. J. B., & Freire-Rubio, T. (2023). Promotion of entrepreneurship through business incubators: Regional analysis in Spain. *Technological Forecasting and Social Change*, 190, 122419. DOI: 10.1016/j.techfore.2023.122419

Rotenstein, L. S., Wickner, P., Hauser, L., Littlefield, M., Abbett, S., Desrosiers, J., Bates, D. W., Dudley, J., & Laskowski, K. R. (2019). An Academic Medical Center-Based Incubator to Promote Clinical Innovation and Financial Value. *Joint Commission Journal on Quality and Patient Safety*, 45(4), 259–267. DOI: 10.1016/j.jcjq.2018.12.004 PMID: 30665836

Roundy, P. T. (2021). Leadership in startup communities: How incubator leaders develop a regional entrepreneurial ecosystem. *Journal of Management Development*, 40(3), 190–208. DOI: 10.1108/JMD-10-2020-0320

Rustiarini, N. W., Arsawan, I. W. E., Rajiani, I., Supartha, W. G., Koval, V., & Suryantini, N. P. S. (2020). Leveraging knowledge sharing and innovation culture into SMEs sustainable competitive advantage. *International Journal of Productivity and Performance Management*. DOI: 10.1108/IJPPM-04-2020-0192

Sabiha, T., & Saida, S. (2024). The role of startups in promoting the development of smart cities–dubai as a model. *International Journal of Professional Business Review*, 9(5), 7. https://dialnet.unirioja.es/servlet/articulo?codigo=9570054

Saffar, A. (2008). Business incubation and support system in Asia-Pacific: Establishing international cooperation among Asian Incubators. Asia Pacific Conference on Business Incubation Asia-and Entrepreneurship Seoul, Korea.

Sanchez, J. C. (2013). The Impact of an entrepreneurship education program on entrepreneurial competencies and intention. *Journal of Small Business Management*, 51(3), 447–465. DOI: 10.1111/jsbm.12025

Sansone, G., Viglialoro, D., Ughetto, E., & Landoni, P. (2023). What is a Startup Studio? Evidence from Europe. *Proceedings - Academy of Management*, 2023(1), 13027. DOI: 10.5465/AMPROC.2023.13027abstract

Sanyal, S., & Hisam, M. W. (2018). The Role of Business Incubators in Creating an Entrepreneurial Ecosystem: A Study of the Sultanate of Oman. *Indian Journal of Commerce and Management Studies*, 9(3), 10–17. DOI: 10.18843/ijcms/v9i3/02

Schein, E. H. (2010). Organizational culture and leadership (Vol. 2). *John Wiley & Sons*.

Schückes, M., & Gutmann, T. (2021). Why do startups pursue initial coin offerings (ICOs)? The role of economic drivers and social identity on funding choice. *Small Bus Econ,57*, 1027–1052. .DOI: 10.1007/s11187-020-00337-9

Schueffel, P. (2017). *The Concise fintech compendium*. School of Management Fribourg.

Schumpeter, J. A. (1934). *The Theory of Economic Development: An Inquiry into Profits, Capital, Credit, Interest, and the Business Cycle*. Harvard University Press.

Schwartz, M., & Hornych, C. (2012). Specialisation versus Diversification: Perceived Benefits of Different Business Incubation Models. *International Journal of Entrepreneurship and Innovation Management*, 15(3), 177. DOI: 10.1504/IJEIM.2012.046599

Scillitoe, J. L., & Birasnav, M. (2022). Ease of market entry of Indian startups: Formal and informal institutional influences. *South Asian Journal of Business Studies*, 11(2), 195–215. DOI: 10.1108/SAJBS-07-2019-0131

Secundo, G., Mele, G., Passiante, G., & Albergo, F. (2023). University business idea incubation and stakeholders' engagement: Closing the gap between theory and practice. *European Journal of Innovation Management*, 26(4), 1005–1033. DOI: 10.1108/EJIM-08-2021-0435

Segal, G., Bogia, D., & Schoenfeld, J. (2005). The Motivation to Become an Entrepreneur. *International Journal of Entrepreneurial Behaviour & Research*, 11(1), 42–57. DOI: 10.1108/13552550510580834

Semenova, V. (2021). Entry Dynamics of Startup Companies and the Drivers of Their Growth in the Nascent Blockchain Industry. New Horizons in Business and Management Studies: Conference Proceedings, 136-148. DOI: 10.14267/978-963-503-867-1_13

Seoane, F. J. F., Rodriguez, G. R., & Rojo, D. A. (2014). The Influence of Training and gender in entrepreneurship through Business Incubators in Galicia (Spain). *International Journal of Social Science and Entrepreneurship*, 1(9), 611–623.

Shandilya, S. K., Datta, A., Kartik, Y., & Nagar, A. (2024). Achieving Digital Resilience with Cybersecurity. In *Digital Resilience: Navigating Disruption and Safeguarding Data Privacy* (pp. 43–123). Springer. DOI: 10.1007/978-3-031-53290-0_2

Shane, S. A. (2003). *A General Theory of Entrepreneurship: The Individual-Opportunity Nexus*. Edward Elgar Publishing. DOI: 10.4337/9781781007990

Shane, S., & Venkataraman, S. (2000). The promise of entrepreneurship as a field of research. *Academy of Management Review*, 25(1), 217–226. DOI: 10.5465/amr.2000.2791611

Sharda, A., Goel, A., Mishra, A., & Chandra, S. (2015). Green Entrepreneurship in India: Global Evaluation, Needs Analysis, and Drivers for Growth. In Manimala, M., & Wasdani, K. (Eds.), *Entrepreneurial Ecosystem* (pp. 261–282). Springer. DOI: 10.1007/978-81-322-2086-2_11

Sharma, A. R., Shukla, B., & Joshi, M. (2019). *The Role of Business Incubators in the Economic Growth of India*. Walter de Gruyter GmbH & Co KG. DOI: 10.1515/9783110640489

Shehata, G. M., Montash, M. A. H., & Areda, M. R. (2021). Examining the interrelatedness among human resources management practices, entrepreneurial traits and corporate entrepreneurship in emerging markets: An evidence from Egypt. *Journal of Entrepreneurship in Emerging Economies*, 13(3), 353–379. DOI: 10.1108/JEEE-08-2019-0117

Shepherd, D. A., Souitaris, V., & Gruber, M. (2021). Creating new ventures: A review and research agenda. *Journal of Management*, 47(1), 11–42. DOI: 10.1177/0149206319900537

Shirokova, G., Osiyevskyy, O., & Bogatyreva, K. (2016). Exploring the Intention-Behavior Link in Student Entrepreneurship: Moderating Effects of Individual and Environmental Characteristics. *European Management Journal*, 34(4), 386–399. DOI: 10.1016/j.emj.2015.12.007

Shneor, R., & Flåten, B.-T. (2015). *Opportunities for Entrepreneurial Development and Growth through Online Communities, Collaboration, and Co-Creation*. In *Entrepreneurial Challenges in the 21st Century*. Palgrave Macmillan.

Silva, D. S., Ghezzi, A., Aguiar, R. B. D., Cortimiglia, M. N., & ten Caten, C. S. (2020). Lean Startup, Agile Methodologies and Customer Development for business model innovation: A systematic review and research agenda. *International Journal of Entrepreneurial Behaviour & Research*, 26(4), 595–628. DOI: 10.1108/IJEBR-07-2019-0425

Singh, S., & Saxena, A. (2023). The impact that employee performance is influenced by organisational citizenship behaviour and workplace happiness variable intervention in organizations. *Institute of Business Management, GLA University Mathura.*

Singh, S., & Saxena, A. (2024). Professional allegiance and beyond a comprehensive study of organization commitment and citizenship behaviour in ncr region. *Institute of Business Management, GLA University Mathura.* https://seyboldreport.net/

Singh, J., Singh, C. D., & Deepak, D. (2024). Effectiveness of green manufacturing in resolving environmental issues: A review. *International Journal of Materials & Product Technology*, 68(1/2), 122–157. DOI: 10.1504/IJMPT.2024.136813

SMEs. (2010). In *OECD studies on SMEs and entrepreneurship*. DOI: 10.1787/9789264080355-en

Sohail, K., Belitski, M., & Castro Christiansen, L. (2023). Developing Business Incubation Process Frameworks: A Systematic Literature Review. *Journal of Business Research*, 162, 113902. DOI: 10.1016/j.jbusres.2023.113902

Somadder, E., & Somadder, E. (2024, May 27). *IIT-Madras set to provide funds to incubate Sports-Tech startups*. Equitypandit. https://www.equitypandit.com/iit-madras-set-to-provide-funds-to-incubate-sports-tech-startups/

Spigel, B. (2017). The Relational Organization of Entrepreneurial Ecosystems. *Entrepreneurship Theory and Practice*, 41(1), 49–72. DOI: 10.1111/etap.12167

Sports Tech Tokyo - Connecting the world to sports innovation. (n.d.). https://sportstech.tokyo

Ssekiziyivu, B., Mwesigwa, R., Kabahinda, E., Lakareber, S., & Nakajubi, F. (2023). Strengthening business incubation practices among startup firms. Evidence from Ugandan communities. *Journal of Enterprising Communities: People and Places in the Global Economy*, 17(2), 498–518. DOI: 10.1108/JEC-08-2021-0131

Staff., & Associates. (2022, July 27). LA Dodgers seeking innovating startups and growth stage companies for global sports Venture Studio. *American Entrepreneurship Today®*. https://americanentrepreneurship.com/news/startup-news/la-dodgers-seeking-innovating-startups-and-growth-stage-companies-for-global-sports-venture-studio

Staniewski, M., & Awruk, K. (2015). Motivating factors and barriers in the commencement of one's own business for potential entrepreneurs. *Ekonomska Istrazivanja*, 28(1), 583–592. DOI: 10.1080/1331677X.2015.1083876

Stephens, S., & Lyons, R. M. (2023). The changing activities of business incubation clients: An Irish case study. *Journal of Science and Technology Policy Management*, 14(3), 612–625. DOI: 10.1108/JSTPM-01-2021-0016

Storey, D. J. (1982). *Entrepreneurship and the New Firm*. Praeger Publishers.

Storey, D., & Johnson, S. (1987). Regional variations in entrepreneurship in the UK. *Scottish Journal of Political Economy*, 34(2), 161–173. DOI: 10.1111/j.1467-9485.1987.tb00276.x

Stryd | Run with Power | Stryd (Global). (n.d.). Stryd (Global). https://www.stryd.com/gl/en

Sun, L., Cao, X., Alharthi, M., Zhang, J., Taghizadeh-Hesary, F., & Mohsin, M. (2020). Carbon emission transfer strategies in supply chain with lag time of emission reduction technologies and low-carbon preference of consumers. *Journal of Cleaner Production*, 264, 121664. DOI: 10.1016/j.jclepro.2020.121664

Surana, K., Singh, A., & Sagar, A. D. (2020). Strengthening science, technology, and innovation-based incubators to help achieve Sustainable Development Goals: Lessons from India. *Technological Forecasting and Social Change*, 157, 120057. DOI: 10.1016/j.techfore.2020.120057

Surya, B., Menne, F., Sabhan, H., Suriani, S., Abubakar, H., & Idris, M. (2021). Economic growth, increasing productivity of SMEs, and open innovation. *Journal of Open Innovation*, 7(1), 20. DOI: 10.3390/joitmc7010020

Szczukiewicz K. (2021). NFT Metaverse Startups and A Possibility of Fundraising Through Token Issuance. *Seria: Administracja i Zarządzanie* (57).

Taged, P., & Ajzen, I. (1991). The Theory of Planned Behaviour. *Organizational Behavior and Human Decision Processes*, 50(2), 179–211. DOI: 10.1016/0749-5978(91)90020-T

Taherdoost, H., & Madanchian, M. (2023). Blockchain-Based New Business Models: A Systematic Review. *Electronics (Basel)*, 12(6), 1479. DOI: 10.3390/electronics12061479

Taylor, M. P. (1996). Earnings, independence or unemployment: Why become self-employed? *Oxford Bulletin of Economics and Statistics*, 58(2), 253–265. DOI: 10.1111/j.1468-0084.1996.mp58002003.x

Techstars Sports accelerator powered by Indy. (n.d.). Techstars. https://www.techstars.com/accelerators/indy-sports

Techstars. (n.d.). Retrieved from https://www.techstars.com/

Teece, D. J., Pisano, G., & Shuen, A. (1997). Dynamic capabilities and strategic management. *Strategic Management Journal*, 18(7), 509–533. DOI: 10.1002/(SICI)1097-0266(199708)18:7<509::AID-SMJ882>3.0.CO;2-Z

Teigland, R., & Wasko, M. M. (2003). Integrating knowledge through information trading: Examining the relationship between boundary spanning communication and individual performance. *Decision Sciences*, 34(2), 261–286. DOI: 10.1111/1540-5915.02341

Tengeh, R. K., & Choto, P. (2015). The Relevance and Challenges of Business Incubators that Support Survivalist Entrepreneurs. Investment Management and Financial Innovations, 12(2), 150–161. https://philarchive.org/rec/TENTRA-3

Terribile, E., & Aquilina, R. (2023). The Impact of a Business Incubation Centre On Business Enterprises in Gozo. *MCAST Journal of Applied Research & Practice*, 7(2), 190–208. DOI: 10.5604/01.3001.0053.7301

The At Home Cycling & Running virtual training app. (n.d.). Zwift. https://www.zwift.com/news/102-the-early-days

The NBA launches a first-of-its-kind new app experience for fans, driven by the power of data. (2024, April 16). https://news.microsoft.com/source/features/digital-transformation/the-nba-launches-a-first-of-its-kind-new-app-experience-for-fans-driven-by-the-power-of-data/

The Role of Incubators for Small and Medium Enterprises, International Forum: Requirements for the Qualification of Small and Medium Enterprises in the Arab Countries. (2006). *Hassiba Ben Ali University, 1.*

Theodoraki, C., Messeghem, K., & Audretsch, D. B. (2022). The Effectiveness of Incubators' Co-Opetition Strategy in the Entrepreneurial Ecosystem: Empirical Evidence from France. *IEEE Transactions on Engineering Management*, 69(4), 1781–1794. DOI: 10.1109/TEM.2020.3034476

Thomas, J., & Reddy, R. (2013). Evaluation of social entrepreneurship educational programs in india. Social Innovation in Social Entrepreneurship: Strengthening the Ecosystem for Scaling Social Innovation, Villgro & IDRC. http://www.villgro.org/~villgrouser/images/social%20innovation%20paper

Thurik, A. R., Carree, M. A., van Stel, A., & Audretsch, D. B. (2008). Does self-employment reduce unemployment? *Journal of Business Venturing*, 23(6), 673–686. DOI: 10.1016/j.jbusvent.2008.01.007

Todorova, T. (2024). Corporate culture and corporate strategy: Some economic aspects of the modern organisation. *International Journal of Business Performance Management*, 25(1), 147–158. DOI: 10.1504/IJBPM.2024.135136

Toganel, A. R. M., & Zhu, M. (2017). Success factors of accelerator backed ventures: Insights from the case of TechStars Accelerator Program.

Torun, M., Peconick, L., Sobreiro, V., Kimura, H., & Pique, J. (2018). Assessing business incubation: A review on benchmarking. *International Journal of Innovation Studies*, 2(3), 91–100. DOI: 10.1016/j.ijis.2018.08.002

Tötterman, H., & Sten, J. (2005). Start-ups: Business incubation and social capital. *International Small Business Journal*, 23(5), 487–511. DOI: 10.1177/0266242605055909

Trethewey-Mould, R. L., & Moos, M. N. (2024). A stakeholder approach towards a consolidated framework for measuring business incubator efficacy. *The Southern African Journal of Entrepreneurship and Small Business Management*, 16(1), 776. DOI: 10.4102/sajesbm.v16i1.776

Tritoasmoro, I. I., Ciptomulyono, U., Dhewanto, W., & Taufik, T. A. (2024). Determinant factors of lean start-up-based incubation metrics on post-incubation start-up viability: Case-based study. *Journal of Science and Technology Policy Management*, 15(1), 178–199. DOI: 10.1108/JSTPM-12-2021-0187

Uctu, R., & Al-Silefanee, R. (2024). Understanding Entrepreneurial Ecosystem in the MIDDLE EAST: Insights from Isenberg's Model. *International Journal of Entrepreneurial Knowledge*, 12(1), 86–109. https://www.ijek.org/index.php/IJEK/article/view/211. DOI: 10.37335/ijek.v12i1.211

Uhlaner, L., & Thurik, R. (2007). Post materialism Influencing Total Entrepreneurial Activity across Nations. *Journal of Evolutionary Economics*, 17(2), 161–185. DOI: 10.1007/s00191-006-0046-0

Uhm, C. H., Sung, C. S., & Park, J. Y. (2018). Understanding the accelerator from resources-based perspective. *Asia Pacific Journal of Innovation and Entrepreneurship*, 12(3), 258–278. DOI: 10.1108/APJIE-01-2018-0001

Under Armour and IBM to transform personal health and fitness, powered by IBM Watson. (n.d.). IBM UK Newsroom. https://uk.newsroom.ibm.com/2016-Jan-06-Under-Armour-And-IBM-To-Transform-Personal-Health-And-Fitness-Powered-By-IBM-Watson

Ushakov, D. S., Ivanova, D. G., Rubinskaya, E. D., & Shatila, K. (2023). The mediating impact of innovation on green entrepreneurship practices and sustainability. In *Climate-Smart Innovation* (pp. 3–18). Social Entrepreneurship and Sustainable Development in the Environmental Economy. DOI: 10.1142/9789811264252_0001

Usman, F. O., Kess-Momoh, A. J., Ibeh, C. V., Elufioye, A. E., Ilojianya, V. I., & Oyeyemi, O. P. (2024). Entrepreneurial innovations and trends: A global review: Examining emerging trends, challenges, and opportunities in the field of entrepreneurship, with a focus on how technology and globalization are shaping new business ventures. *International Journal of Science and Research Archive*, 11(1), 552–569. DOI: 10.30574/ijsra.2024.11.1.0079

Valliere, D., & Nicholls-Nixon, C. L. (2024). From business incubator to crucible: A new perspective on entrepreneurial support. *Journal of Small Business and Enterprise Development*, 31(2), 395–417. DOI: 10.1108/JSBED-04-2023-0181

van den Hooff, B., & Huysman, M. (2009). Managing knowledge sharing: Emergent and engineering approaches. *Information & Management*, 46(1), 1–8. DOI: 10.1016/j.im.2008.09.002

Van Erkelens, A. M., Thompson, N. A., & Chalmers, D. (2024). The Dynamic Construction of an Incubation Context: A Practice Theory Perspective. *Small Business Economics*, 62(2), 583–605. DOI: 10.1007/s11187-023-00771-5

Van Hear, N., Bakewell, O., & Long, K. (2018). Push-Pull Plus: Reconsidering the Drivers of Migration. *Journal of Ethnic and Migration Studies*, 44(6), 927–944. DOI: 10.1080/1369183X.2017.1384135

Van Lancker, E., Knockaert, M., Audenaert, M., & Cardon, M. (2022). HRM in entrepreneurial firms: A systematic review and research agenda. *Human Resource Management Review*, 32(3), 100850. DOI: 10.1016/j.hrmr.2021.100850

van Rijnsoever, F. J., & Eveleens, C. P. (2021). Money Don't matter? How incubation experience affects start-up entrepreneurs' resource valuation. *Technovation*, 106, 102294. DOI: 10.1016/j.technovation.2021.102294

Vanderstraeten, J., & Matthyssens, P. (2012). Service-based differentiation strategies for business incubators: Exploring external and internal alignment. *Technovation*, 32(12), 656–670. DOI: 10.1016/j.technovation.2012.09.002

Vanderstraeten, J., Matthyssens, P., & Van Witteloostuijn, A. (2014). Toward a balanced framework to evaluate and improve the internal functioning of non-profit economic development business incubators. A study in Belgium. *International Journal of Entrepreneurship and Small Business*, 23(4), 478–508. DOI: 10.1504/IJESB.2014.065684

Vardhan, J., & Mahato, M. (2022). Business Incubation Centres in Universities and their Role in Developing Entrepreneurial Ecosystem. *Journal of Entrepreneurship and Innovation in Emerging Economies*, 8(1), 143–157. DOI: 10.1177/23939575211034056

Varma, D., & Dutta, P. (2023). Empowering human resource functions with data-driven decision-making in start-ups: A narrative inquiry approach. *The International Journal of Organizational Analysis*, 31(4), 945–958. DOI: 10.1108/IJOA-08-2021-2888

Vaz, R., de Carvalho, J. V., & Teixeira, S. F. (2023). Developing a digital business incubator model to foster entrepreneurship, business growth, and academia–industry connections. *Sustainability (Basel)*, 15(9), 7209. DOI: 10.3390/su15097209

Vepo do Nascimento Welter, C., Oneide Sausen, J., & Rossetto, C. R. (2020). The development of innovative capacity as a strategic resource in technology-based incubation activities. *Revista de Gestão*, 27(2), 169–188. DOI: 10.1108/REGE-02-2019-0034

Verheugen, G. (2007). CSR and competitiveness: A view from the European Commission. *The State Of Responsible Competitiveness*, 2007, 111.

Verheul, I., Thurik, R., Hessels, J., & van der Zwan, P. (2010). Factors Influencing the Entrepreneurial Engagement of Opportunity and Necessity Entrepreneurs. *In EIM. Research Reports (Montgomery)*.

Vîrjan, D., Manole, A. M., Stanef-Puică, M. R., Chenic, A. S., Papuc, C. M., Huru, D., & Bănacu, C. S. (2023). Competitiveness—The engine that boosts economic growth and revives the economy. *Frontiers in Environmental Science*, 11, 1130173. DOI: 10.3389/fenvs.2023.1130173

Wada, Y., Sakoda, M., Tsuji, H., Aoki, Y., & Seta, K. (2009). Designing Sticky Knowledge-Network SNS for Japanese Science Teachers. In M. J. Smith & G. Salvendy (Eds.), *Human Interface and the Management of Information: Designing Information Environments, Pt I* (Vol. 5617, pp. 447-456). DOI: 10.1007/978-3-642-02556-3_51

Wang, S., & Noe, R. A. (2010). Knowledge sharing: A review and directions for future research. *Human Resource Management Review*, 20(2), 115–131. DOI: 10.1016/j.hrmr.2009.10.001

Wasdani, K. P., Vijaygopal, A., & Manimala, M. J. (2022). Business Incubators: A Need-Heed Gap Analysis of Technology-Based Enterprises. *Global Business Review*, 097215092210740, 09721509221074099. Advance online publication. DOI: 10.1177/09721509221074099

Wasko, M. M., & Faraj, S. (2005). Why should I share? Examining social capital and knowledge contribution in electronic networks of practice. *MIS Quarterly*, 29(1), 35-57.

Whoop. (n.d.). https://www.whoop.com/in/en/

Widén-Wulff, G., & Ginman, M. (2004). Explaining knowledge sharing in organizations through the dimensions of social capital. *Journal of Information Science*, 30(5), 448–458. DOI: 10.1177/0165551504046997

Wierik, T. M. (2019). Analyzing Investment Decision Criteria for Blockchain Startups. http://essay.utwente.nl/78563/

Wiig, K. M. (2002). Knowledge management in public administration. *Journal of Knowledge Management*, 6(3), 224–239. DOI: 10.1108/13673270210434331

Wikipedia contributors. (2024, April 6). *PlaySight Interactive*. Wikipedia. https://en.wikipedia.org/wiki/PlaySight_Interactive

Wilber, P. L., & Dixon, L. (2003). The Impact of Business Incubators on Small Business Survivability. *Journal of Business Venturing*, 10(5), 349–370.

William, P., Shrivastava, A., Aswal, U. S., Kumar, I., Gupta, M., & Rao, A. K. (2023, May). Framework for implementation of android automation tool in agro business sector. In *2023 4th International Conference on Intelligent Engineering and Management (ICIEM)* (pp. 1-6). IEEE. DOI: 10.1109/ICIEM59379.2023.10167328

Winn, J. (2004). Entrepreneurship: Not an easy path to top management for women. *Women in Management Review*, 19(3), 143–153. DOI: 10.1108/09649420410529852

Wright, P. M., & McMahan, G. C. (1992). Theoretical perspectives for strategic human resource management. *Journal of Management*, 18(2), 295–320. DOI: 10.1177/014920639201800205

Yagüe-Perales, R. M., March-Chorda, I., & López-Paredes, H. (2024). Assessing the Impact of Seed Accelerators in Start-Ups from Emerging Entrepreneurial Ecosystems. *The International Entrepreneurship and Management Journal*, 20(2), 1323–1345. Advance online publication. DOI: 10.1007/s11365-024-00956-8

Yang, C., Jiang, B., & Zeng, S. (2024). An integrated multiple attribute decision-making framework for evaluation of incubation capability of science and technology business incubators. *Granular Computing*, 9(2), 31. DOI: 10.1007/s41066-024-00457-7

Yannone, T. (2019, January 31). Five fitness wearables created in Boston. *Boston Magazine.* https://www.bostonmagazine.com/health/2019/01/31/futuristic-fitness-wearables/

Yanuarti, D. W., & Murwatiningsih, M. (2019). Mediating Role of Competitive Strategy and Marketing Capability on The Relationship between EntrepreneurialOrientation and Market Performance. *Management Analysis Journal*, 8(2), 188–195.

Yan, Y., Peng, Z., & Zha, X. (2023). Transactive memory system (TMS) and knowledge sharing: The effects of social capital and task visibility. *Library & Information Science Research*, 45(2), 101233. DOI: 10.1016/j.lisr.2023.101233

Yao, G., Wu, C., & Yang, C. (2008). Examining the content validity of the WHOQOL-BREF from respondents' perspective by quantitative methods. *Social Indicators Research*, 85(3), 483–498. DOI: 10.1007/s11205-007-9112-8

Yau, O. H. M., McFetridge, P. R., Chow, R. P. M., Lee, J. S. Y., Sin, L. Y. M., & Tse, A. C. B. (2000). Is relationship marketing for everyone? *European Journal of Marketing*, 34(9/10), 1111–1127. DOI: 10.1108/03090560010342494

Yuan, X., Hao, H., Guan, C., & Pentland, A. (2022). Which Factors Affect The Performance of Technology Business Incubators in China? An Entrepreneurial Ecosystem Perspective. *PLoS One*, 17(1), e0261922. DOI: 10.1371/journal.pone.0261922 PMID: 35015766

Zane, L. J., & Tribbitt, M. A. (2024). Examining the influence of specific IC elements on alliance formation of new ventures. *Journal of Intellectual Capital*, 25(1), 38–59. DOI: 10.1108/JIC-07-2022-0155

Zeithaml, V. A., Berry, L. L., & Parasuraman, A. (1996). The behavioral consequences of service quality. *the Journal of Marketing, 60*, 31-46. https://www.jstor.org/stable/1251929

Zhang, Y., Lan, M., Zhao, Y., Su, Z., Hao, Y., & Du, H. (2024). Regional carbon emission pressure and corporate green innovation. *Applied Energy*, 360, 122625. DOI: 10.1016/j.apenergy.2024.122625

About the Contributors

Logaiswari Indiran possesses a doctoral degree from Management at the Universiti Teknologi Malaysia (UTM), Malaysia. Throughout her 21-year teaching career, she has made significant contributions to the Faculty of Management, focusing her research efforts on various areas including technology entrepreneurship, innovation, intellectual capital, business incubators, and start-ups. She has published in leading journals and presented in various international conferences. She is a guest speaker in several forums and management institutions in Malaysia, Turkey and UAE.

Ramakrishna Yanamandra is an Associate Dean of Undergraduate Program and Associate Professor in School of Business of Skyline University College, Sharjah, UAE. He is a PhD in Supply Chain Management from Jawaharlal Nehru Technological University (JNTU), Hyderabad, India. His teaching, research and consultancy areas include Logistics and Supply Chain Management, Operations Management, Lean Management, and Quality Management. He has presented in reputed international conferences and published articles in leading journals.

***

Mohd Zaidi Abd Rozan, an Associate Professor in Information Systems at Universiti Teknologi Malaysia. He has 28 years of experience in private and public organizations and is also an entrepreneur. He was selected as one of 16 worldwide participants of the International Visitors Leadership Program (IVLP) USA focusing on the Science and Technology Entrepreneurship Inter-Regional Project in 2021 and he also led the IDEA@KPT- Impact Digital Entrepreneurship Apprentice@KPT National Program in 2021-2022 to boost 42 micro and small enterprises nationwide through Digital Entrepreneurship. He is actively involved in coaching and mentoring start-ups through innovative approaches in product and customer development.

Through his approaches, he has groomed many projects and enterprises owned by young entrepreneurs particularly in Digital domain. Now he is also a Professional Trainer focusing on soft skills and analytics training, which he would like to impact One million lives!

Sameera Afroze is currently serving as an Assistant Professor in Human Resources and Organisation Behaviour area in St. Joseph's Degree and PG College (Autonomous), King Kothi, Hyderabad. She obtained her PhD in Business Administration from Department of Business Management, Osmania University. She qualified UGC-NET & SET (Telangana and AP) in the year 2016. She is the recipient of Maulana Azad National Fellowship from UGC. She has published a book and has presented her work at conferences, workshops and seminars both nationally and internationally.

Saket Narendra Bansod is currently working as an Assistant Professor at Dr. Ambedkar Institute of Management Studies & Research, Nagpur, Maharashtra, India, He received his BBA, and Ph.D. from the Rashtrasant Tukdoji Maharaj Nagpur University and obtained his MMS from the Mumbai University. His areas of expertise are retail management, marketing management, and IMC. He has more than six years of teaching and research experience.

Neeta Baporikar is currently Professor/Director(Business Management) at Harold Pupkewitz Graduate School of Business, Namibia University of Science and Technology, Namibia. Prior to this, she was Head-Scientific Research, with the Ministry of Higher Education CAS-Salalah, Sultanate of Oman, Professor (Strategy and Entrepreneurship) at IIIT Pune and BITS India. With a decade-plus of experience in the industry, consultancy, and training, she made a lateral switch to research and academics in 2000. Prof Baporikar holds D.Sc. (Management Studies) USA, Ph.D. (Management), SP Pune University, INDIA with MBA (Distinction) and Law (Hons.) degrees. Apart from this, she is an external reviewer, Oman Academic Accreditation Authority, an Accredited Management Teacher, a Qualified Trainer, an FDP from EDII, a Doctoral Guide, and Board Member of Academic Advisory Committee in accredited B-Schools. She has to her credit many conferred doctorates, 350+ scientific publications and authored 30+ books in the area of Strategy, Entrepreneurship, Management and Higher Education. She is also a member of the international and editorial advisory board, reviewer for Emerald, IGI, Inderscience, Wiley, etc.

Amitab Bhattacharjee, MBA, has been serving as a lecturer and research associate since 2016. He also holds an affiliate research position at Instituto de Investigación, Universidad Católica de Los Ángeles de Chimbote, in Latin

America. He has successfully coordinated several international research projects in collaboration with the USA, Japan, India, and Malaysia. He is the author of several books and numerous publications. Mr. Bhattacharjee integrates low-emission technological concepts to investigate issues within eco-friendly industrial management and green economic development. His research work encompasses themes such as green technologies, renewable energy, and artificial/augmented intelligence in sustainable business practices; green supply chain management; green entrepreneurship; and sustainability.

Satya Sekhar Gudimetla, M.Com, MBA, M.Phil, Ph.D, Associate Professor and Deputy Director, Centre for Distance Learning, GITAM –Deemed to be University, Visakhapatnam, India., has 20 years of teaching and research experience at Post Graduate level. He has published several books viz. 1) Financial Innovation-Theories, Models and Regulation, Vernon Press, USA, 2)The Indian Mutual Fund Industry, Plagrave Macmilan, London. 3) Mangement of Mutual Funds, Springer Nature, Germany, 4) Currency Risk Management, Vernon Press, USA. He has participated and presented papers in various national and international seminars, and published 50 articles in various national and international reputed journals.

Saba Inamdar is A distinguished educator, accomplished author, and dedicated researcher. Dr. Saba Inamdar is driven by a genuine passion for education, and she harmoniously blends her instructional prowess with a profound dedication to scholarly exploration. Dr. Inamdar holds a notable academic background, with degrees encompassing an MBA, MCOM, and a Ph.D. in Management. Her accomplishments comprises of more than 25 paper presentations and remarkable array of more than 26 research publications including UGC Care listed, Scopus-indexed journals and as book chapters, additionally a reviewer to journals of Web of Science (WoS). Attesting high calibre academia contributions. Dr. Inamdar's quest for knowledge is exemplified by her active participation in over 80 more webinars, seminars, FDPs, and workshops. Additionally, she is an actively engaged member of professional platforms including LinkedIn, ResearchGate, and Academia, further epitomize her commitment to the global academic community.

Mohammad Irfan is presently working as an Associate Professor at School of Business and Management, Christ University, Lavasa, Pune, India. Dr. Irfan has done his Ph.D. from the Central University of Haryana. He is MBA (Finance), M.Com (Account and Law), and MA (Economics). He has qualified UGC-JRF/SRF/NET in Management and Commerce. Dr. Irfan certified NSEs (NCFM) and BSEs certification. He has experience of more than sixteen years in the area of SAPM, Artificial Intelligence, Machine Learning, Blockchain, Cryptocurrency,

Financial Engineering, Fintech, Green Finance, and Alternative Finance. He has to his credit more than 40+ Scopus Indexed articles, includes The Journal of Economic Cooperation and Development (Q2), International Journal of Business Excellence (IJBEX), International Journal of Economics and Management (IJEM), Montenegrin Journal of Economics (Q2), Cogent Business & Management (Taylor & Francis) (Q2), Indian Journal of Finance (IJF) and Journal of Islamic Monetary Economics and Finance (JIMF). His citations reached 365+ along with 12 H-index. Dr. Irfan has published 7 books in Springer, IGI Global Publication (Scopus indexed).

Shankar Subramanian Iyer is an astute and result-oriented engineer, management, and finance expert with nearly two and a half decades of comprehensive techno-commercial experience in sales, marketing, business development, and CRM with profit accountability across various sectors including Engineering, Construction, Mining, Projects, Finance, and Education. Lately, he has been developing program and course curriculum, Quality Assurance for Business, Engineering, and Vocational Courses (KHDA), and assisting in their delivery after receiving approval from the sponsors (Dubai Municipality, Mohammed Bin Rashid Housing Establishment, Dubai Electrical and Water Authority, Dubai Road Transport Authority, Dubai Aluminium, Dubai Petroleum and Gas, and Academicians (EDEXCEL). Dr Shankar has also worked for QAD on TVET Approvals as an Internal Verifier and External Reviewer. His research interests include Blockchain in Education, Data Analysis, Big Data, Artificial Intelligence, Virtual Reality, and Augmented Reality.

Lakshmi Prasad Panda is an esteemed Assistant Professor in the Department of Humanities at the Government College of Engineering Kalahandi, located in Bhawanipatna, Odisha. With a strong academic background, Dr. Panda has dedicated his career to advancing the field of humanities through both teaching and research. His contributions to the college are marked by his commitment to student development and interdisciplinary studies. Dr. Panda's work reflects his passion for education and his dedication to fostering a dynamic learning environment. His expertise and dedication make him a respected figure in the academic community of Odisha.

N. V. Jagannadha Rao is a distinguished professor at the School of Management Studies, GIET University, Gunupur, Odisha, India. With extensive expertise in management education, Dr. Rao has significantly contributed to the academic community through his research and teaching.

Kali Charan Rath is an Associate Professor in the Department of Mechanical Engineering at GIET University, Odisha, India. Dr. Rath has published extensively in national and international journals and actively guides undergraduate, postgraduate and PhD research projects. He participates in various professional organizations and conferences, continually updating his expertise and sharing his knowledge. His dedication to education and research fosters an innovative academic environment at GIET University.

Dhana S. is a vibrant, enthusiastic professional with nearly 13 years of Academic, Research and Industry experience in various institution approved by AICTE/UGC. Ample experience in academic, research, also curriculum design in Management, Tourism and Travel Management courses. Author for book "Multirater Feedback for Succession Planning: A Study on Banking Sector". Contribute regularly in articles for Journals. Proven researcher on various aspects of Management especially Human Resource, Marketing, Tourism and Hospitality Journals. She has published many articles in international and national journals few of the articles in UGC Care List, WOS, Scopus and reputed Journals. She is serving as Editorial Member and Reviewer for Elsevier and Reputed Journals.

Masoumeh Zibarzani, possessing a profound educational foundation in computer engineering and information systems, including a PhD, and a research tenure at the University of Vienna, now serving as an assistant professor at Alzahra University, is an enthusiastic researcher. Her research delves into the intricate spheres of entrepreneurship, digital transformation, and digital marketing, with the goal of fusing cutting-edge technological developments with strategic business insights. Their scholarly endeavors not only enrich the academic dialogue but also equip budding entrepreneurs with the tools to leverage digital innovations effectively.

Index

A

Accelerator 3, 5, 7, 10, 14, 15, 27, 35, 36, 38, 48, 59, 90, 95, 98, 130, 170, 208, 301, 306, 307, 309, 310, 323, 324

B

Blockchain 15, 45, 166, 259, 269, 270, 271, 272, 273, 274, 277, 278, 279, 280, 281, 282, 283, 284, 286, 287, 288, 289, 290, 293, 294, 295, 296, 297, 298, 310

Business 1, 2, 3, 4, 5, 6, 7, 8, 9, 10, 11, 12, 14, 15, 16, 17, 18, 21, 22, 23, 25, 26, 27, 29, 30, 31, 32, 33, 34, 35, 36, 37, 38, 39, 40, 41, 42, 43, 44, 45, 46, 47, 48, 49, 50, 51, 52, 53, 55, 56, 57, 58, 59, 60, 61, 62, 63, 64, 65, 66, 67, 68, 69, 70, 71, 72, 73, 74, 75, 82, 84, 85, 87, 88, 89, 90, 91, 92, 93, 94, 95, 96, 97, 98, 99, 100, 101, 102, 107, 109, 110, 111, 112, 113, 114, 115, 116, 117, 118, 119, 120, 121, 122, 123, 124, 125, 126, 127, 128, 129, 130, 131, 132, 133, 134, 135, 136, 137, 138, 139, 140, 141, 142, 143, 145, 146, 147, 148, 149, 150, 151, 152, 153, 154, 155, 156, 157, 158, 159, 160, 161, 162, 163, 164, 165, 166, 167, 169, 170, 171, 172, 173, 174, 175, 176, 177, 178, 179, 180, 181, 182, 183, 184, 189, 195, 196, 197, 198, 199, 200, 201, 202, 203, 204, 205, 206, 207, 208, 209, 210, 211, 212, 213, 214, 215, 216, 217, 218, 220, 221, 222, 223, 224, 225, 226, 227, 228, 231, 232, 233, 234, 235, 236, 237, 238, 239, 240, 241, 242, 243, 244, 245, 247, 248, 249, 251, 252, 253, 254, 255, 256, 257, 258, 259, 260, 261, 262, 263, 264, 265, 266, 269, 270, 271, 273, 274, 275, 276, 278, 280, 281, 282, 283, 284, 287, 288, 293, 295, 296, 297, 299, 300, 301, 303, 304, 305, 306, 307, 309, 310, 312, 314, 315, 316, 317, 320, 321, 322, 323, 324, 325

Business Incubation 2, 12, 14, 26, 29, 30, 31, 32, 33, 35, 39, 42, 43, 45, 46, 47, 48, 49, 50, 51, 52, 55, 56, 57, 58, 59, 60, 61, 62, 63, 64, 65, 66, 67, 68, 70, 71, 72, 73, 74, 115, 120, 121, 129, 130, 137, 139, 140, 141, 142, 145, 146, 147, 148, 149, 150, 151, 152, 153, 154, 155, 156, 159, 160, 161, 162, 163, 164, 165, 166, 167, 174, 175, 181, 195, 197, 199, 200, 201, 202, 204, 207, 208, 209, 210, 211, 212, 213, 214, 215, 216, 217, 218, 220, 221, 222, 223, 224, 225, 226, 227, 231, 232, 233, 234, 235, 236, 237, 238, 240, 241, 242, 243, 244, 245, 247, 248, 249, 251, 252, 253, 255, 256, 257, 258, 261, 262, 263, 265, 266, 269, 299, 300, 301, 305, 306, 321, 325

Business Incubation Ecosystem 231, 233, 237, 238, 240, 255, 256, 257

Business Incubation Process 29, 30, 32, 47, 51, 202, 227, 232, 233, 235, 236, 237, 247, 256, 258, 261, 265, 266

Business Incubator 2, 8, 14, 22, 25, 26, 30, 37, 40, 41, 47, 49, 50, 56, 59, 60, 66, 68, 71, 121, 123, 130, 132, 142, 169, 172, 175, 178, 180, 181, 196, 197, 199, 200, 202, 204, 206, 213, 215, 232, 240, 258, 260, 261, 265, 266

Business Venture 2, 74

C

Commercialisation 314

Community Engagement 95, 145, 147, 148, 149, 151, 155, 156, 157, 158, 159, 162, 167, 175, 234

Crypto-Currency 281

D

Decentralized Finance 270
Development 1, 2, 3, 4, 5, 8, 9, 10, 12, 13, 14, 15, 16, 17, 18, 21, 22, 23, 24, 26, 29, 30, 31, 33, 34, 35, 36, 38, 39, 40, 42, 43, 44, 45, 46, 48, 49, 50, 52, 55, 56, 57, 59, 60, 61, 62, 63, 64, 65, 66, 67, 68, 69, 70, 71, 72, 73, 75, 86, 87, 88, 89, 90, 91, 92, 93, 94, 95, 96, 99, 100, 108, 109, 111, 114, 115, 116, 117, 118, 119, 120, 121, 122, 124, 127, 128, 129, 130, 131, 132, 133, 135, 136, 137, 138, 140, 141, 142, 143, 145, 146, 147, 148, 149, 150, 151, 152, 155, 156, 157, 159, 160, 161, 162, 163, 165, 166, 167, 170, 171, 172, 173, 174, 175, 176, 179, 180, 181, 201, 202, 203, 204, 205, 206, 208, 209, 211, 212, 213, 214, 215, 216, 217, 218, 219, 220, 221, 222, 223, 226, 227, 228, 231, 232, 233, 235, 237, 238, 239, 241, 247, 253, 254, 255, 256, 257, 259, 260, 263, 264, 265, 272, 284, 296, 297, 299, 300, 301, 303, 304, 309, 311, 313, 315, 316, 320, 321
Diversity and Inclusion 101, 148, 149, 156, 157, 167, 176

E

Economic Growth 4, 10, 11, 12, 16, 17, 21, 22, 23, 26, 33, 36, 42, 43, 44, 45, 56, 57, 78, 91, 94, 106, 116, 120, 123, 126, 131, 143, 146, 147, 148, 149, 156, 157, 158, 159, 161, 162, 163, 166, 167, 170, 172, 175, 176, 228, 232, 235, 241, 247, 254, 256, 257, 266, 299, 300, 302, 321
Economic Impact 16, 91, 147, 148, 149, 152, 153, 154, 155, 158, 159, 160, 161, 162, 176
Economy 1, 3, 4, 10, 35, 41, 43, 47, 55, 56, 57, 68, 71, 91, 113, 116, 118, 119, 123, 124, 129, 131, 136, 137, 146, 148, 149, 153, 157, 158, 165, 169, 170, 174, 175, 176, 181, 202, 259, 263, 265, 266, 283, 295, 300
Ecosystems 5, 21, 22, 44, 49, 52, 55, 78, 87, 91, 118, 138, 142, 150, 162, 163, 164, 167, 170, 171, 172, 173, 174, 176, 194, 210, 218, 258
Entrepreneurial Activity 18, 31, 78, 91, 95, 109, 113, 114, 124
Entrepreneurial Ecosystems 5, 49, 52, 55, 87, 91, 142, 150, 164, 167, 170, 171, 172, 173, 176, 194, 258
Entrepreneurial Support 143, 170, 204, 265
Entrepreneurs 1, 2, 3, 4, 5, 6, 7, 8, 9, 10, 11, 12, 13, 14, 15, 16, 17, 18, 21, 22, 23, 24, 25, 30, 31, 32, 33, 34, 35, 37, 38, 39, 40, 41, 42, 43, 44, 46, 51, 53, 55, 56, 59, 60, 63, 65, 66, 67, 68, 69, 72, 73, 78, 79, 80, 81, 82, 83, 85, 86, 87, 88, 89, 90, 91, 92, 93, 94, 95, 96, 97, 98, 99, 100, 102, 105, 106, 107, 108, 110, 112, 113, 116, 118, 120, 121, 122, 124, 129, 130, 131, 132, 133, 136, 138, 140, 141, 143, 145, 149, 150, 152, 153, 155, 157, 158, 159, 161, 162, 164, 165, 167, 170, 174, 178, 203, 221, 227, 228, 231, 232, 233, 234, 235, 236, 237, 238, 239, 240, 241, 242, 243, 244, 245, 247, 248, 249, 250, 251, 252, 253, 254, 255, 256, 257, 260, 262, 263, 264, 266, 272, 273, 294, 299, 300, 301, 302, 303, 305, 306, 309, 310, 312, 313, 314, 315, 316, 317, 321, 322
Entrepreneurship 2, 3, 5, 8, 10, 13, 14, 15, 16, 17, 22, 23, 24, 25, 26, 27, 31, 33, 34, 35, 37, 38, 42, 43, 45, 47, 48, 49, 50, 51, 52, 55, 56, 57, 58, 59, 60, 62, 65, 66, 67, 69, 70, 71, 72, 73, 74, 77, 78, 79, 80, 81, 82, 83, 84, 85, 87, 88, 89, 90, 91, 92, 93, 94, 95, 96, 97, 98, 99, 101, 102, 104, 105, 106, 107, 108, 109, 110, 111, 112, 113, 114, 115, 116, 118, 119, 120, 121, 122, 123, 124, 128, 129, 131, 132, 134, 135, 136, 137, 138, 139, 140, 141, 142, 143, 145, 146, 147, 148, 150, 151, 152, 157, 158, 160, 161, 162,

163, 164, 165, 167, 169, 170, 171, 172, 173, 174, 175, 176, 180, 181, 200, 203, 204, 205, 207, 208, 210, 211, 212, 213, 214, 218, 220, 221, 222, 223, 225, 226, 228, 231, 232, 233, 235, 247, 255, 259, 261, 262, 263, 264, 265, 266, 295, 299, 300, 301, 302, 305, 306, 313, 317, 318, 320, 321, 322, 323, 324

G

Green Business Incubation 231, 232, 233, 235, 236, 237, 238, 240, 241, 242, 243, 244, 245, 247, 248, 249, 251, 252, 253, 255, 256, 257

Green Innovation 231, 232, 233, 235, 237, 238, 239, 240, 241, 242, 243, 244, 245, 247, 248, 251, 253, 254, 255, 256, 257, 260, 266

Growth 1, 2, 3, 4, 5, 10, 11, 12, 13, 14, 15, 16, 17, 18, 19, 20, 21, 22, 23, 25, 26, 31, 32, 33, 36, 37, 39, 40, 42, 43, 44, 45, 49, 55, 56, 57, 58, 59, 60, 62, 63, 65, 68, 70, 72, 78, 89, 91, 92, 93, 94, 98, 106, 109, 115, 116, 119, 120, 121, 122, 123, 126, 128, 129, 130, 131, 136, 137, 139, 140, 143, 146, 147, 148, 149, 150, 151, 152, 153, 155, 156, 157, 158, 159, 160, 161, 162, 163, 165, 167, 170, 172, 175, 176, 181, 201, 207, 208, 209, 210, 211, 212, 214, 216, 217, 218, 220, 221, 222, 223, 228, 232, 234, 235, 236, 237, 240, 241, 247, 250, 254, 256, 257, 259, 260, 263, 264, 266, 273, 274, 275, 283, 296, 299, 300, 301, 302, 303, 305, 306, 309, 310, 312, 314, 315, 317, 318, 320, 321, 322, 324, 325

H

HRM 207, 208, 209, 210, 211, 212, 213, 214, 215, 216, 217, 218, 219, 220, 221, 222, 223, 226, 227, 228, 262

I

Incubation 1, 2, 9, 11, 12, 13, 14, 15, 16, 18, 21, 22, 23, 25, 26, 29, 30, 31, 32, 33, 34, 35, 36, 39, 40, 41, 42, 43, 44, 45, 46, 47, 48, 49, 50, 51, 52, 53, 55, 56, 57, 58, 59, 60, 61, 62, 63, 64, 65, 66, 67, 68, 69, 70, 71, 72, 73, 74, 115, 116, 117, 118, 120, 121, 122, 123, 129, 130, 131, 134, 137, 139, 140, 141, 142, 145, 146, 147, 148, 149, 150, 151, 152, 153, 154, 155, 156, 159, 160, 161, 162, 163, 164, 165, 166, 167, 170, 172, 174, 175, 180, 181, 182, 183, 187, 195, 197, 198, 199, 200, 201, 202, 204, 205, 207, 208, 209, 210, 211, 212, 213, 214, 215, 216, 217, 218, 220, 221, 222, 223, 224, 225, 226, 227, 228, 231, 232, 233, 234, 235, 236, 237, 238, 239, 240, 241, 242, 243, 244, 245, 247, 248, 249, 250, 251, 252, 253, 255, 256, 257, 258, 261, 262, 263, 264, 265, 266, 269, 286, 299, 300, 301, 302, 305, 306, 308, 309, 310, 311, 313, 314, 321, 322, 325

Incubator 2, 5, 8, 10, 12, 14, 15, 16, 22, 23, 24, 25, 26, 29, 30, 31, 32, 33, 35, 36, 37, 38, 39, 40, 41, 43, 44, 45, 46, 47, 48, 49, 50, 51, 52, 56, 57, 58, 59, 60, 61, 62, 63, 64, 65, 66, 67, 68, 71, 90, 98, 117, 118, 121, 122, 123, 124, 127, 128, 130, 132, 134, 135, 136, 139, 141, 142, 148, 149, 155, 158, 163, 169, 170, 171, 172, 173, 175, 178, 179, 180, 181, 182, 183, 185, 186, 189, 195, 196, 197, 198, 199, 200, 202, 204, 206, 208, 211, 213, 215, 218, 219, 220, 221, 223, 224, 232, 234, 235, 236, 237, 238, 239, 240, 241, 242, 244, 245, 252, 253, 255, 256, 257, 258, 260, 261, 263, 265, 266, 302, 306, 311, 312, 315, 316, 318

Incubator Programs 12, 23, 130, 218, 223

Innovation 1, 2, 3, 5, 8, 9, 10, 11, 14, 16, 17, 18, 21, 22, 23, 25, 26, 27, 30, 31, 32, 33, 35, 37, 39, 42, 43, 44, 45, 47,

48, 49, 50, 51, 52, 56, 57, 59, 61, 62, 64, 65, 70, 73, 74, 78, 80, 86, 88, 91, 92, 93, 94, 95, 96, 97, 99, 106, 112, 115, 116, 118, 120, 121, 123, 125, 126, 127, 128, 129, 130, 131, 133, 134, 135, 136, 137, 138, 139, 140, 141, 143, 145, 146, 148, 150, 151, 152, 153, 156, 157, 158, 159, 160, 161, 162, 163, 164, 165, 167, 169, 170, 171, 172, 173, 174, 175, 176, 177, 179, 180, 184, 202, 203, 204, 207, 208, 209, 210, 211, 212, 213, 214, 215, 216, 217, 218, 220, 221, 222, 223, 224, 225, 226, 227, 228, 231, 232, 233, 235, 237, 238, 239, 240, 241, 242, 243, 244, 245, 247, 248, 251, 253, 254, 255, 256, 257, 258, 260, 262, 263, 264, 265, 266, 277, 299, 300, 301, 302, 304, 306, 307, 308, 309, 310, 311, 313, 314, 316, 317, 318, 319, 320, 321, 323, 324

Innovative Business 56, 99, 111, 269

J

Job Creation 1, 4, 11, 16, 17, 23, 36, 42, 44, 91, 94, 116, 146, 147, 148, 149, 151, 153, 155, 156, 157, 158, 159, 161, 162, 167, 176, 232, 321

K

Knowledge Sharing 12, 126, 160, 169, 177, 178, 197, 200, 201, 202, 203, 204, 205, 206

M

Mentorship 1, 2, 3, 4, 5, 6, 7, 8, 9, 10, 11, 15, 18, 21, 22, 23, 30, 33, 36, 37, 38, 39, 42, 43, 44, 65, 66, 67, 91, 92, 93, 94, 98, 120, 121, 123, 131, 136, 137, 142, 146, 149, 150, 152, 153, 156, 157, 158, 159, 160, 162, 163, 164, 173, 175, 176, 208, 210, 212, 215, 218, 219, 228, 232, 233, 234, 236, 247, 253, 301, 303, 306, 307, 309, 310, 312, 314, 317, 321, 325

Motivation 82, 83, 105, 110, 112, 114, 173, 183, 293

P

Performance 16, 23, 29, 45, 47, 48, 49, 50, 52, 57, 58, 62, 63, 67, 68, 69, 71, 72, 75, 89, 110, 117, 120, 122, 123, 132, 139, 142, 163, 165, 169, 172, 173, 174, 176, 177, 178, 179, 180, 181, 182, 183, 184, 185, 188, 191, 192, 194, 195, 196, 197, 198, 200, 201, 202, 203, 204, 206, 207, 208, 209, 210, 212, 213, 214, 215, 216, 217, 218, 219, 220, 221, 222, 223, 224, 225, 231, 233, 235, 237, 238, 240, 241, 243, 244, 245, 247, 248, 249, 250, 253, 255, 256, 257, 258, 259, 261, 262, 263, 264, 265, 271, 283, 307, 308, 310, 311, 316, 317, 318, 320, 321, 325

Promotion 56, 127, 132, 149, 181, 264

R

Relationship Marketing 177, 201, 202, 206

S

Social Capital 36, 117, 149, 152, 153, 154, 155, 160, 161, 163, 164, 165, 166, 167, 169, 171, 177, 183, 184, 186, 191, 195, 197, 198, 199, 200, 201, 203, 204, 205, 206, 226

Social Entrepreneurship 25, 27, 50, 118, 119, 120, 134, 142, 151, 171, 265

Social Impact 16, 18, 131, 145, 147, 149, 150, 151, 155, 156, 159, 162, 165, 166, 167, 170, 173, 176, 263

Start-Up 22, 26, 30, 31, 32, 33, 38, 39, 40, 41, 45, 49, 50, 56, 60, 62, 63, 66, 67, 69, 78, 87, 91, 94, 96, 98, 111, 116, 117, 118, 124, 125, 130, 131, 132, 137, 139, 140, 148, 159, 170, 173, 174, 203, 214, 221, 222, 224, 225, 227, 261, 263, 264, 265, 311